THOREAU'S COMPLEX WEAVE

The Writing of
*A Week on the Concord and
Merrimack Rivers*

with the Text of the First Draft

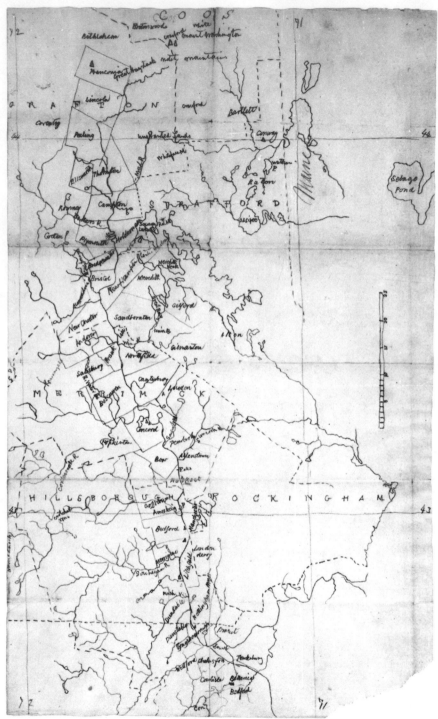

THOREAU'S
Complex Weave

THE WRITING OF

A Week on the Concord and Merrimack Rivers

with the Text of the First Draft

LINCK C. JOHNSON

Published for the Bibliographical Society of the University of Virginia
by the University Press of Virginia, Charlottesville

For Lynn

THE UNIVERSITY PRESS OF VIRGINIA
Copyright © 1986 by the Rector and Visitors
of the University of Virginia

First published 1986

Frontispiece: Thoreau's map of the journey,
ca. 1839. (Courtesy of the Thoreau Collection of
the Clifton Waller Barrett Library, the University
of Virginia Library)

Library of Congress Cataloging-in-Publication Data

Johnson, Linck C., 1946–
    Thoreau's complex weave.

    Includes index.
    1. Thoreau, Henry David, 1817–1862.   A week on the
Concord and Merrimack rivers.   2. Thoreau, Henry
David, 1817–1862—Technique.   3. Thoreau, Henry David,
1817–1862—Journeys—Merrimack River (N.H. and Mass.)
4. Thoreau, Henry David, 1817–1862—Journey—Massachusetts
—Concord River.   5. Literary journeys—New England.
6. Merrimack River (N.H. and Mass.)—Description and
travel.   7. Concord River (Mass.)—Description and travel.
I. Thoreau, Henry David, 1817–1862.   A week on the
Concord and Merrimack rivers. 1985.   II. University of
Virginia. Bibliographical Society.   III. Title.
F72.M7T533   1985   974.2'72   85-17859
ISBN 0–8139–1063–3

Printed in the United States of America

Contents

Acknowledgments

If he had included acknowledgments in *A Week,* Thoreau probably would have thanked members of his family, his mentor, Emerson, others of his friends and associates like Hawthorne, Horace Greeley, Bronson Alcott, and Ellery Channing, as well as a number of libraries, which were among the few institutions he did not disdain. By all rights I too should thank them, since some of those same individuals and institutions were later responsible for preserving the manuscripts and other records upon which this study so heavily relies. But having worked on Thoreau's first book longer than he did, I have been lucky enough to amass other, more pressing debts, which I welcome the opportunity to acknowledge.

For permission to refer to, quote from, edit, and reproduce manuscript materials, I am indebted to The Huntington Library, San Marino, California; the Houghton Library; the Henry W. and Albert A. Berg Collection, The New York Public Library, Astor, Lenox and Tilden Foundations; The Pierpont Morgan Library; the Abernethy Library of American Literature, Middlebury College; the Harry Ranson Humanities Research Center, The University of Texas at Austin; the Beinecke Rare Book Library, Yale University; the Clifton Waller Barrett Library, the University of Virginia Library; and to Mr. W. Stephen Thomas, Rochester, New York.

The efforts of other scholars have greatly facilitated my work. I owe a personal as well as a scholarly debt to William Howarth, who inspired my interest in Thoreau, who encouraged me to study *A Week,* and who has offered guidance and solid support at every stage of this project. Through him I also became involved in *The Writings of Henry D. Thoreau.* I have of course benefited from the work of Walter Harding, who initiated the edition, and from that of all of its other contributors, especially Carl Hovde and Elizabeth Witherell, who along with William Howarth edited the Princeton edition of *A Week.* I am particularly grateful to Wendell Glick, for the good talk and good times while we were working together at the Textual Center in Princeton, and to Thomas Blanding, whose work on the fragmentary Journals of the 1840s opened out the study of Thoreau's early career, and whose expertise and generosity have frequently spared me both effort and error.

I have also been lucky in those who have read my manuscript at various stages. Through early cultivation and judicious pruning, William Howarth and Carlos Baker helped spur its later growth. As the study branched out, it was tended by my friends Neill Joy and Joseph Slater, whose sensitive comments were enormously helpful. Indeed, their knowledge, interest, and support have given genuine meaning to the much-abused word *colleague*. The final shape of the study was influenced by Don Cook, who offered valuable advice, and especially by Joel Myerson, who brought his usual scholarly and critical acumen to the task of reading the manuscript. His careful scrutiny and cogent suggestions made its organization clearer and more coherent, though I of course am responsible for any tangles that remain.

The research, writing, preparation, and publication of this book have been aided by numerous individuals and institutions. Early on, I received a grant from the Huntington Library, where my month-long stay was made all the more pleasant and productive by Dr. James Thorpe and his helpful staff. Research at other libraries as well as the preparation of the manuscript was supported by a series of grants from the Humanities Development Council, Colgate University, and the Colgate Research Council. Patricia Ryan displayed infinite patience as she typed and retyped the manuscript for an author who could rarely leave well enough alone, a burden that was later handed on to my editor, Gerald Trett. His civility, wit, and wisdom have made the task of preparing the manuscript for the printer less onerous and far more instructive than I ever imagined it could be. I am also indebted to Walker Cowen, Director of the University Press of Virginia, both for his suggestions and for his confidence in this study, whose publication has been generously supported by the Bibliographical Society, the University of Virginia.

I have already exhausted the limited vocabulary of acknowledgments, so to all those mentioned above, and to the numerous scholars and critics cited in my notes, I can only add a final *thank you*. I must, however, reserve my warmest thanks and my most heartfelt gratitude to my closest friend and colleague, my wife, Lynn, who constantly took time away from her own work to read and comment on mine, and to whom this book is lovingly dedicated.

Introduction

THOREAU published only two books during his lifetime: *A Week on the Concord and Merrimack Rivers* (1849) and *Walden* (1854). His other books are collections of lectures or essays, arranged or edited by friends after his death in 1862. This does not detract from the value or significance of *Cape Cod* and *The Maine Woods* or of the looser collections of *Excursions* and *Reform Papers,* but it calls special attention to the volumes Thoreau conceived of as books. *Walden,* of course, has received such attention. In fact, its fame has distracted interest from *A Week,* as a bright star draws our attention away from a lesser luminary nearby. Yet *Walden* could not have been written if Thoreau had not first struggled with the stylistic, formal, and structural problems of his earlier book. Those early struggles, which taught him lessons later applied in *Walden,* left their mark on *A Week.* But if Thoreau's first book is flawed, it is a flawed masterpiece. Indeed, as critics have begun to recognize, even if *Walden* had not been written, *A Week* would nonetheless stand as one of the seminal works of the American Renaissance.[1]

The cornerstone of the present study is an edited text of the reconstructed first draft of *A Week.* When I began work, no scholar had suggested that a distinguishable draft had survived or even that Thoreau had written separate drafts. In a groundbreaking dissertation Carl Hovde demonstrated that Thoreau revised *A*

[1] *A Week* has received a good deal of critical attention, especially during the last 25 years. For an exhaustive list of secondary works, see Jeanetta Boswell and Sarah Crouch, *Henry David Thoreau and the Critics: A Checklist of Criticism, 1900–1978* (Metuchen, N.J.: Scarecrow Press, 1981). The most recent selected and annotated bibliography is Michael Meyer's "Henry David Thoreau," in *The Transcendentalists: A Review of Research and Criticism,* ed. Joel Myerson (New York: Modern Language Association, 1984), pp. 260–85, a helpful guide, not only to criticism of *A Week,* but also through scholarship on other aspects of Thoreau's career touched upon in my study.

Week with great care and conceived of it as a unified work of art.[2] Hovde, however, did not have access to a complete census of its surviving manuscripts, so he was able to arrive at only tentative conclusions about the way Thoreau wrote his first book. When I examined microfilms of manuscripts William Howarth had later identified as belonging to *A Week,* however, I discovered that, while they were widely scattered, certain groups of manuscripts bore striking similarities. A physical examination of surviving leaves in the Berg Collection of the New York Public Library, the Pierpont Morgan Library, the Abernethy Library at Middlebury College, the Houghton Library at Harvard University, the Henry E. Huntington Library, and manuscripts in W. S. Thomas's important private collection confirmed that these scattered manuscripts were part of a single first draft of *A Week.* These manuscripts are described in detail in Part 2, which also includes a chapter-by-chapter reconstruction of the first draft, with each leaf listed in its probable original order and referred to its place in the edited text.

My study of the writing of *A Week* in Part 1 is largely based upon the first draft and other previously unpublished materials. At the Textual Center of *The Writings of Henry D. Thoreau,* I had access to a wealth of material, including transcriptions of Thoreau's Journal of 1837–49, much of which was not printed in the 1906 edition of the Journal. As part of my work on *A Week,* I transcribed two volumes of Thoreau's Journal transcripts, the texts of which appear in the first two volumes of the Princeton edition of the Journal. The second of these transcript volumes, the Long Book, contains his initial adaptations and revisions of entries from the Journal for the first draft of *A Week.* After reconstructing the first draft, written in 1845, I transcribed all other

---

[2]"The Writing of Henry D. Thoreau's *A Week on the Concord and Merrimack Rivers:* A Study of Textual Materials and Techniques," Ph.D. diss., Princeton, 1956. Portions of Hovde's dissertation have been published as "Nature into Art: Thoreau's Use of His Journals in *A Week,*" *American Literature* 30 (1958):165–84, and "Literary Materials in Thoreau's *A Week,*" *PMLA 80* (1965):76–83, both of which offer valuable insights into Thoreau's process of composition.

surviving leaves, most of them omitted from a second draft of *A Week*, written in 1846–47 and revised and expanded at intervals during the following two years. I often quote significant passages from these leaves, and I include the texts of some other passages omitted from *A Week* in the Appendix. In the Historical Introduction to the Princeton edition of *A Week*, I have elsewhere outlined the stages of its growth and traced the history of its publication, reception, and later reputation. In this study I am less concerned with its fortunes after the publication of the first edition in 1849. Instead, I focus on the background and composition of *A Week*, offering an analysis of the method by which Thoreau constructed his first book, the impact of events on its emerging form and underlying structure, and the relationship between its design and the overall pattern of his early literary career.

The trip took two weeks; his account of that trip occupied Thoreau on and off for ten years, nearly a quarter of his lifetime. In fact, when he and his brother, John Thoreau, Jr., left Concord, Massachusetts, for a boating and walking tour to the White Mountains on August 31, 1839, Thoreau probably had no thought of writing about their holiday. Then twenty-two, the young schoolteacher had been scribbling busily since his graduation from Harvard two years earlier, but Thoreau had no outlet for the poetry and prose he had accumulated in his Journal. Shortly after the brothers' return to Concord, however, members of the Transcendental Club founded the *Dial*, for which Thoreau soon began to plan a series of articles, among them an essay on the 1839 trip. But, after beginning that account in June 1840, he soon turned to other projects for the *Dial*. His plans for a book emerged only after John's death in 1842. Two years later he gathered material from the Journal of 1837–44 into the Long Book, source of most of the first draft of *A Week*, probably begun after he moved to Walden Pond on July 4, 1845. There he also wrote a second draft, completed in 1847. Unable to find a publisher, he continued to work on the manuscript until 1849, when Thoreau published *A Week on the Concord and Merrimack Rivers* at his own expense.

If the writing of *A Week* had been as simple and straightforward as the paragraph above suggests, my study would hardly justify either its length or its title. But Thoreau's process of composition was far more elaborate and complex. In a celebrated parable of his life and literary vocation at the opening of *Walden,* Thoreau used an illuminating image to describe the writing of *A Week.* After telling of an Indian's unsuccessful efforts to sell baskets in Concord, he continued: "I too had woven a kind of basket of a delicate texture, but I had not made it worth any one's while to buy them. Yet not the less, in my case, did I think it worth my while to weave them, and instead of studying how to make it worth men's while to buy my baskets, I studied rather how to avoid the necessity of selling them." (*Wa* 19).

A Week, which had sold only about two hundred copies by the time *Walden* was published in 1854, was that "basket of a delicate texture," the first great product of Thoreau's craftsmanship. But basket weaving, which suggested the title and organization of my study, is also an apt analogy for the writing of *A Week.* Like the Indian, Thoreau gathered whatever materials were readily available to him. From these he began to fashion a simple utilitarian product, yet one capable of serving the higher uses of art. The design of the basket was suggested by two literary forms: the excursion, which provided strong narrative and symbolic elements, and the elegy, the source of important thematic and structural elements. These elements formed the woof and warp of *A Week.* As he plaited them together, Thoreau also worked in strands of material on reform, colonial history, and literature, thus achieving the variety, complexity, and "delicate texture" of *A Week.*

My first chapter concerns the development of Thoreau's ideas about the excursion, his most successful literary form. From models as diverse as Virgil's *Eclogues,* Bunyan's *Pilgrim's Progress,* Goethe's *Italienische Reise,* and contemporary travel books, Thoreau developed a flexible vehicle for natural and poetic description, imaginative flight, and spiritual quest. Although he began to plan an account of the 1839 trip to the White Mountains as early as 1840, he first experimented with the excursion form in essays published in 1843, "A Walk to Wachusett" and "A Winter Walk," prototypes for the book to come. In these early "walks" Thoreau learned to exploit the symbolic possibilities of rivers and mountains and to organize his experiences in linear and cyclical patterns that would also characterize his first book. As he worked on *A Week,* Thoreau wrote "Ktaadn, and the Maine Woods," which possibly inspired him to depict a series of mountain ascents within the larger journey described in *A Week;* he also completed the first versions of *Walden,* in which he continued the figurative journey begun in *A Week.*

In contrast to *Walden* and his other early excursions, *A Week* was unpremeditated. During the 1839 trip, Thoreau made few, if any, preparations for giving an account of his impressions and experiences. He probably would have sympathized with Mark Twain, who complained that he remembered "next to nothing" about the trip described in *Roughing It,* for when Thoreau began *A Week* he, too, was frustrated by a paucity of materials and was forced to improvise. That *A Week* often seem spontaneous and immediate is a sign of his artistry, for some of its most vivid descriptions were either adapted from unrelated Journal entries, drawn from guidebooks, or based upon his experiences during other journeys, including a return trip to southern New Hampshire in 1848. Indeed, as illustrated in chapter 1, *A Week* is less a journal of the excursion than a reconstruction of that excursion; less a product of direct observation than of research, craft, and imagination.

In *A Week* the narrative and symbolic elements of the excursion are crossed by the elements of the pastoral elegy. In my second chapter I seek to demonstrate how strongly Thoreau's elegiac purpose controlled the theme and structure of *A Week.* His initial efforts to come to terms with the death of his brother, John, in January 1842, notably in letters and Journal entries written in the months following, illuminate his later elegiac strategies in *A Week.* Like Milton in "Lycidas," Thoreau tried to place his brother's death within the context of nature's seasonal cycle of death and rebirth. But, in contrast to Milton, Thoreau looked solely to the natural world for consolation rather than seeking it in a realm of supernatural order. "Natural History of Massachusetts," his first essay following John's death, and poems written in 1843 reveal an emphasis on signs of continuity and permanence in nature, art, and human pursuits, signs that Thoreau also sought to discover in the first draft of *A Week.* Later revisions and additions illuminate his persistent efforts to heighten the drama of grief and reconciliation in the book. His elegiac purpose also explains the seasonal structure of *A Week*. Although the brothers returned to Concord on September 13, eight days before the autumnal equinox, Thoreau devotes much of "Friday" to a meditation on the autumnal landscape. He thus created an imaginary landscape poised between fruition and decay yet offering signs of endurance and intimations of immortality.

The excursion and the elegy form the pattern of *A Week*, but there are three other major strands of material, only a few traces of which are apparent in the first draft. I therefore devote a chapter each to Thoreau's commitment to reform, his uses of colonial history, and his digressions on literary subjects in *A Week*. The order in which I take up these three topics alters the order in which they emerged in his other writings, which revealed first his immersion in literature (his undergraduate essays and contributions to the *Dial*), then his growing preoccupation with reform, culminating in *Walden*, and finally his fascination with the early discovery, exploration, and settlement of America, a major theme in *A Yankee in Canada, The Maine Woods, Cape Cod*, and late essays like "Walking." But surviving manuscripts suggest that my arrangement accurately reflects changing patterns in *A Week* as Thoreau revised and expanded it during 1846–49. His overlapping interests in reform, colonial history, and literature developed much earlier, however, so in each chapter I first trace the development of his ideas within the cultural and historical context and then discuss the ways Thoreau sought to integrate materials on these topics in *A Week*.

The first of these major strands relates to the issue of reform, manifested by Thoreau's growing awareness of social issues during the decade 1839–49. By the time *A Week* was published, he had also completed "Resistance to Civil Government" (better known as "Civil Disobedience") and the early versions of *Walden*, originally scheduled for publication shortly after *A Week*. Even before the 1839 trip, his views had begun to take shape under the influence of Emerson and other Transcendentalists. Although Thoreau avoided direct involvement in reform activities, by the time he began *A Week* he had become increasingly preoccupied

with the controversies simmering in New England. That interest
is apparent in an unpublished lecture on the conservative and
the reformer, drafted early in 1844, and in his tributes to prominent abolitionists: "Herald of Freedom" (1844), a review of the
antislavery newspaper edited by Nathaniel Rogers, and "Wendell
Phillips before Concord Lyceum" (1845). His radical views were
only dimly reflected in the first draft, but after his arrest in 1846
Thoreau began to express a wide range of social, political, and
religious concerns in *A Week*. Since he shifted some passages to
Walden and omitted others, many of which I quote or paraphrase,
the published version of *A Week* does not fully measure the extent
of his critique of life in New England. Nonetheless, as a study
of its background and composition reveals, the book was strongly
influenced by the spirit of dissent and protest that characterized
the age.

The second major strand woven into the elegiac excursion is
apparent in Thoreau's interest in colonial history in *A Week*. That
interest was prompted by his fascination with the American Indian. At Harvard, he made his first forays into the increasingly
voluminous literature concerning Indian tribes and the colonial
past. But he found little place for either the Indians or their epic
struggles with white settlers in his early essays, which tended to
ignore or dismiss what he called the "dark age" of New England.
It was in *A Week* that he discovered the uses of the colonial past.
Beginning with a few scattered references in the first draft, he
created a compelling version of the destruction of the Indians
and of a wilderness paradise in America. I am particularly concerned with the way Thoreau constructed that account, which
reveals his dependence on colonial narratives and local histories,
as well as his growing ability to select, arrange, and recast these
materials for *A Week*.

The uses of the literary past provided Thoreau with the final
strand in his complex weave. His literary habits and tastes developed at Harvard, where he began to read deeply in the classics
of Continental and English literature. He also discovered Emerson, who inspired many of Thoreau's early literary activities. The
excursion seemed to represent his predestined form, but he wrote
mostly poetry, translations, and criticism for the *Dial*. From 1841

to 1844 he also worked on an anthology of English poetry, for which he gathered a good deal of material that later found its way into *A Week*. Although the first draft contained a number of poems and quotations, it included only a few brief passages on literary topics. As he revised and expanded the book, however, Thoreau gathered material on writers and writing from the early Journal and unpublished essays like "Sir Walter Raleigh." He also inserted a series of articles originally published in the *Dial*. His first book consequently included a good deal of material from the period of his literary apprenticeship, but Thoreau arranged these materials in a sophisticated pattern in *A Week,* where he first expresses his ideals of writing, then charts the decline of those ideals from epic poets to writers of more civilized eras, and finally asserts his own potential role in the creation of a native American literature.

A Week thus takes its place in the broader context of America's Declaration of Cultural Independence. But, as I argue in my final chapter, the book was also a product of a series of personal crises and private revolutions. In fact, the writing of *A Week* charts Thoreau's long and difficult struggle to assert himself as a man and as a writer, especially in relation to Emerson, who encouraged, shaped, and directed his young disciple's literary career. An effort to please Emerson informs virtually all of Thoreau's early writing projects, especially his varied contributions to the *Dial*. But his involvement in the *Dial* offered neither remuneration nor recognition, so Thoreau sought other means of establishing himself as a writer and thus fulfilling Emerson's expectations. Through Hawthorne's influence Thoreau published his first essay outside the *Dial* in 1843, the year he moved to New York City in a desperate effort to become a self-supporting writer. There he published two articles in the *United States Magazine and Democratic Review,* an influential political and literary journal whose contributors included Bryant, Whittier, and Hawthorne. He also became friends with Horace Greeley, founder and editor of the *New-York Tribune,* who later acted as an agent for his works, but Thoreau failed to gain a foothold in New York's literary world and soon retreated home to Concord.

That failure and the collapse of the *Dial* in 1844 set the stage for his two books, which he worked on during the next five years. His move to Walden Pond in 1845 marked a crucial turning point, for thereafter Thoreau began to chart his own course in his life and writings, especially in *A Week*. By doing so, he resisted both Emerson's ideas about the direction the book should take and Greeley's advice about the direction his career should take. Even after failing to find a publisher for *A Week* in 1847, a failure that seemed to justify Greeley's advice that he should write for magazines to make a name for himself, Thoreau persevered with *A Week* and *Walden*, which were crucial to his own strategy for gaining literary recognition. Indeed, by publishing *A Week* at his own expense in 1849, Thoreau clearly hoped to escape the invidious comparisons with Emerson he had been subject to since graduating from college and to free himself from the equally onerous necessities of Greeley's literary marketplace. Some critics recognized *A Week* as the work of an original and independent artist, and its commercial failure brought Thoreau's relationship with Emerson to a crisis, after which the two men stood on a more equal footing. In an equally ironic and unanticipated way, the publication of *A Week* also helped liberate Thoreau from the literary marketplace, for, as we have seen, its failure prompted him to study, not how to sell his books, but "how to avoid the necessity of selling them."

As this introduction suggests, I believe a study of the writing of *A Week* illuminates a broad range of issues concerning Thoreau's artistry, the initial direction and overall shape of his literary career, and his reactions to cultural and historical developments during the 1840s. First, it reveals his response to formal problems of style, form, and structure. Second, it indicates the relationship not only between *A Week* and his other early writings but also between his first book and *Walden*, which is perhaps best understood as a sequel to *A Week*. Third, it illustrates the problems Thoreau confronted during his long struggle to become a self-supporting writer. Fourth, it sheds light on his relationships with Emerson, Hawthorne, and other literary figures, as well as his responses to broader movements like Transcendentalism and abolitionism. During the writing of *A Week* Thoreau moved outward from relatively narrow personal, philosophical, and literary concerns to broader social, cultural, and historical questions. I therefore have sought to treat the manuscripts and text of *A Week* not simply as the product of a particular phase in the growth of Thoreau's mind but also as part of a chapter in what Perry Miller called the life of the mind in America. As I suggest in the Epilogue, *A Week* was an American book in every sense of that resonant phrase: a book written by a self-consciously American artist determined to resist the lure of European culture and to discover the resources of art in his native land; a book whose failure underscored the difficulties of writing in a country that offered few rewards to its men of letters; and a book that, despite its commercial failure, may in retrospect be viewed as a herald of a series of masterpieces in the 1850s—*The Scarlet Letter, Moby-Dick, Walden,* and *Leaves of Grass*—that finally began to put American literature on an equal footing with the national literatures of Europe.

Abbreviations

C   *The Correspondence of Henry David Thoreau*. Ed. Walter Harding and Carl Bode. New York: New York Univ. Press, 1958.

CC   *Consciousness in Concord*. The Text of Thoreau's Hitherto "Lost Journal" (1840–1841) Together with Notes and a Commentary by Perry Miller. Boston: Houghton Mifflin, 1958.

CE   *The Complete Works of Ralph Waldo Emerson*. 12 vols. Boston: Houghton Mifflin, 1903.

CP   *Collected Poems of Henry Thoreau*. Enlarged edition. Ed. Carl Bode. Baltimore: Johns Hopkins Univ. Press, 1964.

CW   *The Collected Works of Ralph Waldo Emerson*. Ed. Alfred R. Ferguson et al. 3 vols. to date. Cambridge: Harvard Univ. Press, 1971–.

D   The *Dial: A Magazine for Literature, Philosophy, and Religion*. 4 vols. [1840–44]. New York: Russell & Russell, 1961.

DHT   Walter Harding. *The Days of Henry Thoreau*. Enlarged and corrected edition. New York: Dover, 1982.

EEM   Henry D. Thoreau. *Early Essays and Miscellanies*. Ed. Joseph J. Moldenhauer and William Moser, with Alexander C. Kern. Princeton: Princeton Univ. Press, 1975.

Ex   Henry D. Thoreau. *Excursions*. Volume 5 of *The Writings of Henry D. Thoreau*. 6 vols. Boston: Houghton Mifflin, 1906.

FD   The text of the first draft of *A Week on the Concord and Merrimack Rivers*. Edited below, Part 2.

HDT   Henry David Thoreau.

HM   Manuscripts in the Henry E. Huntington Library, San Marino, Calif. References include the number of the manuscript, the number or title of the division within the manuscript, and, for paginated leaves that were part of the second draft of *A Week*, Thoreau's page numbers (recto and verso).

J   The *Journal* of Henry D. Thoreau. Ed. John C. Broderick et
         al. 2 vols to date. Princeton: Princeton Univ. Press, 1981–.
         Since page proofs are not yet available, I have not included
         page numbers in references to *Journal 3: 1848–1851*
         (forthcoming).

JMN   *The Journals and Miscellaneous Notebooks of Ralph Waldo
         Emerson*. Ed. William H. Gilman et al. 16 vols. Cambridge:
         Harvard Univ. Press, 1961–83.

L   *The Letters of Ralph Waldo Emerson*. Ed. Ralph L. Rusk. 6
         vols. New York: Columbia Univ. Press, 1939.

LMHDT   William L. Howarth. *The Literary Manuscripts of Henry
         David Thoreau*. Columbus: Ohio State Univ. Press, 1974.
         Cited by item numbers.

MH   Manuscripts designated bMS Am 278.5 in the Houghton
         Library, Harvard University. References include the folder
         number within bMS Am 278.5 and, for paginated leaves
         that were part of the second draft of *A Week,* Thoreau's
         page numbers (recto and verso).

MW   Henry D. Thoreau. *The Maine Woods*. Ed. Joseph J.
         Moldenhauer. Princeton: Princeton Univ. Press,
         1972.

RLF   *Records of a Lifelong Friendship, 1807–1882, Ralph Waldo
         Emerson and William Henry Furness*. Ed. H. H. Furness.
         Boston: Houghton Mifflin, 1910.

RP   Henry D. Thoreau. *Reform Papers*. Ed. Wendell Glick.
         Princeton: Princeton Univ. Press, 1973.

S   J. Lyndon Shanley. *The Making of Walden*. Chicago: Univ.
         of Chicago Press, 1957.

TL   Walter Harding. *Thoreau's Library*. Charlottesville: Univ. of
         Virginia Press, 1957.

TLN   *Thoreau's Literary Notebook in the Library of Congress*.
         Facsimile text edited by Kenneth Walter Cameron.
         Hartford: Transcendental Books, 1964.

TN   Textual note. Cited by the page and line references of the
         note.

W   Henry D. Thoreau. *A Week on the Concord and Merrimack
         Rivers*. Ed. Carl F. Hovde, William L. Howarth, and
         Elizabeth Hall Witherell. Historical Introduction by Linck
         C. Johnson. Princeton: Princeton Univ. Press, 1980.

49 W   Henry D. Thoreau, *A Week on the Concord and Merrimack Rivers*. Boston: James Munroe, 1849.

Wa   Henry D. Thoreau, *Walden*. Ed. J. Lyndon Shanley. Princeton: Princeton Univ. Press, 1971.

PART ONE

The Writing of *A Week on the Concord and Merrimack Rivers*

1
Early Excursions, 1839-49

THE GROWTH OF *A Week* from inception to publication, 1839-49, illustrates the development of Thoreau's ideas about the literary excursion.[1] He took only a few meager notes during a vacation he and his elder brother, John, took to the White Mountains of New Hampshire in September 1839, but Emerson apparently encouraged him to write an account of that trip. For models Thoreau relied upon the travel books and pastoral poetry he had begun to read at Harvard. In passages drafted in June 1940 for a projected essay, he thus depicted the journey as a withdrawal from the village to an unspoiled poetic world where he and his brother achieve a closer communion with nature. After John's death in 1842 Thoreau began to plan a book. Before he began work in 1844, he wrote two preliminary excursions, "A Walk to Wachusett" and "A Winter Walk." In them, Thoreau used the excursion as a vehicle for an imaginative and spiritual quest. He also began to exploit the symbolic possibilities of rivers and mountains, the central features in the landscape of *A Week*.

A Week was less a product of direct observation than of recollection, imagination, and craft. By the time he began to gather materials for the book, Thoreau had written but little about the 1839 trip. He therefore reconstructed it by adapting unrelated entries from the Journal, 1837-44. Depicting a voyage of exploration and discovery, Thoreau in the first draft, written in 1845, charted its course with the aid of factual books like the *New England Gazetteer*. But he continued to stress the symbolic nature of traveling through a pastoral and primitive landscape toward a distant mountain. Inspired by his ascent of Mount Katahdin in

[1]For discussions of the travel-writing tradition and the form of the literary excursion, see Leo Marx, "Thoreau's Excursions," *Yale Review* 51 (1962):363–69; and Lawrence Buell, *Literary Transcendentalism: Style and Vision in the American Renaissance* (Ithaca, N.Y.: Cornell Univ. Press, 1973), pp. 188–207.

Maine in 1846, Thoreau in 1847 inserted a portion of "A Walk to Wachusett" in "Monday" and greatly expanded the account of the ascent of Saddleback Mountain (now better known as Greylock) in "Tuesday." The metaphor of traveling and the theme of spiritual elevation played an equally important role in the first version of *Walden,* also drafted in 1847 and closely related to *A Week*. He gathered additional material for *A Week* during a walking tour of southern New Hampshire in 1848, when he confronted the results of the rapid growth of the Merrimack valley since 1839. By the time it was published in 1849, *A Week* was thus composed of a carefully orchestrated series of excursions through New England, at once a pastoral realm, a primitive wilderness, and a bustling industrial region.

In *A Week* Thoreau describes a river excursion, passing over in a few brief paragraphs the days he and John had spent hiking and mountain climbing. But the pair probably conceived of the voyage simply as a convenient and inexpensive means of reaching the White Mountains. Their trip preceded the "Golden Age of the White Mountains," as Frederick Tuckerman called the years 1840-60,[2] but by 1839 Mount Washington, the highest peak, had already attracted a distinguished list of visitors, including Timothy Dwight, author of *Travels in New England and New York* (1821-22); the English writer Charles Joseph Latrobe, whose *Rambler in North America* (1832-33) was dedicated to his companion Washington Irving; and Harriet Martineau, who described her visit in *Retrospect of Western Travel* (1838). In 1832 Nathaniel Hawthorne climbed Mount Washington and explored the surrounding area, the setting of tales like "The Ambitious Guest" (1835) and "The Great Carbuncle," subtitled "A Mystery of the White Mountains" (1837). Thoreau may have read some of these

[2]Quoted in F. Allen Burt, *The Story of Mount Washington* (Hanover, N.H.: Dartmouth Publications, 1960), p. 63, which contains an excellent survey of the early visitors to the White Mountains. Detailed accounts of the brothers' experiences during their week in the White Mountains include Christopher McKee, "Thoreau's First Visit to the White Mountains," *Appalachia* 31 (1956): 199–209; and *Thoreau in the Mountains* (New York: Farrar Strauss Giroux, 1982), a collection of Thoreau's writings with commentary by William Howarth, pp. 207–23.

accounts; he had certainly at least heard a good deal about the area from Emerson, who had first visited the White Mountains in 1832 when he was making his momentous decision to resign from the Unitarian ministry. In fact, it was probably no coincidence that Emerson joined his second cousin George Bradford for a return visit to the White Mountains shortly before his young friends Henry and John Thoreau embarked from Concord on Saturday, August 31, 1839, aboard the *Musketaquid,* a boat they had built that spring and christened with the Indian name for the Concord River.

Thoreau's initial record of that jaunt bears about as much resemblance to *A Week* as an offhand sketch of a boat bears to Thomas Cole's series of paintings *The Voyage of Life,* an apposite and equally ambitious work begun in 1839. On Saturday, Thoreau recorded some excited impressions of night at their first campsite on the banks of the Concord. The next day he added a description of the river between Ball's Hill and Billerica, jotted down while he rested by the side of the Middlesex Canal, connecting link between the Concord and the Merrimack. Thereafter he tersely recorded each day's progress up the Merrimack. The river voyage ended Wednesday night near the village of Hooksett, New Hampshire, where he and John left their boat the next morning and "walked to Concord—10 miles."[3]

Thoreau was no more expansive about their tour of the White Mountains. On Friday they took a stagecoach to Plymouth, from which they walked to Tilton's Inn in Thornton. "The scenery commences on Sanbornton square, Whence the White Mountains are first visible," Thoreau observed in the stilted, self-conscious tone of a tourist about to encounter the sublime. "In Campton it

[3]In the Journal Thoreau's excursion notes appear under the date "June 21st 1840" (J 1:134–37). He wrote "Copied from pencil" above the notes and put them in quotation marks to set them off from interpolated comments and from the following entry. In the fall of 1841 he transcribed the surviving contents of his three early Journal volumes into five smaller volumes, so it is not possible to determine when he first transcribed his notes "Copied from pencil." Thus, the Journal entries for 1837 through the fall of 1841 are transcripts, while his notes "Copied from pencil" are apparently transcripts of transcripts.

is decidedly mountainous." But he did not record his impressions of the scenery the brothers enjoyed as they hiked from Thornton through Peeling and Lincoln to Franconia. In fact, although he mentions the main tourist attractions they took in—the basin and flume at Lincoln, Franconia Notch, and the Old Man of the Mountains, visible from Echo Lake—the only thing he found worth recording in detail were the dimensions of the flume, "the measurements of some scientific person—according to Mr. Gurnsey who keeps the inn, and furnishes these facts." On Sunday, breaking the sabbath as usual, he and John walked from Franconia to the most famous of the White Mountain inns, Thomas J. Crawford's "Notch House," a comfortable hotel where they stayed for two nights before ascending Mount Washington on Tuesday. As was usual with parties from Crawford's, before their descent the brothers may have joined in singing "Old Hundred" (the Doxology), proclaiming their youthful joy in the glory of God's creation. But, although the experience on the summit would later assume great symbolic importance in *A Week,* Thoreau in his notes simply recorded, "Sept. 10th ascended the mountain and rode to Conway." From there the weary pair took other stagecoaches back through Concord to Hooksett, where they retrieved their boat and embarked for the two-day return voyage on Thursday, September 12.

Thoreau's sketchy record suggests that he did not originally plan to write about the trip; if so, a number of factors may have changed his mind. After returning on September 2 from the White Mountains, where he "found few striking experiences," Emerson in his journal complained about "the perpetual self preservation of the traveller," who could not "forget himself & yielding to the new world of facts that environ him, utter without memory that which they say" (*JMN* V.II:234-36). On September 14, the day after Henry and John returned to Concord, Emerson implicitly compared his own disappointing journey by railroad and stagecoach to their voyage: "Now here are my wise young neighbors who instead of getting . . . into a railroad-car where they have not even the activity of holding the reins, have got into a boat which they have built with their own hands[,] with sails which they have contrived to serve as a tent by night, & gone up the river

Merrimack to live by their wits on the fish of the stream & the berries of the wood" (*JMN* VII:238). His enthusiasm for the river voyage, which Emerson viewed as natural mode of travel, and his emphasis on their ingenuity and self-reliance possibly caused Thoreau to perceive the literary and philosophical uses of the jaunt. His tentative title for a lecture or essay—"Memoirs of a Tour—A Chit-chat with Nature"—suggests that by 1840 he had begun to view it as an illustration of man's intimacy and communion with nature.[4] But if that title reveals the impact of Emerson's views, it also bears witness to Thoreau's early interest in travel books like Henry Brackenridge's *Journal of a Voyage up the River Missouri* (1815), Thomas L. McKenney's *Sketches of a Tour to the Lakes* (1827), and Ross Cox's *Adventures on the Columbia River* (1832), all of which he read at Harvard, as well as Goethe's *Italienische Reise*, which he discussed in the early Journal and later in *A Week*.[5]

Italienische Reise illuminates some of the difficulties Thoreau faced when he attempted to give an account of the journey to the White Mountains. When Goethe left Weimar for Italy in 1786, he was thirty-seven and an experienced writer. Although he did not write *Italienische Reise* until twenty-five years later, Goethe was able to base his account on the copious letters and journals he wrote during his two-year stay. Moreover, while Italy offered topics such as manners, history, and art (all the topics writers like Irving, Cooper, and Hawthorne despaired of finding in America), the White Mountains seemed to offer only nature. Thoreau no doubt welcomed the opportunity to turn his eye to nature, but unlike Goethe, who had developed his gift for observation through

[4]The title is included in a list of potential lecture or essay topics in "Index rerum" (HM 945), p. 19. For the complete list, see below, p. 208.

[5]Thoreau's withdrawals from the Harvard College Library are listed in Kenneth W. Cameron, *Emerson the Essayist*, 2 vols. (Raleigh, N.C.: Thistle Press, 1945), II:191–208. For a discussion of parallels between *A Week* and Brackenridge's account, see John Aldrich Christie, *Thoreau as World Traveler* (New York: Columbia Univ. Press, 1965), pp. 251–52.

the study of anatomy, botany, and geology, Thoreau had just begun to train himself as an observer of nature.

If he lacked Goethe's experience and skills as an observer, Thoreau shared with the German master a pastoral vision that strongly influenced his conception of the 1839 tour. During his last term at Harvard, Thoreau in the spring of 1837 read and studied Milton's poetry, taking twelve pages of notes on "L'Allegro," "Il Penseroso," "Comus," and "Lycidas." Since he wrote an assigned theme on "L'Allegro" and "Il Penseroso," his interest may have been purely academic, but his comments were highly appreciative (*EEM* 73-78). His enthusiasm apparently prompted him to seek out other examples of pastoral poetry, for he soon read and took extracts from *The Paradise of Dainty Devices* and *England's Helicon.*[6] The common source of these Renaissance pastorals was, of course, Virgil's *Eclogues,* which Thoreau reread in the fall of 1837, about the same time he read *Italienische Reise.* "I would read Virgil, if only that I might be reminded of the identity of human nature in all ages," he commented in the Journal. "It was the same world, and the same men inhabited it" (*J* 1:14; cf. FD 32, W 90). As Ethel Seybold has noted, however, the lines Thoreau quoted in the Journal and later in *A Week* "were from the world and nature rather than from men and human nature."[7]

Although the vision of a pastoral Golden Age began to cast its spell on him, Thoreau was aware of the gap between the classical ideal and the mundane realities of New England. In an attempt to reconcile the real and ideal, he sought a new perspective. "One must needs climb a hill to know what a world he inhabits," he observed on November 21, 1837, the day after he commented on Virgil's *Eclogues* (*J* 1:14). For Thoreau, the ascent from the plain

[6]Kenneth Cameron, "Thoreau's Notes on Harvard Reading," *The Transcendentalists and Minerva,* 3 vols. (Hartford: Transcendental Books, 1958), I:154 ff.

[7]Ethel Seybold, *Thoreau: The Quest and the Classics* (New Haven: Yale Univ. Press, 1951), p. 29. Quotations in *A Week* are identified by William Brennan, "An Index to Thoreau's Quotations in *A Week on the Concord and Merrimack Rivers,*" *Studies in the American Renaissance 1980,* ed. Joel Myerson (Boston: Twayne, 1980), pp. 259–90.

to the hilltop was a poetic act. "Here at the top of Nawshawtuct, this mild August afternoon, I can discern no deformed thing," he wrote in the Journal on August 29, 1838. "The prophane haymakers in yonder meadow are yet the haymakers of poetry—forsooth Faustus and Amyntas." The perspective that transforms these "prophane haymakers" into the shepherds of pastoral poetry also refines the "base-metal" of man's works into nature's "gold" (J 1:53-54). Similarly, describing the view from Annursnack Hill in the summer of 1839, a few weeks before the brothers' trip, Thoreau exclaimed: "How little matters it all they have built and delved there in the valley—it is after all but a feature in the landscape— Still the vast impulse of nature breathes over all" (J 1:75). He no doubt underestimated man's impact on nature, but by celebrating her "vast impulse" Thoreau sought to preserve the world of Virgil for the budding poet in New England.

He soon began to conceive of the 1839 journey as a kind of sacerdotal withdrawal from the village. In a Journal entry dated June 11, 1840, he called it their "White Mountain expedition" and stressed the regenerative and sacramental overtones of their departure. For Thoreau the trip was a voyage of body, mind, and spirit: "Gradually the village murmur subsides—as when one falls into a placid dream and on its Lethe tide is floated from the past into the future.— or as silently as fresh thoughts awaken us to new morning or evening light" (J 1:125; cf. FD 5, W 19-20). Through the use of present tense he suggested the timeless nature of their voyage, giving it an aura that underscored the spiritual dimension of their goal. "We hear it muttered of some village far up amid the hills, and look to our chart and guide book to learn of its mountains, and caves, and rivers," he wrote in August 1840. "For the livelong day there skirts the horizon the dark blue outline of Crotched Mountain, in Goffstown, as we are told. Every sweep of the oar brings us nearer to 'the far blue mountain' " (J 1:169; cf. W 255). As in his descriptions of the view from Nawshawtuct and Annursnack, the village "amid the hills" is absorbed into the natural landscape. Although Crotched Mountain is located in Goffstown, Thoreau looks beyond that town to glimpse "the far blue mountain," a transcendent place of physical and spiritual regeneration.

He described a withdrawal to a timeless world, but he probably recognized that he could not ignore the present inhabitants along the Concord and Merrimack. Wordsworth, whose "Resolution and Independence" Thoreau recalled when he began to reconstruct his own excursion in June 1840, may have provided him with hints about how to dignify rural life without relying on either a distant perspective or a transcendental vision (see *J* 1:127). Characteristically, however, he found even greater inspiration in a classical work. After reading Virgil's *Georgics* at the end of 1840, he meditated in the Journal: "Our Golden Age must after all be a pastoral one, we would be simple men in ignorance, and not accomplished in wisdom. We want great peasants more than great heroes. The sun would shine along the highway to some purpose, if we would unlearn our wisdom and practise illiterate truth henceforth" (*J* 1:212).

Despite his emphasis on the need for "illiterate truth," Thoreau was not rejecting literature. Rather, alluding to the convention established by Virgil and followed by virtually every major English poet, that the writer must begin with humble forms before aspiring to write an epic, Thoreau affirmed the importance of that convention for life as well as art. But he made little distinction between the *Eclogues* and the *Georgics*. Although he quoted Virgil's description of "the end of the Golden Age and the commencement of the reign of Jupiter" (*J* 1:213), a decline that forced man to labor in the field, Thoreau associated husbandry with the pastoral and the Golden Age. He was possibly also influenced by his own decision to buy a farm. But even after his agreement to buy the Hollowell Place on Sudbury River fell through in the spring of 1841, his classical vision of rural wisdom and simplicity continued to influence his conception of man's life along the Concord and the Merrimack.

Thoreau increasingly sought to integrate man and nature. After boating with him along Concord River one evening in early June 1841, Emerson exclaimed that his young friend, "the good river-god," had introduced him to "a lovely new world lying as close & yet as unknown to this vulgar trite one of streets & shops as death to life or poetry to prose. Through one field only we went to the boat & then left all time, all science, all history behind us and entered into Nature with one stroke of a paddle" (*JMN* VII:454). As Thoreau had done a year earlier, Emerson described a withdrawal to a timeless poetic realm. But by the summer of 1841 Thoreau was no longer satisfied with such sharp distinctions between the profane and vulgar town and the world of nature. "This town too lies out under the sky," he observed in the Journal in July, "a port of entry and departure for souls to and from Heaven" (*J* 1:314; cf. FD 1, *W* 15). His effort to depict the town as part of the natural and celestial order is also revealed by his plans for "a poem to be called Concord," which Thoreau described in the Journal for September 4, 1841: "For argument I should have the River—the Woods—the Ponds—the Hills—the Fields—the Swamps and Meadows—the Streets and Buildings— and the Villagers. Then Morning—Noon—and Evening—Spring Summer— Autumn and Winter—Night—Indian Summer—and the Mountains in the Horizon" (*J* 1:330). He thus emphasized the natural phenomena of Concord, but he nonetheless found a place for its streets, buildings, and villagers in the panoramic landscape between the river and the mountains in the horizon.

The "argument" of Thoreau's poem illuminates his continuing plan to write an essay about the 1839 voyage. At the top of a list of writing projects jotted down in the late summer or fall of 1841, he inscribed "Merrimack & Musketaquid."[8] In contrast to "Memoirs of a Tour—A Chit-chat with Nature," in which nature is a personified abstraction, "Merrimack & Musketaquid" is sharply focused. These two streams, one dead and stagnant, as its old Indian name "Musektaquid," or "Grass-ground River," suggests (*W* 5), the other swiftly flowing, "not a dead but a living stream" (*W* 88), ultimately offered him all he needed for argument—the cycle of the day and of the seasons, the amplitude of natural forms, and, ultimately, the drama of human life. That drama unfolded before him in January 1842, when John Thoreau, Jr., died from lockjaw. As a consequence Thoreau abandoned his plan for an essay and began to plan a book to commemorate his brother's death. Although he did not have the opportunity to begin

[8]"Index rerum" (HM 945), front endpaper [verso]. For the complete list, see below, p. 211.

extended drafting of *A Week* until 1844, during 1842 and 1843 he wrote two preliminary "excursions," prototypes for the book that was to come.

The earliest version of "A Walk to Wachusett," which Thoreau revised and compressed for publication in the *Boston Miscellany of Literature* for January 1843, indicates that he conveived of the excursion primarily as a vehicle for an inward journey of mind and spirit.[9] "Nor shall the shortness of the journey be any objection if our industry can make it long," he explained. "These continents and hemispheres are the prey of a speedy familiarity, but always an unexplored and infinite region makes off on every side from the mind, as far as Cathay and as near too, into which we can make no highway or beaten track, but immediately the grass springs up in the path. To travel and 'descry new lands' is to think new thoughts, and have new imaginings." In an effort to extend in time and space the brief trip he and his student Richard Fuller had made in July 1842, Thoreau included a series of digressions in the account. In addition to passages on Wordsworth, Virgil, and the Robin Hood ballads, all of which appear in the published version, the earliest version contained an extended passage on the value of classics, a long quotation from *Italienische Reise,* and a disquisition on the economy of nature. In that draft he also underscored the spiritual dimension of their walk. "Morning is the time to set out on a pilgrimage," he remarked in a passage later revised and expanded for *A Week* (see Appendix, no. 4), and he repeatedly referred to the companions as "pilgrims." Describing the sunset from the top of the mountain, Thoreau observed, "The sun fell on us two alone of all New England men — And we were reminded that we had only to rise a little higher that the sun might never set to us" (cf. *Ex* 145).

As his first literary excursion indicates, mountains were at the center of the landscapes Thoreau had begun to explore in his life

---

[9]All quotations from the earliest version of "A Walk to Wachusett" are from an unpublished draft of the essay in a notebook in the Berg Collection of the New York Public Library (*LMHDT*, C4a). The notebook, whose other contents are discussed in chap. 2 below, will hereafter be identified as "Nature and Bird Notes."

and art. At the opening of "A Walk to Wachusett," he inserted the poem "With frontier strength ye stand your ground," in which the mountains are associated with the Golden Age and the Celestial City: "I fancy even/Through your defiles windeth the way to heaven;/And yonder still, in spite of history's page,/Linger the golden and the silver age" (*Ex* 134). Thoreau and his companion thus resemble Bunyan's pilgrims, who catch their first glimpse of the gate to heaven from the Delectable Mountains. His feeling of liberation and transcendence is apparent in the published version, where Thoreau concludes, "There is elevation in every hour, as no part of the earth is so low that the heavens may not be seen from, and we have only to stand on the summit of our hour to command an uninterrupted horizon" (*Ex* 151). But he was even more explicit in the earliest version, which continued: "We can at least occupy this sacred and solitary peak, as if we had descended on eagles wings; for an eagle has stooped to his perch on the highest cliff, and has never climbed the rock, but stands more by his wings than by his feet." As those who wait upon the Lord "shall mount up with wings as eagles . . . *and* they shall walk, and not faint" (Isaiah 40:31), so the companions in "A Walk to Wachusett" gain the strength and vision to retain their perch upon the sacred mountaintop even after their return to the profane plain.

Rivers played an equally important role in Thoreau's symbolic landscapes of New England. During his extended stay on Staten Island in 1843, he wrote Emerson, "Yet will my thoughts revert to those dear hills and that *river* which so fills up the world to its brim, worthy to be named with Mincius and Alpheus still drinking its meadows while I am far away" (*C* 123). When Emerson requested a contribution to the *Dial*, Thoreau responded with a Concord excursion, "A Winter Walk." In it, he adumbrated the central image of *A Week:* "The river flows in the rear of the towns, and we see all things from a new and wilder side. The fields and gardens come down to it with a frankness, and freedom from pretension, which they do not wear on the highway. It is the outside and edge of the earth. Our eyes are not offended by violent contrasts. The last rail of the farmer's fence is some swaying willow bough, which still preserves its freshness, and here at length all fences stop, and we no longer cross any road" (*Ex* 178).

Like a mountain, the river offers a new perspective. Instead of flowing before or through towns, Thoreau's river flows in the *rear* of towns. In contrast to *frontage,* with its associations of artfulness, ostentation, and loftiness, the lands along its banks "come *down* to it with a frankness, and freedom from pretension, which they do not wear on the *high*way." In "With frontier strength ye stand your ground" Thoreau observes that the mountains stand on "the earth's edge." The river, which he also associates with the frontier, "is the outside and edge of the earth." From that vantage point the visual conflict between man's works and nature is resolved. As the rail of a farmer's fence is finally a "swaying willow bough," so the rigid divisions man imposes on the landscape become increasingly fluid and natural, until all barriers are removed from the traveler's path.

Thoreau also stressed the ease of river travel. "We may go far up within the country now by the most retired and level road, never climbing a hill, but by broad levels ascending to the upland meadows," he continues in "A Winter Walk." "It is a beautiful illustration of the law of obedience, the flow of a river; the path for a sick man, a highway down which an acorn cup may float secure with its freight" (*Ex* 178). The effortlessness of descending the river contrasts to the stern discipline of mountain climbing. An "illustration of the law of obedience," a river indicates how healthy man's life might be if he would simply yield himself to natural laws. Ascending a mountain restores the spirit, floating down a river, "the path of a sick man," restores the body. Both journeys are emblems of human life. As Thoreau remarked in an uncompleted essay entitled "Travelling," probably begun shortly after he completed "A Winter Walk": "No Tale pleased my youthful imagination more than the Journey of a Day or A Picture of Human Life, and to my maturer years it suggests the form at least in which many thoughts might pleasantly be cast. Life is such a journey, such a progress—that the traveller seems only another name for a man."[10]

Thoreau's early excursions prepared him to write *A Week*. First,

[10]The surviving leaf is at the Beinecke Rare Book Library, Yale University (see *LMHDT,* D8f).

although nothing about his walk to Wachusett or his ramble around Concord was particularly remarkable, especially compared to contemporary accounts of journeys through unexplored tracts of Asia, Africa, and the Americas, he discovered that the most mundane journey might become a vehicle for an ambitious, imaginative quest. Second, he learned to exploit the symbolic possibilities of rivers and mountains. Finally, he experimented with different structural patterns. Perhaps inspired by Milton's "L'Allegro," which he quoted in the essay, Thoreau organized "A Winter Walk" around the events of a single day, thus complementing the more linear pattern of "A Walk to Wachusett." He would utilize both patterns in *A Week*, in which each chapter describes a movement from morning to night, while the narrative as a whole describes the movement from Concord to a mountain and back to Concord. By the end of 1843 Thoreau had thus established the form, theme, and structure of his projected book: that, of course, left the small matter of actually writing *A Week*.

If he needed additional impetus to begin work, Thoreau may have received it from Margaret Fuller's *Summer on the Lakes*.[11] In May 1843 Fuller set off with friends to Niagara Falls, where they boarded a steamboat to Chicago. From there they traveled through northern Illinois into Wisconsin, an area Fuller found as tame as New England. Eager to catch a climpse of the true wilderness, she therefore ventured on alone to Mackinaw Island, where the Chippewa and Ottawa tribes were gathered to receive their annual payments from the government. Her description of the frontier, and of that scene in particular, must have fascinated Thoreau, whom she visited on Staten Island during her return trip in September. He encouraged Fuller's plan to turn her journal of the trip into a book, which she began that fall. "Some leaves are written of my record of the West," she wrote Emerson in November from Cambridge, where she was doing research on

[11]For a more detailed account of the trip and of the writing of the book, see Arthur W. Brown, *Margaret Fuller* (Boston: Twayne, 1964), pp. 69–71. The impact of *Summer on the Lakes* on *A Week* is briefly discussed by Perry Miller, ed., *Margaret Fuller: American Romantic* (Garden City, N.Y.: Anchor, 1963), p. 116.

western travel in the Harvard Library. "I shall bring in with brief criticisms of books read there, a kind of letter box, where I shall put in part of one of S[amuel Gray] Ward's letters, one of Ellery [Channing]'s and apropos to that July moon beneath whose influences I received it, a letter containing [the poem] Triformis" (*L* III: 220n, brackets supplied). Consequently, in *Summer on the Lakes* Fuller's account of the trip is interspersed with extracts from earlier narratives of western travel, letters, poetry, and literary criticism. Thoreau of course had introduced similar materials into essays like "A Walk to Wachusett" and "A Winter Walk," but never on such a large scale, so Fuller's methods of research and composition may have offered useful hints about how to construct a book about the brothers' own late-summer tour, which he finally began a few months after *Summer on the Lakes* was published in June 1844.

Before 1844 Thoreau had drafted a small amount of material specifically for *A Week;* that fall and winter he began to reconstruct the voyage by adapting unrelated entries from the Journal. The first entry he revised and copied into the Long Book was originally titled "Sailing with and against the Stream" in the Journal of November 3, 1837, nearly two years before he and John embarked from Concord: "If one would reflect let him embark on some placid stream, and float with the current. He cannot resist the Muse. As we ascend the stream, plying the paddle with might and main, snatched and impetuous thoughts course through the brain. We dream of conflict—power—and grandeur. But turn the prow downstream, and rock, tree, kine, knoll, assuming new and varying positions, as wind and water shift the scene—favor the liquid lapse of thought, far-reaching and sublime, but ever calm and gently undulating" (*J* 1:10).

Thoreau's revision of this Journal entry represents a distinct improvement. At the opening of the entry he immediately linked boating with meditation. He was consequently less concerned with physical impressions than with the mental process of reflection. In the Long Book, however, he honed the overwrought Journal entry into one nicely balanced sentence: "While we ascended the stream, plying the oars, or shoving our way along, with might and main, the current of our dreams also was somewhat ruffled and impetuous; but when we turned the prow down stream, rock, tree, kine, knoll, silently assuming new and varying position, as wind and tide shifted the scene, we yielded ourselves to the liquid undulating lapse of thought" (J 2:3). Here the activities of rowing against and floating with the current come first, so the analogy between the current of the river and the current of their dreams develops naturally out of the experience of boating. What was a generalized depiction of boating became a far more specific and concrete description of the brothers' impressions while sailing on the Merrimack, a development that continued in drafts of *A Week* (cf. FD 40, W 339, 349).

Comparison of another entry on boating in the Journal with the revised version in the Long Book illustrates Thoreau's ability to adapt material to a radically different context:

> June 30th 1840   I sailed from Fair Haven last evening as gently and steadily as the clouds sail through the atmosphere. The wind came blowing blithely from the South west fields, and stepped into the folds of our sail like a winged horse—pulling with a strong and steady impulse. The sail bends gently to the breeze as swells some generous impulse of the heart—and anon flutters and flaps with a kind of human suspense. I could watch the motions of a sail forever, they are so rich and full of meaning. I watch the play of its pulse, as if it were my own blood beating there. (J 1:145)

> Sept 13th we sailed along as gently and steadily as the clouds sailed through the atmosphere over our heads—watching the receding shores and the motions of our sails. The north wind stepped readily into the harness we had provided for it—and pulled us along with good will—   We were not tired of watching the motions of our sail—so thin and yet so full of life, now bending to some generous impulse of the breeze. And then fluttering and flapping with a kind of human suspense. We watched the play of its pulse as if it were our own blood beating there. (J 2:16-17)

The revision reveals shifts in tone and intensity as well as locale. Changing "I" to "we," and the wind "blowing blithely from the South west fields" to the "north wind," Thoreau transformed a mild summer evening on the Concord to a brisk day on the Merrimack below Chelmsford. In 1840 he had used the "pulse" of the sail as an example of the happy correspondence between man and nature; in 1844, more than two years after John's death, Thoreau stressed the frailty and suspense of human life. While formerly he was "blown on by God's breath" (J 1:145), now the brothers remained "always at the mercy of the breeze" that pulled their small boat down the Merrimack (J 2:17; cf. FD 94-95, W 360).

Because he had planned an account of the voyage since 1840, Thoreau had occasionally described his life in Concord with an eye to the projected work. "As I walk across the yard from The barn to the House—through the fog—with a lamp in my hand," he wrote on August 6, 1841, "I am reminded of the Merrimack nights—and seem to see the sod between tent ropes. The trees seen dimly through the mist suggest things which do not at all belong to the past, but are peculiar to my fresh New England life. It is as novel as green peas. The dew hangs every where upon the grass—and I breathe the rich damp air in slices" (J 1:316-17).

Characteristically, Thoreau sharply revised and compressed this entry in the Long Book. "When we looked out from under our tent—the trees were seen dimly through the mist, and a cool dew hung upon the grass," he wrote. "And in the damp air we seemed to inhale a solid fragrance" (J 2:22-23). Omitting the abstract comment about the quality of life in New England, he stressed the brothers' immediate physical impressions. But he also sacrificed two striking images, "as novel as green peas" and "I breathe the rich damp air in slices," substituting a somewhat less specific and evocative image. Whether or not the revision was a complete success, it reflects the critical gaze Thoreau cast upon his early Journal entries as he gathered material for A Week (cf. FD 88, W 332).

His descriptions of boating and recollections of Merrimack nights were obvious choices for inclusion in the Long Book, but other entries Thoreau revised and recopied there reveal his sharp eye for useful material. As an illustration that the "Gods are of no sect—they side with no man," on April 15, 1841, he noted in the Journal: "When I imagined that nature inclined rather to some few earnest and faithful souls, and specially existed for them— I go to see an obscure individual who lives under the hill letting both gods and men alone and find that strawberries and tomatoes grow for him too in his garden there, and the sun lodges kindly under his hill side—and am compelled to allow the grand catholicism of nature, and the unbribable charity of the gods" (J 1:301). On first glance the entry hardly promises to provide matter for A Week. But, in the Long Book, Thoreau ingeniously, and rather disingenuously, remarked, "Away up among the hills here I learn that nature is very catholic and impartial— Strawberries and tomatoes grow as well in one man's garden as anothers, and the sun lodges kindly under his hill side" (J 2:21; cf. W 290-91).

His revisions of two other entries from April 1841, apparently a rather desultory month for journalizing, reveal how carefully Thoreau sifted the Journal to collect bits and pieces in the Long Book. On April 24 he had noted, "It has been a cloudy drizzling day with occasional brightenings in the mist, when the trill of the tree-sparrow seemed to be ushering in sunny hours" (J 1:303). Changing "has been" to "was," he copied the sentence into the Long Book, where it described the sixth day of the excursion, September 5, 1839 (J 2:21; cf. FD 82, W 299-300). As he was able to make one day serve another, Thoreau was also able to make certain quotations serve a second purpose. On April 30 he had concluded a discussion of a natural literary style with a quotation from Nathaniel Morton's New England's Memorial: " 'For summer being ended, all things,' said the pilgrim, 'stand in appearance with a weather-beaten face, and the whole country full of woods and thickets represented a wild and savage hue' " (J 1:306). He initially ignored the remarks about literary style, later to become a major theme in A Week, but Thoreau copied the quotation into the Long Book, where he prefaced it with the comment "The country has not much changed since the days of the pilgrims" (J 2:22; cf. FD 89).

His emphasis on the unchanging scenery is revealing. In contrast to travelers like Timothy Dwight, whose dominant theme was the "conversion of New England from a wilderness into a civilized society,"[12] Thoreau sought to discover the wilderness that survived in New England. Embarking on the rivers, "the guides which conducted the footsteps of the first travellers" (FD 2, W 12), the adventurous pair become explorers of a New World. In "Saturday," Thoreau called Ball's Hill "the St. Anne's of Concord voyageurs" (FD 7, W 22), a reference to the point just below Montreal on the St. Lawrence River that was considered the jumping-off place for voyages to the interior (J 2:393n). Like the early navigators, when the brothers pass an island, a "piece of unexplored America," they name it (FD 19; cf. W 44). As they proceed up the Merrimack, the scenery becomes increasingly primitive. Drawing upon an 1842 Journal entry revised in the Long Book (J 1:445, 2:56), Thoreau observed in "Thursday": "In many parts the Merrimack is as wild and natural as ever, and the shore and surrounding scenery exhibit only the revolutions of nature. The pine stands up erect on its brink, and the alders and willows fringe its edge, only the beaver and the red man have departed" (FD 84). As "many parts" suggests, his description was vague and generalized, less a depiction of a specific locale than a picture of the primitive wilderness through which he and John had ostensibly voyaged.

Thoreau used several aids as he charted the voyage in the first draft. Sometime after their trip he had drawn up a detailed map of the area between Concord and the White Mountains, marking their nightly campsites with small triangles, or tents.[13] Added to his excursion notes, which he recopied in the Long Book, the map probably helped Thoreau delineate each day of the voyage

[12]Timothy Dwight, *Travels in New England and New York,* ed. Barbara Miller Solomon with Patricia M. King, 4 vols. (Cambridge: Harvard Univ. Press, 1969), I:xxxiii. It is not clear whether he read Dwight before the publication of *A Week,* but the *Travels* had a marked impact on Thoreau's writings during the 1850s. See Walter Harding, "Thoreau and Timothy Dwight," *Boston Public Library Quarterly* 10 (1958): 109–15.

[13]The map is reproduced in Robert F. Stowell, *A Thoreau Gazetteer,* ed. William L. Howarth (Princeton: Princeton Univ. Press, 1970), p. 2, and in this volume as frontispiece.

by indicating towns and landmarks they had passed that day. His familiarity with the Concord gave weight to the descriptions in "Concord River," "Saturday," and the opening of "Sunday." But in descriptions of the territories along the Merrimack, he tended to rely upon the *New England Gazetteer*. "As we rested in the shade or rowed leisurely along we had recourse from time to time to the gazeteer, which was our Navigator," he noted in "Sunday." "And from its bald natural facts extracted the pleasure of poetry" (FD 32, *W* 90). Thoreau, however, also extracted a good many of its "bald natural facts." His first-draft description of the Merrimack River compresses the *Gazetteer* entry for "Merrimack River, N. H.," portions of which read:

> One of the principal rivers of New England, is formed of two branches. The N. branch called Pemigewasset, rises near the Notch of the White mountains. . . . The E. branch is the Winnepisiogee, through which pass the waters of the lake of that name. . . . The confluent stream bears the name of Merrimack, and pursues a S. course, 78 miles, to Chelmsford, Mass.; thence an E. course, 35 miles, to the sea at Newburyport. . . . The Merrimack, whose fountains are nearly at a level with the Connecticut, being much shorter in its course, has a far more rapid descent to the sea than the latter river. Hence the intervals on its borders are less extensive, and the scenery less beautiful, than on the Connecticut. . . . The name of this river was originally written *Merramacke* and *Monnomake,* which in the Indian language signified a *sturgeon*.[14]

While he roughly followed the arrangement and even the wording of the original passage, Thoreau made it his own. Placing the description within the context of a meditation on the ways natural boundaries "balk the efforts of restricting legislatures,"

[14]John Hayward, *The New England Gazetteer* (Concord, N.H.: Boyd and White, 1839), unpaged (see *TL* 57). Hereafter all quotations from the *Gazetteer* will be identified by titles of entries in this edition.

he began, "The *Merrimack* or as its name signifies the *Sturgeon* River is the main artery of New Hampshire though this state should have a mountain boundary on the west and east instead of a river which divides it against itself and makes it face both ways" (FD 30-31; cf. W 83). He also added brief comments on navigation and on the flora and fauna of the state, all of which he extracted from Jeremy Belknap's description of the Merrimack in the *History of New-Hampshire.*[15] Although the result was not as effective as "Concord River," it served as an apt introduction to the Merrimack River and a striking illustration of Thoreau's efforts to compensate for his lack of first-hand knowledge.

Despite the material he had harvested from the Journal and books like the *Gazetteer* and Belknap's *History,* Thoreau had some difficulty creating a convincingly detailed version of the excursion in the first draft of *A Week.* Too often his impressions seem vague or insubstantial. He habitually prefaced descriptions with "occasionally," "from time to time," and "perchance," expressions that undermined the directness and immediacy of his account. Many of his revisions reveal an effort to make the narrative more specific, for example, at the end of "Sunday," where he revised "Usually having reached some retired part of the river" to "Having reached a retired part of the river" (FD 35). But, perhaps inevitably, the account remained somewhat static and repetitive. The opening of "Tuesday" reveals the difficulty Thoreau faced, for he noted that the brothers embarked early in the morning, "anticipating another pleasant day" (FD 49). He later omitted the comment but added what was implicit in the first draft: that they had prepared to embark "as usual" and had been enveloped in fog "as usual" (W 179). Finally, for long stretches of the first draft, he seemed to have abandoned the excursion. "But think not that we have been becalmed all this while," he wryly remarked following a series of digressions in "Sunday," "for we arrived at the Billerica falls, before noon" (FD 27). Thoreau quickly picked up the thread of the narrative, establishing the rhythm of action and reflection, advance and withdrawal, that

[15]Jeremy Belknap, *The History of New-Hampshire,* 3 vols., 2d ed. (Boston: Bradford and Read, 1813), III:45–47.

forms the essential rhythm of *A Week*. But, after devoting the bulk of "Wednesday" to a long disquisition on friendship, he lamely concluded the chapter, "Thus we sailed between the territories of Manchester & Goffstown" (FD 81).

Thoreau soon recognized that he should expand the narrative and descriptive portions of *A Week*. In an 1845 Journal entry later indexed as "houses on Merrimack," he wrote: "I repeat it that if men will believe it—there are no more quiet Tempes or more poetic & Arcadian life than may be lived in these New E. dwellings— It seemed as if their employment by day would be to tend the flowers & herds—and at night like the shepherds of old to cluster & gives names to the stars" (J 2:197; cf. W 243). The description of these houses and their inhabitants reflects his continuing effort to discover signs of classical purity and simplicity in New England. In fact, the Journal entry probably had less to do with Thoreau's recollections of the 1839 voyage than with his serene existence at Walden Pond and his memory of Virgil's description of the husbandman's happy life in Book II of the *Georgics* (ll.458 ff.).

A classicizing tendency is also apparent in a passage on the sources of the Merrimack in the August 1846 Journal. Describing the Pemigewasset, flowing by "many a pastured Pielion and Ossa where unnamed muses haunt, and receiving the tribute of many an untasted Helicon," Thoreau added, "For every mountain stream is more than Helicon, tended by oreads dryads Naiads" (J 2:266). Ossa and Pelion, the highest mountains in Thessaly, which the brothers Otus and Ephialtes piled upon Mount Olympus in order to reach heaven and attack the gods, thus took a place in the poetic geography of the White Mountains, which two other brothers ascend toward heaven. In "Sunday," where Thoreau later inserted the passage at the opening of his description of the Merrimack, he corrected Helicon, the sacred mountain in Boetia, to Hippocrene, the spring on Mount Helicon. From that spring, sacred to the muses, man continues to receive pure draughts of divine inspiration: "Such water do the gods distill / And pour down hill / For their new England men" (J 2:266; cf. W 84).

In the 1846 Journal the description of the sources of the Mer-

rimack introduced reminiscences about the 1839 walking tour of
the White Mountains, a section probably drafted to link the two
"Thursday" chapters in the first draft. There, Thoreau passed over
their experiences in three brief paragraphs: he alluded to the ascent of Mount Washington, called by its Indian name Agiocochook, but, drawing upon an entry from the 1843 Journal, concluded, "Why should we take the reader who may have been
tenderly nurtured—through that rude country—where the crags
are steep and the inns none of the best, and many a rude blast
would have to be encountered on the mountain side" (FD 83; cf.
J 1:476). Like the first draft, the 1846 Journal contains no references to stagecoaches, but it includes fond descriptions of some
of the villages and rude inns he and John had visited. Shortly
after his 1839 trip to the White Mountains, Emerson had gloomily
remarked, "In New Hampshire the dignity of the landscape made
more obvious by the meanness of the tavern[-]haunting men"
(JMN VII:236). At a mollifying distance of seven years, Thoreau
offered a different vision of those men and their habitats, including
Tilton's Inn in Thornton, of which he observed, "The remembrance of an entertainment still remains and among publicans
Tiltons name still stands conspicuous in our diary" (J 2:268).

Such comments would not have been out of place in a pamphlet
like the *White Mountain and Winnepissiogee Lake Guide Book*
(Boston, 1846), published in response to the annually increasing
number of visitors to the area. Significantly, however, Thoreau
later used only a few sentences from the Journal account in
"Thursday," where he charts a movement away from other men
to primitive nature. In the Journal he noted that they had "crossed
a rude wooden bridge over the Amonnoosuck and breathed the
free air of the Unappropriated Land" (J 2:268); in *A Week* they
cross the stream "on prostrate trees." Implicitly, since they are
"*enabled* to reach the summit of AGIOCOCHOOK" (W 314, emphasis added), their journey is made possible, not by man or man-
made improvements, but by the consent of nature and the Indian
gods of Agiocochook.

Thoreau possibly drafted the reminiscences of the White
Mountains in anticipation of his journey to Mount Katahdin in
Maine in September 1846. The two trips bore striking similarities.

In 1839 he and John embarked on August 31, the same day Thoreau left Concord in 1846. He traveled by various means in 1839 and 1846, but much of each trip was spent on rivers. As the voyage on the Concord and Merrimack anticipated the voyage on the Penobscot, the ascent of Mount Washington, the highest peak in New England, anticipated the ascent of Katahdin, the highest peak in Maine. But after devoting years to reconstructing the 1839 trip from meager notes, Thoreau kept a more detailed diary during his ten days in Maine. More importantly, after his return to Concord, in the fall of 1846 he revised and expanded his jottings, filling 170 pages of the Journal with a preliminary account of the Maine trip.

That account had a marked impact on *A Week*.[16] Most directly, it eventually contributed a number of passages, including a discussion of ancient fables in "Sunday" (*W* 58 ff.; cf. *J* 2:334) and a brief digression on commerce in "Tuesday" (*W* 212-13; cf. *J* 2:315-16). Its description of the ascent of Katahdin also anticipated mountain episodes in *A Week*. Climbing "toward the clouds," Thoreau entered a mysterious twilight world reminiscent "of the creations of the old epic and dramatic poets, of Atlas, Vulcan, the Cyclops, and Prometheus" (*J* 2:339). As the reference to Prometheus suggests, Thoreau treated the ascent as a violation of a sanctuary. Upbraided for his insolence and presumption, man is confronted by "Vast Titanic inhuman nature," which asks, "Why seek me where I have not called you and then complain that I am not your genial mother?" (*J* 2:339-40; cf. *MW* 64). That theme, which emerged even more strongly in the published version, was obviously not appropriate to *A Week*, in which Thoreau had continually stressed the brothers' communion and harmony with nature. But the depiction of mountaintops as "sacred and mysterious tracts," the haunts of spirits and gods, possibly prompted him to make Agiocochook as remote and as mysterious

---

[16]For a discussion of Thoreau's experiences, which they view as "a source of an important qualification of his transcendentalism," see John G. Blair and Augustus Trowbridge, "Thoreau on Katahdin," *American Quarterly* 12 (1960): 508–17. Thoreau's Journal account is described by R. C. Croseby, "Thoreau at Work: The Writing of 'Ktaadn,' " *Bulletin of the New York Public Library* 65 (1961): 21–30.

as Katahdin and to extend the geography of *A Week* to include other mountains in New England.

As he worked on the second draft of *A Week*, Thoreau began to draw upon his experiences during the excursions to Mount Wachusett and Saddleback Mountain. Early in 1847 he began to revise "A Walk to Wachusett." Working from the published version, with occasional references to the earliest version, he drafted a third version of the essay, apparently for inclusion in *A Week*.[17] Although he ultimately decided to omit this new version, he included portions of the published version at the end of "Monday," where it prefigures his account of the ascent of Saddleback Mountain, which he sketched in the first draft and later revised and expanded. Together, these episodes anticipate the climb to the summit of Agiocochook in "Thursday," the final ascent in a series that ultimately formed a strong counterpoint to the river voyage in *A Week*.

In the 1847 version of "A Walk to Wachusett," Thoreau focused on the pair's experience atop the mountain. "One pleasant summer morning, (July 19th 1842,) we started to walk to Wachusett," he began, "carrying a tent that we might pass a night on the summit, and provision for mind and body in our knapsacks." In the context of *A Week*, that "we" would have suggested that the brothers had made the trip. By omitting the poem "With frontier strength ye stand your ground" and compressing the account of their walk to the mountain, Thoreau in the 1847 version moved more swiftly to their experience on the summit. In the published version he had written that, as the sun rose, "we began to realize the extent of the view, and how the earth, in some degree, answered to the heavens in breadth, the white villages to the constellations in the sky" (*Ex* 146). In the 1847 version he dropped the strained analogy between the earth and heavens and instead underscored their sense of discovery: "And now [we] first began to discover where we were, and to realize the extent of the view."

[17]All quotations from the 1847 version are from the draft of the essay at the Houghton Library (MH 10). In "Thoreau at Work: Four Versions of 'A Walk to Wachusett,' " *Bulletin of the New York Public Library* 69 (1965):3–16, Lauriat Lane called the Houghton draft the first version of the essay. It is correctly identified as part of the surviving manuscripts of *A Week* in *LMHDT,* D5k.

He also omitted a disquisition on the importance of mountains and a description of a bird's flight over the mountains; consequently, in the 1847 version their stay atop the mountain ended with the vision of Monadnock, which, Thoreau noted, "will longest haunt our dreams."

He apparently felt that even the compressed 1847 version of "A Walk to Wachusett" was too long for inclusion in *A Week,* so he drew up yet another version for insertion in "Monday." In contrast to the 1847 version, Thoreau remarks that he made the trip "with another companion" (*W* 162). He also heightened the symbolic nature of that journey to "those Delectable Mountains," the Emmanuel's Land within sight of the Celestial City in the *Pilgrim's Progress.* What follows that introductory paragraph, however, is simply a transcription of the opening pages of the published version, to the point where Thoreau notes that he and his companion "had resolved to scale the blue wall which bounded the western horizon, though not without misgivings that thereafter no visible fairy land would exist for us" (*W* 165, *Ex* 135). But instead of continuing the account, he abruptly remarks that he has no time to describe that "pilgrimage." "We have since made many similar excursions to the principal mountains of New England and New York, and even far in the wilderness [Katahdin in Maine]," Thoreau continues, blurring the distinction between his brother and his various other companions, "and have passed a night on the summit of many of them" (*W* 165-66). Consequently, even as Wachusett and Monadnock retreat "once more among the blue and fabulous mountains in the horizon," the brief episode in "Monday" serves as a tantalizing prelude to the account of his ascent of Saddleback Mountain, which Thoreau expanded from a 200-word vignette in the first draft to a 3,500-word digression in *A Week.*

Thoreau did not fully exploit the Saddleback Mountain episode in the first draft. He had climbed the mountain during a trip to the Berkshires and Catskills in the summer of 1844, shortly before beginning intensive work on *A Week.*[18] He may have been

---

[18]The significance of the trip and its place in that "transitional and preparatory year" of 1844 are dealt with by Thomas Woodson, "Thoreau's Excursion to the Berkshires and Catskills," *ESQ* 21 (1975):82–92.

prompted to give an account by an article in the October 1844 *Democratic Review,* "The Journey of a Day; or, A Sequel to the Berkshire Jubilee." In that leisurely and rather conventional account, the author described a trip to Greylock, or Saddleback Mountain, concluding with a rapt description of sunrise from the summit. Thoreau, who obviously followed a well-worn path to the mountain, skipped over the trip to focus on the sunrise from the summit. After describing a fog that enveloped the river, he remarked at the opening of "Tuesday" in the first draft, "I once saw the day break from the top of Saddle back mountain in Massachusetts when the whole earth was invested with clouds" (FD 49). Unlike the people "of the lower world," he had continued to inhale "the pure atmosphere of a July morning." Thoreau swiftly drew the moral of the story. Following a brief description of the scene, in which the "world of clouds" answered "to the terrestrial world it veiled," he concluded, "Such morning experiences methinks should not be lost upon an cloudy philosophy" (FD 49, 50). The episode initially served as a striking instance of the correspondence between inward and outward worlds, and a simple, if somewhat heavy-handed, illustration of transcendence. But as he began to revise and expand the episode at the end of 1846 (*J* 2:359 ff.), shortly after completing the Journal account of his trip to Maine, Thoreau realized that an account of his ascent of Saddleback Mountain might also dramatize the process by which one achieved such transcendence.

In *A Week,* he develops the allegorical overtones of the excursion. He approaches Saddleback Mountain carrying a "staff" and embarks on a path that seems like "a road for the pilgrim to enter upon who would climb to the gates of heaven" (*W* 180, 181). At the next to the last house he meets a seductive young woman "full of interest in that lower world from which I had come" (*W* 182). She bears a striking resemblance to Madame Bubble, the dark and comely woman who boldly accosts Stand-fast on the "dangerous road" to the Celestial City in the *Pilgrim's Progress.* Thoreau, a pretty fair Stand-fast himself, resists temptation and passes on to the last house, where a man calls out that there is no path to the summit. But, as Charles Anderson has noted, "like Bunyan's Pilgrim, Thoreau knew that the true way to heaven was steep and hard."[19] Yet he also insists that such difficulties are illusory. "So far as my experience goes, travellers generally exaggerate the difficulties of the way," he observes, perhaps casting an ironic glance at the *Pilgrim's Progress:* "Like most evil, the difficulty is imaginary" (W 183-84). Although the trees begin "to have a scraggy and infernal look, as if contending with frost goblins," he reaches the summit without difficulty, "just as the sun was setting" (W 184).

Despite the symbolic overtones of this episode, Thoreau's narrative treatment is initially casual and undramatic. He seems more interested in describing the sights and sounds along the way than in constructing a parable. Within the digression he further digresses about his memories of Staten Island and, later, about newspapers. The leisurely pace heightens what he calls the "pith" of the digression—sunrise over Saddleback Mountain: "As the light increased I discovered around me an ocean of mist, which by chance reached up exactly to the base of the tower, and shut out every vestige of the earth, while I was left floating on this fragment of the wreck of a world, on my carved plank in cloudland; a situation which required no aid from the imagination to render it impressive. As the light in the east steadily increased, it revealed to me more clearly the new world into which I had risen in the night, the new terra-firma perchance of my future life" (W 188).

Thoreau's description of this "new world" transcends everyday reality. In contrast to the first draft, where the clouds were simply spread about him, here they reach "exactly to the base of the tower," leaving him "floating on this fragment of the wreck of a world." Where he earlier stressed that he continued to inhale "the pure atmosphere of a July morning" (FD 49), he here adds the qualification "if it were July there," for this world is outside of time as well as place (W 188). As numerous critics have remarked, the passage that follows in *A Week,* expanded from its first-draft version, bears a striking resemblance to Wordsworth's description of "a silent sea of hoary mist" (l. 42) in the Mount Snowdon ep-

[19]*Thoreau's Vision: The Major Essays,* ed. Charles R. Anderson (Englewood Cliffs, N.J.: Prentice-Hall, 1973), p. 22.

isode at the beginning of the fourteenth book of *The Prelude* (1850).[20] But Wordsworth's imagery of light and dark, silence and tumult, contrasts sharply with Thoreau's pure, ethereal paradise. "As there was wanting the symbol," he emphasizes, "so there was not the substance of impurity, no spot nor stain" (*W* 188). In *The Prelude* the shaping power of imagination is lodged in the "rift" (l. 56) that disturbs the scene; in *A Week,* Thoreau has "climbed above storm and cloud": "But when its own sun began to rise on this pure world, I found myself a dweller in the dazzling halls of Aurora, into which poets have had but a partial glance over the eastern hills,—drifting amid the saffron-colored clouds, and playing with the rosy fingers of the Dawn, in the very path of the Sun's chariot, and sprinkled with its dewy dust, enjoying the benignant smile, and near at hand the far-darting glances of the god" (*W* 189).

With its string of Homeric epithets, Thoreau's description—like the remainder of the section—is self-consciously literary and artificial. As he had transformed the streams in the White Mountains into sacred fountains, "tended by oreads dryads and Naiads" in the 1846 Journal, he here transforms Saddleback Mountain into Helicon or Olympus. The "god," whose smiling aspect also reminds us of Winnepisiogee Lake, "signifying 'The Smile of the Great Spirit' " (*W* 83), is not Jehovah but Apollo, god of radiance, purity, and poetry, whose re-creation of the world from clouds inspires Thoreau's own creativity.[21] Like the Mount Snowdon episode, this experience on Saddleback Mountain suggests a renaissance of imaginative power. The experience, however, proves transitory, so a section that begins with a burst of refulgent light concludes with a dense series of allusions to and quotations from

[20]See especially Christopher Collins, *The Uses of Observation* (The Hague: Mouton, 1971), pp. 73–76. James McIntosh, who discusses Wordsworth's influence on Thoreau in some detail, compares the account to the Simplon Pass episode from *Prelude* VI in *Thoreau as Romantic Naturalist* (Ithaca, N.Y.: Cornell Univ. Press, 1974), pp. 163–65. The quotations from Wordsworth are taken from *The Prelude,* ed. Ernest de Selincourt, 2d ed. rev. Helen Darbisher (Oxford: Clarendon, 1959).

[21]Anderson, p. 22. The relationship between Thoreau's vision and the style of the section is discussed by William Bysshe Stein, "Thoreau's *A*

Shakespeare's Sonnet 33, where a morning's vision of heavenly glory is swiftly obscured by dark clouds, with their strong suggestions of human sinfulness and mortality. But Thoreau determines to continue his quest, for as he sinks down "into that 'forlorn world,' from which the celestial Sun had hid his visage," he casts his eye on "the summits of new and yet higher mountains, the Catskills, by which I might hope to climb to heaven again" (*W* 190).

In an intermediate draft of the Saddleback Mountain episode, Thoreau ended on an anticlimatic note. Describing his descent into the valley, where "the inhabitants affirmed that it had been a cloudy and drizzling day wholly" (*W* 190), he continued, "I was of that age when an unexplored country road furnishes objects of interest enough . . . and we proceed with the adventurous feeling of childhood, not knowing what we shall see next." After a catalog of some of the mundane sights that had "charmed" him and made him feel that he was "in a new country and not far from the end of the world," he concluded:

> It takes many years to learn what seem to the man
> very simple and common things, as for instance that
> the world is all so like that part of it in which we live,
> for the young ever expect greater variety and sublimity
> than they find. They do not know but at the next turn
> of the road there may be a gulf or unfathomable depth,
> or a tree of unheard of dimensions. Mountains and
> falls never come up to the expectation of children.
> Mountains are but steeper hills to them. They had
> expected to see the rocks piled up in a more Titanic
> manner greater height & depth & size, so as to strike

Week and *OM* Cosmograpy," *American Transcendental Quarterly* 11 (1971):15–37; and John Carlos Rowe, " 'The Being of Language: The Language of Being' in *A Week on the Concord and Merrimack Rivers*," *Boundary* 7, no. 3 (1979):91–115. Stein argues that "the pedantry of a bookworm underscores the insincerity of the rapture" (p. 24), while Rowe suggests that "the failure of such inauthentic poeticizing" brings the ascent of Saddleback into Thoreau's larger quest for the origins of poetry (pp. 96–98).

the beholder dumb, and think that if they were in the
place of nature they could do better themselves. And
no doubt they could, and they may have a chance to
try one day. (MH 15, L)

With the exception of a few lines (W 192), Thoreau omitted
this passage from his earlier essay on "Travelling" from *A Week*.
By relating the ascent of Saddleback Mountain to his youthful
enthusiasm for travel, he tended to trivialize the experience, as
if his discovery of that "new world" were somehow analogous to
his naive belief that he was in "a new country and not far from
the end of the world." Although the discovery that "the world is
all so like that part of it in which we live" is integral to *Walden*,
it undermined the importance of the series of ascents in *A Week*.
The fact that mountains never fulfill the expectations of children
implies that nature cannot compete with the sublime visions of
man and that man need only raise himself above himself in order
to discover a vast, unexplored realm of mind and imagination.
But, however he had achieved that insight, Thoreau in *A Week*
gave it enduring literary form by describing an excursion away
from that part of the world in which he lived. Indeed, as *Walden*
reveals, it was impossible for him to depict even the life in his
native town without depending upon the potent metaphor of
traveling.

"I have travelled a good deal in Concord," Thoreau proclaimed
at the opening of the first draft of *Walden*, which he wrote while
working on the second draft of *A Week* in 1847. He established
the same relation between the works as between "A Walk to Wachusett" and "A Winter Walk," for in *A Week* he enacts a journey
toward a mysterious and remote mountain, while in *Walden* he
discovers the unknown amid familiar territory. In the opening
pages of *Walden*, traveling through his native town simply revealed the desperate lives of its inhabitants, but toward the end
of the draft he used such travel to suggest the kind of life that
might be lived in Concord: "Why not live always a rude and frontier life—full of adventures and hard work—learn much—travel
much—though it be only through these woods & fields! There
is no other country than this—here is the field and the man.—

The daily boundaries of life are expanded & dispersed and I see in what field I stand. Roam far and wide—grasp at life and conquer it. Learn much and live" (S 189).

As the passage indicates, Thoreau could not describe life without suggesting movement. He begins by defining a "frontier life," but it soon becomes clear that the hard work and adventure he has in mind involves the exploration rather than the settlement of the country. By defining *live* in terms of the verbs *to learn* and *to travel,* both of which in the nineteenth century implied toil and exertion, he sets life in motion. The centrifugal force of the passage is momentarily checked by his references to *these* woods and fields, and to *this* country, which introduce a sentence in which movement and stability are carefully balanced: "The daily boundaries of life are expanded & dispersed and I see in what field I stand." But "see" and "stand" immediately give way to a series of active verbs—*roam, grasp, conquer, learn,* and *live.* After urging his audience not to rest "every night in villages nor in the same place," he effectively summarizes the passage by concluding, "But we should go beyond our shadow at sunrise, and come home from far—from adventures and perils—from enterprises and discoveries every day" (S 189; cf. *Wa* 207-8).

The "enterprises and discoveries" adumbrated in the first draft of *Walden* were closely related to those described in *A Week.* With each ascent in *A Week,* Thoreau rises a little higher, from Wachusett, one of the Delectable Mountains, to Saddleback, home of benign classical deities, to Agiocochook, highest point of physical and spiritual elevation in *A Week.* He attains a similar elevation on the hill above Walden Pond. For a brief moment atop Saddleback Mountain, Thoreau dwells in "the dazzling halls of Aurora" (*W* 189). In *Walden* he compared his cabin to certain "mountain houses," which retained a "fresh auroral atmosphere about them." Alluding to a visit to a sawmiller's house during his 1844 trip to the Berkshires and Catskills, Thoreau continued, "On the tops of mountains, as everywhere to hopeful souls, it is always morning" (S 138). The truth glimpsed in *A Week* is thus grasped in *Walden.* The pond, "formerly a place of eagles," once again became the home of one who rises up with wings as eagles. As the transcendent power of man's imagination is illustrated by the se-

ries of ascents in *A Week*, it is demonstrated by the discovery of
the long lost bottom of the pond in *Walden*. In *A Week* he remarks
that the height of mountains is always "ridiculously small" compared to what we imagine (*W* 192); in *Walden* he makes a similar
discovery about the depth of the pond. "The amount of it is," he
concludes, "the imagination, give it the least license, dives deeper
and soars higher than Nature goes" (*Wa* 288).[22]

The discovery that the physical universe is not commensurate
with imagined realms did not keep Thoreau at home. As he had
hiked to Wachusett in 1842, traveled to the Berkshires and Catskills in 1844, and journeyed to Katahdin in Maine in 1846, he
joined Ellery Channing on a four-day walking tour of southern
New Hampshire in the summer of 1848. Although his Aunt Maria
complained, "I wish [Thoreau] could find something better to do
than walking off every now and then" (*DHT* 234), during the
1848 tour, as on his earlier trips, he gathered material for his
writings. In fact, it amounted to a research trip for *A Week*. Their
route took them through Tyngsborough, Dunstable, Goffstown,
Hooksett, Hampstead, Plaistow, and Haverhill, most of which he
and John had passed through nine years earlier. He and Channing
also visited Moore's Falls, which the brothers had bypassed by
means of locks, and climbed the pinnacle near Hooksett Falls.
But, as usual, the high point of the 1848 trip was ascent of a
mountain. Appropriately, Mount Uncannunuc, "the far blue
mountain" of the early Journal, was the last of those principal
mountains of New England that Thoreau climbed between the
voyage of 1839 and the publication of *A Week* in 1849.

Among the numerous passages on the 1848 tour absorbed into
A Week, two references to the ascent of Uncannunuc are particularly revealing. Although he does not name the mountain, Thoreau alludes to the ascent of Uncannunuc in "Sunday," where
he tells of being accosted by a minister, "because I was bending
my steps to a mountain-top on the Sabbath, instead of a church,
when I would have gone further than he to hear a true word
spoken on that or any day" (*W* 75-76). Ironically, self-righteous

---

[22]Since three leaves are missing (S 199), it is not clear whether the
first draft of *Walden* included this observation.

Christianity seems to represent the greatest danger to the lone pilgrim as he journeys to the mountaintops in *A Week*. In a revision of the Journal entry on "the far blue mountain," Thoreau remarked in 1848, "Uncannunuc mountain in Goffstown, which we have since ascended, is visible from this part of the river, five or six miles westward" (HM 13195, "Wednesday," 10; cf. *J* 1:169). He finally revised the passage to read: "Uncannunuc Mountain in Goffstown was visible from Amoskeag, five or six miles westward. It is the north-easternmost in the horizon, which we see from our native town, but seen from there is too ethereally blue to be the same which the like of us have ever climbed" (*W* 255). In contrast to the misleading statement "which we have since ascended," the final version is ambiguous: the brothers see the mountain from Concord, but it is not clear that both have actually ascended it.

As his references to Uncannunuc illustrate, Thoreau never alludes to Ellery Channing or even to a companion in his accounts of the 1848 trip in *A Week*. In a passage deleted from "Tuesday," however, he described their stop near Moore's Falls: "On the rocky shore in front of Moore's Falls I have since prepared a rather sumptuous but somewhat more innocent repast than our last, when travelling this way one summer day with another companion. It was composed of crusts of bread which the farmers had refused, hens eggs, for one of which we waited till it was laid, and a hasty pudding boiled on the rocks amidst the roar of the rapids, and almost sprinkled with the foam—for our means were small, though our appetites were great—and we studied economy as well as the landscape" (HM 13195, "Tuesday," 2).

Thoreau probably omitted this paragraph to avoid introducing "another companion" who might detract from the brothers' experiences. Even more revealingly, after mentioning Massabesic Pond in "Wednesday" (*W* 236), he commented in the manuscript, "It is a wild and dark looking Indian lake, with a pine clad shore, in whose cold waters we have since bathed" (HM 13195, "Wednesday," 3). Since only he and Channing had visited the spot, the comment was deceptive. It, too, was omitted. In all the remaining references to the 1848 trip in *A Week*, Thoreau speaks in the first person singular, as in the description of Hooksett Pinnacle in "Thursday," where he remarks, "I have sat upon its summit . . . in fairer weather, when the sun was setting and filling the river valley with a flood of light" (W 302). Thus, with the exception of a passing reference to "another companion" at the opening of the brief extract from "A Walk to Wachusett" (W 162), Thoreau consciously limited A Week to the brothers' shared experiences or, ostensibly at least, to his own solitary excursions through New England.

Although the 1848 walking tour provided a good deal of useful material for A Week, it cast a shadow over the narrative, for it brought home to Thoreau how much the valley of the Merrimack had changed since 1839.[23] Even in 1839 the Gazetteer commented that "some of the most flourishing towns in the state" were situated on its banks ("Merrimack River, N. H."). Thoreau, however, tended either to ignore these towns or simply to use them as guideposts to chart the brothers' progress upstream. In a brief description of Nashua, New Hampshire, he noted in the first draft that while one of them "threaded the town his companion rowed steadily on to meet him" at the mouth of the Nashua River (FD 45). But even that brief sojourn was expunged from A Week, where he emphasized what he had also observed in the first draft, that near its mouth the river "is obstructed by falls and factories, and we did not pause to explore it" (W 162). Similarly, responding to the Gazetteer, which had proudly proclaimed that the people of Manchester were "laying the foundation of another Lowell" ("Manchester, N. H."), Thoreau in a comment added to the description of Amoskeag Falls contemptuously remarked, "But we did not tarry to examine them minutely, making haste to get past the village here collected, and out of hearing of the hammer which was laying the foundation of another Lowell on its banks" (W 245).

As he recognized, a major reason for the growth of manufacturing along the Merrimack was its numerous falls, but Thoreau found a different value and a far greater significance in those

[23]For a discussion of these changes, see The Concord and Merrimack, ed. Dudley C. Hunt (Boston: Little, Brown, 1954), p. xiii; and Raymond P. Holden, The Merrimack (New York: Rinehart, 1958).

natural resources. "As we have said, we did not pay much heed to the Falls, being better able today to appreciate the fall of still water," he observed in the second draft, shortly after the description of Amoskeag Falls:

> Wild animals and wild men naturally enough linger about falls and rapids. They are already a sort of natural factory in the woods where many operations are carried on, working in stone and in wood, turning boring, filing, polishing, bleaching, rotting. Their rainbow sprays, and the sun shining on their slippery rocks serve to distinguish such localities even at a distance. It is pleasant to sit on the bank of a rapid river in the primitive forest, on damp & shelving rocks, clinging with your hands & feet, and see the waters rush past you, wild and beautiful, ceaseless impetuous and graceful; talking to the rocks in its bed, now hoarsely as thunder, now sweetly as a rill, and now in smooth inaudible whispers; every square yard an unravelled plot of adventures and escapes; so smooth, so cool, so swift! Great masts of trees all bare and polished chafing and panting in midstream between the rocks; a mile of storied rocks, scored over with an ancient chronicle in nature's runes, which no learned society can decypher, mementoes of a river's struggle & a river's victory. (MH 15, O)[24]

Thoreau found it increasingly difficult to sustain that vision of wild and unspoiled nature. As late as 1848 he omitted the evocative passage, which had earlier survived exhaustive revisions of the second draft, possibly because his trip that year revealed how completely such natural factories had been displaced by the textile mills along the Merrimack, where an altogether different chronicle

[24]This is the third and final version of the passage (ca. 1848), which followed the ironic salute to the inhabitants of Litchfield in "Wednesday" (W 255–56). Two earlier versions from the second draft, one on a leaf paged 297–98 and the other on a leaf paged 320–21, are also in MH 15, O.

of victory was being scored in the ancient stones. The swiftness of that conquest was dramatized by the growth of Manchester, which after 1848 Thoreau could no longer so contemptuously dismiss. Indeed, as John Hayward, who in the *Gazetteer* had prophesied its golden industrial future, proudly announced in 1849: "The growth of the village of Manchester is unrivalled by any place in the world except Lowell, and is a magnificent specimen of the enterprise and skill of the New England people. The population within the limits of the city in 1838 was about 50; in 1848 the city contained 12,000 inhabitants."[25]

If Thoreau could not exclude Manchester from the landscape of *A Week,* he at least sought to tame the fact of its existence. In a passage added to "Wednesday" after his 1848 trip, he made reference to the remarkable growth of Manchester's population, which he had some difficulty establishing (see W TN 245.30). Initially, he also observed that its name had been "changed to Manchester in 1810 at the suggestion of Samuel Blodgett, who already foresaw that old Derryfield would become the Manchester of America" (HM 13195, "Wednesday," 6). The manufacturing possibilities of the site, with its ample waterpower, had indeed prompted the change of the village's name, but Thoreau later deleted the comment. Most likely, he did not wish to raise in "Wednesday" the specter of "sooty Manchester," as Carlyle referred to the English commercial and industrial center, whose filthy rivers, squalid slums, and social strife had by the 1840s come to symbolize the modern age, not only to a wide range of English social critics and novelists, but also to foreign writers like Alexis de Tocqueville and Friedrich Engels, whose book *The Condition of the Working Classes in England* (1845) paved the

[25]John Hayward, *Gazetteer of New Hampshire* (Boston: John P. Jewett, 1849), p. 96. Thoreau's response to industrialization is treated by Joseph Lawrence Basile, "Technology and the Artist in *A Week*," *American Transcendental Quarterly* 11 (1971):87–91; and John Conron, "Bright American Rivers: The Luminist Landscapes of Thoreau's *A Week on the Concord and Merrimack Rivers*," *American Quarterly* 32 (1980):144– 66. As Conron observes, "For the mills at Lowell and Manchester [Thoreau] has no pictorial imagination at all. They are blank spaces on his mental map" (p. 156).

way for *The Communist Manifesto* of 1848.[26] Even Emerson, who
was relatively sheltered during a lecture tour of England in 1847-
48, movingly described "the tragic spectacles" of Manchester's
streets in a letter to his family, with whom Thoreau was then
living (*L* III:442).

Thoreau, however, sought a different prospect on—and imagined brighter prospects for—the Manchester of *New* England.
"The sunlight on cities at a distance is a deceptive beauty," he
had observed in March 1841, "but foretells the final harmony of
man with nature" (J 1:283). In an attempt to place Manchester
in that characteristic perspective of the early Journal, Thoreau
in the passage revised for "Wednesday" continued, "From a hill
on the road between Goffstown and Hooksett, four miles distant,
I have seen a thunder shower pass over, and the sun break out
and shine on a city there, where I had landed nine years before
in the fields" (*W* 245). But even viewing Manchester at a distance,
and in the best possible light, with the flag of its museum waving
proudly over a city that also boasted of its "Athenaeum and Gallery
of the Fine Arts" (*W* 246), could not obscure the fact that Lowell,
"the city of spindles" and true "Manchester of America" (*W* 83),
had become the pattern for development along the Merrimack.
That river, which initially receives "the tribute of many an untasted Hippocrene," thus emerges from the last of the factories
as "a mere *waste water* . . . bearing little with it but its fame" (*W*
84, 87).

The industrialization of the Merrimack valley was speeded by
the advance of the railroad, the *Atropos* Thoreau confronted in
A Week and *Walden*. As he noted in the first draft of *A Week*,
during their first night on the Merrimack the brothers had been
"kept awake by the boisterous sport of some Irish laborers on the
railroad" (FD 35, *W* 116). It was an ominous sound, for the railroad spelled the end of the river as he and John had known it.
Thoreau was later forced to conclude his description of the Merrimack in "Sunday" by acknowledging that, in the southern

[26]A useful summary of criticisms and defenses of Manchester is given
by Asa Briggs, *Victorian Cities* (New York: Harper and Row, 1963), pp.
85–135.

reaches of the river, its true channel was the "iron channel" of the railroad and that "instead of the scream of a fish-hawk scaring the fishes, is heard the whistle of the steam-engine arousing a country to its progress" (*W* 87). By 1848 the railroad had been extended all the way to Concord, New Hampshire, beyond the farthest reach of their 1839 voyage. At the conclusion of an extended celebration of canal boats, which play such an important role in *A Week,* Thoreau consequently added: "Since our voyage the railroad on the bank has been extended, and there is now but little boating on the Merrimack. All kinds of produce and stores were formerly conveyed by water, but now nothing is carried up the stream, and almost wood and bricks alone are carried down, and these are also carried on the railroad. The locks are fast wearing out, and will soon be impassable, since the tolls will not pay the expense of repairing them, and so in a few years there will be an end of boating on this river" (*W* 213).

The passing of the canalboats from the Merrimack and the consequent destruction of locks and canals were not, of course, what Thoreau had foreseen when, in a description of the Middlesex Canal in the first draft, he spoke of the works of man passing "out of the hands of the architect into the hands of nature" (FD 28, *W* 62). Rather, his elegiac meditation is one of the most poignant reminders of the toll the passage of time had exacted. But another and far more shattering loss lurked behind all these signs of change and decay, for Thoreau's attempt to come to terms with the rapid changes he observed in 1848 played a small part in the larger drama of *A Week,* his effort to come to terms with his brother's death. Indeed, if his effort to depict New England as a kind of natural paradise, at once primitive and pastoral, reflected his yearning for wildness and his love of the classics, it also revealed his struggle to deal with the problem of John's death by placing it within a world in which nature's cycle of decay and rebirth is unimpeded by the forces of human progress.

2
The Elegiac Mode

THE CLOSENESS BETWEEN Thoreau and his elder brother, which is so movingly evoked in *A Week,* developed years before the voyage the book depicts. Born almost exactly three years apart, in 1814 and 1817, the two children became close playmates.[1] Indeed, the outgoing and popular John offered his younger brother the companionship Thoreau found it so difficult to establish with his other playmates, many of whom viewed him as withdrawn and unsympathetic. In a nostalgic essay on childhood, Thoreau in 1835 wrote: "In the freshness of the dawn my brother and I were ever ready to enjoy a stroll to a certain cliff, distant a mile or more, where we were wont to climb to the highest peak, and seating ourselves on some rocky platform, catch the first ray of the morning sun, as it gleamed upon the smooth, still river, wandering in sullen silence far below" (*DHT* 69-70). The scene, remembered in terms that echo "Lycidas"—"Together both, ere the high Lawns appear'd/Under the opening eyelids of the morn,/ We drove afield" (11. 25 ff.)—anticipated his depiction of a similar landscape in *A Week*. In fact, that book, initially conceived in pastoral terms, became one of the most ambitious of all pastoral elegies, in which Thoreau, like Milton, sought to assuage his grief for the loss of a companion of his youth.[2]

[1]Henry was born on July 12, 1817. Harding gives the year of John's birth as 1815 (*DHT* 10), but Thomas Blanding has discovered that he was born on July 5, 1814 ("Beans, Baked and Half-Baked [13]," *Concord Saunterer* 15, no. 1 [1980]:16–18).

[2]All quotations from Milton are taken from *John Milton: Complete Poems and Major Prose,* ed. Merritt Y. Hughes (New York: Odyssey, 1957). Hughes's headnote to "Lycidas" (pp. 116–20) contains an excellent survey of critical and scholarly approaches to the poem. The classic study of its pastoral background, against which *A Week* may also be viewed, remains J. H. Hanford's "The Pastoral Elegy and Milton's *Lycidas,*" *PMLA* 25 (1910):403–47.

The loss was made all the more painful by the savagery of John's death from lockjaw, a dreaded form of tetanus. In "Heroism," printed in *Essays* (1841), Emerson used "a lockjaw, that bends a man's head back to his heels" as an example of "a certain ferocity in nature," which "must have its outlet by human suffering" (*CW* II:148). That ferocity was evidenced by John's case, which began with a trivial razor cut on a finger of his left hand early in January 1842. A week later the finger had become infected, first causing acute pain in various parts of his body, then violent spasms as lockjaw set in, and finally periods of delirium. Yet through it all John remained calm and composed. When told that the doctors could do nothing to prevent his speedy and painful death, he replied, "The cup that my Father gives me, shall I not drink it?" (*DHT* 134). And Thoreau, who nursed his brother through three agonizing days, later wrote his friend Isaiah T. Williams that John "was perfectly calm, even pleasant while reason lasted, and gleams of the same serenity and playfulness shone through his delirium to the last" (*C* 66), which came on the afternoon of Tuesday, January 11, when his brother died in Thoreau's arms.

At first Thoreau, too, displayed a calm that belied his own agony. "He says John is not lost but nearer to him than ever," Emerson's wife Lidian wrote her sister Lucy Jackson Brown a week later, "for he knows him better than he ever did before and to know a friend better brings him nearer."[3] But he became increasingly withdrawn from others until, on January 22, he began to exhibit the symptoms of John's disease. Although he began a slow recovery from the psychosomatic attack of lockjaw on the twenty-fourth, by which time his family had given up hope, Thoreau never completely recovered from the shock of his brother's early death, which haunted him for the remaining twenty years of his life.

[3]Quoted in Joel Myerson, "More apropos John Thoreau," *American Literature* 45 (1973):106. Thoreau's effort to come to terms with John's death is treated by Sherman Paul, *The Shores of America* (Urbana: Univ. of Illinois Press, 1958), pp. 103 ff.; and Richard Lebeaux, *Young Man Thoreau* (Amherst: Univ. of Massachusetts Press, 1977), pp. 167 ff. Lebeaux's second volume, *Thoreau's Seasons* (1984), which contains a stimulating reading of *A Week*, was published after my study was completed.

His grief was shared by all who knew John. Shortly before Thoreau's own death in 1862, Emerson remembered two examples of John's kindness and thoughtfulness. First, he had put up a bluebird's box on Emerson's barn, "and there it is still with every summer a melodious family in it, adorning the place, & singing his praises." Second, he had taken Emerson's beloved son Waldo to a daguerrotypist, seeing that the portrait was well done, a "wise & gentle piece of friendship" that had assumed even greater significance when Waldo died two weeks after John (*JMN* XV:165). In his funeral eulogy for John, the Reverend Barzillai Frost also stressed the young man's "benevolence," which "appeared in his love of animals, in the pleasure he took in making children happy, and in his readiness to give up his time to oblige all," as well as his love of nature. "He spent many of his leisure hours in straying over these hills and along the banks of the streams. There is not a hill, nor a tree, nor a bird, nor a flower of marked beauty in all this neighborhood that he was not familiar with, and any new bird or flower he discovered gave him the most unfeigned delight, and he would dwell with and seem to commune with it for hours" (*DHT* 135).

John's special closeness to nature gives added point to his brother's efforts to cope with grief in the early months of 1842. Three years earlier, shortly after they returned from the White Mountains, Thoreau had noted in the Journal, "The lively decay of autumn promises as infinite duration and freshness, as the green leaves of spring" (*J* 1:100). That celebration of the natural process, in which change and continuity are balanced and resolved, reflected his faith in nature's permanence. More importantly, he perceived that what was true in nature might also be true for human life, an analogy that served as an emotional lifeline to him after John's death. In a letter to Emerson, Thoreau wrote on March 11: "How plain that death is only the phenomenon of the individual or class. Nature does not recognize it, she finds her own again under new forms without loss." After insisting that death was not an accident, but a law of life, he continued:

Every blade in the field—every leaf in the forest—
lays down its life in its season as beautifully as it was

taken up. It is the pastime of a full quarter of the year.
Dead trees—sere leaves—dried grass and herbs—are
not these a good part of our life? And what is that
pride of our autumnal scenery but the hectic flush—
the sallow and cadaverous countenance of vegetation—
its painted throes—with the November air for canvas—
    When we look over the fields are we not saddened
because the particular flowers or grasses will wither—
for the law of their death is the law of new life   Will
not the land be in good heart *because* the crops die
down from year to year? The herbage cheerfully
consents to bloom, and wither, and give place to a
new.
    So it is with the human plant. We are partial and
selfish when we lament the death of the individual,
unless our plaint be a paean to the departed soul, and
a sigh as the wind sighs over the fields, which no
shrub interprets into its private grief.
    One might as well go into mourning for every sere
leaf—but the more innocent and wiser soul will snuff a
fragrance in the gales of autumn, and congratulate
Nature upon her health. (*C* 64-65)

By placing the sudden and seemingly "accidental" deaths of
John and Waldo within the annual cycle of decay and regeneration, Thoreau adopted the basic strategy of the pastoral elergy.[4]
What was initially probably an instinctive gesture of defense
against pain ultimately determined his artistic response to his
brother's death. As Emerson commemorated Waldo's death by
writing "Threnody," in which the natural process is affirmed even

    [4]See Ellen Zetzel Lambert, *Placing Sorrow: A Study of the Pastoral
Elegy Convention from Theocritus to Milton* (Chapel Hill: Univ. of North
Carolina Press, 1976). Other useful studies include Renato Poggioli, *The
Oaten Flute* (Cambridge: Harvard Univ. Press, 1975), which contains
an illuminating discussion of what Poggioli calls the pastoral of friendship,
and Harold E. Toliver, *Pastoral Forms and Attitudes* (Berkeley: Univ.
of California Press, 1971), especially Toliver's discussion of the ways in
which various romantic poets and writers adapted pastoral modes.

at the cost of a son, Thoreau, too, sought to reaffirm his own belief in nature's restorative powers in *A Week*. At once a lament and a pastoral of friendship, the book was his "paean to the departed soul," whose death is alluded to in the opening elegiac hymn, whose praises are sung in the essay on friendship in "Wednesday," and whose loss is dramatically resolved in a meditation on the autumnal landscape in "Friday."

Thoreau had already begun to transform his dead brother into the idealized friend celebrated in *A Week*. On March 2, after describing his response to John's death in a letter to Lucy Brown, he observed: "I do not wish to see John ever again—I mean him who is dead—but the other whom only he would have wished to see, or to be, of whom he was the imperfect representative. For we are not what we are, nor do we treat or esteem each other for such, but for what we are capable of being" (C 62). That division between the actual man and his ideal self, a theme he developed in the essay on friendship (see W 265), helps explain one of the peculiarities of *A Week*, in which John is neither described nor characterized. Freed from the limitations of human life, John had begun to assume to Thoreau the status of a pure idea, one that tended to displace the historical person. In fact, Thoreau seemed to feel that any effort to see—or to help others see—John was somehow equivalent to opening a grave and exposing the all too perishable remains. His reluctance to depict John was also anticipated by the letter to Isaiah Williams, where, after reporting the circumstances of John's death, Thoreau abruptly concluded: "But I will not disturb his memory. If you knew him, I could not add to your knowledge, and if you did not know him, as I think you could not, it is now too late, and no eulogy of mine would suffice—For my own part I feel that I could not have done without this experience" (C 66).

In his reply to the letter, which had also informed him of Waldo's death, Williams tactlessly questioned the adequacy of Emerson's philosophy at such a time, posing as an alternate "the consolations that a christian faith offers the bereaved & afflicted" (C 70). But Thoreau, who never again wrote to Williams, had sought consolation elsewhere. In the March 2 letter to Lucy Brown, he looked forward to the coming of spring, when the ice would melt, the birds would sing along the river which John had frequented, and the flowers would spring again from the old stocks where Waldo had plucked them the year before (*C* 62-63). That same day he observed in the Journal, "We can understand the phenomenon of death in the animal better if we first consider it in the order next below us—the vegetable" (*J* 1:368). His rather pedantic tone suggests studied detachment, a stance that could not disguise the urgency of the problem, which he confronted again and again in the Journal. Meditating on the difference between living, "a condition of continuance," and dying, "a transient phenomenon," he insisted on March 12, "Nature presents nothing in a state of death" (*J* 1:372). "There seem to be two sides to this world presented us at different times—as we see things in growth or dissolution—in life or death," he continued on March 14, the day he wrote to Williams about John and Waldo. "For seen with the eye of a poet—as God sees them, all are alive and beautiful, but seen with the historical eye, or the eye of the memory, they are dead and offensive. If we see nature as pausing immediately all mortifies and decays—but seen as progressing she is beautiful" (*J* 1:372-73).

Thoreau sought to shift attention from his personal loss to a larger process into which that loss was absorbed. On one level that process is simply the law of nature, in which there can be no progress without decay and death. But his emphasis on the different ways we may perceive nature suggests that Thoreau was also concerned with another creative process, the growth of his own knowledge and understanding. Indeed, in the March 14 Journal entry he unknowingly echoed one of the greatest poems of spiritual growth, *The Fall of Hyperion: A Dream,* which Keats had first drafted as *Hyperion* in the fall of 1818, when his beloved brother Tom was dying before his eyes, and revised and recast in 1819, though the fragment was not published until 1856.[5] At the climax of the second version, after the revelation of the "high

---

[5]Sensitive discussions of the history and biographical context of Keats's poem include Walter Jackson Bate, *John Keats* (New York: Oxford Univ. Press, 1963), pp. 388 ff.; and Robert Gittings, *John Keats* (Boston: Little, Brown, 1968), pp. 245 ff. Quotations are from *The Poems of John Keats,* ed. Jack Stillinger (Cambridge: Harvard Univ. Press, 1978).

tragedy" of human life—symbolized by the passing of the Saturnalian golden age but informed by Tom's agonizing death from tuberculosis—there grows within the poet a power "of enormous ken,/ To see as a God sees" (ll.303-4), an expanded awareness Thoreau described as to see "with the eye of a poet—as God sees." To achieve such insight and distance, the poet must first pass through the stage of powerful empathy with human suffering, an initiation both Keats and Thoreau had undergone at the bedside of a dying brother. That, perhaps, is what Thoreau meant when he told Williams that he could not have done without the experience. But whereas in *The Fall of Hyperion* the poet's vision, at once painful and liberating, is granted by Moneta, the immortal "Shade of memory," Thoreau sharply distinguished between "the eye of a poet" and "the eye of the memory," thus turning from history, the realm of suffering humanity, to the timeless beauty of the natural order.

His almost desperate faith in nature also found expression in "Natural History of Massachusetts," a review-essay written that spring and published in the July 1842 *Dial*. Drawing upon a Journal entry from December 31, 1841, less than two weeks before John's death, Thoreau early in the essay reaffirmed: "To the sick, indeed, nature is sick, but to the well, a fountain of health. To him who contemplates a trait of natural beauty no harm nor disappointment can come" (*Ex* 105; cf. *J* 1:353-54). He praised naturalists like Audubon, but Thoreau's own approach was more poetic than scientific. Thus, in introductory remarks to his translation of Anacreon's ode to the cicada, he observed, "There were ears for these sounds in Greece long ago" (*Ex* 107); he also commented that, in "The Return of Spring," the "old Teian poet sing[s] as well for New England as for Greece" (*Ex* 109). The juxtaposition of ancient Greece and modern New England illustrated nature's continuity, a central theme in the essay. That continuity is built into its very structure, for in his review of the *State Reports—on the Fishes, Reptiles, and Birds; the Herbaceous Plants and Quadrupeds; the Insects . . . and the Invertebrate Animals of Massachusetts,* Thoreau traced representative species of each phylum or group through a full year.

A poetic census of the birds of Massachusetts, the longest section in the essay, was perhaps intended as a kind of oblique memorial to John, who had spurred Thoreau's own interest in ornithology. In fact, as he worked on "Natural History of Massachusetts," Thoreau gained inspiration and some information from an album, "Nature and Bird Notes," John and their sister Sophia had begun in 1836. Following three pages of notes on the birds of Massachusetts from Peabody, Nuttall, and Audubon, the beginning of the album was devoted to an ornithological calendar, with descriptions of birds and their habits jotted down on the page headed with the month in which the birds made their appearance in Concord. Working from the back of the album, John then headed pages with the names of roughly two dozen species of birds, later recording sightings and additional brief descriptions under many of the headings. He made most of those entries in May and June 1837, adding several more in June 1840, after which he apparently laid the album aside. After his death it was taken up by Thoreau, who made seven additional entries between March 27 and June 3, 1842. His penultimate entry, an exquisite description of a brood of partridges, was later revised for *Walden* (*Wa* 226-27), but the abortive project had a more immediate impact on "Natural History of Massachusetts." There, evidently taking a cue from the ornithological calendar and the dated sightings in the album, Thoreau began his survey of native birds with those "which spend the winter with us," traced others through spring and summer, especially May and June when "the woodland quire is in full tune," and concluded with those arriving in autumn, which, he noted, "begins in some measure a new spring" (*Ex* 108, 111, 112).

Nature's seasonal patterns of return and renewal were complemented by other signs of her ongoing health and vitality. Pausing to admire the trees in a winter landscape, Thoreau observed: "They do not wait as man does, but now is the golden age of the sapling. Earth, air, sun, and rain are occasion enough; they were no better in primeval centuries. The 'winter of *their* discontent' never comes" (*Ex* 125). Implicity, in nature there is no memory, no past tense, for the "golden age" and the "primeval centuries" are constantly present in the natural process. These trees "express a naked confidence," inspiring a corresponding faith in their observer. In fact, to the skilled observer, even the hardest and seemingly most inorganic materials revealed the secret of nature's miraculous process. At the end of a description of "ice-foliage" he had observed some years earlier, Thoreau concluded, "In some places the ice-crystals were lying upon granite rocks, directly over crystals of quartz, the frostwork of a longer night, crystals of a longer period, but, to some eye unprejudiced by the short term of human life, melting as fast as the former" (*Ex* 129). To see with such an unprejudiced, godlike eye was to understand that in all things the law of nature is the law of change, or metamorphosis.

"Natural History of Massachusetts" suggests that, after his own "winter of discontent," Thoreau began to look to the future with renewed hope, but John's death nonetheless left him bereft of his closest friend and companion. That loss is reflected in two poems written during 1842 and 1843. In "Great Friend," which he later included in the first draft of *A Week,* he began: "I walk in nature still alone/And know no one" (*CP* 144; cf. FD 73-74). In contrast to "A Walk to Wachusett" and "A Winter Walk," written during the same period, walking does not in the poem lead to discovery but rather underscores his isolation from man and from nature. His quest for the friend "Who does with nature blend,/Who is the person in her mask" is an effort to discover the identity of nature, which otherwise remains blank and expressionless. An embodiment of the intellectual, spiritual, and vital laws of nature, the friend is the poet's link to the cosmos:

> The center of this world,
> The face of nature,
> The site of human life,
> Some sure foundation
> And nucleus of a nation—
> At least a private station.

The friend represents a force that binds together the "world," "nature," and "human life," which otherwise remain separate and discordant. As the three unrhymed opening lines suggest, without such a friend the form the unity achieved in the concluding triplet

is impossible. The triplet also reveals a profound yearning for society. As he begins, "I walk in nature still alone," Thoreau poign-
antly concludes, "We twain would walk together," just as he and
John had once traveled together.

In "Brother where dost thou dwell?"—which Thoreau sent to
his sister Sophia on May 23, 1843, noting that it had been written
"some time ago" (C 108)—he again confronted the problem of
John's death. After a series of opening questions, culminating
with "Are not the fates more kind/Than they appear?" Thoreau
refers to the "ugly pain" and "fears" of his brother's final moments,
but notes:

> Yet thou wast cheery still,
>   They could not quench thy fire,
> Thou didst abide their will,
>   And then retire.

As in the letter to Emerson, where he had insisted that the
"herbage cheerfully consents to bloom, and wither, and give place
to a new," Thoreau here stresses that his brother cheerfully abided
the will of the fates. By submitting to natural laws, John had not
died out of nature but had retired into it. But when Thoreau seeks
his "presence" among familiar scenes, along "the neighboring
brook" and on the shore of "yonder river's tide," the search is
fruitless. Alluding to their mutual interest in ornithology, he asks,
"What bird wilt thou employ/To bring me word of thee?" The
birds, however, share the poet's grief, for they sing a "sadder
strain" and have "slowlier built their nests," those emblems of
ongoing life. Nature stands mute and at rest:

> Where is the finch—the thrush
>   I used to hear?
> Ah! they could well abide
>   The dying year.
>
> Now they no more return,
>   I hear them not;
> They have remained to mourn,
>   Or else forgot.

Instead of assuaging the poet's grief, nature shares or mirrors it. Even her seasonal patterns of return and renewal, eloquently described in the survey of birds in "Natural History of Massachusetts," are interrupted by John's death.

As Sherman Paul has pointed out, "Brother where dost thou dwell?" is an elegy in the tradition of "Lycidas," but the differences between the two poems are illuminating.[6] In "Lycidas" nature initially mourns the Shepherd (ll. 37ff.); like the daystar, however, Lycidas is finally

> sunk low, but mounted high,
> Through the dear might of him that walk'd the waves,
> Where other groves, and other streams along,
> With *Nectar* pure his oozy Locks he laves. (ll. 172-75)

Milton's analogy between the daystar and Lycidas suggests the correspondence between the diurnal cycle and human life, but such transcendence is achieved only through the intercession of Christ, "him that walk'd the waves," who redeems both man and nature. Although he begins by questioning nature about his friend's fate, Milton ends with a vision of Lycidas in the transfigured landscape of "the blest Kingdoms meek of joy and love" (l. 177). In contrast, Thoreau refused to deal with John's death in such orthodox Christian terms, so he continued to seek consolation within the natural world rather than in a vision of supernatural order. In "Brother where dost thou dwell?" his effort ended on a note of pathos; in *A Week,* which may be read as a continuation of that elegy, he sought and achieved far greater resolution.

[6]Paul, p. 104. The sympathetic participation of nature in mourning the dead youth was, of course, a conventional device of the pastoral elegy. Compare the grieving spring of "Brother where dost thou dwell?" to "Adonais": "Grief made the young Spring wild, and she threw down/Her kindling buds, as if she Autumn were,/Or they dead leaves; since her delight is flown,/For whom should she have waked the sullen year?" (ll. 136–39) (*The Complete Poetical Works of Shelley,* ed. Thomas Hutchinson [London: Oxford Univ. Press, 1948]).

The continuity between the two works is illustrated by four lines of poetry which Thoreau jotted down on the first page of the Long Book (see illustration) and later used as the opening epigraph in *A Week:*

> Where'er thou sail'st who sailed with me,
> Though now thou climbest loftier mounts
> And fairer rivers dost ascend
> Be thou my muse, my Brother. (*J* 2:3, *W* 3)

In this opening invocation, Thoreau hints at the central concerns of *A Week*—death and a brotherhood that transcends death. He echoes Milton's line, "Where other groves, and other streams along," but he depicts a natural paradise rather than a Christian heaven. As he had earlier sought John's presence among familiar scenes in "Brother where dost thou dwell?" he here places his brother within a landscape of rivers and mountains that mirrors the landscape of *A Week*. With characteristic reticence Thoreau does not refer to his brother by name, or even explicitly refer to his brother's death. Instead, as Jonathan Bishop has observed, John "disappears into the 'we' who together constitute the anonymous sensibility of the narrator."[7] John thus remains a living presence, taking his pace by Thoreau's side during the excursion, and, as his muse, during the writing of *A Week*. There, Thoreau frequently refers to "our journal" of the voyage, implying that it was based on a detailed record the pair kept, when, in fact, the book was the result of his own determined efforts to vivify their happy time together in 1839.

[7]"The Experience of the Sacred in Thoreau's *Week*," *ELH* 33 (1966):89–90. Bishop's article (pp. 66–91), which remains one of the most convincing readings of *A Week*, also illuminates Thoreau's efforts to discover variants of the sacred within personal, natural, cultural, and historical experiences. For a more detailed discussion of the interplay between "I" and "we," which he views as one of Thoreau's means of resisting the establishment of any clearly defined persona in the book, see Steven Fink, "Variations on the Self: Thoreau's Personae in *A Week on the Concord and Merrimack Rivers*," *ESQ* 28 (1982):24–35.

Thoreau's elegiac purpose accounts for some of his initial selections of entries from the 1837-44 Journal for use in *A Week*. He copied out numerous passages on friendship, then already destined to be its most extended digression, into the Long Book. He gathered other kinds of material from the Journal of late September and October 1842, dating those entries so that he could later place the phenomena described in them in an accurate sequence in the meditation on autumn in "Friday," for which he also copied into the Long Book an extended description of the autumn cattle show, poems concerning the season, and a series of quotations, including lines from "Autumn" in Thomson's *The Seasons*. Since the 1839 voyage had ended on September 13, eight days before the true autumnal equinox, Thoreau clearly did not plan to write a literal account of the trip. Instead, the autumnal scene—like the narrative of the voyage itself—offered a context within which he would seek to resolve the emotional and spiritual problems posed by John's death. "Am I not as far from those scenes though I have wandered a different rout, as my companion who has finished the voyage of life?" Thoreau asked in the Long Book. "Am I not most dead who have not life to die, and cast off my sere leaves?" (*J* 2:60).

Having established the theme and seasonal structure of *A Week*, he had not yet achieved a fully articulated form. A comparison of the first draft and the published version, as well as a textual study of surviving intermediate states, reveals that as he revised and expanded the manuscript Thoreau sought to make each chapter play a more effective part in the larger drama of *A Week*. He thus heightened the tension between transience and permanence in "Concord River" and "Saturday"; underscored the brothers' increasing harmony with man and nature in "Sunday," "Monday," and "Tuesday"; prepared for and gave added weight to the digression on friendship in "Wednesday"; firmly established the transitional role of "Thursday"; and persistently developed the autumnal motifs in "Friday." Indeed, Thoreau's effort to integrate his elegiac concerns into the narrative was so successful that critics have only recently begun to recognize how central those concerns are to an understanding of *A Week*.

"Concord River" serves as an apt introduction to the physical and spiritual topography of *A Week*. In his opening description of the streams that mingle to form Concord River, which in turn joins the Merrimack in its final run to the sea, Thoreau establishes the significance of his native river. He initially asserts that it is as old as the Euphrates or Nile, on whose banks the first civilizations sprang up. He then associates it with the Ganges and the Mississippi, rivers of crucial importance to later civilizations. Finally, he describes the Concord as a representative of universal laws: "Many a time had I stood on the banks of the stream, watching the lapse of the current, and apt emblem of all progress, following the same law with the system, with time, with all that is made. The weeds at the bottom gently bending down the stream, shaken by the watery wind, still planted where their seeds had sunk, but ere long to die and go down the stream" (FD 3, W 12-13).

Standing alone on the banks of the river, Thoreau meditates on time and transience. The law that governs "all that is made" is, of course, the law of life and death. Like the weeds at the bottom of the stream, men, too, soon "die and go down the stream," an echo of the ever-popular hymn, "Time, like an ever rolling stream,/Bears all its sons away." By the time Thoreau drafted "Concord River," that current had already borne his brother away, which doubtless accounts for the prominent "I" in the introductory chapter of a book dominated by "we." His tone is restrained, but Thoreau is not detached. Observing that the objects floating by, "fulfilling their fate," were "of singular interest to" him, he originally concluded, "And at length I had resolved to launch myself on its current, and float *like them* whither it might bear me" (FD 3; emphasis added). Although he later omitted the explicit likeness between himself and the flotsam (W 13), by embarking on the river in *A Week* Thoreau implicitly affirms his own place in the natural process, though it initially seems to promise only death and oblivion.

The somber mood of "Concord River" is partially offset by the opening of "Saturday." The rain that threatened to delay their departure gives way to "a mild afternoon, as serene and fresh, as if nature were maturing some greater scheme of her own" (FD

4, *W* 15). In an effort to establish the favorable auspices of the voyage, Thoreau adapted Journal entries from July 28 and September 12, 1842, decking out the banks of the river with a gay array of flowers, all seemingly at the height of their beauty. "Indeed nature seemed to have attired herself for our departure," he observed, "with a profusion of fringes and curls" (FD 7, *W* 21).

That unseasonable array is the first of numerous signs of nature's dispensation discovered in *A Week*. But Thoreau also used the flowers as emblems of the transience of life. The entry dated July 28, 1842, in the Long Book begins, "The banks of the river are in the height of their beauty at this season" (*J* 2:10). In the first draft, where it describes the scenery on August 31, 1839, Thoreau revised the sentence to read: "The banks of the river had perhaps passed the height of their beauty, and some of the brighter flowers showed by their faded tints that the season was verging toward the afternoon of the year" (FD 6, *W* 20). He did not revise the remainder of the passage accordingly, but his reference to the "faded tints" of these flowers, like Milton's description of the "sad embroidery" of the flowers in "Lycidas" (ll. 132 ff.), suggests the inevitability of decay and death. Adding that the brothers had missed the water lily, "the queen of river flowers," he concluded the description on an ominous note: "He makes his voyage too late perhaps by a true water clock—who delays so long" (FD 7, *W* 21).

Thoreau's preoccupation with time and the river underlies his depiction of fishermen in "Saturday." "Human life is to him very much like a river," he observed, " 'aie renning downward to the see' " (FD 9, *W* 24). He later added a recollection of an old man, "the Walton of this stream," whom he had ostensibly observed fishing along the river: "I think nobody else saw him; nobody else remembers him now, for he soon after died, and migrated to new Tyne streams" (*W* 25). The passage is saved from sentimentality by the subtle irony of "migrated," a term that also relates the life of the fisherman to the life cycle of fish, especially to the migratory fish which "were formerly abundant in this river ... until the dam and afterward the canal at Billerica, and the factories at Lowell put an end to their migrations hitherward" (FD 13, W 33).[8]

The extended digression on the fish of the Concord River is informed by Thoreau's elegiac purpose in *A Week*. As species, the fish illustrate the health and vitality of nature; as individuals, they dramatize the frailty and transience of life. Although he apparently gathered information from the reports reviewed in "Natural History of Massachusetts," Thoreau stressed the human characteristics of fish. "How many young finny contemporaries have I in this water," he remarked. "And methinks it will not be forgotten by *some* memory that we *were* contemporaries" (FD 9; cf. W 37). He identifies most strongly with the migratory shad, denied access to the river by the dams and canal but still "revisiting their old haunts as if their stern Fates would relent" (FD 14, W 37). Like John, who was "cheery still" when confronted by the seemingly cruel "fates" (C 109), the shad confront their "stern Fates" with equanimity: "Not despairing utterly when whole myriads have gone to feed those sea monsters, during thy suspense, but still brave, indifferent, on easy fin there, like shad reserved for higher destinies" (FD 15, W 37).

The veiled link between the shad and his brother perhaps explains the intensity of Thoreau's apostrophe to the shad. In biblical, prophetic terms, he concluded: "The time is not far off when thou shalt have thy way up the rivers, up all the rivers of the globe, If I am not mistaken, and thy nature prevail. If it were not so but thou were to be over looked at first *and* at last—then would not *I* take their heaven" (FD 15). Adding an anthropomorphic touch, he later deleted "and thy nature prevail," which suggests mere brute instinct, and inserted, "Yea, even thy dull watery dream shall be more than realized" (W 38). If the shad's dream should not be realized, if their migratory cycle of life, death, and

---

[8]In "Circular Imagery in Thoreau's *Week*," *College English* 26 (1965):350–55, J. J. Boies suggests that the migratory fish are "an analogue of all nature," since their cycle of life recapitulates nature's rhythm of return and renewal. Cf. Joseph J. Moldenhauer, "Images of Circularity in Thoreau's Prose," *Texas Studies in Literature and Language* 1 (1959):245–63; and Stephen L. Tanner, "Current Motions in Thoreau's *A Week*," *Studies in Romanticism* 12 (1973):763–76.

rebirth should continue to be impeded, it would make a mockery of man's own dreams of heaven. Conversely, signs that nature's continuity is unbroken, signs that Thoreau soon begins to discover in *A Week,* suggest that man's belief in a corresponding spiritual rebirth is more than a dream.

The descriptions of the flowers along the banks and the fish of the Concord River introduce the theme of fruition and decay, transience and permanence, life, death, and rebirth; they also introduce the reader to a pastoral world in which the drama of grief and reconciliation is enacted. The voyage away from the village is a journey back to a primeval Golden Age. "It seemed insensibly to grow lighter as the night shut in," he observed in the first draft, "and a distant and solitary hamlet was revealed which before might have lurked in the shadows of the noon" (FD 16). This luminous night suggested that a transformation had taken place, and he later underscored the brothers' joint discovery of a new world, or rather an old world made new. Changing "hamlet" to "farmhouse," Thoreau added, "There was no other house in sight, nor any cultivated field." Although he notes that they had voyaged only seven miles from Concord, the details of the scene—the pine woods, the shrub oaks, the grapevines and ivy—are those of a primeval "leafy wilderness." Comparing this magical pastoral world, "a place for nymphs and satyrs," to Ostia, the port of Rome, he remarks, "What of sublimity there is in history was there symbolized" (W 39-40; cf. FD 16).

For Thoreau, sound is a vehicle of the correspondence between past and present. They first hear the barking of dogs, "which we did not fail to hear every night afterward" (FD 17, W 41). This sign of continuity during their voyage prepares for an even more striking instance of continuity through history. Upon hearing a dog pursuing a fox, he comments, "How long this natural bugle must have rung in the woods of Attica and Latinum before the horn was invented" (FD 17, W 41). After the images of mutability earlier in "Saturday," these sounds are a source of hope, embodied by "the shrill clarion of the cock—with wakeful hope—even from the very setting of the sun—prematurely ushering in the dawn" (FD 18, W 41). Revising an entry in the Journal of March 3, 1841 (J 1:276-77), Thoreau succinctly concludes, "All these sounds

. . . are evidence of nature's health and *sound* state" (FD 18, *W* 41-42). His confident assertion of nature's continuity and health anticipates his shift from grief to joy and assurance in *A Week*.

Just as he revised the end of "Saturday" to underscore the primitive and pastoral elements of the scene, Thoreau revised the opening of "Sunday" to emphasize its wild, unsettled aspect. In the first draft, for example, he wrote that "for long reaches" between Ball's Hill and Billerica, there was "no house in sight hardly any cultivated field" (FD 19). In *A Week* his comment is far more emphatic: "For long reaches we could see neither house nor cultivated field, nor any sign of the vicinity of man" (*W* 44). The extended description of land, air, and water that follows underwent even more extensive changes as Thoreau revised, rearranged, and expanded it, seeking to unify the somewhat disparate impressions gathered together in the first draft. Each version, however, evokes the magical and poetic qualities of the scene; and each concludes with a description of two men in a skiff from the Journal of September 1841 (FD 23, *W* 48-49; cf. *J* 1:330-31). These men, a mirror image of the brothers, serve as an apt emblem of human life in harmony with nature.

In "Sunday," Thoreau also offers cultural equivalents of such a natural life. He first contrasts the civil inhabitants of Billerica with the Indian, and modern arts and sciences with "those more venerable arts of hunting and fishing and perhaps of husbandry" (FD 25, *W* 57). While he later shifted the comments on primitive shelters to *Walden* (*Wa* 28), he expanded the digression on ancient times by inserting passages on fables from the Journal of late 1845 and 1846. There, after insisting that the reader of a fable should be less concerned with "the historical truth" than with "a higher poetical truth," thus offering us a hint about how to read *A Week* and *Walden*, he wrote, "We seem to hear the music of a thought and care not if our intellect be not gratified" (*J* 2:185). Changing "our intellect" to "the understanding," he continued in *A Week*, "For their beauty, consider the fables of Narcissus, of Endymion, of Memnon son of Morning, the representative of all promising youths who have died a premature death, and whose memory is melodiously prolonged to the latest morning" (*W* 58).

That reference to Memnon is probably an oblique allusion to John Thoreau. As the story is told in Ovid's *Metamorphoses* and interpreted in Alexander Ross's *Mystagogus Poeticus,* both of which Thoreau read during the early Walden period, when Memnon's body was burned on the funeral pyre, he was by the prayers of Aurora transformed into a bird, which, with other birds called the Memnones, flew out the pile.[9] For Ross this metamorphosis was an emblem of the Resurrection. For Thoreau, who in "Brother where dost thou dwell?" had earlier asked, "What bird wilt thou employ/ To bring me word of thee?" (*CP* 152), it possibly served as a vivid example of the "higher poetical truth" of fables. The ancient fable prolonged the memory of Memnon, "representative of all promising youths who have died a premature death"; *A Week* prolongs the memory of another such youth to yet later mornings.

The Merrimack River reveals other patterns of recurrence. As Thoreau introduced his digression on antiquity by praising its "venerable arts," he began his account of the voyage up the Merrimack by remarking that "we began again busily to put in practice those old arts of rowing steering and paddling" (FD 29, *W* 80). By revising and inserting passages from the 1846 Journal, in which he described the river flowing through a primitive pastoral landscape (*W* 83-84), he established the Merrimack as a link between the ancient past and modern New England. It also served as an emblem of nature's health and vitality. "Unlike the Concord it has a swift current," he noted in the first draft (FD 31). In *A Week* he describes the river in far more resonant terms: "Unlike the Concord, the Merrimack is not a dead but a living stream" (*W* 88). He was ultimately forced to acknowledge the damage locks and dams had done to its fisheries, but, in contrast to "Saturday," where he mourned the disappearance of the shad from Concord River, Thoreau in "Sunday" celebrated their annual ap-

[9]See *Metamorphoses*, Bk. 13, ll. 576–623, and Alexander Ross, *Mystagogus Poeticus, Or The Muses Interpreter* (London, 1648), pp. 278–83; rpt. *The Renaissance of the Gods*, no. 30 (New York: Garland, 1976). For a list of passages from *Mystagogus Poeticus* used in *A Week*, see Seybold, p. 59.

pearance in the Merrimack, concluding, "It cannot but affect our philosophy favorably to know of these schools of migratory fishes . . . which penetrate up the innumerable rivers of our coast in the spring . . . and again of the young fry which in still greater numbers wend their way downward to the sea" (FD 32, W 89). His recognition that this cycle of life is unbroken forms a fitting prelude to the brothers' own cyclical voyage up and back down the Merrimack.

Thoreau's effort to discover signs of continuity in art as well as in nature was reflected in a brief digression on books of "Sunday." At the opening of the digression in the first draft, he commented, "I should read Virgil if only to be reminded of the identity of human life in all ages" (FD 32; cf. *Ex* 138). Quoting two lines from the *Eclogues,* one describing buds swelling in the spring and the other describing apples scattered on the ground in the fall, he observed, "Such sentences were written while grass grew and water ran" (FD 33, W 90). Implicitly, Thoreau sought to fulfill a similar requirement in *A Week,* for at the end of the chapter he remarked that they pitched their tent upon a "gently sloping grassy bank," where they wrote the "journal" of the voyage, "or listened to the wind or the rippling of the river" (FD 36, W 115).

After exploring nature and art in "Sunday," Thoreau in "Monday" discovers the continuity of man's spiritual ideas from the earliest times to the present. "There dwelt the subject of the Hebrew scriptures and the Esprit des Lois," he remarked. "All that is told of that mankind—of the inhabitants of the upper Nile— and the Sunderbunds and Timbuctoo—and the Orinoko—is experience here" (FD 38-39, W 123). As the brothers contemplate "the lapse of the river and of human life" (FD 39, W 124), their thoughts revert "to Arabia—Persia and Hindostan" (FD 40, W 126). Like Greek fables and Latin literature, Hindu scripture is characterized by its timelessness: "In the New England noontide are more materials for oriental history than the Sanscrit contains. In every man's brain is the sanscrit" (FD 42; cf. W 153). Added to his other discoveries, the comments suggest that the past is not past but everpresent. The river, which initially serves as an emblem of flux, increasingly reveals the most permanent and enduring qualities of life.

As he preceded his comments on Hindu scripture with a disquisition upon the fluid nature of all materials, he followed it with a meditation on nature's simplicity and fertility. "What an impulse was given some time or other to vegetation that now nothing can stay it," he exclaimed, "but every where it is nature's business constantly to create new leaves and repeat this type in many materials" (FD 43). Behind Thoreau's vision of unity amid multiformity stands Emerson's comment "Metamorphosis is Nature," as well as Goethe's *Metamorphosis of Plants,* with its description of "the Arch plant, which, being known would give not only all actual but all possible vegetable forms."[10] After drafting an intermediate version of the passage (MH 15, L), Thoreau deleted the catalog of the various forms the leaf takes, which echoed the "ice foliage" passage in "Natural History of Massachusetts." But he retained the half-whimsical suggestion that "from rustling leaves she came in the course of ages to the loftier flight and clear carol of the bird" (FD 44, W 160). As language serves man, so does the leaf serve nature as a mode of expression. Thoreau's extension of Goethe's idea from the vegetative to the animal realm also placed the underlying problem of *A Week* against the backdrop of nature's miraculous process, which is constantly impelling vegetable and animal life through higher and higher forms of existence. When we recall that shortly after John's death Thoreau insisted that "nature presents nothing in a state of death" (*J* 1:372), we recognize that his efforts to resolve the problems associated with that death were rarely far below the apparently serene surface of *A Week*.

According to Perry Miller, Thoreau failed to confront the problem of death directly. Describing some of the surviving manuscripts of the digression on graveyards, which Miller believes indicate "the agonized effort that lies behind the pages" in "Monday," he concludes, "The subject became too much for [Thoreau], he could not master it" (CC 68). Thoreau reworked the digression at least three times and finally omitted more than

[10]Quoted in Daniel Shea, "Emerson and the American Metamorphosis," in *Emerson: Prophesy, Metamorphosis, and Influence,* ed. David Levin (New York: Columbia Univ. Press, 1975), pp. 29, 39.

half of it, but he lavished a similar amount of work on other sections in *A Week,* so his efforts in "Monday," though urgent, were not necessarily "agonized." Nor is it clear that Thoreau could not "master" the problem of death. Instead, the manuscripts reveal that, for aesthetic and literary reasons, he finally decided to deal with one aspect of the problem at the expense of another.

The digression on graveyards began as a disquisition on burials and developed into a meditation on fame. In the earliest version Thoreau described Christian burial practices as "heathenish" and insisted that, instead of being placed under a heavy monument "for fear he should rise before his time," a man's body should either be plowed into the ground to restore nature's fertility or burned, "for so the body is most speedily and cleanly returned to dust again, and its elements dispersed throughout nature" (MH 15, J). He soon added a leaf containing a brief discussion of epitaphs, two of which he had earlier copied into the Long Book (MH 15, J; cf. *J* 2:86). He incorporated the passage on epitaphs in a revised and expanded version, in which he first meditated on monuments, epitaphs, and fame, as in "Monday," and then launched into a bitter tirade against graveyards, most of which he later omitted from *A Week.*

As it stands in "Monday," the meditation in the Dunstable Graveyard evokes Gray's "Elegy Written in a Country Churchyard," which Thoreau briefly discussed in the early Journal (*J* 1:435). Standing in a simple rural graveyard, both authors describe the graves, tombstones, and epitaphs, and speculate about the humble lives of those now at rest there. But their attitudes are radically different. Gray's countryfolk rest "Beneath those rugged elms, that yew tree's shade" (l. 13). In sharp contrast Thoreau observes, "It is remarkable that the dead lie every where under stones,—/'Strata jacent passim *suo* quaeque sub' *lapide*—/*corpora,* we might say, if the measure allowed" (*W* 169). The Latin line is a grotesque version of a line from the *Eclogues* earlier quoted in "Sunday," " 'Strata jacent passim sua quaeque sub arbore poma.'/ The apples lie scattered every where, each under its tree" (*W* 90). In "Sunday," Virgil's line illustrates the fertile relationship between art and "living nature"; the variant in "Monday" describes a barren, sterile place whose only fruits are stones.

A "frail memorial" in Gray's "Elegy" implores "a sigh," a plea-
surable feeling of melancholy and pathos (ll. 78-80); the heavy
slabs in the Dunstable Graveyard prompt Thoreau's contempt and
loathing, as do "all large monuments over men's bodies, from the
pyramids down" (W 169). Gray observes that these memorials
supply the "place of fame and elegy" (l. 82) and concludes his
poem by ostensibly quoting the epitaph to "A youth to Fortune
and to Fame unknown" (ll. 117-28). Thoreau quotes a series of
epitaphs, but he objects, "Why should the monument be so much
more enduring than the fame which it is designed to perpetuate,—
a stone to a bone?" (W 170).

His comments on fame also recall "Lycidas." Mourning Edward
King, "dead ere his prime," Milton asks why a poet should seek
fame if he may die before it is won. Phoebus replies that true
fame is not a product of this world ("no plant that grows on mortal
soil"), "But lives and spreads aloft by those pure eyes/And perfect
witness of all-judging *Jove*" (ll. 78, 81-82). Thoreau, mourning
the death of another young man who died before fulfilling his
early promise, also distinguishes between false rumor and true
fame. But in contrast to Milton, who places the judgment before
Jove, Thoreau asserts that friends should "leave it to posterity to
write the epitaph" (W 170). The judgment is therefore ultimately
handed down in this world rather than the next. The resolution
of the problem is no more satisfying than Milton's tentative so-
lution in "Lycidas," but it helped Thoreau to remove memories
of his brother from the barren realm of graves, tombstones, and
epitaphs to *A Week*, his own loving memorial to John. Remarking
that he has "little love" of graveyards (something of an under-
statement), Thoreau in the final paragraph of the digression thus
asserts, "I have no friends there" (W 170-71).

The final paragraph is a distillation of one of the most violent
diatribes Thoreau ever penned (see Appendix, no. 3). Insisting
that "we should not retard but forward" the economies of nature
(W 171), he continued in the manuscript version: "She incessantly demands manures. Every carcass should be husbanded,
nothing be lost. Keep the ball a moving. Instead of a stinking
graveyard, let us have blooming and fertile fields. Any body can
smell a slaughter-house. When Caspar Hauser went abroad he

smelt the graveyards. If an angel were to come on earth he would smell the graveyards everywhere, and inquire—Why dont you dispose of your dead? Aye, he would smell the living also, and ask—Why dont you bury these too?"

Thoreau probably omitted this passage, and other passages in a similar vein, because it contrasted too violently with the dominant images of life, growth, and fruition in *A Week*. As burials violate the natural process, so graveyards violate the pastoral world, those "blooming and fertile fields" glimpsed throughout the narrative. Although his attitude is initially detached and even flip, he quickly adopts the angry tone that characterizes his jeremiad in "Economy," drafted about the same time. Here, Thoreau envisages the world as a vast charnel house, whose odor of corruption is immediately apparent to a visitor from another realm. Here, too, the living are but one more manifestation of the living-dead in "Economy," who "begin digging their graves as soon as they are born" (*Wa* 5). But, as his decision to omit the bulk of the tirade against graveyards suggests, Thoreau in *A Week* was ultimately less interested in castigating those "who are said to live in New England" (*Wa* 4) than in discovering and celebrating those who actually *live* there.

One of the most important exemplars of life in New England is a man called Rice whom Thoreau met during his 1844 trip to the Berkshires and later described in "Tuesday." Although he stayed with Rice the night before his ascent of Saddleback Mountain, Thoreau treats the events as separate episodes in "Tuesday." In contrast to his private experience atop the mountain, where he finds himself "a dweller in the dazzling halls of Aurora," completely detached from the inhabitants of the neighboring valleys (*W* 189-90), his trip through those same valleys, where he first encounters "a few mild and hospitable inhabitants" and then meets Rice (FD 53 ff., *W* 202 ff.), introduces an important social dimension in *A Week*. Thoreau is intentionally vague about the time of their meeting, but he was originally explicit about the man's emblematic character, calling him Satyrus instead of Rice (FD TN 53.30). In the first draft he also alluded to Rice's heavy drinking and rudeness. Thoreau later omitted the references to drinking but stressed Rice's uncivil manner in order to heighten the contrast between manner and character. At the end of their encounter he detected "a beam of true hospitality and ancient civility" in Rice's eyes (FD 56). Marking this ancient quality, he later added, "It was more significant than any Rice of those parts could even comprehend, and long anticipated this man's culture" (W 207).

Rice is but the first of many signs of continuity between ancient and modern life that Thoreau discerns in "Tuesday." His is ostensibly reminded of Rice by a boatman, "a rude apollo of a man," whom the brothers meet while waiting to get through some locks (FD 52, W 201). After describing his encounter with Rice, he again turns to the boatmen, whose occupation looks like "some ancient oriental game . . . handed down to this generation" (FD 58, W 210-11). Like Rice, these men live in harmony with nature and unconsciously embody the vigor and nobility of ancient times. As the brothers pass some carpenters mending a scow on the bank, Thoreau perceives yet another enduring activity. "Thus did men begin to go down upon the sea in ships," he remarked in the first draft. "There was Iolchos and the launching of the argo" (FD, 59). He omitted the reference to Jason and the Argonauts in the 1849 edition but later replaced it with a line from the *Metamorphoses*, which Thoreau translates, "and keels which had long stood on high mountains careened insultingly (*insultavêre*) over unknown waves" (W TN 216.16-20). As he well knew, in the passage preceding this line Ovid described shipbuilding as the first sign of man's "damned desire of having" in the debased Age of Iron. But for Thoreau, eagerly seeking illustrations of historical continuity, it is "as ancient and honorable an art as agriculture" (FD 58-59, W 216).

Other activities described in "Tuesday" and "Wednesday" also reveal that various aspects of ancient and primitive life were preserved along the banks of the Merrimack. As the brothers voyage upriver in "Tuesday," they glimpse lumberers rolling timber down to the river (FD 61), an activity later shifted to "Thursday," where it awakens "primeval echoes" (W 315); an "industrious damsel" (evidently one of the few who had resisted recruiters from the mills at Lowell) practicing the old art of making leghorn bonnets (FD, 61, W 233); and some masons repairing the locks in "a wild and solitary part of the river" (FD 62, W 234). Even more than these simple folk, the inhabitants of houses along the Merrimack described in "Wednesday" establish the correspondence between the ancient past and the New England present and embody the ideals explored earlier in *A Week*. Approaching the house of a lockman, Thoreau notes that he fears to disturb the "oriental dreamers," refers to the housewife as "some Yankee-Hindoo woman," describes the "devotions" of the inhabitants, a transfigured version of Rice's "ancient civility," and concludes with an eloquent encomium to their "poetic and Arcadian lives" (W 241-43). This imaginary encounter, first drafted in the Journal of the early Walden period, also serves as an apt prelude to the long digression on friendship, which, as Thoreau had noted in the first draft, "is not only at the bottom of all romance and chivalry, but of all rural—pastoral—poetical life" (FD 72).

No subject preoccupied Thoreau and other Transcendentalists more than friendship. As early as April 1838 he wrote a poem on "Friendship," a "close connecting link/Tween heaven and earth" (J 1:40). Perhaps inspired by his growing friendship with Emerson, Thoreau began to draft extended passages on the subject in the fall of 1839 (J 1:98-100), shortly before Emerson began to draft "Friendship" in 1840. Thoreau included the topic in lists of projected writing projects in 1840 and 1841. After his brother's death in 1842, the subject assumed even greater importance, for John was to Thoreau what Charles Emerson, who died in 1836, had earlier been to Emerson, "a brother and a friend in one" (CE I:410n). In an effort to commemorate this sacred bond, Thoreau revised and recopied numerous entries on friendship in the Long Book, later gathering them together in "Wednesday" in the first draft of *A Week*. It was by far the longest disgression in the first draft, and Thoreau later revised and expanded it for the second draft in 1847, and once more for a projected lecture early in 1848.[11] Even after the publication of *A Week* in 1849 he continued

---

[11]Describing the success of his lecture on Katahdin, Thoreau in a letter to Emerson on January 12, 1848, reported, "I have also written what will do for a lecture on Friendship" (C 204). The remark has caused considerable confusion about the writing of *A Week*, since it led various biographers and critics to conclude that Thoreau inserted the digression on friendship in 1848.

to tinker with the digression, making more than two dozen additions that were incorporated in the revised version published in 1868.

Although it would require a chapter in itself to describe the growth of the digression on friendship, the changes Thoreau made in a single paragraph are suggestive of the whole process of revision. Apparently adapting an entry from the Journal of 1844, he wrote in the Long Book:

> My friend thou art not of some other race or family of men—thou art flesh of my flesh, bone of my bone. Has not nature associated us in many ways. Water from the same fountain—lime from the same quarry—grain from the same field, compose our bodies. And per chance our elements but reassert their ancient kindredship. Is it of no significance that I have so long partaken of the same loaf with thee, have breathed the same air summer and winter—have felt the same heat and cold—the same fruits of summer have been pleased to refresh us both—   And thou hast never had a thought of different fibre from my own. (J 2:86-87)

His description of the kinship between friends was possibly inspired by "Lycidas." Milton proclaims his right to mourn Edward King by stating, "For we were nurst upon the self-same hill,/Fed the same flock, by fountain, shade, and rill" (ll. 23-24). Thoreau, too, alluded to the friends' common experiences, but he was even more insistent, stressing their absolute physical and intellectual identity. After jotting the paragraph in the Long Book, he added, "Our kindred—of one blood with us. With the favor and not the displeasure of the gods, we have partaken the same bread" (J 2:87). Somewhat incoherent and repetitive, the comment was probably intended as a preliminary revision rather than as an extension of the paragraph.

He made other and far more significant revisions when he copied the paragraph into the first draft of A Week (FD 71). In contrast to the Long Book, where he addressed the friend directly, Thoreau in the first draft adopted an indirect form of address. At the same time he revised "Has not nature . . ." to "Have not the fates as-

sociated us in many ways." In order to underscore the unity of
friends, he also changed "I . . . with thee" to "we," and "thou . . .
from my own" to "we . . . the one from the other." Implicitly, in
friendship there could be no "I" and "thou," no suggestion of
individual thought or identity.

In the published versions the paragraph reveals subtle shifts
in emphasis. Sometime before publication of the 1849 edition
Thoreau omitted "Water from the same fountain—lime from the
same quarry—grain from the same field, compose our bodies.
And our elements but reassert their ancient kindredship" (FD
71), and added: "He is my real brother. I see his nature groping
yonder so like mine. We do not live far apart" (W 284). The emphasis on spiritual brotherhood, which recalls his neighbor's "savor of holiness groping for expression" at the end of *Walden* (*Wa*
315), represented a marked improvement over his earlier suggestion that friendship resulted from "elements" reasserting their
"ancient kindredship." But it also marks a retreat from the communal "our" to "his" and "mine," from friends being identical to
friends being similar but still separate. Indeed, the word *yonder*
and the comment "We do not live far apart" suggest that there
is always a certain distance between friends. Perhaps in an effort
to balance that suggestion, sometime after 1849 he added a quotation from the *Vishnu Purana:* "Seven paces together is sufficient
for the friendship of the virtuous, but thou and I have dwelt together" (W 284 and TN 284.27-30).

Thoreau's revisions of the paragraph on the kindredship of
friends were probably influenced by his decision to shift it from
near the beginning to the end of the digression. In the first draft
it immediately establishes the bonds between friends; in the published versions it reestablishes those bonds after Thoreau, possibly
influenced by his eroding relationship with Emerson, had devoted
a substantial portion of his commentary to the obstacles confronting friendship. In the latter position the paragraph also prepares for Thoreau's eloquent testament to the continuing bond
between himself and his brother. After relating his love of a friend
to his love of nature, he continued in the 1849 edition: "Even
the death of Friends will inspire us as much as their lives. They
will leave consolation to the mourners, as the rich leave money

to defray the expenses of their funerals, and their memories will be incrusted over with sublime and pleasing thoughts, as their monuments are overgrown with moss" (49 W 299).

Combining sentences from the Journal of February 20 and March 13, 1842, copied into the Long Book but overlooked or rejected in his first draft, Thoreau again sought to resolve the crisis that followed John's death. In the Journal he had noted, "The sad memory of departed friends is soon incrusted over with sublime & pleasing thoughts—as their monuments are overgrown with moss" (J 1:372). In the Long Book he omitted "sad" and revised the final clause to read, "as the monuments of others are overgrown with moss" (J 2:38). The 1849 edition reads "as their monuments," but Thoreau later revised it to "as monuments of other men are overgrown with moss" and added the paradoxical assertion "for our Friends have no place in the graveyard" (W 286). Echoing his earlier remark, "I have no friends there," in the digression on graveyards in "Monday" (W 171), he suggests that John is not in the graveyard and is therefore not explicitly mourned in A Week because he lives in memories of their friendship, which in turn are transmuted into the living art of A Week. The continuities Thoreau discovers in nature, art, and the pursuits of mankind thus culminate in an even greater source of permanence, the everlasting bond between friends.

In the first draft the digression on friendship stood virtually alone in "Wednesday," but Thoreau later framed it with related commentaries on the condition of man. In the second draft it was preceded by a disquisition on physical and spiritual health, which he later revised and compressed (W 256-57). He also drafted an extended meditation on the life of the imagination, which served as an appropriate coda to "Wednesday." Together, these sections reveal his faith in mankind as well as his hostility to those whose actions, beliefs, and teachings undermined the faith of others.

As in the digression on graveyards in "Monday," Thoreau omitted the most controversial portions of the disquisition on health in "Wednesday" (Appendix, no. 9). Musing about the various prescriptions for physical and spiritual welfare, he contemptuously described the "quackery" of doctors and priests. "There is need of a physician who shall minister to both soul and body at once, that is to man," he concludes the section in "Wednesday." "Now he falls between two stools" (*W* 257). But in two manuscript versions he continued: "Is not Death a sovereign remedy? For certain diseases I should write—'Kill the patient.' I would put him out of misery as I would an insect." Thoreau developed three arguments in defense of mercy killing. First, as his earlier comments imply, the physician's efforts to prolong life at all costs reveal a lack of faith in life after death. Second, by seeking to keep the sick, infirm, and deformed alive, physicians "strive right against nature." Finally, if a man faces "too prolonged an agony, shocking to humanity to witness," kindness and respect for life demand that his friends "gently cut his thread and let him go." Echoing "Brother where dost thou dwell?"—where he had earlier suggested that the seemingly cruel fates were kind to end John's agony so swiftly—Thoreau asked, "May not a man be kind heroically, and as the fates are kind?"

He probably omitted the defense of mercy killing because its emphasis on sickness and infirmity was out of place in a chapter dominated by the digression on friendship and concluding with a celebration of the vigor and endurance of human life. He marked two passages in the Long Book concerning the sublimity of man's visions for insertion in "Wednesday" (*J* 2:43), but he apparently overlooked them when he wrote the first draft. Those passages later formed the germ of an extended meditation on man's inward life at the end of the chapter. After describing the absolute sovereignty of imagination, Thoreau in an early draft of the section confronted its greatest obstacle:

> What means this change which is at the bottom of all
> tragedy? Where is the House of Change? The
> individual that stands before you shall tell with a sigh
> of intervals as great as the heavens and earth are
> asunder—   Yet where is the pregnant circumstance
> that has produced this revolution?—   The eye is
> dimmed and sees but its own humors. The mother
> tells her falsehoods to her child, but the healthy child
> does not believe them, for it does not stand in its
> mother's shadow. The winds blow as they were wont,

grass grows and water runs, and we enjoy one
opportunity with all that is created, and with the
creator himself. We are never born too late, nor too
early;—we are never too old, nor too young.
Opportunity never fails.— Our mother's faith has not
grown with her experience. Her experience is too
much for her, and the lesson is too hard to be
learned.[12]

Although Thoreau retained only the cryptic question "Where
is the House of Change?" in "Wednesday" (W 292), shifting three
other sentences to "Sunday" (W 77), his original commentary is
revealing. If change "is at the bottom of all tragedy," by denying
the power of change he implicitly denies that life is tragic. Like
Emerson in "Experience," begun in 1843, at least partly in response to Waldo's death a year earlier, Thoreau attributes the
darkness of life to the failure of man's perceptions.[13] But where
Emerson viewed that failure as inevitable in all but a few "liberated
moments," Thoreau insists that it is a result of false teaching. In
contrast, nature reveals that change does not exist and that the
present moment is equal to all other moments past or future.
Man cannot be born too late or too early, cannot be too young or
too old, for at every moment he enjoys "one opportunity with all
that is created, and with the creator himself." Those whose faith
has grown with their experience recognize that nature and the

[12]The early draft of the digression, written on two leaves in the Harry
Ransom Humanities Research Center, the University of Texas at Austin,
probably dates from 1846 or 1847 (see LMHDT, D7f). A leaf in the
Houghton Library (MH 15, E) contains a compressed version, probably
drafted in 1848.

[13]David W. Hill has challenged the prevailing assumption that "the
uncertainty and darkness of tone" in "Experience" is solely attributable
to the death of Waldo, demonstrating through an analysis of its composition that the essay "taps in a complex way veins of feeling which
stretch back to the journals of the 1820's" ("Emerson's Eumenides:
Textual Evidence and the Interpretation of 'Experience,' " in Emerson
Centenary Essays, ed. Joel Myerson [Carbondale: Southern Illinois Univ.
Press, 1982] , pp. 107–21).

universe do not fail man, but that man fails them. As an illustration of this thesis, Thoreau quoted fifteen scattered lines from
Coleridge's "Dejection: An Ode," concluding "Ah! from the soul
itself must issue forth,/A light, a glory, a fair luminous cloud/
Enveloping the Earth" (ll. 53-55), and two stanzas from *Don Juan*.

His earlier use of the stanzas from *Don Juan* underscores their
significance in the manuscript of *A Week*. In the letter to Isaiah
Williams written in March 1842, Thoreau first described John's
death two months earlier and continued, "What you express with
regard to the effect of time on our youthful feelings—which indeed
is the theme of universal elegy—reminds me of some verses of
Byron—quite rare to find in him, and of his best I think" (*C* 66).
He quoted the two stanzas, beginning "No more, no more! Oh
never more on me/The freshness of the heart can fall like dew"
and concluding "The illusion's gone forever" (Canto I, stanzas
214-15). Perry Miller observed that Thoreau "could hardly have
been unaware that the last stanza ends with one of Byron's ironic
twists" (*CC* 74), but since he had originally copied the stanzas
from Emerson's commonplace book, he may not have been aware
of their context in *Don Juan*.[14] In either case, Thoreau in the
letter to Williams responded to the lament for lost youth by
stressing the timelessness of truth, virtue, and faith and insisting
that man shapes his own destiny. Anticipating *A Week*, he concluded, "The soul which does shape the world is within and central" (*C* 68).

In contrast to Coleridge and Byron, who mourned the passing
of the power of what one called the "soul" and the other called
the "heart," Thoreau in *A Week* again celebrated the continuity
of man's imagination. In his urgent and willed version of reality,
the imagination did not simply invest experience with radiance;
it also freed man from all the accidents and circumstances of life.
After omitting the quotations and compressing the rest of his
commentary on the power of imagination into one paragraph (*W*
292-93), he added an extended passage beginning, "I am aston-

[14]In the margin of the page containing the truncated stanzas from
Don Juan, Thoreau in his commonplace book noted, "From R. W. E.s
Common Place Book" (*TLN* 54).

ished at the singular pertinacity and endurance of our lives" (*W* 293 ff.). He also included a revised version of "The Inward Morning," a poem in the Journal of December 1841 (*W* 294-95; cf. *J* 1:340-42). With its mood of joyful anticipation, the poem is Thoreau's response to the dejection described by Coleridge and Byron.

Thoreau concludes with a paragraph suggested by another entry from December 1841. Describing moments, "the memory of which is armor that can laugh at any blow of fortunes," he had written in the Journal on December 29: "A man should go out nature with the chirp of the cricket, or the trrill of the veery ringing in his ear. These earthly sounds should only die away for a season, as the strains of the harp rise and swell— Death is that expressive pause in the music of the blast" (*J* 1:349-50). With slight modifications Thoreau included these lines in *A Week* (*W* 295-96), as if he unconsciously sought to suggest that John's death two weeks after they were first written had failed to shake his own serene faith, just as that death had failed to destroy their enduring friendship.

At least partly because he wished to fulfill the optimistic promise of "Wednesday," Thoreau greatly expanded the opening of "Thursday." Early in 1847 he added the poem "My books I'd fain cast off," a humorous response to Wordsworth's "Expostulation and Reply." A surviving manuscript, however, reveals that the poem was originally followed by a more serious prose commentary. "There is no where any apology for despondency," Thoreau asserted. "There is always life, which rightly lived implies a divine satisfaction" (HM 1225; cf. *J* 1:86). After briefly chastising Christianity, scholars, and philosophers for failing to learn this simple lesson, he continued:

> It is a singular but consoling fact that it is as hard for
> a melancholy man to speak from the depth of his
> sadness, as for the poet to give utterance to his
> inspirations. While he lives, and in the sunshine, he
> cannot be earnestly sad enough to convey his real
> meaning, and he even derives a secondary sadness
> from this source. Nature refuses to sympathize with
> our sorrow she has not provided for, but by a thousand

contrivances against it   She has bevelled the margins
of the eyelids that the tears may not overflow on the
cheek. The injured man with querulous tone resisting
his age .& destiny is like a tree struck by lightning,
which rustles its sere leaves the winter through, not
having vigor enough to cast them off. (HM 13182, I,
25)

After heavily revising this passage, Thoreau deleted it along
with the rest of the commentary on "My books I'd fain cast off."
But his comments on the relationship between human suffering
and nature serve as an illuminating gloss on his concerns in *A
Week*. For the man who truly understands the natural process,
as the brothers have implicitly come to understand it by the end
of their voyage up the Merrimack, sadness and sorrow are a violation of nature, which does everything in her power to deny
the appropriateness of grief. His analogy between the injured man
and a tree struck by lightning is apt, for it suggests that to resist
"age & destiny" is equivalent to resisting a natural process in
which leaves must fall in the autumn in order to prepare for new
growth in the spring.

That analogy also reflects Thoreau's increasing preoccupation
with the seasonal structure of the narrative, in which "Thursday,"
initially a transition between the two parts of the voyage, became
a seasonal transition between summer and autumn. In a passage
on the brothers' campsite in the first draft, he simply depicted
the trees seen through the mist (FD 88). But, after describing
the sound of the wind and of the river, "whirling and sucking,
and lapsing downward," he later added, "There seemed to be a
great haste and preparation throughout Nature, as for a distinguished visitor" (W 332-33). That visitor is, of course, autumn,
whose arrival is announced in a passage added to the opening of
"Friday": "That night was the turning point in the season. We
had gone to bed in summer, and we awoke in autumn; for summer
passes into autumn in some unimaginable point of time, like the
turning of a leaf" (W 334).

By "anticipating in some measure the progress of the year" (W

349), Thoreau created an imaginary landscape answering in each particular to man's condition—a landscape poised between fruition and decay yet offering signs of endurance and intimations of immortality. In a description of the autumn foliage in the first draft, he noted that by the beginning of October "the woods are in the height of their beauty and the leaves fairly ripened for the fall" (FD 90). Revising the comment to read, "In all woods the leaves were fast ripening for their fall" (W 335), he echoed Shakespeare's "Ripeness is all," a sentiment that might stand as an epigraph to "Friday," for Thoreau, too, has come to accept decay and death as conditions of life.[15] While he is sensitive to the melancholy aspects of the scene, exemplified by the quotations from Frances Quarles (FD 89, W 335, 353), Thoreau offers a different image of autumn, "not the dry and sere leaves of the poets—not the tints of decay but of maturity—more lively than the green   Not a withering but a ripening" (FD 90; cf. W 335).

In an effort to reveal social and cultural analogues to nature's vitality, Thoreau gives an account of the autumn cattle show. After a bout of bronchitis, he noted in the Journal on February 26, 1841, "I who have been sick hear cattle low in the street, with such a healthy ear as prophesies my cure" (J 1:274). The remark indicates the importance of the cattle show to Thoreau, who first described it in the Journal of 1843, immediately after an entry on the brothers' trip through the White Mountains (J 1:446-47). There, as in the revised version in the first draft, he quoted Marlowe's *Hero and Leander,* which may have inspired him to depict the cattle show as a reenactment of ancient games and festivals. Like the Egyptians, Greeks, Etruscans, and Romans, "the farmers crowd to the fair today—in obedience to the same ancient law of the race" (FD 92, W 338). Just as his earlier descriptions of the people along the banks of the Merrimack reveal continuities between past and present, between the pastoral Golden Age and New England, his account of the farmers at the

[15]Cf. Paul David Johnson, "Thoreau's Redemptive *Week,*" *American Literature* 49 (1977):33.

cattle show suggests the continuing life and vitality of a seemingly outmoded form of celebration, for "the old custom still survives while antiquarians & skolars grow grey in commemorating it" (FD 92, W 338). His comparison of these farmers to wild apples, which survive where more palatable varieties perish, thus suggests that human life may mirror the health, vigor, and permanence of nature.

Thoreau linked the account of the cattle show to a section on migratory birds. The farmers, who "sweep by in crowds amid the rustle of leaves, like migrating finches" (FD 91, W 337), follow the same natural laws with birds, which Thoreau, of course, closely associated with his lost brother. Expanding brief paragraphs on the bobolink, lark, and purple finch in the first draft (FD 90), he later drafted an extended digression on migratory birds, "the truest heralds of the seasons" (Appendix, no. 12). In the second draft it followed his long poem "The Fall of the Leaf," one stanza of which Thoreau retained in *A Week* (W 349). Two later versions of the digression, in which Thoreau described the oriole, goldfinch, lark, bobolink, and linnet in the order of their appearance, moving smoothly from midsummer to early autumn, followed an extended meditation on man's central place in the universe, which concludes, "There is something even in the lapse of time by which time recovers itself" (W 351). After that powerful assertion of permanence, a description of the transient and transitory migrations of birds would be anticlimatic. Omitting the digression on birds, whose migrations to the "haunts of summer" serve as "a passing warning to man," Thoreau instead focused on the flowers of autumn, "which abide with us the approach of winter" (FD 93, W 355).

Flowers, which also were charged with associations for him, thus became the central symbols in *A Week*. John's funeral eulogy, in which it was noted that "any new bird or flower he discovered gave him the most unfeigned delight," was delivered on two appropriate biblical texts: "For what *is* your life?" (James 4:14) and "He cometh forth like a flower, and is cut down" (Job 14:2). The first is echoed in Quarles's "And what's a life? The flourishing array/Of the proud summer meadow, which to-day/Wears her green plush, and is to-morrow hay" (*W* 353). The second, from Job's elegy on the human condition, informs Thoreau's description of the flowers along the banks of the Concord River, which "showed by their faded tints that the season was verging toward the afternoon of the year" (FD 6, *W* 20). In contrast, the autumn flowers along the banks of the Merrimack "express all the ripeness of the autumn" (FD 93, *W* 354). Indeed, if the flowers in "Saturday," as in Job's simile and like the flowers in "Lycidas," are pathetic reminders of the frailty and transience of human life, the seemingly unfading flowers in "Friday" are emblems of immortality.

Thoreau revised the description of autumn flowers to emphasize the relationship between human life and plant life. He first expanded the section by combining paragraphs on the "floral solstice" and the symbolism of flowers from "Tuesday" with descriptions in "Friday" (FD 61-62, 93-94; cf. MH 15, E, G). Omitting passages on the medicinal, literary, and spiritual uses of flowers, he added seven stanzas from Ellery Channing's "Autumn," with its description of the passing of summer flowers, its celebration of the autumnal scene, and its ultimate concern with decay, death, and immortality: "So fair we seem, so cold we are,/So fast we hasten to decay,/Yet through our night glows many a star,/That still shall claim its sunny day" (*W* 355). The analogy between flowers and human life explains the "peculiar interest belonging to the still later flowers," for the fact that shrubs like the witch hazel flourish and bloom after other flowers have passed away suggests that man's life may be equally rugged and enduring (*W* 355; cf. FD 93).

Shifts in context betray the significance Thoreau attached to the autumn flowers in "Friday." In the first draft the description was followed by a sequence on the light, atmosphere, and celestial phenomena of autumn, including a paean to the autumnal moon from Thomson's *The Seasons*. Adding two stanzas from Ralegh's "Praise of his sacred Diana" and lines from the *Iliad*, which "carries us back to a moonlight night in the country 3000 years ago" (MH 15, H), Thoreau in the second draft used that sequence to introduce the "floral solstice," which consequently became the climactic autumnal phenomenon described in "Friday."[16] But he later dropped the introductory sequence, which reflected more the glow of a reading lamp than the luminescence of autumn, and drafted a new introduction to the description of flowers: "We saw now along the shore, and on the hills and meadows mostly dried specimens of a summer, but still sweet and clean & invigorating to our senses—all whose death and decay was pregnant with new life." His somewhat incongruous remark offered an occasion for some animadversions upon museums, "the catacombs of nature," and their visitors. "I have had my sight-perceiving sense so disturbed in these haunts," he concluded, "as for a long time to mistake a veritable living man in the attitude of repose, musing like myself, as the place requires, for a stuffed specimen" (Appendix, no. 13). Thoreau finally omitted that passage too, perhaps because, like the attack on graveyards in "Monday," which it recalls, and the defense of mercy killing in "Wednesday," his foray in "Friday" sounded a sour note in a chapter devoted to the vigor and endurance of life. Consequently, instead of seeing "mostly dried specimens of a summer," the brothers climb a hill "in haste to get a nearer sight of the autumnal flowers," which "expressed all the ripeness of the season" (W 353-54).

In two poems, "I am the autumnal sun" and "The moon no longer reflects the day," Thoreau rounded off his description of the autumnal scene and recapitulated the movement from grief to reconciliation in *A Week*. A comparison of these verses with the greatest of all poems devoted to the season, Keats's "To Autumn," is instructive. As Arthur Davenport has observed, "The music of Autumn which ends [Keats's] poem is a music of living

[16]In a surviving sequence of six leaves from the second draft completed in early 1847, the section on migratory birds (paged 369–72: HM 13182, III, 5–6) is followed by a description of the light and atmosphere of autumn (paged 373–74: MH 15, O) and by a celebration of the splendors of the autumn moon, which introduces the section on autumn flowers (paged 375–78: MH 15, H). The final leaf, originally paged 379–80, was renumbered 428–29 (MH 15, E) in the expanded draft completed in mid-1847, where it followed a revised opening of the section on autumn flowers, drafted on two leaves, paged 425–26 and 427-[verso blank] (MH 15, G). See Appendix, no. 13.

and dying, of staying and departure, of summer-winter."[17] The music in "Friday" is similar, but unlike Keats, who harmonized seemingly discordant tones, Thoreau arranged two poems antiphonally, first sounding a dirge, then responding with a hymn. In the last of his major odes, written less than a year after the death of his brother Tom, Keats achieved a complex balance between two opposing views of the season, and of human life; in contrast, Thoreau enacts a progressive movement from one view to the other, reminding us that shortly after John's death he had written, "There seem to be two sides to this world presented us at different times—as we see things in growth or dissolution— in life or death" (J 1:372). Following a depiction of autumn in terms of darkness and decay, the first poem in "Friday" concludes, "And the rustling of the withered leaf/Is the constant music of my grief" (FD 99, W 378). But, abruptly shifting from that perspective, which reveals only death and dissolution, Thoreau in the second poem (transformed into a prose poem in A Week) treats autumn in terms of growth and life, of fruition and permanence, a time when "Asters and golden rods reign along the way/And the life-everlasting withers not" (FD 99; cf. W 378). As that symbolically charged rendering of the autumnal scene suggests, the "true harvest of the year" is not physical but spiritual, a recognition that, though "he cometh forth like a flower," man need not be cut down like the frail flowers in "Saturday" but may endure and flourish like the rugged varieties in "Friday."

Thoreau originally sought to deal with the problem of life, death,

---

[17]"A Note on 'To Autumn,' " Reassessment (1958), p. 96; quoted in The Poems of John Keats, ed. Miriam Allott (London: Longman, 1970), p. 653n. In her annotations Allott also identifies many of Keats's sources, including the Aeneid and Thomson's The Seasons, with both of which Thoreau was equally familiar. He may also have known of "To Autumn," since Keats's brother George sent the original manuscript of the poem to Anna Barker in November 1839, less than a year before her marriage to Samuel Gray Ward, close friend of Emerson and Margaret Fuller. Although those two had little taste for Keats's poetry, others of the Transcendentalists, notably James Freeman Clarke, were staunch supporters of the English post. See Hyder Edward Rollins, Keats's Reputation in America to 1848 (Cambridge: Harvard Univ. Press, 1946).

and immortality in terms of this world rather than the next. In the first draft he followed the two poems with a brief meditation on the relationship between man and nature: "Men no where, east or west, live as yet a natural life. . . . A life of equal simplicity and sincerity with nature" (FD 99, W 379). But he excepted a few "earth-born" men, whose motions are "graceful and flowing as if a place were already found for them—like rivers flowing through vallies" (FD 100, W 380). His depiction echoed a passage earlier in "Friday," where Thoreau described the "great & current motions" of sailing in harmony with wind and water (FD 94, W 360), so he clearly intended the voyage to serve as an illustration of the harmony between man and nature. Instead of looking to the hereafter, he thus implied that such life-giving harmony invested man's life with a kind of immortality in this world.

As he revised and expanded the brief paragraphs in the first draft into an extended digression in *A Week,* Thoreau's attention shifted from the world of nature to the realm of spirit.[18] To suggest the divinity of life in harmony with nature, he quoted two lines from Virgil's description of the Elysian fields in Book VI of the *Aeneid* (W 380). Drawing upon an 1845 Journal entry inspired by Christ's words, "In my father's house are many mansions," he added, "The borders of our plot are set with flowers, whose seeds were blown from more Elysian fields adjacent" (W 381; cf. *J* 2:167-68). He emphasized the continuity between these adjacent realms, even insisting that man "need pray for no higher heaven than the pure senses can furnish, a *purely* sensuous life" (W 382). Yet, like Emerson in *Nature,* Thoreau ultimately treats the physical world as a bridge to a transcendent spiritual realm. "I have interest but for six feet of star, and that interest is transient," he remarks of astronomy. "Then farewell to all ye bodies, such as I have known ye" (W 387). The digression, which began

[18]The growth of the digression between 1845 and 1849 helps explain what Frederick Garber, *Thoreau's Redemptive Imagination* (New York: New York Univ. Press, 1977), pp. 195-97, views as the contradiction between Thoreau's initial embrace and final "rejection of the earthly experience in the digression." For another interesting discussion of the interplay between naturalism and idealism in "Friday," see McIntosh, pp. 171–78.

as the celebration of "a natural life" in the first draft, ends in *A Week* with a quotation concerning the death of Saadi, the Persian poet honored as a saint by the Muslims: "The eagle of the immaterial soul of Shaikh Sadi shook from his plumage the dust of his body" (W 388).

Images of natural harmony and spiritual transcendence are fused as the brothers near the end of their voyage. "Thus we go home to find some autumnal work to do," Thoreau remarked, "& help in the revolution of the seasons" (FD 101, W 388-89). Addressing the "gods of the shore" in the poem "All things are current found," an assertion of the continuity between matter and spirit, he concluded, "I hear the sweet evening sounds/From your undecaying grounds/Cheat me no more with time,/Take me to your clime" (FD 100-101, W 389). As if to suggest that the prayer had been answered, he described the evening of their return as "so rich a sunset as would never have ended but for some mysterious reason unknown to men, and surely to be marked with brighter colors than ordinary in the scroll of time   the evenings have no principle of decay in them" (FD 101). He later omitted the second sentence but retained a cryptic reference to "some reason unknown to men" (W 389), thus hinting at a divine cosmic order into which the diurnal cycle, like the cycle of the seasons, is finally absorbed and transfigured. Thoreau appropriately concluded the description of the sunset with a glimpse of the stars, which "are distant and unobtrusive, but bright and enduring—like our fairest and most memorable experience" (FD 102, W 391), an experience grown more luminous in memory and with the loss of the companion who shared it, like the voyage depicted in *A Week*.

Their return to Concord is charged with literary associations. Virgil's description of the Elysian fields—which Thoreau translated, "Here a more copious air invests the fields, and clothes with purple light; and they know their own sun and their own stars" (W 380)—informs his own depiction of the brothers' approach "to the fields where our lives had passed" amid "the warm purple colors" of sunset (FD 101, W 389). Observing that "the shadows of the hills were beginning to steal over the stream," Thoreau placed himself with Virgil at the end of the first eclogue

("and longer shadows fall from the mountain-heights") and with
Milton at the end of "Lycidas" ("And now the Sun had stretch't
out all the hills"). In the final line of "Lycidas," Milton turns "to
fresh Woods, and Pastures new"; at the end of his elegy Thoreau
returns to the fields of Concord, which have been transformed
by the brothers' experience into the Elysian fields, where the
spirits of heroes, bards, and philosophers disport.

Thoreau's vision of that new world and its putative inhabitants
also relates *A Week* to the most ambitious undertakings of his
more immediate predecessors among the English Romantic poets,
notably Wordsworth. In the Prospectus to *The Recluse,* an extraordinary attempt to write the equivalent of *Paradise Lost* for
his own age, Wordsworth rhetorically asked:

> Paradise, and groves
> Elysian, Fortunate Fields—like those of old
> Sought in the Atlantic Main—why should they be
> A history only of departed things,
> Or a mere fiction of what never was? (ll. 47-51).[19]

Wordsworth affirmed that paradise was neither fictional nor irrevocably lost. Instead, it was to be regained by the marriage of
"the discerning intellect of Man" to "this goodly universe" (ll. 52-
53), a union from which would spring a new "creation." Under
the strong influence of Emersonian idealism, Thoreau sometimes
tipped that Wordsworthian balance in favor of the mind. Consequently, the paradise transferred from a supernatural to a nat-

---

[19]*The Poetical Works of William Wordsworth,* ed. Ernest de Selincourt
and Helen Darbisher, 5 vols. (London: Oxford Univ. Press, 1940–49),
V:4. The significance of this passage is developed by M. H. Abrams,
Natural Supernaturalism (New York: Norton, 1971), pp. 26–27, which
contains a superb discussion of *The Recluse* and related works written
in England and Germany during the decades following the French Revolution. Thoreau's relationship to European romanticism is treated by
McIntosh and in two seminal articles: R. P. Adams, "Romanticism and
the American Renaissance," *American Literature* 23 (1952):419–32; and
Perry Miller, "Thoreau in the Context of International Romanticism,"
New England Quarterly 24 (1961):147–59.

ural frame of reference by Wordsworth, who insists that it will be "A simple produce of the common day" (l. 55), sometimes in *A Week* seems to transcend time and place. But as they near the end of their voyage, traveling westward toward the sunset, the way of mortal life, the brothers clearly see their world in a new light: they are not simply returning to their native village, but *home,* to a kind of earthly paradise restored on native grounds through the movement of a new spirit upon the face of the waters in *A Week,* Thoreau's own version of a seven-days' creation.

In a paragraph in which loss and recovery, permanence and change, are carefully balanced, Thoreau concluded the book on a note of triumphant innocence and expectancy.[20] As its keel recognizes "the Concord mud where the flattened weeds still preserved some semblance of its own outline having scarce yet recovered themselves since its departure," the brothers leap "gladly on shore" and attach their boat "to the little apple tree whose stem still bore the mark which its chain had worn—in the chafing of the spring freshets" (FD 128, W 393). In contrast to the dead "weeds" and "stems of trees" that float by, "fulfilling their fate," at the end of "Concord River" (FD 3, W 13), these resilient weeds and tough little tree are final examples of the rugged varieties discovered in the course of the voyage. Indeed, that apple tree, which has survived the chafing of experience and whose wound is slowly healing, is a fit icon for its creator, whose recovery from the trauma of John's death is enacted in *A Week*. With those "spring freshets," sure signs of the seasonal renewal promised by the autumnal landscape in "Friday," Thoreau thus completed the transformation of the river from an emblem of time and transience to a symbol of nature's permanence, a final reaffirmation of the signs of continuity celebrated earlier in *A Week*.

By depicting their voyage as a withdrawal to a timeless, pastoral world, Thoreau at once commemorated John's death, resolved

---

[20]For different readings of the language, tone, and imagery of the final paragraph, and of the mood of the book as a whole, see the chapter on *A Week* in Eric J. Sundquist, *Home as Found* (Baltimore: Johns Hopkins Univ. Press, 1979); and Richard Bridgman, *Dark Thoreau* (Lincoln: Univ. of Nebraska Press, 1982).

the problems associated with that death, and adumbrated the kind of life that might be led in *New* England, the natural frame for his vision of a brave new world. But, in the first draft at least, he sustained that idealized vision only by ignoring the actualities of his native region. A darker side of its life is glimpsed in the digression on graveyards in "Monday," the attack on physicians and priests in "Wednesday," and the foray against museums in "Friday," all of which reveal his disenchantment with the customs of New England. Significantly, Thoreau drafted these sections after 1846, when his growing involvement in the social, political, and religious controversies of the time began to have a significant impact on his conception of *A Week*.

3

The Abuses of the Past

ONE OF THE most persistent criticisms of *A Week* is that it does not reflect the full range of Thoreau's concerns. The "Thoreau of *A Week on the Concord and Merrimack Rivers* is primarily the mystic and the lover of the primitive, not yet much the critic of society," Joseph Wood Krutch asserted. "And as a result the book does not present the complete man."[1] Even if this were an accurate appraisal, Krutch's remark would be deceptive, for it suggests that *A Week* was written before Thoreau's social, political, and religious views had fully developed. By the time he published the book in 1849, however, he had also completed "Resistance to Civil Government" (better known as "Civil Disobedience"), published the same month as *A Week,* and the first three versions of *Walden,* originally scheduled for publication shortly after *A Week*. Although he was profoundly affected by the events of the early 1850s, especially the passage of the Fugitive Slave Bill in 1851, the Thoreau of *A Week* was already well on his way to becoming the social critic of *Walden*.

His radical views developed early. At Harvard he was strongly influenced by Orestes Brownson's *New Views of Christianity, Society, and the Church* and by Emerson's *Nature,* both published in 1836. Thoreau became friends with Emerson shortly before the latter delivered the "Divinity School Address" (1838), fueling a debate within Unitarianism that continued in works like Theodore Parker's "A Discourse of the Transient and Permanent in Christianity" (1841). Thoreau was also influenced by the spirited abolitionists in his own household. But, as his comments in the Journal and in early essays like "The Service" reveal, he believed in individual rather than group reform. He was therefore highly critical of organized reformers and avoided direct involvement in their activities. By the time he began to gather materials for *A*

[1]Joseph Wood Krutch, *Henry David Thoreau* (New York: William Sloane, 1948), p. 97.

Week, however, Thoreau had become increasingly preoccupied with the controversies simmering in New England. His growing concern is apparent in an unpublished lecture on the conservative and the reformer, as well as in "Herald of Freedom" (1844) and "Wendell Phillips before Concord Lyceum" (1845), tributes to prominent abolitionists that were published by the time he wrote the first draft of *A Week.*

Although his interest in reform is only dimly reflected in the first draft, after his arrest in 1846 Thoreau began to use *A Week* as a vehicle for expressing a wide range of social, political, and religious concerns. He consequently attacked the church in "Sunday" and the state in "Monday." He continued to dissociate himself from organized reformers, especially in extracts from his unpublished lecture apparently intended for "Monday," but other surviving manuscripts indicate that Thoreau continued his own attack in later chapters, where he inserted a series of sharp critiques of his countrymen's social customs and economic practices as well as a revised version of "Herald of Freedom." Probably because he wished to stress the promise of life in New England, figured by the brothers' idyllic journey,Thoreau omitted "Herald of Freedom," the extracts on reformers, and numerous other passages, some of which he revised for *Walden. A Week* therefore does not measure the full extent of his critique of New England or fully reveal his ambivalence toward those who sought to reform New England. Nonetheless, a study of its background and composition indicates how strongly Thoreau's first book was influenced by the spirit of dissent and protest that characterized the age.

In "Historic Notes of Life and Letters in New England," Emerson observed: "There are always two parties, the party of the Past and the party of the Future; the Establishment and the Movement. At times the resistance is reanimated, the schism runs under the world and appears in Literature, Philosophy, Church, State and social customs. It is not easy to date these eras of activity with any precision, but in this region one made itself remarked, say in 1820 and the twenty years following."[2]

²*The Transcendentalists,* ed. Perry Miller (Cambridge: Harvard Univ. Press, 1950), p. 494.

Emerson's delineation of the issues that divided the party of the Future from the party of the Past suggests the breadth of the revolt, a revolt in which the Transcendentalists, or "New School," played an important role. At once a product and an heir of Transcendentalism, Thoreau, like many other young men, received his introduction to the ideas of the New School while attending Harvard, the bastion of the Old School. During a brief leave in 1836 he stayed with Orestes Brownson, then engaged in writing *New Views of Christianity, Society, and the Church*, a condemnation of Protestantism, and particularly rational Unitarianism, as the rebellion of Materialism against Spiritualism. *New Views,* "one of the seminal books in American Transcendentalism" (*DHT* 46), was published in November, only two months after Emerson's *Nature*, which Thoreau read in the spring of 1837.[3] As his comments at a commencement conference on "The Commercial Spirit of Modern Times" indicate, the impact of these works was immediate. Like Brownson, Thoreau feared that materialism would make man "selfish" in his social relations and soulless in his relations with God; and, like Emerson, Thoreau celebrated the relationship between man and nature. Insisting that the universe is more to be enjoyed than used, he prefigured the divisions of days in *A Week*: "The order of things should be somewhat reversed,—the seventh should be man's day of toil . . . and the other six his sabbath of the affections and the soul, in which to range this wide-spread garden, and drink in the soft influences and sublime revelations of Nature" (*EEM* 117).[4]

During the fall and winter of 1837-38 Thoreau began to absorb Emerson's ideas at first hand. Significantly, the two men became friends while Emerson was preparing a frontal attack on the orthodox Unitarianism taught at Harvard Divinity School. In a rebellious mood himself, Emerson was delighted with what he described as Thoreau's spirit of "rebellion" (*JMN* V:460), which was probably spurred by the violent public reaction to the "Divinity

[3]Kenneth Cameron, "Thoreau Discovers Emerson," *Bulletin of the New York Public Library* 57 (1953): 319–34.

[4]Cf. Brownson's comment in *New Views*: "The Material predominates over the Spiritual. Men labor six days for this world and at most but one for the world to come" (*The Transcendentalists*, p. 118).

School Address," delivered on July 15, 1838. In an entry entitled the "Sabbath Bell," Thoreau a few weeks later wrote in the Journal: "It is as the sound of many catechisms and religious books twanging a canting peal round the world. . . . One is sick at heart of this pagoda worship" (*J* 1:51; cf. *W* 77). His growing hostility to the church and its accouterments anticipated Thoreau's formal signing off from the First Parish Church in 1840 and, more significantly, his radical critique of Christianity and the church in *A Week*.

Thoreau's attitude toward the church was revealed in "The Service," an essay on bravery completed in the summer of 1840. Like Emerson, he affirmed the integrity of the individual and rejected all external supports, especially those of organized religion. The coward "recognizes no faith but a creed," he asserted, "thinking this straw, by which he is moored, does him good service, because his sheet anchor does not drag" (*RP* 5; cf. *W* 78). Although he was less interested in attacking those creeds than in establishing man's true relations to God and the universe, Thoreau described life as a kind of moral crusade against hypocrisy and falsity. "I see Falsehood sneaking from the full blaze of truth," he exclaimed exuberantly, "and with good relish could do execution on their rearward ranks with the first brand that came to hand" (*RP* 13).

If he entertained the idea of taking arms against evil, Thoreau expected to fight alone, not as part of a group. In fact, he had no more use for organized reform than for organized religion. In contrast to Emerson, whose lectures on reform in 1840 and 1841 reflected his emotional involvement with and toleration of reformers, Thoreau viewed their activities with contempt. Both men declined invitations to join Brook Farm, but Emerson did so only after a long and painful period of self-questioning, while Thoreau dismissed the venture with the comment "As for these communities—I think I had rather keep batchelor's hall in hell than go to board in heaven" (*J* 1:277). As he reiterated in *A Week*, he believed reform was a matter of individual action: "The true reform can be undertaken any morning before unbarring our doors. It calls no convention. I can do two thirds the reform of the world myself. . . . When an individual takes a sincere step, then all the gods attend, and his single deed is sweet" (*J* 1:299; cf. *W* 127).

Thoreau was clearly more concerned with the relationship of man to nature and God than with the relationships among men in society. For example, on May 31, 1841, a few days after he moved in with the Emersons, he noted in the Journal: "That title— The Laws of Menu—with the Gloss of Culluca—comes to me with such a volume of sound as if it had swept unobstructed over the plains of Hindostan" (*J* 1:311). Thus at the very moment when controversy was raging over Theodore Parker's "Discourse of the Transient and Permanent in Christianity," a sermon delivered two weeks earlier which challenged the absolute authority of the Bible, Thoreau was excitedly discovering the ancient lawgiver Manu (Sanscrit, "man"), whose ordinances impose "with authority on the latest age" (*J* 1:316). That spring and summer he returned to the volume again and again, praising its style, wisdom, and spirituality. Moreover, after completing "Natural History of Massachusetts," he drafted an essay on the *Laws of Menu*.[5]

As in "The Service," Thoreau in his essay on Manu was less interested in confronting specific issues than in defining a way of life. Possibly with Parker's distinction between the permanent truths of Christianity and its transient manifestations in testaments, creeds, and churches still fresh in his mind, he observed, "It is now easy to apply to this ancient scripture such a catholic criticism as it will become the part of some future age to apply to Christianity, when the design and idea which underlie it will be considered, and not its narrow and partial fulfillment" (MH 15, A). But his jibe at sects and churches was deceptive. Like Brownson, who in *New Views* cited the interest in Hindu literature and philosophy as a sign of modern man's longing for a changeless spiritual world, Thoreau used the silent and contemplative East

---

[5]Thoreau later incorporated two leaves from this unpublished essay in the first draft of *A Week* (see FD TN 42.13–43.5). Other surviving leaves are preserved in the Houghton Library (MH 15, A) and at the Fruitlands Museums. The impact of the *Laws of Menu* and other Hindu scriptures on Thoreau is discussed by Arthur Christy, *The Orient in American Transcendentalism* (New York: Columbia Univ. Press, 1932); and Robert D. Richardson, Jr., *Myth and Literature in the American Renaissance* (Bloomington: Indiana Univ. Press, 1978), which contains the best general treatment of Thoreau's uses of various mythologies, especially Indic, Nordic, and Greek.

as a foil to the din and activity of New England. But where Brownson remarked the nostalgia for the East to illustrate the failure of modern society and religion, Thoreau exemplified that nostalgia by writing an enthusiastic but rather abstract and vaporous appreciation of the *Laws of Menu*. The bulk of the essay, however, would ultimately play a part in a far more radical critique of New England life in *A Week*.

However ardently he embraced philosophical alternatives to the social and religious values of his native region, Thoreau continued to resist the lure of utopian communities. In the spring of 1843, as the Millerites prepared for the Second Coming, expected on October 22, Bronson Alcott and his English disciple Charles Lane made plans for a new community, a "second Eden to be planted in which the divine seed is to bruise the head of Evil and restore Man to his rightful communion with God in the Paradise of Good."[6] But as Alcott and Lane sought out a site for Fruitlands, Thoreau headed for New York City, seeking a larger audience for his writings. In June he was invited to join Fruitlands, which had been established on a farm overlooking the Nashua River in Harvard, Massachusetts, a few miles west of Concord. "It is very remotely placed, nearly three miles beyond the village, without a road, surrounded by a beautiful green landscape of fields and woods, with the distance filled up by some of the loftiest mountains in the State," Lane seductively observed. "On the estate are about fourteen acres of wood, part of it extremely pleasant as a retreat, a very sylvan realization, which only wants a Thoreau's mind to elevate it to classic beauty" (C 115). But Thoreau, who at the opening of the Journal had jotted two lines from Marvell's "The Garden," "Two Paradises 'twere in one,/To live in paradise alone," declined the invitation to this pastoral paradise, a miniature of the landscape of *A Week* and *Walden*. Moreover, in a review of J. A. Etzler's *The Paradise within the Reach of All Men*, a book heavily influenced by the utopian socialism of Charles Fourier, whose ideas had by then inspired the creation of a number of communities and soon spurred a reorganization of Brook Farm,

---

[6]Quoted in Odell Shepard, *Pedlar's Progress: The Life of Bronson Alcott* (Boston: Little, Brown, 1937), p. 338.

Thoreau took the opportunity to reply to the Fourierists among his friends and associates.[7]

For Thoreau, Etzler was the reformer in extremis, a man who not only wanted to reform the world but to transform the face of the earth. After an extended summary of the fantastic scheme to create paradise in ten years by mechanical means, Thoreau reached the nub of his argument in "Paridise (to be) Regained." Quoting Etzler's assertion "Nothing great, for the improvement of his own condition, or that of his fellow men, can ever be effected by individual enterprise," he responded: "Alas! this is the crying sin of the age, this want of faith in the prevalence of a man" (*RP* 41-42). He thus concluded the review with a paean to the individual and to the force of God's love blowing upon the individual soul, a power which, Thoreau insisted, had never been fully applied. "It has patented only such machines as the almshouses, the hospital, and the Bible Society, while its infinite wind is still blowing, and blowing down these very structures, too, from time to time" (*RP* 47).

The conflict between individualism and institutionalism also provided the unifying theme in Thoreau's long lecture on the conservative and the reformer, apparently written in early 1844, shortly after he returned to Concord.[8] Opening with an attack on

[7]Walter Harding and Michael Meyer, *The New Thoreau Handbook* (New York: New York Univ. Press, 1980), p. 38. Hawthorne, who used his influence to get Thoreau's review printed in the *Democratic Review*, satirized Etzler's scheme in "The Hall of Fantasy." See Buford Jones, " 'The Hall of Fantasy' and the Early Hawthorne-Thoreau Relationship," *PMLA* 83 (1968): 1429–38.

[8]The manuscript of the lecture, from which all quotations are taken, is in the Houghton Library (MH 18, A). I am grateful to Thomas Blanding for providing me with a copy of his transcript of the manuscript, which is described and briefly discussed in *LMHDT,* C10a. In "Reforming the Reformers: Emerson, Thoreau, and the 1844 Lecture Series at Amory Hall," a paper read in 1985 as part of the Seminar on American Literary History at the American Antiquarian Society, I recently presented evidence that Thoreau delivered the lecture on March 10, 1844 at Amory Hall, Boston, where Emerson had delivered "New England Reformers" a week earlier, on March 3. Other speakers in the series, which concerned various aspects of reform, included Charles Lane, Wendell Phillips, and William Lloyd Garrison.

the conservative, who "belongs to a decaying family, and has not yet learned that he who seeks to save his life shall lose it," Thoreau challenged "the superstition about institutions." In effect, he applied Parker's argument in "A Discourse of the Transient and Permanent in Christianity" to government, equating the Bible, creeds, and traditions of the church with the constitution, laws, and precedents of the state. Since government had no divine sanction, it had no absolute authority, he insisted: like the church, the state should therefore be viewed as a transient rather than as a permanent form. But turning from those who sought to preserve to those who sought to reform such institutions, Thoreau was equally critical. "In the midst of all this disorder and imperfection in human affairs comes the Reformer," he continued, "the Impersonation of disorder and imperfection—to heal and reform them." Although he acknowledged the need for reform, he punningly remarked that radicals were not radical enough, since they "got this name rather by meddling with the exposed roots of innocent institutions than with their own." Following his comments on the failure of government, his reference to "innocent institutions" sounds rather disingenuous; but for Thoreau institutions were "innocent," or blameless, because they devolved from man, whose personal ills were the true source of social problems. In a passage that anticipates his own withdrawal to Walden Pond, he thus compared the healthy man to a tree, whose roots are attracted "to a moist and fertile spot in the earth," and stressed the private and public advantage of taking root in one's own native soil.

Thoreau's advocacy of individual rather than group reform was tested by the struggle over slavery. From the time he left Harvard, the Thoreau household had been dominated by members of the Women's Anti-Slavery Society, including his mother and sisters, as well as Mrs. Joseph Ward and her daughter Prudence (*DHT* 73-74). Despite, or perhaps because of, their support of the abolitionist activities of William Lloyd Garrison, Thoreau remained aloof from the issue, which he rarely, if ever, alluded to in either his early essays or the Journal. Yet over the strong objections of a minority of the members of the Concord Lyceum, who argued that "the vexed and disorganizing question of Abolition or Slavery should be kept out of it," Thoreau invited Wendell Phillips to lecture on the topic in December 1842.[9] Phillips lectured there again in January 1844, shortly before Thoreau drafted the lecture on the conservative and the reformer. In it, he clearly sought to dissociate himself from the radicals, but his comments on law and government betray the strong influence of agitators like Garrison and Phillips. Moreover, at about the same time he wrote the lecture, Thoreau also penned a brief tribute to another of the radical abolitionists, Nathaniel Rogers, the editor of the *Herald of Freedom,* an antislavery newspaper published in Concord, New Hampshire.

"Herald of Freedom," which appeared in the *Dial* in April 1844, reveals Thoreau's ambivalent attitude toward reform. For him, what distinguished Rogers from other reformers was his style, which Thoreau associated with the rivers and mountains of New Hampshire, as well as his healthy and cheerful attitude. But he also praised Rogers's involvement in and commitment to the cause of abolition. As Wendell Glick has pointed out, Thoreau's comments "marked his first departure from the ideal of the reformer who remains aloof and apart, in communion with the moral universe."[10] After offering a series of extracts from the *Herald of Freedom,* he concluded, "Such timely, pure, and unpremeditated expressions of a public sentiment, such publicity of genuine indignation and humanity, as abound every where in this journal, are the most generous gifts which a man can make" (*RP* 56). Thoreau never saw fit to withdraw his praise, for he later revised "Herald of Freedom" for *A Week,* where Rogers temporarily served as an embodiment of the ideal reformer.

Thoreau gathered materials for *A Week* in an atmosphere of political turmoil. Shortly before he began to copy entries into the Long Book, he arranged for the meeting at which Emerson de-

[9]The surviving records of the Concord Lyceum are printed in *The Massachusetts Lyceum during the American Renaissance,* ed. Kenneth Cameron (Hartford: Transcendental Books, 1969), pp. 101–90.

[10]Quoted in *The New Thoreau Handbook,* p. 39. See also Wendell Glick, "Thoreau and the 'Herald of Freedom,'" *New England Quarterly* 22 (1949): 193–204.

livered "Emancipation in the West Indies" on August 1, 1844. About the time Thoreau completed his transcriptions, the directors of the Concord Lyceum voted on March 5, 1845, to invite Wendell Phillips to address it a third time. After two men resigned as curators in protest, Emerson and Thoreau filled the vacancies. The controversy over the role of the Lyceum prompted some kind words about reformers. Almost immediately after jotting down the final paragraph of *A Week*, Thoreau wrote in the Long Book: "We can afford to lend a willing ear occasionally to those earnest reprovers of the age—   Let us treat them hospitably—   Shall we be charitable only to the poor. What though they are fanatics—their errors are likely to be generous errors—and these may be they who will indeed put to rest the american Church and the American Government, and awaken better ones in their stead" (*J* 2:117).

In contrast to his comments on reformers in the early Journal and in his 1844 lecture, Thoreau adopted the tone of amused toleration and grudging respect that had characterized Emerson's lectures on reform and reformers, especially "New England Reformers," published in *Essays: Second Series* (1844). Although he was most concerned with the issue of free speech, for the first time Thoreau indicated that institutional as well as individual reform might be necessary. In "Wendell Phillips before Concord Lyceum," drafted in the Long Book (*J* 2:120-24) and published as a letter to the editor in Garrison's *Liberator* on March 28, 1845, he went even further. "It was the speaker's aim to show what the state, and above all the church, had to do, and now, alas! have done, with Texas and slavery," he observed, "and how much, on the other hand, the individual should have to do with church and state" (*RP* 59).

Given his growing radicalism, it is remarkable how little the first draft of *A Week* mirrors Thoreau's social and political concerns. But his effort to keep the pressures of a troubled present from impinging on that account of an idyllic past was undermined by events during his first year at Walden Pond. The annexation of Texas in December 1845, which Garrison called "a crime unsurpassed in the annals of human depravity," gave added impetus to the struggle over slavery.[11] Thoreau was even more outraged by the outbreak of the Mexican War in the spring of 1846. That July he was arrested for failing to pay the poll tax. His arrest was the last straw. In a Journal entry later revised for *A Week*, a few days after his arrest Thoreau savagely denounced "dead institutions," the church and the state. These were no longer the "innocent institutions" of his earlier lecture but "grim and ghostly phantoms like Moloch & Juggernaut." Alluding to the man who arrested him and to the volunteers marching off to the Mexican War, in which "there probably never were worse crimes committed since time began," he insisted that whatever virtue a man might possess was lost in the service of institutions, "the stereotyped and petrified will of the past" (*J* 2:262-64).

Thoreau's fury at those "dead institutions" had a marked impact on *A Week*. In the first draft he celebrated friendship, his ideal of human society. After his arrest he increasingly focused attention in the book on the institutional and traditionary obstacles that mankind must overcome before such an ideal might be realized. As he revised and expanded the manuscript, for example, he added a sweeping critique of the Christian church to "Sunday." In addition to his denunciation of the state, he inserted in "Monday" the 1842 essay on the *Laws of Menu* as well as a commentary on the *Bhagavad-Gita*, used as a counter to Western religious and political traditions. Extracts from his lecture on the conservative and the reformer intended for *A Week* indicate that Thoreau had not changed his mind about reformers, but in portions of "The Service" inserted at the end of "Monday" and throughout the later chapters of *A Week*, he contrasted those who live in harmony with natural laws to those who abide by the artificial conventions of society. Pointing up the conflict between the permanent laws of nature and God and the transient laws of man, he added extracts from Sophocles' *Antigone* to "Monday" and a revised version of "Herald of Freedom" to "Thursday." Thoreau ultimately omitted the tribute to Rogers as well as a number

[11]Quoted in Walter M. Merrill, *Against Wind and Tide: A Biography of Wm. Lloyd Garrison* (Cambridge: Harvard Univ. Press, 1963), p. 210.

of other passages on the subject of reform, partly because he dealt with these topics more fully in "Resistance to Civil Government" and *Walden* and partly because an emphasis on society's ills conflicted with his effort to depict the brothers' ideal society within a timeless pastoral world. Nonetheless, as he revised and expanded *A Week* during 1846-49, he consistently sought to contrast their life-giving voyage to the deadening social, political, and religious traditions of New England.

Probably as a result of his growing hostility to the church, Thoreau played down the Christian associations of the brothers' spiritual journey. In the Journal of July 1841 he called the village of Concord "a port of entry and departure for souls to and from Heaven" (*J* 1:314). He omitted the reference to heaven at the opening of the first draft, remarking instead that Concord was "a port of entry and departure for human souls" (FD 1). In order to emphasize the bond between the spiritual and the physical, he later revised the remark to read "for the bodies as well as the souls of men" and shifted it to the opening of "Saturday," where it follows an epigraph from Quarles's "Christ's Invitation to the Soul": "Come, come, my lovely fair, and let us try/These rural delicates" (*W* 15). By quoting out of context, Thoreau transformed the lines into an invitation to a terrestrial rather than a heavenly paradise. His strategy was typical, for, as Carl Hovde has pointed out, Thoreau "avoids the predominantly Christian tone of many of the poets whose lines he borrows for use in *A Week*."[12]

Thoreau also expunged allusions to Christianity from his own prose and poetry in *A Week*. In "Saturday," after describing the water lily unfolding to the sun's rays, he initially remarked, "So forward is purity to greet its Lord" (FD 7). He later omitted the comment, possibly because he wished to avoid any confusion between that benign lord and the harsh Jehovah worshipped in New England. Equally revealing are his revisions of "Morning," a poem at the opening of "Sunday." In the first draft, it began, "Thou unconverted Saint/Early Christian without taint" (FD 19). Tho-

---

[12]Hovde, "The Writing of *A Week*," p. 74. Thoreau originally identified Quarles's poem as "Invitation to the Soul" rather than as "Christ's Invitation to the Soul" (49 *W* 15).

reau altered the second line to "Free from noontide or evening taint" and omitted the concluding lines, which underscored the symbolic overtones of the brothers' journey eastward. "The morning broke for us two alone as for a thousand more," he continued in the first draft, "and with such serenity as if it too observed the sabbath which man had appointed" (FD 19). In *A Week* the morning is far less pious and conventional, for Thoreau substituted this: "It was a quiet Sunday morning, with more of auroral rosy and white than of the yellow light in it, as if it dated from earlier than the fall of man, and still preserved a heathenish integrity" (*W* 43). Instead of observing the sabbath, nature challenges the fundamental premise of Christianity and anticipates Thoreau's assault on the Christian church later in "Sunday."

The hushed mood of the "natural sabbath" is broken when the brothers pass through the Middlesex Canal, where they confront a group of more conventional worshippers. "The people were coming out of church in crowds," Thoreau noted on a leaf inserted in the first draft, "and passing over the bridge as we floated under" (FD 28). The comment introduced a quotation from the *History of New-Hampshire,* in which Belknap proudly proclaimed that most of the people in the state were Christians. Defending those few whom Belknap contemptuously dismissed as "sort of *wise men,* who pretend to reject it" but had "not yet been able to substitute a better in its place," Thoreau responded: "Probably they believed practically some of the principles which the others only professed, but were naturally unable to substitute practice for profession among the rest" (FD 28-29). Since the canal is in Massachusetts, not New Hampshire, Thoreau apparently realized the passage was also out of place, for he later shifted Belknap's comment to "Monday," where, ironically, it is used as evidence that "free thinking men" lived in New Hampshire even in the eighteenth century (*W* 123). In its place in "Sunday" he added that the people coming out of church "indulged in some heathenish comparisons" (*W* 63), thus heightening the contrast between these bigoted Christians and the "humane" lockman, "who over stepped his prescribed duty and helped us through the locks discerning through our disguise that we were breaking no law of Gods that sunday" (FD 29; cf. *W* 79).

The reference to God's law raised the issue of religious authority. Quoting from the papers of an old trader, "who was also a deacon and a justice of the peace"—an illustration of the unholy alliance between commercial, civil, and ecclesiastical authority—Thoreau contrasted the brothers with two men who had been arrested for traveling on the sabbath (FD 29-30). But lest this serve as an example of the growth of toleration and freedom, he concluded: "Some things men will do from age to age and some things they will not do. If the ligature is found to be loosened in one quarter it is only drawn the tighter in another" (FD 30). To drive home the point, he later revised these sentences to read: "Society has relaxed a little from its strictness, one would say, but I presume that there is no less *religion* than formerly. If the *ligature* is found to be loosened in one part, it is only drawn the tighter in another" (W 64). By ignoring the probable root of *religion* ("religio," a bond between man and the gods), and stressing its possible common root with *ligature* ("ligare," to bind or fasten), Thoreau suggests that, at least in practice, religion is a trap for the unwary. His comment serves as an apt introduction to the critique of Christianity that follows in *A Week* (W 64-79).

The critique, which he began to draft in 1846-47 and continued to revise and expand, illuminates the background and design of *A Week*. Essentially it is Thoreau's contribution to the controversy initiated by Brownson's *New Views of Christianity, Society, and the Church* and continued in Emerson's "Divinity School Address" and Parker's "Discourse of the Transient and Permanent in Christianity." There was also ample precedent for inserting such a digression into *A Week,* since church satire was an important element of pastorals like Spenser's *Shepherd's Calendar,* portions of which Thoreau copied into a commonplace book (*TLN* 276), and "Lycidas." Significantly, Thoreau inserted his satire just as the brothers are entering the Merrimack, where they begin to chart a more heroic and active course against the current. The voyage upriver thus came to serve as a potent symbol of Thoreau's resistance to the social, political, and religious "currents" of New England.

Thoreau's opening remarks were clearly designed to shock an orthodox audience. He first alludes to the conflict between scientific evidence and the literal truth of Genesis. He then contrasts "the liberal divinities of Greece" with Jehovah, "my country's God" (*W* 64; cf. *J* 2:183). Perhaps recalling the passage on the decay of pantheism in the *History of the World,* which he had earlier quoted in "Sir Walter Raleigh" (*EEM* 206), Thoreau continued: "In my Pantheon, Pan still reigns in his pristine glory . . . for the great God Pan is not dead, as was rumored. No god ever dies. Perhaps of all the gods of New England and of ancient Greece, I am most constant at his shrine" (*W* 65). As Perry Miller has remarked, "This is Byronism less strident than Byron's but more unrepentant" (*CC* 173n). It is also strategic, for, by treating Jehovah as but one in a long line of gods, Thoreau sought to shake his audience out of its complacency and to undermine its faith in the absolute authority of the Bible.

For Thoreau, like Emerson, authority was the central issue in the debate within Unitarianism. He thus describes the gods worshipped in civilized countries as embodiments of "the overwhelming authority and respectability of mankind combined" (*W* 65). Turning from the Hebrew to "the Christian fable," he recapitulates the argument of the "Divinity School Address," in which Emerson complained that Christianity had become a "Mythus," in which Christ had been transformed into a "demigod" (*CW* I:81-82). Thoreau, too, believed that by denying Christ's humanity Christians degraded mankind. "It would seem as if it were in the progress of our mythology to dethrone Jehovah," he remarks, "and crown Christ in his stead" (*W* 67).

The assault offered an opportunity to express his long-standing hostility to priests, the executors of the church's will. Following the poem "I make ye an offer," with its assertion "I'll be slave to no God" (*W* 69), Thoreau in an early manuscript described two Yankee priests (Appendix, no. 1). His satirical sketches of these men, one shrewd and greedy, the other vapid and ridiculous, hang in a long gallery of similar portraits, from the horse-loving Monk and rapacious Friar in the *Canterbury Tales* to the "spectral" minister in the "Divinity School Address." Significantly, Thoreau described one's actions before entering the church and the other's actions as he descends from the pulpit, for, between them, these priests make a mockery of divine service. Their prayers are, as he remarks about the second priest, no better than practical jokes or mischievous tricks played upon the congregation. But Thoreau perhaps realized that the false heartiness, labored humor, and open contempt of these sketches contradicted his assertion that he had "no spite against the priest," for he omitted the passage. In its place he substituted more general comments on all those who rigidly adhere to a "scheme of the universe" based on the shaky authority of the Old Testament, "a sort of family history of God" in which "some old poet's grand imagination is imposed on us as adamantine everlasting truth, and God's own word!" (*W* 69, 71).

Thoreau's remarks on the New Testament reflect his sympathy with Parker's attempt to distinguish between the doctrines of the church and the enduring truths of religion. Following the portraits of the Yankee priests, Thoreau in the manuscript noted: "The New Testament is a capital book, though I confess to having been slightly prejudiced against it in my very early days by the Church and the Sabbath School" (MH 15, R). He possibly felt that "capital" sounded a bit too irreverent, for he altered it to "invaluable." He also interlined comments on the *Pilgrim's Progress,* "the best sermon which has ever been preached from this text" (MH 15, R; *W* 71). Like Bunyan, the great nonconformist who had been jailed for unlicensed preaching, Thoreau stresses the radical message of the New Testament. "I know of no book that has so few readers," he paradoxically insists: "There is none so strange, and heretical, and unpopular" (*W* 72). After citing a few of the "severe things in it," most of them from the Sermon on the Mount, he remarks that if even one of these sentences were read from a pulpit, "there would not be left one stone of that meeting-house upon another" (*W* 73).

Despite his attraction to the radical message of the New Testament, he was ambivalent about Christ's teaching. Quoting his directions to the apostles, "Heaven and earth shall pass away, but my words shall not pass away" (Luke 21:23), Thoreau remarks, "I draw near to him at such a time" (*W* 73). Following the lead of Parker, who preached on the same text in the "Discourse," Thoreau applauded Christ's abiding faith in the word of God. But he also faulted Christ for directing all his thoughts to another world. His failure to teach man how to live in this world is magnified by his apostles and priests, whom Thoreau compares to politicians and policemen. Like those other manifestations of a diseased society, priests inculcate false lessons and demand obedience to authority. As an illustration, he added a brief account of being accosted by a minister for traveling on the sabbath, which took place during the walking tour through southern New Hampshire in 1848. Sometime after the publication of *A Week*, he also added a description of "a preacher shouting like a boatswain in a gale of wind," whom he overheard in a village on Cape Cod in 1850 (*DHT* 273). And yet, Thoreau exclaims indignantly, if he were to ask to preach in a pulpit, his request would be denied because he (perhaps he was also recalling Bunyan) was not ordained (*W* 76).

By the late 1840s Thoreau's attitude toward the church had hardened, but his views had not changed substantially in the decade since he left Harvard. He thus concludes with a pastiche of six extracts from the early Journal (*W* 76-78). After contrasting the health and vitality of the northern hunter with the sickness of "sedentary sects" and the consolations offered by their preachers, "the creed of the hypochondriac," he observed on January 1, 1842: "There is no infidelity so great as that which prays— and keeps the Sabbath—and founds churches. The sealer of the south pacific preaches a truer doctrine. The church is the hospital for men's souls, but the reflection that he may one day occupy a ward in it should not discourage the cheerful labors of the able-bodied man. Let him remember the sick in their extremities— but not look thither as to his goal" (*J* 1:355).

Although Thoreau was possibly hesitant to include this angry indictment of the church in "Natural History of Massachusetts," where he placed a portion of the entry (*Ex* 105), he made it even harsher in *A Week*. In an apparent reference to his neighbors in Concord, who completely renovated the First Parish Church in the early 1840s, he revised "founds churches" to "rebuilds the churches." Following the comment that the church is "the hospital for men's souls," he continued in *A Week*, "and as full of quackery as the hospital for their bodies." He also added, "Those who are taken into it live like pensioners in their Retreat or Sailor's

Snug Harbor, where you may see a row of religious cripples sitting outside in sunny weather" (*W* 76). His nautical imagery underscores the contrast between what the church provides and what *A Week* offers: a choice between a "Sailor's Snug Harbor" (a reference to the home for infirm seamen he had visited on Staten Island) and a spiritual adventure or voyage of discovery for what Thoreau now calls the "able-souled man." Revising two entries he had earlier combined in "The Service," he thus concluded:

> A man's real faith is never contained in his creed, nor is his creed an article of his faith. . . . And yet he clings anxiously to his creed, as to a straw, thinking that that does him good service because his sheet anchor does not drag.
> In most men's religion, the ligature, which should be its umbilical cord connecting them with divinity, is rather like that thread which the accomplices of Cylon held in their hands when they went abroad from the temple of Minerva, the other end being attached to the statue of the goddess. But frequently, as in their case, the thread breaks, being stretched, and they are left without an asylum. (*W* 78; cf. *J* 1:55, 153, and *RP* 5)

As Thoreau introduces his critique of Christianity by playing upon the root meaning of *ligature* and *religion*, he concludes by redefining those terms. Instead of binding or restraining man, the ligature of religion should serve as a bond to divinity. But even this bond is transient, for the "umbilical cord" nourishes man only until he is reborn in spirit, a union with God celebrated in a long quotation from Saadi (*W* 78-79). With this definition Thoreau returns to his original point of departure, where the "serene and liberal-minded" lockman exceeds his Sabbath duties and presents the brothers with the "freedom of the Merrimack" (*W* 79).

In order to illustrate the contrast between the freedom of their voyage and the constrictions of life on shore, Thoreau at the end of "Sunday" in the first draft described another pair, "travellers who had been way laid by the sabbath" (FD 35, *W* 112). Confronting an "unsympathizing river," these men resemble Christian and Hopefulness in the *Pilgrim's Progress,* which possibly suggested the episode to Thoreau.[13] Like Bunyan's pilgrims, who looked "this way and that" but could find no way "by which they might escape the River [of Death]," the pair on the banks of the Merrimack seek a miraculous deliverance, for "once more they tried the river here, and once more there, to see if water still indeed was not to be walked on" (*W* 113). Christian is told, "You shall find it deeper or shallower, as you believe in the King of the place." Translating this into an assertion of nature's primacy, Thoreau concluded, "Thus does nature put the busiest merchant to pilgrim's shifts, and soon drives him to staff and scrip and scallop shell" (FD 35). In *A Week,* the moral—and the contrast—is more explicit: "We could not help being struck by the seeming, though innocent, indifference of Nature to these men's necessities, while elsewhere she was equally serving others. Like a true benefactress, the secret of her service is unchangeableness. Thus is the busiest merchant, though within sight of his Lowell, put to pilgrim's shifts, and soon comes to staff and scrip and scallop shell" (*W* 113-14).

The ironic juxtaposition of the merchant's vision of Lowell and Christian's vision of the Celestial City suggests the debasement and commercialization of life in New England, a theme Thoreau introduces in "Sunday" and develops in "Monday." Following the question "Where is the man who is guilty of direct and personal insolence to Him that made him?" (*W* 66), the 1849 edition continued: "Yet there are certain current expressions of blasphemous modes of viewing things,—as, frequently, when we say, 'He is doing good business,' more profane than cursing and swearing. There is sin and death in such words. Let not the children hear them" (49 *W* 70; cf. *J* 1:302). That passage was later omitted, but Thoreau's hostility to the commercial mores of his countrymen emerges with almost equal force and even greater fitness at the opening of "Monday." In the first draft, he briefly alluded to pas-

---

[13]Thoreau took three pages of extracts from the *Pilgrim's Progress* sometime during the 1840s (*TLN* 355–57). All quotations are from the edition he owned (New York: Tiebout, 1811).

sengers crossing the river "on the business of the week" (FD 37); he later added an extended description of the ferry, which is compared to the boat Charon rows across the Styx. "It is only a *transjectus*," Thoreau remarks, "a transitory voyage, like life itself, none but the long-lived gods bound up or down the stream" (W 118). He is especially scornful of the ministers, "good religious men, with love of men in their hearts, and the means to pay their toll in their pockets" (W 119). In contrast, the brothers escape the "toll," ostensibly the two-cent fare, but implicitly the death-in-life their countrymen experience.

The addition of the passage concerning the ferry is noteworthy, for, as Lawrence Buell has pointed out, it serves notice that the critique begun in "Sunday" will continue in "Monday."[14] To that end Thoreau also added digressions on reformers (W 126-29), the political state (W 129-35), and Hindu scriptures, which serve as foils to western religious and political traditions (W 135-44, 147-54). Combined with his comments on graveyards near the end of the chapter, these digressions reflect his conviction that reform was not simply a social issue but a matter of life and death. Yet despite his increasing preoccupation with the external symptoms of a diseased society, Thoreau remained committed to the inward life first described in "The Service," portions of which he inserted at the conclusion of "Monday."

In 1846 or 1847 he revised and recopied twelve pages of extracts from his lecture on the conservative and the reformer, possibly for inclusion in "Monday," where he had briefly alluded to their activities in the first draft (FD 40).[15] "When a zealous Reformer

---

[14]Buell, p. 217.

[15]The six leaves are in the Houghton Library: the first five in MH 18, B, and the final leaf in MH 15, V. At the end of the extracts, on the verso of the final leaf, Thoreau later jotted, "We had now passed &c," indicating that he initially incorporated the extracts into the manuscript of *A Week*. But, with the exception of two lines of poetry (W 215) and three scattered sentences (W 267, 272), he omitted the extracts, recopying portions of them in the first draft of *Walden* (S 135–36). For a different view of these extracts, which he edited as part of a later version of the original lecture, see Wendell Glick's Textual Introduction to "Reform and the Reformers" (*RP* 379 ff.).

would fain discourse to me," he began, "I would have him consider first if he has anything to say to me" (MH 18, B). As that introductory comment suggests, he emphasized violations of the laws of human companionship, abuses characteristic of both preachers and reformers: "It is hard to make those who have talked much, especially preachers & lecturers, deepen their speech, and give it fresh sincerity and significance" (MH 18, B). In "Sunday" Thoreau berates preachers who cling to "that old Jewish scheme" of the universe and thus "presume to fable of the ineffable" (W 70); in the extracts he lashed out at the reformers, illustrations of "the death that presumes to give laws to life . . . [and] perseveres in maturing its schemes of life till its last days are come" (MH 18, B). The preacher's scheme, "his conformity to tradition," violates the sanctity of God; the reformer's schemes, efforts to establish equally rigid traditions, violate nature's laws of life, growth, and metamorphosis. In the concluding passage of the extracts, Thoreau thus exhorted him: "Now ye Reformer, let us have an institution that is worth the while. Let us not repeat the old error, but leave life as free to those who are to come, as we complain that it was not left to us. Let us not stiffen the currents of life. . . . New things are continually arriving—let us not hold fast to any of the old—nor to any of the new" (MH 15, V).

Although he omitted most of the lecture extracts from *A Week*, Thoreau expanded the brief comments on reformers in the first draft. In contrast to the sharp, incisive tone of the extracts, his critique in "Monday" reveals a quietism more in keeping with the brothers' peaceful "nooning" on the banks of the Merrimack. Instead of stressing the constant changes in nature and human life, he affirms an underlying continuity: "Go where we will, we discover infinite change in particulars only, not in generals" (W 124). To the man who contemplates this immutable order, the activities of "the restless class of Reformers" are an affront to life. "What if these grievances exist?" he asks. "So do you and I" (W 126). In their anxiety to change the world, reformers defer living in the world. Like Christ, whose "thoughts were all directed toward another world" (W 73), reformers live on anticipation and cannot teach man to live in the present. Observing how easy it is "to establish another durable and harmonious scheme," Thoreau also implies that when a reformer's scheme is instituted it occasions the same conformity as the old routine: "Only make something to take the place of something, and men will behave as if it were the very thing they wanted. . . . There is always a present and extant life, be it better or worse, which all combine to uphold" (*W* 128; cf. *J* 1:105). The wise man therefore will not rush off to reform the world, but, like the pair on the banks of the Merrimack, rest in serene contemplation of the universal laws of man, nature, and God.

Thoreau attempts to dissociate himself from reformers before mounting his own attack on one of their primary targets, the political state. In the digression, an expanded version of the Journal entry written after his arrest in 1846, he sought to achieve the same detached tone that characterizes his relatively restrained critique of reformers in "Monday." He therefore added an introductory paragraph, beginning: "To one who habitually endeavors to contemplate the true state of things, the political state can hardly be said to have any existence whatever. It is unreal, incredible, and insignificant to him" (*W* 129). As in his comments on reformers, he insists that social revolutions are of only passing interest, especially when compared to the revolutions of nature. His effort to sound indifferent is also revealed by his revisions of the Journal entry, which began, "In my short experience of human life I have found that the outward obstacles which stood in my way were not living men—but dead institutions" (*J* 2:262). Since the political state "could hardly be said to have any existence," it could hardly represent one of these "outward obstacles"; so Thoreau added "if there were any such" (*W* 130).

His indifference to institutions was more apparent than real. Although he omitted the reference to "grim and ghostly phantoms like Moloch & Juggernaut," he retained the depiction of "some monster institution," which in *A Week* is described as crushing "its free members in its scaly folds" (*W* 130). After noting that the state had arrested him, he also added a passage beginning, "Poor creature! if it knows no better I will not blame it." His dismissive tone recalls "Resistance to Civil Government," where, after describing his arrest, Thoreau remarked: "I saw that the State was half-witted, that it was timid as a lone woman with her silver spoons, and that it did not know its friends from its foes, and I lost all my remaining respect for it, and pitied it" (*RP* 80). But his anger, vividly revealed in the 1846 Journal, had not completely subsided by the time he drafted "Resistance to Civil Government" and revised the Journal entry for *A Week,* both probably in late 1847. In the Journal, he observed, "I love mankind   I hate the institutions of their forefathers" (*J* 2:262). He first revised this to "institutions which unsurp their place" before he arrived at the highly charged phrasing of *A Week:* "I love man—kind, but I hate the institutions of the dead unkind. Men execute nothing so faithfully as the wills of the dead, to the last codicil and letter. *They* rule this world, and the living are but their executors" (*W* 131). Like the church, which demands fidelity to its own last will or testament, the state demands obedience to its constitution and laws. As an individual the constable may have "human virtues," but as an officer of the state he is simply "the tool of an institution" (*W* 131).

Thoreau develops his critique of the political state and its servants in terms of the central polarities of *A Week:* youth and age, health and sickness, life and death. In the Journal, after insisting that men are buried in "the grave of custom," he asserted: "Better are the physically dead, for they more lively rot" (*J* 2:264). In *A Week* the same comment introduces a diagnosis of society's stagnant condition adapted from an entry in the 1842 Journal: "A man's life should be constantly as fresh as this river [the Journal reads "a river"]. . . . Most men have no inclination, no rapids, no cascades, but marshes, and alligators, and miasma instead" (*W* 132, *J* 1:390). He forged an additional link between the critique and voyage by contrasting youthful faith with what he describes as the "infidelity" of old age: "The same hopes and prospects are not for him who stands upon the rosy mountain-tops of life, and him who expects the setting of his earthly day" (*W* 133). Unlike the brothers, bound upriver toward the mountains, men who cling to the "order and expediency" of institutions sign their own death warrants (*W* 134).

The attack on the political state concludes with brief extracts from Sophocles' *Antigone* (*W* 134-35). As Richard Drinnon has pointed out, Thoreau in "Resistance to Civil Government" "made quite clear his rejection of the Periclean argument of Creon that the highest responsibility of the individual must be to the state and his rejection of the later Platonic assumption of a pleasing harmony between the laws of man and the laws of the gods."[16] Thoreau takes a similar stand in "Monday," where he prefaces the extracts from *Antigone* with the comment "The expedients of the nations clash with one another, only the absolutely right is expedient for all" (*W* 134). Antigone's dialogues with Ismene and Creon illustrate the conflict between law and conscience and indicate that this conflict is an ancient as Western culture. By inserting the extracts from *Antigone,* Thoreau thus acknowledged his own debt to Sophocles and formed a transition to a digression on an even more ancient text, the *Bhagavad-Gita* (*W* 135-44), an extension of his 1842 essay on the *Laws of Menu,* which he had also inserted in "Monday" (*W* 147-54).

Despite their close proximity in *A Week,* the commentaries reveal markedly different approaches to Hindu scripture. In 1842 Thoreau praised the style and sublimity of the *Laws of Menu;* after 1846, however, he was as concerned with the political and religious implications of the *Bhagavad-Gita* as with its literary qualities. In his comments on it he thus uses Hindu scripture as a foil to the Western traditions that he criticizes elsewhere in *A Week.* Adapting an entry from the Journal of 1841, before he had read the *Bhagavad-Gita,* he begins by contrasting the conservatism of the Hindu, whose law "was the custom of the gods before men used it," with that of New England: "The fault of our New England custom is that it is memorial. What is morality but immemorial custom? Conscience is the chief of conservatives" (*W* 135; cf. *J* 1:313). In contrast to Christ, "the prince of Reformers and Radicals" (*W* 137), the Brahman is completely absorbed in the contemplation of God. Because of its emphasis on practical morality, the New Testament has no room for poetry or for anything "regarded in the light of beauty merely" (*W* 137). To combat the insularity of Western culture, Thoreau includes a series of extracts from the *Bhagavad-Gita* and concludes with a call for

[16]Richard Drinnon, "Thoreau's Politics of the Upright Man," *Massachusetts Review* 4 (1962): 127.

the publication of "the collected Scriptures or Sacred Writings" of mankind. "Such a juxtaposition and comparison might help to liberalize the faith of men," he asserts, recalling the criticism of bigoted Christians in "Sunday." "This would be the Bible, or Book of Books, which let the missionaries carry to the uttermost parts of the earth" (*W* 144).

The sublime visions of the *Bhagavad-Gita* answered Thoreau's own efforts to "communicate with the gods" (*W* 140), but he was also critical of its deterministic view of man's relationship to the universe. "The Brahman never proposes courageously to assault evil," he remarks. "His active faculties are paralyzed by the idea of cast, of impassable limits, of destiny and the tyranny of time" (*W* 140). The idea of caste is faintly mirrored in the conservatism of the West, which says "forsake not your calling, outrage no institution, use no violence, rend no bonds, the State is thy parent" (*W* 141). Implicitly, the heroic man, whose soul is in harmony with the universe, will accede neither to the limitations of time and destiny nor to the tyranny of the state. Despite the attractions of the *Bhagavad-Gita,* Thoreau continued to conceive of the inward or comtemplative life in the active and heroic terms of "The Service," portions of which he also inserted in "Monday."[17]

In his initial efforts to adapt portions of "The Service" to *A Week,* Thoreau made little effort to reconsider his earlier notions about soldiers, heroism, and war in the light of contemporary events. At least partly in reaction to the numerous discourses on peace and nonresistance in 1840, Thoreau in "The Service" had used the soldier as a paradigm of the brave man.[18] When he revised and recopied three pages of extracts from the essay in 1846, he thus included the opening paragraph of "What Music Shall We Have?" in which he celebrated the martial music and chivalric spirit of war (MH 4, D). Even after the outbreak of the Mexican

[17]For a more detailed discussion, see the author's article "Contexts of Bravery: Thoreau's Revisions of 'The Service' for *A Week,*" *Studies in the American Renaissance 1983,* ed. Joel Myerson (Charlottesville: Univ. Press of Virginia, 1983), pp. 281–96.

[18]*The Service,* ed. F. B. Sanborn (New York: C. E. Goodspeed, 1902), p. x.

War, he retained the paragraph in two drafts of the digression
on music at the end of "Monday" (MH 15,O, paged 195-96, 210-
11). Following the comment "As polishing expresses the vein in
marble and the grain in wood, so music brings out what of heroic
lurks anywhere," the second of these drafts continued: "The brave
man is the sole patron of music, and recognizes it as his mother
tongue. The steady flux of his thought constitutes its time. According to the ancients Harmony was begotten of Mars and Venus.
The soldier especially always insists on agreement & harmony.
If he marches to the sack of a town even he must be preceded
by drums and trumpets, which will identify his cause with the
concordant universe. It is the friendship there is in war that makes
it chivalric & heroic. It was the dim sentiment of a noble friendship
for the purest soul in history that gave to Europe a crusading
era" (MH 15, O, paged 210-11; cf. *RP* 9).

Given his growing hostility toward the military and his revulsion
from the Mexican War, Thoreau's decision to include this paragraph in the second draft of *A Week* is surprising. He did not
precisely equate the soldier and the brave man, but it is difficult
to distinguish between them. It was one thing casually to refer
to soldiers marching to the sack of a town in 1840, when America
had not yet awakened to its Manifest Destiny; it was quite another
thing to refer to it in 1847, when American forces were laying
siege to Vera Cruz in March, two months before Thoreau first
submitted the manuscript of *A Week,* probably including the passage quoted above. By then he no longer believed that war was
"chivalric & heroic"; and as American troops continued their
triumphant march toward Mexico City that spring and summer,
he surely recognized that friendship, and especially "friendship
for the purest soul in history," had little to do with the crusade
south of the Rio Grande.

Thoreau was apparently aware of some of the contradictions
between the idealized notions of "The Service" and the realities
of the Mexican War. In an effort to distinguish the brave man
from the soldier, he later interlined, "That harmony which exists
naturally between the heroe's moods & the universe, the soldier
would fain imitate with drum & trumpet." In a revised and expanded version, probably drafted in late 1847 or early 1848, he

placed the sentence at the opening of his comments on the soldier's insistence on music and harmony. More significantly, following a paragraph from "The Service" concerning the coward's
"universal wail" (cf. *RP* 11), he continued:

> I have heard a strain of music issuing from a
> soldier's camp in the dawn which sounded like the
> morning hymn of creation. The birches rustling in the
> breeze, and the slumberous breathing of the crickets
> seemed to hush their murmuring to attend to it.
>   The soldier is the degenerate hero, as the priest is
> the degenerate saint, and the soldier and priest are still
> as closely related as hero and saint. Their virtue has
> but one name originally in all languages. The ones
> discipline will well bear comparison with the others.
>   Mankind still pays to the soldier the honors due only
> to the hero, as to the priest those due only to the saint.
> All guilds and corporations are taxed to furnish him
> with fit harness and equipment—to adorn him with
> silver and gold, and the colors of the rainbow. Music is
> for him especially and his life is a holiday. (MH 2; cf. *J*
> 1:94)

As this passage suggests, Thoreau had difficulty reconciling
the martial imagery of "The Service" and his hostile attitude toward the military. Following his reference to the stirring sounds
from the soldier's camp, suggested by a passage in "The Service"
(*RP* 10-11), his comparison of the soldier and the priest is distracting and incongruous. In a further attempt to dissociate the
soldier and the hero, whom his imagery tended to link, Thoreau
interlined, "But true virtue is a bravery beside which that of the
soldier & the priest are cowardice." Nonetheless, compared with
his savage critique of soldiers and the Mexican War in "Resistance
to Civil Government," drafted about the same time, his comments
are mild indeed. In the essay the soldier is described as "a mere
shadow and reminiscence of humanity, a man laid out alive and
standing, and already, as one may say, buried alive under arms
with funeral accompaniments" (*RP* 65-66). Despite Thoreau's ef-

forts in the manuscripts of *A Week* to distinguish the soldier from the hero, the two tended to blur into a single compound figure whose equipment takes on "the colors of the rainbow" and whose life becomes a "holiday."

Thoreau ultimately abandoned his effort to balance two radically different views of the soldier and, with it, his attempt to salvage substantial portions of "The Service" in *A Week*. With the exception of a few sentences from "What Music Shall We Have?" (*W* 175) and a favorite sentence about the "clarion sound and clang of corselet and buckler" (*W* 177; cf. *J* 1:167, *CC* 143n, and *RP* 17), he omitted all of the extracts from "Monday." In the only remaining reference to soldiers in the digression on music, Thoreau briefly dismisses their claim to heroism and sharply differentiates between the soldier and the hero. Anticipating the "different drummer" passage in *Walden* (*Wa* 326), he observes: "That harmony which exists naturally between the hero's moods and the universe the soldier would fain imitate with drum and trumpet. . . . Marching is when the pulse of the hero beats in unison with the pulse of Nature, and he steps to the measure of the universe; then there is true courage and invincible strength" (*W* 175).

That celebration of the hero's harmony with nature forms a smooth transition to "Tuesday," which opens on an equally active and heroic note. In the first draft he briefly alluded to their preparations; he later added an exuberant description of their activities. As in *Walden,* where Thoreau seeks to anticipate the dawn, the brothers participate in nature's awakening: "Long before daylight we ranged abroad with hatchet in hand, in search of fuel, and made the yet slumbering and dreaming wood resound with our blows. Then with our fire we burned up a portion of the loitering night. . . . We tramped about the shore, waked all the muskrats, and scared up the bittern and birds that were asleep upon their roosts." Implicitly, their participation in the natural cycle releases them from the moral elements of human life, for he concludes, "So, *shaking the clay from our feet,* we pushed into the fog" (*W* 179; emphasis added). About the time he added the account of their morning ritual, Thoreau also expanded his earlier remarks on man's "morning courage" (Appendix, no. 4; cf. FD 49). The contrast between the health and vitality of the morning man and the sickness of the "afternoon man," who "has an interest in the past, and sees indifferently well either way," illuminates Thoreau's effort to shake off the dead hand of the past, whether its grasp is exerted through the church and the state, his targets in "Sunday" and "Monday," or through various social customs and institutions, which he sniped at in "Tuesday" and the chapters following in *A Week*.

Compared to the abuses of church and state, social usages now seem rather trivial objects of reform. To Thoreau's contemporaries, however, such conventions assumed a good deal of importance. As noted above, Emerson in "Historic Notes on Life and Letters in New England" observed that the division between the party of the Past and the party of the Future appeared "in Literature, Philosophy, Church, State *and social customs*" (emphasis added). Emerson dealt with those customs in early lecture series including "The Philosophy of History" and "The Times." During the winter of 1842-43 he offered a new series, "The Manners and Customs of New England," in New York City. One of the longest chapters in *Essays: Second Series* (1844), which also included "Politics" and "New England Reformers," was "Manners." In it Emerson sought to distinguish "between *fashion*, a word of narrow and often sinister meaning, and the heroic character which the gentleman imports" (*CW* III:73). But he was broadly tolerant of social customs. "Manners aim to facilitate life," he remarked. "They aid our dealing and conversation, as a railway aids travelling, by getting rid of all avoidable obstructions of the road, and leaving nothing to be conquered but pure space" (*CW* III:75).

As usual, Thoreau was far less tolerant. In digressions omitted from "Tuesday" he first attacked social etiquette and then criticized the foolish fashions of society (Appendix, nos. 5-6). He viewed etiquette as but another name for conformity. By refusing to "meet on the ground of their real acquaintance and actual understanding of one another," men degrade themselves into "puppets of convention." Like the church and the state, social institutions impose artificial barriers between men. "If Zoroaster, or Homer, or Socrates should come on earth again," he asked, "would they need letters of introduction to the prominent characters?"

Because they deny us the spiritual resources of other men, such rigid forms destroy the very bonds they were ostensibly designed to strengthen. Thoreau's fulmination against fashion, later revised for *Walden*, where he dealt more systematically with the diseased state of society in New England, was equally scornful. Stressing the foolishness of all finery, he observed that the fashionable lady and gentleman "seem to have counted only on fair weather, and that all things will go on smoothly without jostling." In effect, fashion fails to prepare us for life, or death. "When the soldier is hit by a canon ball rags are as becoming as purple, and purple is perhaps as becoming as rags," he continued. "As soon, in fact, as a man engages to eat, drink, walk, work, and sit, and meet all the contingencies of life therein, his costume is hallowed, and may be the theme of poetry."

As his commentaries on etiquette and fashion indicate, Thoreau believed that the object of all reforms was to help men to live and to bring men closer together. His essay on friendship in "Wednesday" is thus a manual of true reform. "All those abuses which are the subject of reform with the philanthropist—the statesman & the housekeeper," he affirmed in the first draft, "are unconsciously amended in this intercourse" (FD 77). Appropriately, he later added two lines from his lecture on the conservative and the reformer: "It takes two to speak the truth,—one to speak, and another to hear. . . . Only lovers know the value and magnanimity of truth, while traders prize a cheap honesty, and neighbors and acquaintance a cheap civility" (W 267). In contrast to the family, the neighborhood, and the state, friendship demands the noblest behavior. He also insists that this behavior has nothing whatever to do with "the Christian duties and humanities," since when one "treats his Friend like a Christian . . . Friendship ceases to be Friendship, and becomes charity" (W 275, 276). But he insists that friendship is neither selfish nor exclusive. Instead, it strengthens the bonds between all men. The truest benefactors are consequently not philanthropists or reformers but friends, whose "superfluity and dispersed love is the humanity which sweetens society" (W 277).

The voyage dramatizes the ways in which friendship enhances

human society. In "Wednesday," Thoreau uses the analogy of men traveling "harmoniously" together to define the qualities perfect friendship requires (W 282). His earliest surviving account of the brothers' arrival in Concord, New Hampshire, implied that their harmonious journey had also strengthened their bond with other men: "We were hospitably entertained in Concord New Hampshire, which to the confusion of the inhabitants we persisted in calling *New* Concord, as we had been wont, to distinguish it from our native town from which we had heard that it was named, and in part originally settled. This would have been the proper place to conclude our voyage. Our boat was moored some miles below its port, but we fancied that if its prow had once touched its wharf, uniting Concord with Concord by this meandering river, it would have stirred a chord indeed, whose vibrations might have been heard even by the fishes" (HM 13182, I, 25; cf. W 303). Thoreau humorously plays upon the refusal of certain details of their voyage to conform to the design of *A Week,* but the conclusion of the voyage upstream reveals a deeper truth. Through friendship he and John had, indeed, arrived at a "New" Concord. Although he later omitted the fanciful remark that their boat might have stirred a musical chord, the union of "Concord with Concord" suggests the harmony the brothers had achieved with their fellow man. Descended from the same stock, the men of these towns are bound by the ties of brotherhood, a friendship that exists among all men.

Thoreau's description of the arrival in Concord later occasioned two long digressions. As a preface to it he adapted an unpublished 1843 essay entitled "Conversation." At the same time, he followed it with a revised version of "Herald of Freedom," his tribute to Nathaniel Rogers, the editor of the abolitionist newspaper published in Concord.[19] Both sections were ultimately omitted from

---

[19]This conclusion is based on the argument developed in the author's article " 'Native to New England': Thoreau, 'Herald of Freedom,' and *A Week," Studies in Bibliography* 36 (1983): 213–20. For a different view, see Wendell Glick's Textual Introduction to "Herald of Freedom" (*RP* 287–95).

A Week, but they reveal Thoreau's effort to resolve the conflict between his own ideals and the social and political realities of life in New England.

His discussion of conversation concerned what was for Thoreau one of the greatest barriers between men (Appendix, no. 10). He introduced the topic with an account of the brothers' meeting with a garrulous man who wanted them "to walk and talk both at his pace." Thoreau, however, swiftly got to the point. With measured detachment he continued, "What is called talking is a remarkable though universal phenomenon of society." Throughout the seven-page disquisition on this odd phenomenon, Thoreau sounds like a lecturer describing the quaint customs of some native tribe to a Lyceum audience. Predictably, he stressed the artificiality and absurdity of a group of people "chattering like a flock of blackbirds in the spring, endeavoring to cement society and hasten on the millennium." In fact, as he also observed in the extracts on reformers, such cheap talk has the opposite effect. But the custom is so strong that men refuse to abandon the "disguise" of speech or the "refuge" of conversation. Echoing his similar commentary on etiquette, he insists: "They stand upon ceremony who have no other ground to stand on." Wherever they are enacted, these ceremonies destroy true communication and falsify the relations among people.

After marking a few passages for insertion in the digression on friendship in "Wednesday," Thoreau omitted the description of the old man and the remarks on conversation, a section that formed a rather incongruous prelude to the brothers' "hospitable" reception in Concord. His decision to omit the revised version of "Herald of Freedom" is more puzzling. Although he and John did not meet Rogers during their trip, Thoreau's review of his newspaper fitted smoothly into "Thursday." Following the paragraph concerning their arrival in Concord, he continued, "It was here that the Herald of Freedom was published at this time" (MH 15, O). Moreover, the revised version served a number of purposes in "Thursday." First, it was a moving tribute to Rogers, who died in 1846. Second, it reaffirmed Thoreau's own social and literary ideals. Finally, it formed an effective transition between the river voyage and their jaunt through the White Mountains.

Thoreau's decision to rework "Herald of Freedom" for *A Week* was most likely prompted by the publication of a collection of Rogers's newspaper writings in June 1847.[20] Thoreau, who had called for such a volume at the end of his 1844 review, must have discovered much of interest in the collection. The editor obviously shared Thoreau's enthusiasm for Rogers's descriptive powers, since the collection contained a good deal of travel writing, including an extended account of a trip through the White Mountains, reprinted as "Anti-Slavery Jaunt to the Mountains." As he read the abolitionist's fierce editorials, Thoreau was probably also struck by the congruity between his own political positions and Rogers's comments on the military, on moral versus political action, and on the individual's relation to the state. In fact, Thoreau would soon discuss all of these issues in his lecture "The Rights and Duties of the Individual in Relation to Government," delivered early in 1848.

Probably before he began to draft the lecture, he revised "Herald of Freedom". With the exception of two of Rogers's eloquent calls to antislavery conventions in New England, Thoreau omitted all of the extracts included in the *Dial* version. Drawing upon two pages of notes from the collection of Rogers's writings, he also drafted a new conclusion.[21] Whereas in the *Dial* he concluded with a call for a collection of Rogers's writings and a comment, "Long may we hear the voice of this Herald" (*D* IV:512), Thoreau began the new conclusion: "Such timely, pure, and unpremeditated expressions of a public sentiment, such publicity of genuine indignation and humanity, as abound every where in this journal, are the most generous gifts which a man can make. But since our voyage Rogers has died, and now there is no one in

[20]*A Collection from the Newspaper Writings of Nathaniel Peabody Rogers* (Concord, N.H.: J. R. French, 1847 [publisher's notice is dated June 24, 1847]). Thoreau probably used the copy obtained by Emerson, who also admired Rogers. See Walter Harding, *Emerson's Library* (Charlottesville: Univ. of Virginia Press, 1967), p. 231.

[21]The leaf of notes and two leaves of fair-copy material are in the Houghton Library (MH 11), from which all quotations from the revised conclusion are drawn. For descriptions of this material, see *RP* 293–94 and *LMHDT*, D8e.

New England to express indignation and contempt which may still be felt at any cant or inhumanity."

The contrast between the first sentence, carried over from the *Dial,* and the second sentence, which forms a transition to the additional material drafted for *A Week,* reveals a marked shift in attitude. In 1844 Thoreau praised Rogers's expressions of "indignation and humanity"; in 1847 he mourned that there was no one left to express "indignation or contempt." During the intervening years Thoreau's own contempt for cant and inhumanity had grown apace, fueled by his arrest in 1846, the Mexican War, and the failure of New England's political and religious establishment to oppose slavery. That hostility to the establishment is reflected in his critique of Christianity in "Sunday" and his attack on the political state in "Monday." Similarly, in the new conclusion to "Herald of Freedom" he approvingly quoted Rogers's stern rebuttal to one who argued that Christ never preached abolition. In short, Rogers denied the premise, but asserted that, if true, Christ *"did'nt do his duty."*

He applauded Rogers for rejecting external authority when it conflicted with the demands of conscience, but Thoreau continued to stress the poetry rather than the philosophy of the abolitionist's writings. With the exception of the fierce comment about Christ, all of the extracts included in the revised version of "Herald of Freedom" illustrated Rogers's feeling for New England. Indeed, Thoreau clearly sought to distinguish between Rogers's political writings, which revealed all the faults of a reformer, and Rogers's descriptive writings, which contained "as true and pleasing pictures of New England life & scenery as are anywhere to be found." He thus served as a paradigm of a man whose commitment to a transient cause did not blind him to the permanent truths of nature and human life.

Those "pictures of New England life & scenery" formed an effective transition in "Thursday." Following a long extract from Rogers's celebration of Swamscot, Massachusetts, a fishing village whose bold and adventurous inhabitants demonstrated the rugged independence of the New England character, Thoreau continued, "He was born and bred far up this stream, under the shadow of the higher hills." By quoting Rogers's descriptions of his native

town on the upper reaches of the Merrimack, Thoreau subtly
shifted the reader's attention back to the narrative in "Thursday."
The arrival in Concord occasioned the tribute to Rogers; the revised version of "Herald of Freedom" concluded with glimpses
of Plymouth, the next stop on the journey to the White Mountains.

Although Thoreau omitted his review of Rogers's newspaper,
instead evoking the historical associations of Concord (*W* 303-
4), he inserted brief extracts from the *Herald of Freedom* elsewhere in *A Week*. Earlier in "Thursday," for example, he lauds
Rogers's faith in man and nature, observing, " 'Nothing that naturally happens to man, can *hurt* him, earthquakes and thunder
storms not excepted,' said a man of genius, who at this time lived
a few miles further on our road" (*W* 300). Similarly, in the description of the Merrimack in "Sunday," where he also identifies
Rogers in terms of locale rather than by name, Thoreau quotes
one "born on its head waters," who wrote: "Down out at its mouth,
the dark inky main blending with the blue above. Plum Island,
its sand ridges scalloping along the horizon like the sea serpent,
and the distant outline broken by many a tall ship, leaning, *still*,
against the sky" (*W* 85). The extract is particularly apt, for, by
echoing Samuel Sewell's poetical tribute to Plum Island in *The
New Heaven upon the New Earth* (1697), an eloquent prophecy
that New England would become the New Heaven promised to
the faithful in Revelations, Rogers affirmed the promise of his
native region, a promise Thoreau reaffirmed in *A Week*.

Thoreau's emphasis on the possibilities of life in New England,
rather than on its failures and limitations, partially accounts for
the omission of another section from "Thursday." The section is
memorable, if only because it contained one of his most famous
lines, which originally read, "The great mass of mankind live lives
of quiet desperation" (Appendix, no. 11). In revised form, that
line and portions of the paragraph that followed in "Thursday"
survive in *Walden* (*Wa* 8), but the man who prompted those remarks joined numerous others in the limbo of surviving manuscripts of *A Week*. In his account of the brothers' encounter with
"a poor wretch" who had traveled all the way from New York to
the White Mountains in a futile search for work, Thoreau adumbrated his full-scale critique of American economy in *Walden*.

Like the stranded businessmen in "Sunday," the man travels in the wrong way and for the worst possible reasons. Because "he would not budge an inch in the direction of reform and a good conscience," he has become lost. In terms of either material or spiritual economy, his effort to gain a living has been a complete failure. "He only wished to convince the fates that he was willing to do his part when he knew that he was not," Thoreau sternly remarked. "And so he would go on if his constitution held out to the Gulf of St. Lawrence, where he would probably jump in." In sharp contrast to the brothers' life-enhancing voyage, the man's fruitless journey, like the desperate enterprises described in "Economy," is a form of suicide.

Thoreau later expanded a meditation on traveling which the meeting had occasioned. Initially, he simply sought to illustrate the ways one might "earn his living on the road"; later he stressed the absurdity of traveling for that purpose: "But I never thought of travelling simply as a means of getting a livelihood. . . . True and sincere travelling is no pastime, but it is as serious as the grave, or any other part of the human journey, and it requires a long probation to be broken into it" (W 304, 305-6). Because they had forgotten that life is a pilgrimage, Americans neglected the true business of life and sacrificed themselves to false economic gods.

The theme of profit and loss, possession and dispossession, is developed more fully in the opening chapters of *Walden,* but Thoreau's concern is also evident at the end of *A Week.* "How fortunate were we who did not own an acre of these shores, who had not renounced our title to the whole," he exclaims in "Friday": "One who knew how to appropriate the true value of this world would be the poorest man in it. The poor rich man! all he has is what he has bought. What I see is mine. I am a large owner in the Merrimack intervals" (W 350). As he illustrates in "Where I Lived and What I Lived For" and in "Friday," his countrymen cannot understand this paradox. When the brothers ask a canal-boatman about Wicasuck Island, for example, the man suspects they have a claim upon it and offers to buy their title. In the earliest version of the episode, Thoreau concluded: "And so I have found in many instances that my countrymen have no conception of what a poet travels for. . . . But they will suspect some concealed pecuniary speculation to be at the bottom of it" (MH 15, P; cf. W 358). By omitting that rather obvious comment, he allowed the episode to speak for itself. Added to his description of the businessmen stranded near the same island in "Sunday," the incident in "Friday" eloquently conveys the debasement of his countrymen's values.

Thoreau further deepened the significance of the Wicasuck Island episodes by adding a brief history of the island to "Sunday." Quoting various historical sources, he recounts how the island was first sold by the Penacooks in order to free their chief from jail; then restored to them by the General Court; and finally granted to Jonathan Tyng, who earned his title to it by refusing to abandon his position during King Philip's War (W 110-12). The boatman's reference to the disputed title, which initially served as yet another isolated example of false values, thus takes its place in a kind of parable of American history in which the Indians and the white settlers had struggled over title to New England. Unlike Tyng, Thoreau's countrymen had not earned their title to the land, whose promise was being destroyed by their adherence to dead traditions.

The history of Wicasuck Island is but one of many signs of a shift in emphasis in *A Week*. From the time of his arrest in 1846, when he denounced institutions as "the stereotyped and petrified will of the past," Thoreau sought to confront these dead and deadening institutions in *A Week*. He thus attacked the Christian church in "Sunday," the state in "Monday," and, in later chapters, the social and economic customs of his country. At the same time he was denouncing these abuses of the past, however, he was also discovering the uses of the past. Consequently, while he omitted numerous passages of social criticism, Thoreau added a substantial amount of historical material to *A Week*, in which he repeatedly looks beyond the present realities of New England to glimpse a more heroic age when "*Indian* chiefs and Christian warriors/Joined in fierce and mortal fight" (W 167).

4
The Uses of the Past

OUR AGE IS RETROSPECTIVE," Emerson announced at the opening of *Nature*. "It builds the sepulchres of the fathers. It writes biographies, histories, and criticism. The foregoing generations beheld God and nature face to face; we, through their eyes. Why should not we also enjoy an original relation to the universe? Why should not we have a poetry and philosophy of insight and not of tradition, and a religion by revelation to us, and not the history of theirs?" (*CW* I:7).

Emerson's statement underlies Thoreau's various efforts in *A Week*. The ideal of "an original relation to the universe" illuminates his decision to give an account of the journey to "Unappropriated Land" as well as his emphasis in *A Week* on the pastoral and primitive aspects of New England. In his attacks on New England's stifling social, political, and religious traditions, Thoreau in effect sought to remove obstacles in man's relation to nature and God. But the Transcendentalists' rejection of tradition was not a rejection of the past. As Sherman Paul has pointed out, "When Emerson inveighed against history he was only attempting to change subservience to mastery—he was teaching his generation the uses of history, how through consciousness and idea to appropriate the past."[1] *A Week* represents Thoreau's sustained effort to apply Emerson's lesson about the uses of the past to the colonial history of New England. That history was thus not useful to Thoreau insofar as it remained past, but only insofar as it could be made present, could be revivified in his own life and writings.

Thoreau's interest in colonial history was prompted by his fascination with the American Indian. His quest for the Indian began

[1]Paul, p. 158. Thoreau's views are discussed by David G. Hoch, "Theory of History in *A Week:* Annuals and Perennials," *Emerson Society Quarterly* 56 (1969):32–35; and Jamie Hutchinson, " 'The Lapse of the Current': Thoreau's Historical Vision in *A Week on the Concord and Merrimack Rivers,"* ESQ 25 (1979):211–23.

at Harvard, where he made his first forays into the increasingly voluminous literature concerning Indian tribes and colonial history. Initially, however, his interest was less historical or anthropological than philosophical and literary. The epitome of natural man, the American Indian, like those equally exotic Indians of the Hindu scriptures, served as useful foil to the artificiality and materialism of white civilization, while the conflicts between Indians and whites evoked an earlier heroic age in New England. But Thoreau found little place for either the Indians or their epic struggles with white settlers in his early essays, in which he tended to dismiss what he described as the "dark age" of New England. It was during the writing of *A Week* that he began to discover the uses of the colonial past. Beginning with a few scattered references to its history in the first draft, Thoreau constructed what Robert Sayre calls "a condensed history, in an inferential, poetic form, of Indian-European relations in America."[2] At once a commentary on white man's history, an allegory of the destruction of a wilderness paradise in America, and an elegy on the Indians, whom he implicitly associates with his own lost brother, Thoreau's history reveals his dependence on colonial narratives and local histories as well as his growing ability to select, arrange, and reweave materials from these sources in order to transform the dead particulars of history into the living truths of poetry in *A Week*.

A wealth of historical material was available to Thoreau. Indeed, Emerson was right: the age was retrospective. Among the earliest efforts to mine the rich lode of New England history were Thomas Hutchinson's *History of the Colony and Province of Massachusetts-Bay* (1764-1828) and Jeremy Belknap's *History of New-Hampshire* (1784-92), both of which Thoreau read. Spurred, as Belknap was, by the rapid changes in New England during the decades following the Revolution and by a desire to assert their

[2]Robert F. Sayre, *Thoreau and the American Indians* (Princeton: Princeton Univ. Press, 1977), p. 28. Sayre's is the most detailed and illuminating explication of Thoreau's treatment of the Indians and colonial history in *A Week*. His emphasis on the coherence and continuity of Thoreau's history of Indian-European relations is particularly helpful.

regional identity, scholars formed historical societies in Massachusetts (1791), New York (1804), Maine (1822), Rhode Island, (1822), and New Hampshire (1823), as well as the American Antiquarian Society (1812) and the Essex Historical Society (1821). In their collections these societies published new and often heavily annotated editions of colonial historians, as well as biographical sketches and topographical descriptions of towns and villages, many of which proved invaluable to Thoreau as he worked on *A Week*.

Interest in the colonial past was not limited to the historical societies. Commercial publishers reprinted other early works. An important series of colonial narratives was edited by Samuel G. Drake of Boston. The most popular of these, Drake's edition of Benjamin Church's *History of King Philip's War*, was reissued thirteen times between 1825 and 1846, largely because of the enthusiasm of readers like Thoreau, who acquired a copy of Church's *History* (*TL* 40-41) and took extracts from Drake's *Biography and History of the Indians of North America* (*TLN* 26). Meanwhile, amateur historians began to publish histories of towns such as Concord, Chelmsford, Dunstable, and Haverhill, all of which Thoreau drew upon for *A Week*.

Local history had a marked impact on poets and novelists in New England. Although Longfellow's popular poems did not begin to appear until the 1850s, other poets paved the way. Whittier, whose first book, *Legends of New England* (1831), has been described as an "ambitious attempt to demonstrate the poetic validity of local material," published *The Supernaturalism of New England* in 1847.[3] Portions of the latter appeared in the *Democratic Review* in the fall of 1843. Thoreau, whose essays "The Landlord" and "Paradise (to be) Regained" appeared in the *Democratic Review* at the same time, was probably familiar with Whittier's work, as well as at least some stories by the journal's most distinguished contributor, Nathaniel Hawthorne. By the time Hawthorne moved into the Old Manse in 1842, he had already published *Twice-Told Tales* (1837) and *Grandfather's Chair* (1841), a three-volume

[3]John Greenleaf Whittier, *Legends of New England,* ed. John B. Pickard (Gainesville, Fla.: Scholars Facs., 1965), p. vii.

history of America for children. The stories he wrote during his stay in Concord suggest that Hawthorne felt that he had exhausted the historical romance, but his presence probably spurred Thoreau's interest in the New England past.

Not surprisingly, travel writers also exploited local materials. Concerned that the people of New England, intent as they were on the future, would lose sight of their past, Timothy Dwight incorporated numerous historical episodes into *Travels in New England and New York* (1821-22). Many of these episodes, including his account of Lovewell's Fight and the captivities of Mary Rowlandson and Hannah Duston, were examples of Indian brutality, intended to support Dwight's "contention that survival of the colonists had required the subjection of the Indians."[4] But the virtual annihilation of the eastern tribes sharpened interest in surviving tribes in the West, described in popular romantic narratives like Irving's *A Tour on the Prairies* (1835), with its picturesque Osage and idealized wilderness, *Astoria* (1836), and *Adventures of Captain Bonneville* (1837), as well as in more literal and factual accounts of western travel like those Thoreau read at Harvard.

Although his curiosity about the Indian developed early, Thoreau found less use for factual portraits of American tribes than for the mythical and already somewhat shopworn figure of the noble savage. In an 1837 letter to his brother, who two weeks earlier had joined him in a search for Indian relics, their heads "full of the past and its remains" (*J* 1:9), Thoreau assumed the role of Tahatawan, sachem of the Musketaquid, or Concord River. As the editors observe, the letter, "written in what is supposedly conventionalized Indian dialect, gives a sidelight on the brothers' interest in Indian lore" (*C* 18n). That shared interest helps explain the elegiac strategy in *A Week*, in which Thoreau mourns both the loss of his brother and the passing of the Indians from the American scene. But in the letter, as elsewhere in his early writings, he tended to treat the Indian as an abstraction rather than a historical entity. In an undergraduate review of William Howitt's *The Book of the Seasons*, for example, he described the deprivation

[4]Dwight, I: xxxvii.

of men "whose sordid views extend no further than the profitable, who cannot contemplate the meandering brook, without, in imagination, polluting its waters with a mill-wheel" by contrasting such men to "The poor Indian, whose untutor'd mind/Sees God in clouds, or hears him in the wind" (*EEM* 27). By quoting two lines from a longer passage in *An Essay on Man* (I. 99-100), he subtly subverted Pope's meaning. For both, the Indian represented natural man; but whereas Pope directed a portion of his irony against the Indian's naive religious conceptions, Thoreau suggested that the Indian's sensitivity to nature brought him closer to God. The Indian consequently served as a foil to a society whose materialism threatened to cut it off from nature and from God.

Thoreau also opposed the Indian's freedom to the constraints of civilized life. "The charm of the Indian to me is that he stands free and unconstrained in nature," he remarked in the Journal on April 26, 1841; "is her inhabitant—and not her guest—and wears her easily and gracefully" (*J* 1:304). His reference occasioned a meditation on "civilized man," whose "house is a prison" and who "walks as if he sustained the roof." Since he had just moved in with the Emersons (the entry is headed "At R.W.E.'s"), the satirical sketch was implicitly a warning to himself not to pick up the "habits of the house." He thus abruptly concluded, "It is a great art to saunter." To learn to saunter, to travel through nature with the ease and grace of the Indian, was an antidote to the oppressive burdens of civilized life in both his life and in his works.

Despite his effort to emulate the Indian, Thoreau described him as a radically different variety of man. After walking across the Concord fields, "strewn with the relics of a race which has vanished as completely as if trodden in with the earth," he wrote in the Journal early in 1842: "Another species of mortal men but little less wild to me than the musquash they hunted— Strange spirits—daemons—whose eyes could never meet mine. With another nature—and another fate than mine— The crows flew over the edge of the woods, and wheeling over my head seemed to rebuke—as dark winged spirits more akin to the Indian than I. Perhaps only the present disguise of the Indian" (*J* 1:381).

Characteristically, Thoreau spoke of the Indian in a generic rather than a historical sense. Stripped of its admiring tone, his description of the Indians as "spirits" and "daemons" is more akin to colonial writings than to contemporary nineteenth-century studies of the language, character, and customs of the Indians of North America. Moreover, in contrast to writers like William Cullen Bryant, who, in "An Indian at the Burial-Place of his Fathers," viewed the destruction of the Indians as a sign that the white man might also vanish, "And leave no trace behind,/Save ruins o'er the region spread,/And the white stones above the dead," Thoreau viewed the Indians' fate with equanimity. Although he later related the annihilation of the Indians to the destruction of the natural world by dams and factories, and, implicitly, to the loss of his brother, Thoreau in 1842, six weeks after John's death, insisted that their "fate," like their "nature," was alien to himself. Indeed, the Indians were for him more akin to the musquash or the crow than to the white settlers who had displaced them.

The analogy between the Indian and the crow apparently caught Thoreau's fancy, for he used it again in "Natural History of Massachusetts." In support of the contention that the crow was indigenous to America, he observed: "He is no spaniel to follow our steps; but rather flits about the clearings like the dusky spirit of the Indian, reminding me oftener of Philip and Powhatan than of Winthrop and Smith. He is a relic of the Dark Ages" (*Ex* 113). As the crow had earlier served to describe the Indian, the Indian here serves to describe the crow. Like nature, history served Thoreau as a source of analogies rather than facts. He invoked Philip and Powhatan, Winthrop and Smith, not as historical figures but as mythical beings from a dark, remote, and alien past.

Thoreau again alluded to the dark ages of New England in "A Walk to Wachusett," written later in 1842. Describing the fields and groves of Lancaster, he remarked: "This, it will be remembered, was the scene of Mrs. Rowlandson's capture, and of other events in the Indian wars, but from this July afternoon, and under that mild exterior, those times seemed as remote as the irruption of the Goths. They were the dark age of New England" (*Ex* 149). His allusion to Mrs. Rowlandson's captivity seems to promise yet another telling of that ever-popular story and therefore to anticipate a technique he later used so successfully in *A Week;* but, instead, Thoreau continued: "On beholding a picture of a New England village as it then appeared, with a fair open prospect, and a light on trees and river, as if it were broad noon, we find we had not thought the sun shone in those days, or that men lived in broad daylight then. We do not imagine the sun shining on hill and valley during Philip's war, nor on the war-path of Paugus, or Standish, or Church, or Lovell, with serene summer weather, but a dim twilight or night did those events transpire in. They must have fought in the shade of their own dusky deeds" (*Ex* 149-50).

This passage, later incorporated into a long meditation on history following his account of Hannah Duston's captivity in "Thursday" (*W* 324), disappoints our literary expectations and challenges our historical preconceptions. Influenced by Emerson's "History," the first chapter in *Essays*, Thoreau plays off historical facts against our subjective awareness of the past. In contrast to the picture of a sunlit village "as it then appeared," our conceptions of the colonial past are vague and shadowy. By substituting a meditation on the remoteness of that age for an account of Mrs. Rowlandson's captivity, however, Thoreau implicitly acknowledged his own inability to make the events of the Indian wars vivid and immediate, or, in short, to make the past present. In contrast to Hannah Duston, whose experiences are vividly evoked in "Thursday," Mrs. Rowlandson is simply a name with historical associations but without human qualities or contemporary relevance.

Thoreau continued his meditation on man's relation to the past in "Dark Ages," a brief essay on history printed in the *Dial* in April 1843 and later revised for *A Week* (*W* 154-57). "Time hides no treasures," he asserted in the opening paragraph; "we want not its *then* but its *now*." His insistence that "the living fact commemorates itself" helps explain his predilection for historical events like Hannah Duston's escape from the Indians, a story that had been passed down from generation to generation before Thoreau retold it in *A Week*. He was therefore impatient with those who sought to recover dead facts. Historians and antiquarians might have answered that by seeking to preserve the past man paid homage to his ancestors and bestowed a precious gift upon his descendants. For example, in the Preface to *The History of Chelmsford,* which Thoreau later consulted for *A Week,* Wilkes Allen asserted: "It is a duty, which men owe to their posterity, to transmit the knowledge of their ancestors. Minute and circumstantial accounts of our friends, fathers and progenitors acquire an interest in our feelings and impart a joy to our hearts, which the stranger intermeddleth not with."[5] But for Thoreau the efforts of such compilers were self-defeating. "Strictly speaking, the historical societies have not recovered one fact from oblivion," he argued, "but are themselves instead of the fact that is lost" (*EEM* 143).

Thoreau's disdain for those who simply sought to preserve the past helps explain the paucity of references to the history of Concord in his early writings. By all accounts he was very proud of Concord, which had as rich and as well-documented a history as any town in New England. During the first few months after his graduation from Harvard, for example, he gathered local traditions about the Revolution, including recollections from Anna Jones, whom he described as "a precious relic of days which the man and patriot would not willingly forget" (*EEM* 121).[6] He was also familiar with Lemuel Shattuck's *A History of the Town of Concord* (1835; see *TL* 87), but, with the exception of a brief passage on the early fur trade in "Natural History of Massachusetts," Thoreau made little use of this source in his early essays. Increasingly aware that the Revolution had failed to make men truly free, he may have felt that Concord's pride in its past was only partially justified. He also may have believed that its preoccupation with its place in history blinded the citizens of Concord to its place in nature. "When we withdraw a little from the village—and perceive how it is embosomed in nature," he wrote in the Journal on August

---

[5] Wilkes Allen, *The History of Chelmsford* (Haverhill, Mass.: P. N. Green, 1820), p. 5.

[6] Kenneth Cameron, "Thoreau's Three Months Out of Harvard and His First Publication," *Emerson Society Quarterly,* no. 5 (1956), pp. 2–12. The article includes a useful bibliography of "Books on Indians Which Thoreau Did Know or Might Have Known by November, 1837."

14, 1843, "we wonder if the life of its inhabitants might not also be thus natural and innocent reflecting the aspects of nature" (*J* 1:458-59; cf. FD 100). In "A Winter Walk," drafted earlier that summer, he had described precisely such a physical and meditative withdrawal from Concord, which he curtly referred to as that "gadding town," possibly in order to check the historical associations its name might evoke (*Ex* 168).

As long as Thoreau conceived of his account of the brothers' voyage as a withdrawal into nature similar to "A Winter's Walk," he demonstrated little interest in the history of the towns along the Concord and Merrimack. Walter Harding has suggested that before the 1839 journey Thoreau "prepared himself by reading all the histories of the area he could place his hands on."[7] But since his usual practice was to gather material about an area only after he had visited it, Thoreau probably did little research before the trip. He may have consulted some sources in the early 1840s, but, if so, it was some time before he began to understand their use in giving an account of the excursion. The material he transcribed and drafted in the Long Book, for example, contained few references to towns along the rivers and none to their history.

The first draft contains the first hints of the role colonial history would ultimately play in *A Week*. In "Monday," Thoreau quoted and briefly commented upon some lines from "The Ballad of Lovewell's Fight," a popular account of one of the most famous episodes of the Indian wars. Asserting that the "incidents and exploits" of Lovewell's War "would furnish materials for one book of the Iliad at least," he nonetheless ignored its epic possibilities and simply used it to contrast an earlier heroic age with the mundane realities of commercial New England as its embarked on the business of the week (FD 37-38). He recognized, however, that this commercial spirit was rooted deeply in the New England past, for in "Tuesday" he quoted a passage from the *Gazetteer* concerning Cromwell's Trading Post, the first house erected on the banks of the river in Merrimack, New Hampshire (FD 59-60). Enraged at Cromwell's deceptive practices, a party of Penacooks burned the trading post, but the conflicts initiated by the

---

[7] *The New Thoreau Handbook,* p. 43.

greed of the white settlers had ultimately led to the destruction of the Indians. Perhaps to suggest this sequence of events, Thoreau in "Wednesday" included an elegiac meditation on that "vanished" race (FD 65-68).

In his remarks in the first draft, Thoreau stressed the difficulties of writing the history of the Indian. Drawing upon a description of "Amoskeag Falls & Village, New Hampshire" in the *Gazetteer,* he introduced the section in "Wednesday" with a reference to Sachem Wannalancet, whose tribe had concealed provisions in the cavities of rocks in the upper part of the falls. But Thoreau attributed these facts to "tradition," possibly to support his contention that white historians had ignored Indian deeds. "The future reader of history will associate this generation with the red man in his thoughts," he remarked. "But such are not our associations. The Indian has vanished as completely as if trodden into the earth; absolutely forgotten but by a few persevering poets" (FD 65). In the Journal entry from March 19, 1842, from which portions of this section were adapted, he had also asserted that the Indian had "vanished" (*J* 1:380); his qualification in the first draft, "absolutely forgotten but by a few persevering poets," reveals his own nascent desire to become one such poet. He was aware, of course, that historians had not forgotten the Indian, but he insisted that a true history could only be written by one with a special sympathy with the race. "For Indian deeds there must be an Indian memory," he continued; "the white man will remember only his own" (FD 65).

Thoreau sought to demonstrate his own sympathy with the Indian through an extended description of Indian relics, "evidence of the vital energy of the people that made them" (FD 65). Although familiar with such relics, which he had an uncanny knack of turning up in the fields around Concord, he drew heavily upon descriptions in the chapter "Monuments and relics of the Indians" in Jeremy Belknap's *A History of New-Hampshire*.[8] Without acknowledging his debt to Belknap, Thoreau thus relied on one of the white historians whom he accused of forgetting the Indian. But in contrast to Belknap, who viewed these implements

[8]Belknap, III: 63–72.

as examples of the primitive level of Indian culture, which in turn justified their conquest by the more advanced white settlers, he observed, "It is doubtful whether one of our mechanics, with all the aids of Yankee ingenuity, could soon learn to copy one of the thousands under his feet" (FD 67). For Thoreau the simplicity and necessity of their forms made these implements worthy to stand "beside the latest improvements of art" (FD 68). Yet, despite his effort to use these implements as a key to Indian culture and history, he also asserted that many of these relics were "symbols which cannot be interpreted at this day" (FD 68). Indeed, his comments reveal that he was less interested in restoring the Indian's place in history than in transferring the Indian to the realm of myth, "an era which can never have its history—which is older, or more primitive, than history itself" (FD 67).

If the first draft reflects Thoreau's growing interest in colonial history and Indian culture, it also reveals the limitations of his interest in those subjects. His use of historical sources is more noteworthy for what he ignored than for what he extracted for the first draft. For example, while he borrowed some of Belknap's descriptions of Indian relics and quoted other brief passages from that "pleasant & observant historian" (FD 50), Thoreau drew all of this material from the third volume of Belknap's *History,* which contained descriptions of the geography, natural resources, and social organizations of New Hampshire. He ignored the first two volumes, which contained the history of the state. Similarly, the "Ballad of Lovewell's Fight" was reprinted in the third volume of Farmer and Moore's *Collections,* but he apparently did not consult the first two volumes, which contained Reverend Symme's account of the fight (cited in notes to the ballad), a biographical sketch of John Stark, to whom Thoreau later paid tribute in "Wednesday" (W 253), and articles like "Indian Troubles at Dunstable," an account that included numerous references to Farwell, later described in "Monday" as "an indispensable hero to New England" (W 168).[9] Hayward's *New England Gazetteer,*

[9]*Collections, Topographical, Historical and Biographical, Relating Principally to New-Hampshire,* ed. J. Farmer and J. B. Moore, 3 vols. (Concord, N.H.: Hill and Moore, 1822–24).

which Thoreau had carried along on the voyage and often consulted as he drafted *A Week,* also contained a wealth of historical lore, at which the brief allusions to Cromwell and Sachem Wannalancet only hint. To adopt a distinction made in *A Week,* Thoreau was clearly still far less concerned with "the *annals* of the country" than with "the natural facts, or *perennials,* which are ever without date" (*W* 219).

After completing the first draft, however, he sought out other episodes from colonial history for use in the narrative. He began to draw heavily upon authors he was already familiar with, including Hayward, Shattuck, and Belknap. But he also discovered new sources of information. His search was probably aided by Hermann E. Ludewig's *The Literature of American Local History* (1846; see *TL* 68). A bibliography conveniently organized by state, county, and town, Ludewig's book listed virtually every source that Thoreau consulted as he revised and expanded *A Week.* The sources themselves were plentiful, for, as Ludewig noted, "there is hardly a town of some extent in New England, the historical events of which have not been recorded in some work, particularly written for that purpose, or in centennial sermons, lectures or notices garnered up in the collections of their historical societies."[10]

Thoreau gathered the historical material in *A Week* over a long period, but with ever-increasing zeal. In 1846, probably spurred by his forthcoming trip to Maine, where he immersed himself in the last surviving wilderness in New England, he read Samuel Penhallow's *History of the Wars of New England with the Eastern Tribes* in the *Collections of the New Hampshire Historical Society,* which ultimately provided a wealth of useful material. He soon discovered Wilkes Allen's *History of Chelmsford* (1820) and B. L. Mirick's *History of Haverhill, Massachusetts* (1832; see *TL* 74). Mirick's account of Hannah Duston's captivity inspired Thoreau's own masterly re-creation of that episode, which he began to draft in the Journal in early 1847 (*J* 2:377). *The History of Chelmsford* proved of less direct use, but it contained numerous

[10]Hermann Ernest Ludewig, *The Literature of American Local History* (New York: Craighead, 1846), p. xvi.

references to Daniel Gookin's *Historical Collections of the Indians in New England* and *History of the Christian Indians,* both of which Thoreau consulted, probably sometime later in 1847 or early in 1848. At about the same time he read an edition of Robert Rogers's *Reminiscences of the French War* (1831), which contained a useful account of the adventures of General John Stark, whose grave was among the historical sites Thoreau visited during the walking tour of southern New Hampshire in the summer of 1848.[11]

That tour provided abundant local lore for *A Week.* During the trip he purchased Charles J. Fox's *History of the Old Township of Dunstable,* published only two years earlier (*DHT* 233). With its strong emphasis on conflicts between Indians and the white settlers of Dunstable, Fox's book provided Thoreau with more historical material than any other source he had consulted. He also visited many of the scenes described by Fox. Combined with the research he had done since writing the first draft, the information and impressions he gleaned during the tour helped give *A Week* its strong local flavor. But, as Harry B. Henderson has pointed out, the historical incidents described in the book "are not merely local, but national in their communal resonance, and belong to the national legend of expansion into the wilderness as surely as do Filson's *Narrative* of Boone, the novels of Cooper, and the works of Parkman."[12]

From the opening sentences of *A Week,* Thoreau sought to unite a strong sense of local history and tradition with a far-reaching vision of the implications and consequences to America of the struggle that raged along the banks of the Concord and the Merrimack. Announcing the theme of conflict between the races at

[11]This chronology of Thoreau's reading in colonial history during 1846–48 is based on references in the surviving Journal and in the manuscripts of *A Week.* Thoreau may have begun his "Indian Books" as early as 1847, but only one quotation in *A Week* is duplicated in the extracts in "Indian Book I," most if not all of which he apparently gathered in 1849. See the author's article "Into History: Thoreau's Earliest 'Indian Book' and His First Trip to Cape Cod," *ESQ* 28 (1982):75–88.

[12]Harry B. Henderson, *Versions of the Past* (New York: Oxford Univ. Press. 1974), pp. 8–9.

the opening of "Concord River," he begins to develop that theme in "Sunday." There, he stresses the radical differences between the white farmers and missionaries and the Indians whom the European settlers dispossessed of their land and culture. In his accounts of battles between the races in "Monday," however, Thoreau reveals similarities between Indian warriors and soldiers like Farwell, who swiftly adapted to the wilderness of the New World. The movement toward commerce between the races, briefly adumbrated in "Tuesday," is fulfilled in the friendship between Wawatam and Alexander Henry in "Wednesday." But their brief idyll of peace and friendship is symbolically destroyed by Hannah Duston in "Thursday," where that remote event of colonial history is made vivid and immediate, a crucial source of our national identity. The elegiac tone of his account of Hannah Duston's fateful act, which Thoreau associates with the Fall of Man, recurs in his meditation on Elisha's apple tree in "Friday." But just as the loss of his brother is resolved in his meditation on the autumnal landscape in "Friday," so his grief about the destruction of the wilderness and the extinction of the Indian is assuaged by his recognition of nature's restorative powers.

A comparison of the epigraph to "Concord River" in the first draft and the one substituted in the published verson reveals Thoreau's deepening interest in the conflict between the Indians and the white settlers for wilderness America. In the first draft he used two lines then attributed to Pindar: "Were it the will of Heaven, an osier bough/Were vessel safe enough the seas to plough" (FD 1). With their emphasis on heavenly dispensation, these lines served as an apt preface to his account of the idyllic voyage. Later, however, he shifted these lines to "Saturday" (W 16), replacing them with a passage from Emerson's poem "Musketaquid," which concludes: "Here, in pine houses, built of new-fallen trees,/Supplanters of the tribe, the farmers dwell" (W 5). By concluding with these lines, Thoreau transformed Emerson's poem, which goes on to praise these farmers, into an elegy for the tribe that the white settlers had supplanted.

The revised opening of "Concord River" reasserts the Indians' claim to the land. In the lines from "Musketaquid," Emerson refers to the Concord as "our Indian rivulet," which "Winds mindful still of sannup and of squaw." In order to shift the emphasis to this "Indian rivulet," Thoreau dropped the opening sentences in the first draft, devoted to the town of Concord, so that the first paragraph of the published version begins, "THE MUSKETAQUID, or Grass-ground River." With this rhetorical gesture he returns the river to those who originally named it, or rather adopted its natural name, "Grass-ground." He also questions the intentions of the original white settlers. In the first draft he noted that the river received the name Concord "from the quiet and peaceable lives of these men, both with one another and with the Indians" (FD 1). He later revised this remark to read, "from the first plantation on its banks, which *appears* to have been *commenced* in a spirit of peace and harmony" (emphasis added). Implicitly, he suggests that if the settlement had begun on such a harmonious note, the white settlers had ultimately destroyed this concord. Playing upon the theme of possession and dispossession, he continues: "It will be Grass-ground River as long as grass grows and water runs here; it will be Concord River only while men lead peaceable lives on its banks. To an extinct race it was grass-ground, where they hunted and fished, and it is still perennial grass-ground to Concord farmers, who own the Great Meadows, and get the hay from year to year" (W 5).

Thoreau implies an analogy between the settlers' treatment of the Indian and their relationship to nature. As Robert Sayre has pointed out, the provision "as long as grass grows and water runs" was included in Indian treaties "as an expression for the furthest imaginable future."[13] Thoreau's allusion to this "extinct race" suggests that in Concord and throughout New England the white settlers' provisional claim to the land had ended when the peace was broken. Two consequences of their desire to own or possess the land were the destruction of the Indians and the devastation of the natural world. In contrast to the Indian, who sought to live in harmony with nature, the white man seeks to harness the forces of nature. Although Thoreau notes that the river "is still perennial grass-ground" to the farmers in the Great Meadows, he swiftly reveals that portions of these meadows have been destroyed by

[13]Sayre, p. 30.

the dams built downstream. Where "white honeysuckle or clover" once grew, "now there is nothing but blue-joint and sedge and cut-grass there, standing in water all the year round" (W 6). The same combination of greed and technology that destroyed the Indians now threatens nature itself.

As a counterweight to the opening of "Concord River," in which he stresses the ravages of time and history, Thoreau describes a voyage up the river, where he discovers signs of continuity and permanence (W 7-9). Encountering "such healthy natural tumult as proves the last day is not yet at hand," he confidently affirms that neither man nor nature has decayed. Unlike men in towns, the rude settlers on the upper reaches of the river retain something of the Indian's independence and harmony with nature. In his celebration of these pioneers, "who were out not only in '75 and 1812, but have been out every day of their lives" (W 8), Thoreau originally sounded an uncharacteristically patriotic and even jingoistic note. Following the poem "The respectable folks," he continued in a manuscript version: "Such is the race which has long had a foothold in this land, and which these vagrant immigrants shall never displace. Yet there is room for all." He then concluded the section with the poem "Our Country," with its evocation of the glories of America and its celebration of the triumph of the Anglo-Saxon race. After the elegiac allusions to the destruction of the Indians at the opening of "Concord River," the poem's cheerful vision of the "red race" sullenly retreating before the whites—"Emptying their graves, striking their wigwam tents" (HM 13182, III, 3; cf. CP 134)—sounded a discordant note. If the poem did not exactly justify the destruction of the Indians, it at least made the triumph of the superior Anglo-Saxon race seem inevitable. Thoreau therefore wisely omitted both the poem and his introductory comment, thus balancing the claims of Indian and white America in "Concord River."[14]

Although he introduces the theme of two Americas in "Concord

[14]The quotations in "Concord River" from Edward Johnson's *Wonder-Working Providence,* which describe the early settlement of Concord (W 10–11), were added after the publication of *A Week* in 1849. Thoreau quoted related passages from Johnson's history in *Walden* (Wa 38–39).

River," Thoreau does not begin to develop that theme until "Sunday." Transferring the original epigraph to the body of the text, he replaced it with lines from Ellery Channing's "Boat Song" and a sentence from Sieur de Monts's *Relations of the Jesuits*. Channing's description of a river flowing where "ne'er the cheer of men/Has stirred its mute repose" and Sieur de Monts's report that "the Indians tell us of a beautiful River lying far to the south, which they call Merrimac" together evoke a vision of an unexplored Indian wilderness, through which the brothers float. That vision, however, is interrupted by a glimpse of Billerica, which prompts a meditation on the theme of civilization versus wildness. Not surprisingly, Thoreau takes his stand with the Indian, whose "intercourse with nature is such as admits of the greatest independence of each" (FD 24; cf. W 56).

Ironically, his paean to "the hunter's and forest life" reveals how fully Thoreau accepted certain assumptions about the Indians and their place in American society. A decade earlier Albert Gallatin, the "Father of American Ethnology," had insisted that the annihilation of the Indians was inevitable unless they became cultivators of the soil: "A nation of hunters cannot exist, as such, when brought into contact with an agricultural and industrious people. . . . [The Indians] must be brought to work, to till the ground, in short, in the same manner as our own people, the sons of our industrious farmers."[15] Thoreau echoed that argument in a passage drafted on some leaves inserted in the Long Book, where he developed the thesis that "for the Indian there is no safety but in the plow. If he would not be pushed into the Pacific, he must seize hold of a plow-tail and let go his bow and arrow, his fishspear and rifle. This the only Christianity that will save him."[16]

[15]Albert Gallatin, "A Synopsis of the Indian Tribes within the United States East of the Rocky Mountains, and in the British and Russian Possessions in North America," *Transactions and Collections of the American Antiquarian Society* 2 (1836):159.

[16]The passage is printed in *The Journal of Henry D.Thoreau*, ed. Bradford Torrey and Francis H. Allen, 14 vols. (Boston: Houghton Mifflin, 1906), I:444–46. For a fuller discussion of the passage in the context of nineteenth-century "savagism," see Sayre, chap. 1, especially pp. 21–25.

There, as in *A Week*, he expressed his strong sympathies with "the Indians and hunter men," but Thoreau, like Gallatin and so many others, conveniently ignored the fact that many of the eastern Indians were both hunters and tillers of the soil, perhaps not so radically different from the early white settlers of New England. Instead, he described those differences as absolute, a division between the savage life "of the forest and the outlaw" and the "quiet and civil life" of Billerica, the town that prompts the digression in "Sunday."

Thoreau's treatment of Billerica changed markedly as he revised and expanded *A Week*. In two brief paragraphs in the first draft, he poked gentle fun at the town's meek, cultivated aspect ("Even the cultivators are the cultivated"), but the portrait was by no means unflattering (FD 23). Later, however, he denounced the town and its institutions. He chose an apt target, since Billerica was the very embodiment of the New England way. Dwight, for example, had noted that the "manners of the plain inhabitants appear, like many of their houses, to retain in an uncommon degree the ancient simplicity of New England."[17] Thoreau, too, views Billerica as a symbol of ancient traditions, but he treats those traditions in a sharply different manner: "Here was a village not far off behind the woods, Billerica, settled not long ago, and the children still bear the names of the first settlers in this late 'howling wilderness;' yet to all intents and purposes it is as old as Fernay or as Mantua, an old gray town, where men grow old and sleep already under moss-grown monuments, outgrow their usefulness. This is ancient Billercia, (Villa-rica?) now in its dotage, named from English Billericay, and whose Indian name was Shawshine. I never heard that it was young. See, is not nature here gone to decay, farms all run out, meeting-house grown gray and racked with age?" (*W* 49-50).

That contemptuous description again raises the issue of supplantation. In contrast to Concord, whose name had neither an English nor a Biblical precedent, the very name Billerica indicates the process by which Old World values were transplanted to the New World. Although it was "settled not long ago," the town is

[17]Dwight, I:285.

as old as the most ancient cities in Europe, since its inhabitants carried along with them outmoded traditions that Thoreau savagely associates with sleep and death. In the process the inhabitants had not only changed the Indian name, they had also blighted the promise of the New World. For Thoreau, a major reason for the white settlers' failure to fulfill its promise of a new start was the church, a bastion of the old ways. The old gray meetinghouse, whose bell "startled the dreaming Indian, and frightened his game" (W 50), represents the first violation of the Indian and the wilderness. After wearily recounting the early disputes between Carlisle and Bedford about forming a separate parish, "a tedious question," he concludes with a brilliantly compressed version of the planting of New England. Under the mild guise of agriculture, the pious and industrious settlers destroyed the wilderness and supplanted the Indian. "The white man's mullein soon reigned in Indian corn-fields, and sweet scented English grasses clothed the new soil," Thoreau notes. "Where, then, could the Red Man set his foot?" (W 52-53).

Just as Billerica prompted a meditation on the first stage of the white man's advance, the conversion of the wilderness into an English garden, Chelmsford occasioned remarks on an even more fateful conversion. "As we glided over the broad bosom of this river between Middlesex & Tyngsboro," he remarked in the first draft, "at a third of a mile over the water we heard distinctly the children repeating their catechism in a cottage on shore" (FD 30). Since the town of Tyngsborough was part of Middlesex County, his reference to the location was vague and confusing, so Thoreau later revised it to read "between Chelmsford and Dracut." But his reference to Chelmsford, the site of Wamesit, or Pawtucket, one of the first settlements founded for the praying Indians, was also strategic, for he added, "Two hundred years ago other catechising than this was going on here" (W 80). Billerica testifies to the seizure of Indian lands; Chelmsford recalls the destruction of Indian culture that inevitably followed.

In order to dramatize the impact of white missionaries on Indian culture, Thoreau gathered material from Gookin's *Historical Collections*, Winthrop's *History of New England*, and a letter from the General Court to Cromwell describing the progress of the Bay

Colony's effort to convert the Indians (*W* 80-82). Highlighted by Gookin's account of Wannalancet's weary but dignified submission to the Christian religion, these extracts serve as a spiritual equivalent to the conversions of Billerica from a wilderness to civilization. "What journeyings on foot and on horseback through the wilderness, to preach the gospel to these minks and muskrats!" Thoreau exclaims, "who first, no doubt, listened with their red ears out of natural hospitality and courtesy, and afterward from curiosity or even interest, till at length they were 'praying Indians' " (*W* 82). Like the industrious farmers at Billerica, these indefatigable missionaries take advantage of the Indians' "natural hospitality and courtesy" in order to deprive them of their lands and native traditions. In fact, Thoreau exaggerated the success, and consequently the destructive effects, of such missionary activity. But following his critique of the Christian church in "Sunday," the account of efforts to convert the Indians offers a vivid example of what he viewed as the church's narrowness, bigotry, and hypocrisy.

Although the entry into the Merrimack initially reminds Thoreau of missionary activities, it soon evokes radically different associations. "It was in fact an old battle and hunting ground through which we had been floating," he continues, "the ancient dwelling-place of a race of hunters and warriors" (*W* 82). Having first dramatized the Indians' loss of their hunting grounds to towns like Billerica and their weapons and traditions to the Christian church, he suddenly transforms them from passive victims into tough adversaries. The white settlers undergo a similar transformation from farmers and missionaries to embattled soldiers. In the history of Wicasuck Island, which initially seems but another example of the dispossession of the Indians, he emphasizes the role of Jonathan Tyng, who "sat himself down in the midst of his savage enemies, alone, in the wilderness, to defend his home" (*W* 111). Wannalancet's conversion took place in 1674; Tyng's heroic stand took place during King Philip's War in 1675. Thoreau does not call attention to the close proximity of the dates, but the sequence in "Sunday" implies what incidents described in the following chapters illustrate: that New England was not won by the Bible but by the sword.

The history of Wicasuck Island, which was probably not added to "Sunday" until 1848, when Thoreau acquired Fox's *History*, foreshadows his account of Lovewell's Fight at the opening of "Monday." Quoting from a 1694 law "that every settler who deserted a town for fear of the Indians, should forfeit all his rights therein," he continues in "Sunday," "But now . . . a man may desert the fertile frontier territories of truth and justice, which are the State's best lands, for fear of far more insignificant foes, without forfeiting any of his civil rights therein" (W 112). Similarly, in the first draft he had used extracts from "The Ballad of Lovewell's Fight" as a counterpoint to the commerical present, opposing such heroic pioneers to their ignoble offspring in New England. "Alas our brave forefathers have exterminated all the Indians," he remarked, "and their degenerate children . . . rust in disgraceful peace perchance, while enemies as active are still in the field" (FD 38; cf. W 120). But as he read more deeply in colonial history, Thoreau began to realize that, while Lovewell provided a useful contrast to these "degenerate children," the hero of Pequawket also represented an important source of their identity.

Thoreau's account of Lovewell's Fight grew by accretion from various historical sources. At the end of the extracts from "The Ballad of Lovewell's Fight" in the first draft, he interlined a brief comment about two white survivors, whom he read about in Shattuck's *History of the Town of Concord* (FD 38). Drawing upon Shattuck's account, Thoreau later expanded his comments on the fate of these survivors, identified as Eleazer Davis and Josiah Jones (W 120-22). The effect of these details was to underscore the one-sidedness of white man's history. "But alas! of the crippled Indians, and their adventures in the woods," he exclaims, "there is no journal to tell" (W 122). From Fox's *History* he borrowed four stanzas of the mawkish poem describing the death of the English chaplain (W 121), as well as a description of Lovewell's contemptuous response to a warning about Indian ambuscades (W 122). In a late manuscript, Thoreau drew upon Belknap and Penhallow for an account of an earlier hunting expedition, in which Lovewell and forty of his men ambushed a sleeping party of ten Indians and triumphantly marched back to the settlements with the scalps elevated on poles, for which they received a bounty of a hundred pounds. Noting that the incident had earlier been spoken of with "an air of exhultation," as "a capital exploit," he observed: "To us at *this* distance of time, it seems to have been fair enough, as the world goes, considering the intentions of the Indians, but not particularly heroic; four to one, and that one asleep!" (Appendix, no. 2).

In his treatment of Lovewell's expeditions, Thoreau obviously sought to counter the approach taken by earlier historians. Penhallow's major theme, for example, was the "matchless perfidity" of the Indians. Similarly, in a preface to the edition of Penhallow's *History* published by the New Hampshire Historical Society, Benjamin Colman observed: "The Reader must not expect much entertainment or curiosity in the story of a barbarous war with cruel and perfidious savages. It is the benefit of posterity in a religious improvement of this dry and bloody story, that we aim at, in preserving some rememberance thereof."[18] Thoreau's aim was hardly so pious, for by placing the account of Lovewell's earlier success at the end of the section of Lovewell's Fight, he shifted the reader's sympathies to the Indians and set the colonists' mercenary motives in stark relief. But the account, and especially the concluding catalog of the colonists' plunder, destroyed the careful balance between admiration and irony he had achieved in the rest of the section. In effect, what had begun as an intentionally naive evocation of a fierce and heroic battle ended with a skeptical account of a cold-blooded massacre. Possibly for that reason Thoreau omitted the "hunting expedition," thus concluding with Fox's description of Lovewell bending down a small tree to demonstrate how he would treat the Indians. That gesture, made just before his last march, served as a final, ironic comment on the arrogant Lovewell and on these who persisted in viewing him as the "hero" of Pequawket.

To forge a link between the distant past of the Indian wars and the voyage, Thoreau later in "Monday" described the site of the

[18]Samuel Penhallow, *The History of the Wars of New England with the Eastern Indians*, rpt. *Collections of the New-Hampshire Historical Society*, 1 (1824):2 (see *TL* 76). Hereafter cited as *CNHHS*.

house of John Lovewell, "the father of 'famous Captain Lovewell' " (W 161). As Thoreau learned from Fox, John Lovewell had fought in the army of Oliver Cromwell, engaged in the Narragansett swamp fight during King Philip's War, and finally settled on the frontier before 1690. His house on Salmon Brook, where "the hero of Pequawket was born and bred," was also the first house Hannah Duston reached after her escape from the Indians, which in *A Week* represents the final tragic act of the Indian wars. Thoreau, who apparently visited the site during his 1848 tour, is struck by the proximity of these events to his own time. "I have stood in the dent of his cellar on the bank of the brook," he remarks, "and talked there with one whose grandfather had, whose father might have, talked with Lovewell" (W 161). But as he notes of the past in "Dark Ages," the *Dial* essay inserted in the chapter, "It is not a distance of time, but a distance of relation, which makes thus dusky its memorials" (W 156-57, *EEM* 145). In his final account of Indian warfare in "Monday," he seeks to penetrate that darkness and to reveal the living presence of the past along the banks of the Merrimack.

His initial version of the capture of two colonists and the subsequent ambush of a rescue party sent after them was a model of compression (HM 13195, "Monday," 3). Drawing upon a brief account in Penhallow's *History* and its editor's extended elaboration of the incident, Thoreau compressed his own account to roughly two hundred words. The editor, for example, was eager to record facts that would be of interest to both descendants of the early colonists and to the present inhabitants of Nashua. He therefore named the most important actors in the drama, commented in detail on their activities, and carefully recorded the location of each event, even noting that French, the leader of the rescue party, was killed "under an oak tree now standing in a field belonging to Mr. Lund in Merrimack."[19] Thoreau alludes to that bit of local lore in "Tuesday" (W 198), but in the account in "Monday" he stripped the incident to its bare essentials. He thus omitted the names of the captured men, the causes for alarm about them, and the explanation of their ultimate fate. Instead,

[19]*CNHHS,* I:109n.

he focused on the conflict between the rescue party and the Indians. In contrast to Penhallow, who attributed the colonists' defeat to the Indians' superior numbers, and to the editor, who stressed the antagonism between French and Farwell, his chief lieutenant, Thoreau discovered a different lesson in the defeat. By ignoring French, the stubborn and hot-headed leader of the party, he underscored the role of Farwell, whose wary knowledge of the wilderness led to his survival. His emphasis on Farwell also related this isolated incident to Lovewell's Fight, where Farwell, who was clearly unlucky in his commanders, finally "left his bones in the wilderness" (W 168).

Like his commentary on Lovewell's Fight, Thoreau's account of the ambush at Thornton's Ferry began with a specific incident and developed into a more generalized meditation on the past. For example, whereas the initial version ends with Farwell's escape and Thoreau's adaptation of four lines from the poem "Rio Verde," he later alluded to the burial at Dunstable, which reminds him of lines from the Robin Hood ballads (W 167). These two poems, one concerning the conflict between the Spanish and the Moors, the other a product of English folklore, suggest the universality and timelessness of the brief encounter depicted in A Week. He also added an anecdote he had been "told by an inhabitant of Tyngsboro', who had the story from his ancestors" (W 166), others from Fox's History, and Gookin's comment that before King Philips' War "the English soldiers made a nothing of the Indians, and . . . many reckoned that it was no other but Veni, vidi, vici" (W 168). As a counterpoint to these foolish soldiers, precursors to the arrogant Captain Lovewell, Thoreau in the penultimate paragraph celebrates Farwell, "whose name still reminds us of twilight days and forest scouts on Indian trails" (W 168). But the word twilight reveals the true theme of his discourse, the unreality and inaccessibility of colonial history. Remarking that "posterity will doubt if such things ever were," he concludes: "Now, only a few arrow-heads are turned up by the plow. In the Pelasgic, the Etruscan, or the British story, there is nothing so shadowy and unreal" (W 168-69).

Thoreau's effort to delineate that spectral past takes a different form in "Tuesday," in which his theme is commerce between

Indians and whites. Initially he seems to acknowledge that such commerce had resulted in further conflict and the ultimate displacement of the Indians. In the first draft he noted that their course lay between "Merrimack and Litchfield once called Brenton's Farm, and the Indian Natticott" (FD 52). Probably after reading Fox, he revised and expanded the remark to stress the significance of that series of names: "Our course this morning lay between the territories of Merrimack, on the west, and Litchfield, once called Brenton's Farm, on the east, which townships were anciently the Indian Naticook. Brenton was a fur trader among the Indians, and these lands were granted to him in 1656" (W 194). Cromwell's Trading Post teaches the same lesson, for, although the Indians drove Cromwell away, when the brothers ostensibly visit the site, the only visible signs of the earliest inhabitants are a few relics scattered about a spot "where plainly there had once stood a wigwam of the Indians with whom Cromwell traded, and who fished and hunted here *before he came*" (W 197; emphasis added). Implicitly, the trader's arrival signaled the beginning of the end of the Indians' activities along the banks of the Merrimack.

Despite the implications of Cromwell's story, which suggests that traders spearheaded the conquest of the wilderness and of the Indians, Thoreau sought to distinguish between trade, or exploitation, and commerce, or mutual enrichment. In a brief digression on commerce added to his celebration of the boatmen in "Tuesday," he took a much more positive view of commerce. Inspired by Melville's *Typee*, which he apparently read shortly after its publication in 1846, Thoreau originally drafted the passage on commerce in the Journal account of his trip to Maine (J 2:315-16). He later revised and compressed it for A Week, where he asks, "Who can help being affected at the thought of the very fine and slight, but positive relation, in which the savage inhabitants of some remote isle stand to the mysterious white mariner, the child of the sun?" (W 212). Like *Typee*, the passage in A Week is shot through with wishful thinking and longing. But in contrast to Melville, who stressed the destruction wrought by the traders and by the missionaries who followed, Thoreau ignores the consequences of this first idyllic meeting of the races. Instead, his emphasis in "Tuesday" on the "positive relation" inspired by this commerce between savages and whites modulates between the conflicts described in "Monday" and the friendships between Indians and whites celebrated in "Wednesday."

Thoreau's preoccupation with the initial contacts between the races is inspired by the brothers' movement up the Merrimack, which offers brief glimpses of the primal wilderness. "Sometimes this forenoon the country appeared in its primitive state," he notes early in "Tuesday," "and as if the Indian still inhabited it" (W 194). Toward the end of the chapter he briefly digresses on Alexander Henry's *Travels and Adventures in Canada and the Indian Territories* (1809), which "reads like the argument to a great poem on the primitive state of the country and its inhabitants" (W 219, J 2:261). In fact, Henry's *Adventures* took place between 1760 and 1776, by which time white settlers had pushed far west of the Merrimack. But Thoreau's reference to "the primitive state of the country" sets the scene for a historical note on a series of meetings that took place much earlier, when Indian tribes struggled along the banks of the Merrimack.

The note on the war between the Penacooks and Mohawks reveals the tension between then and now: between the thrilling past and the peaceful present. As Fox pointed out, the war paved the way for white domination, since the greatest part of the Penacooks, who had initially resisted efforts to Christianize them, were destroyed, and the "remnant, dispirited and powerless, united with the Wamesits, and became *'praying Indians.'* "[20] The two letters included in "Tuesday" indicate that the war forced the Penacooks to seek protection from the settlers (W 220, 221), but Thoreau does not stress the connection between these events and the conversions described in "Sunday." Indeed, he seems less interested in the historical consequences of the war than in the fact that these two warlike tribes—"one of which is now extinct, while the other, though it is still represented by a miserable remnant, has long since disappeared from its ancient hunting grounds"—had ever existed along the banks of the river. "Pen-

---

[20]Charles J. Fox, *History of the Old Township of Dunstable* (Nashua, N.H.: Charles T. Gill, 1846), p. 20.

acooks and Mohawks!" he exclaims, *"ubique gentium sunt?"* (*W* 220). Stressing the changes along the Merrimack, he contrasts the Penacooks to the brothers, who go "unalarmed" on their peaceful way, "reading the New England Gazetteer, and seeing no traces of 'Mohogs' on the banks" (*W* 221).

Thoreau was nonetheless eager to demonstrate that the heroic spirit of the Indians and the early pioneers still survived in New England. The *Musketaquid* was laden with "guns and ammunition enough to stock a galleon," he noted in the first draft, part of the outfit that proves of so much interest to the masons encountered at the end of "Tuesday" (FD 4, 62). In a revised and expanded version of the opening of "Wednesday," Thoreau later added that, the following morning, the masons stumbled upon their campsite, where they paused to examine the brothers' equipment. "They handled our guns with especial pleasure," he remarked, "and thought that they should like to join us for the sake of the game." That demonstration of the tenacity of the hunter's instinct prompted a surprisingly un-Thoreauvian digression on the gun, a link between the early settlers and the present inhabitants of New England: "Like the first settlers who rarely went to the field, or even to church, without their guns, we their descendents have not yet quite outgrown this habit of pioneers" (Appendix, no. 7).

The gun was a potent symbol of the frontier spirit, but Thoreau, like Cooper, found it difficult to dissociate guns from the effects they had wrought. "If the Indian and the bear are exterminated," he lamely asserted, "the partridge and the rabbit are left." The survival of small game hardly compensated for the extermination of the Indian, nor did it do much to dignify what Thoreau called man's "reminiscence of the hunter life." In fact, elsewhere in *A Week* Thoreau describes the brothers' "disgust" after killing some squirrels for their supper, the "practice of a barbarous era" (*W* 224). There, he anticipated the argument of "Higher Laws," where he defended hunting as part of a boy's education but insisted, "No humane being, past the thoughtless age of boyhood, will wantonly murder any creature, which holds its life by the same tenure that he does" (*Wa* 212). His evolving concern for the sanctity of all life probably prompted Thoreau to omit both the reference to their arsenal and the incongruous paean to the gun from *A Week*, in which he mourns the death of his brother, the destruction of the wilderness, and the extermination of the Indians.

Signs of their extermination are everywhere apparent in "Wednesday." Although Thoreau omitted the digression on Indian relics, possibly because it relied so heavily on Belknap and smacked of antiquarianism, he substituted far more evocative references to the Indian remains along the Merrimack. For example, after reading of some Indian graves near Bedford in the *Collections of the New Hampshire Historical Society*,[21] he added a charged description of those "graves of the aborigines" to "Wednesday": "The land still bears this scar here, and time is slowly crumbling the bones of a race. Yet without fail every spring since they first fished and hunted here, the brown thrasher has heralded the morning from a birch or alder spray, and the undying race of reed-birds still rustles through the withering grass. But these bones rustle not. These mouldering elements are slowly preparing for another metamorphosis, to serve new masters, and what was the Indian's will ere long be white man's sinew" (*W* 237).

The passage represents one of the most despairing meditations in *A Week* on the fate of the Indian. Alluding to Ezekiel's vision in the valley of dry bones (Ezekiel 37), Thoreau implicitly suggests that these bones will *not* live. Even the seasonal renewal of nature, the crucial source of hope and optimism in *A Week*, seems to offer no rebirth to the remains of the Indian. In his meditation on Elisha's grave in "Friday," he predicts a radically different "metamorphosis" for these "mouldering elements"; in "Wednesday" he can only prophesy the Indian's bondage to his "new masters." To emphasize further the crushing fate set in motion by the white settlers, Thoreau later in "Wednesday" bitterly notes: "The monuments of heroes and the temples of the gods which may once have stood on the banks of this river, are now, at any rate, returned to dust and primitive soil. The murmur of un-

---

[21]"A Topographical and Historical Sketch of Bedford, in the County of Hillsborough," *CNHHS*, I:295.

chronicled nations has died away along these shores, and once more Lowell and Manchester are on the trail of the Indian" (*W* 249).

The reference to those "unchronicled nations" reveals Thoreau's continuing hostility to white man's history, but in "Wednesday" he also uses that history to memorialize two of the Indians' unsung heroes, Passaconaway and Wannalancet. Expanding the brief references to Wannalancet in the first draft (FD 65), he later added a memorial to the two great sachems of the Penacooks, beginning with Passaconaway, who kept his tribe out of war with the English. As Thoreau noted, he was a powwow, whose people believed

> ["that he could make water burn, rocks move, and trees dance, and metamorphose himself into a flaming man; that in winter he could raise a green leaf out (*W* 252)] of the ashes of a dry one, and produce a living snake from the skin of a dead one"   He was a sort of transcendentalist in his day. His son Wonolansett was also the friend of the English, and withdrew to Penacook, now Concord, from the scene of the war. On his return afterward he visited the minister of Chelmsford, and "wished to know whether Chelmsford had suffered much during the war; and being informed that it had not, and that God should be thanked for it, Wonolansett replied, 'Me next.' " In his old age he at length "brought his mind to believe in christianity," and is reported to have said, "I must acknowledge I have all my days been used to pass in an old canoe, and now you exhort me to change and leave my old canoe, and embark in a new one, which I have hitherto been unwilling; but now I yield up myself to your advice, and enter into a new canoe, and do engage to pray to God hereafter." (MH 15, O, paged 297-98)

The memorial to Passaconaway and Wannalancet underwent changes that radically altered its impact. In this early version

Thoreau quoted Belknap's description of Passaconaway's reputed powers, Allen's account of Wannalancet's return to Chelmsford, and Gookin's famous report of Wannalancet's conversion in a sequence that illustrated the Indian's gradual loss of autonomy. As Thoreau knew from reading Gookin, powwows, who were reputed to "hold familiarity with the devil," were prohibited from exercising their "diabolical practices" within English jurisdiction, since they were considered "great hinderers of the Indians in yielding obedience unto the gospel."[22] That fact, added to Belknap's description of Passaconaway's reputed powers, gave added edge to Thoreau's ironic remark that the Indian chief was "a sort of transcendentalist in his day." But it also made Wannalancet's conversion to Christianity all the more poignant, since it represented the son's final yielding of his father's power and potency. Thoreau, however, later shifted Wannalancet's speech to "Sunday," adding an account of Passaconaway's farewell speech to the Penacooks, which Gookin compared to Balaam's prophecy in Numbers (W 253). The changes were dramatic, for, in the altered sequence in "Wednesday," Thoreau first describes Passaconaway in his role of powwow and prophet, then states that his son followed his advice about avoiding war with the English, and concludes with Wannalancet's triumphant remark to the minister of Chelmsford (W 252-53). Instead of a weary convert to Christianity, Wannalancet in "Wednesday" remains the powerful chief of the Penacooks, by whose grace Chelmsford escaped the ravages of King Philip's War.

The tribute to the leaders of the Penacooks reveals the one-sidedness of American history. They had guaranteed the survival of settlements like Chelmsford, yet their friendship to the white settlers had gone unrewarded and unrecorded. Following a description of a monument to Major General John Stark, the hero of the Battle of Bennington, Thoreau in an early manuscript remarked, "The graves of Passaconoway and Wonolansett are marked by no monument, & their native river knows them no more." With characteristic restraint, he later revised it to read,

[22]Daniel Gookin, *Historical Collections of the Indians in New England,* rpt. *Collections of the Massachusetts Historical Society,* 1 (1792):154.

"The graves of Passaconoway and Wonolansett are marked by no monument on the banks of their native river" (MH 15, P; cf. *W* 254). In contrast to Stark, and even to the lawyers, doctors, and ministers eulogized in the *Gazetteer,* which Thoreau gleefully plundered for the ironic catalog of their banal deeds in "Wednesday" (*W* 254-55), the Indian heroes of the American past were doomed to oblivion by the white settlers who dispossessed them of their land and their rightful place in history.

Although he contrasts Stark's fame to the oblivion of Passaconaway and Wannalancet, Thoreau found much to admire in the general, whom he read about in a reprint of Robert Rogers's *Reminiscences of the French Wars.* Born in a frontier settlement along the Merrimack, Stark became Rogers's chief lieutenant during the French and Indian wars. Moreover, in contrast to the leader of the Rangers, who later abandoned America, Stark went on to become a hero of the American Revolution, during which he fought at the Battle of Bunker Hill and won the Battle of Bennington. But what most attracted Thoreau was the fact that Stark had been a captive of the Indians, from whom he learned the lore of the wilderness. Following a brief account of Stark's life, Thoreau in an early version of the tribute described that captivity in detail (Appendix, no. 8).

Thoreau treated it as the central episode in Stark's life. He closely followed the language and arrangement of the account by Luther Roby, who made a similar point about its impact on the hero: "During this captivity, Stark acquired that thorough knowledge of the Indian character, and of their stratagems of war, which he turned to such good account against them, and their allies the French, in the war which ensued."[23] But, in contrast, Thoreau related the captivity to Stark's exploits during the Revolution rather than to his efforts during the French and Indian wars, in which Stark had fought against the tribe that, as Thoreau notes, had granted him "the title of young chief, with the honor

[23]Robert Rogers, *Reminiscences of the French War,* [ed. Luther Roby] (Concord, N.H.: Luther Roby, 1831), p. 174. For an interesting discussion of this volume, see Richard Slotkin, *Regeneration through Violence* (Middletown, Conn.: Wesleyan Univ. Press, 1973), pp. 444–46.

of adoption into the tribe." Thoreau also ignored the fact that, when Stark was captured, his brother narrowly escaped death and another man was killed. His capture and captivity were thus transformed into a kind of heroic idyll, a demonstration of the kinship between a white man and the Indians that transcended the history of conflicts between the races.

Thoreau possibly omitted the story of Stark's captivity because it distracted from the account in "Wednesday" of Wawatam and Alexander Henry, a far more compelling story of friendship between the races. As Richard Slotkin has observed, Henry was one of the first writers to portray his captivity in terms that reflected "a sympathy for the Indian life."[24] In a compressed version of episodes in Henry's *Adventures,* Thoreau in the first draft briefly portrayed "the simple but determined friendship which Wawatam testified for Henry the fur-trader" (FD 77). Like Stark, Henry had been captured by the Indians, who later adopted him into the tribe. But Thoreau avoided references to Henry's captivity and referred to Henry and Wawatam as brothers rather than as adoptive father and son. Stressing the timeless dimension of their friendship, Thoreau began his account in the past tense, with the friendship the Indian warrior "testified" for the fur trader, but continued in the present tense: "The stern imperturbable man comes to his lodge, and affirms that he is the white brother whom he saw in his dream, and adopts him henceforth. And they practise not hostility but friendship thereafter as children of one father. Having a welcome always ready for each other. Wawatam buries the hatchet as it regards his friend, and they feast and hunt together, no longer coveting each other's scalps" (FD 77; cf. W 274-75).

Thoreau revised this passage to underscore the austere nature of their friendship. Identifying the source of the episode, he added that Wawatam came to Henry's lodge "after fasting, solitude, and mortification of body." (For Wawatam, no less than Thoreau, friendship was clearly a serious business.) He omitted the second and third sentences, which were awkward and redundant, and revised the final sentence to read, "and they hunt and feast and

[24]Slotkin, p. 328.

make maple-sugar together." Whatever significance he may have attached to making maple sugar, Thoreau was clearly eager to avoid the implication that Henry and Wawatam had *ever* coveted each other's scalps. Initially, Thoreau also played down the fact that Wawatam was hostile to other whites, for in the first draft he deleted a description of Wawatam's protection of Henry when the warrior "would drink the fire water—or sip his bowl of soup made of his English prisoners" (FD TN 77.36). But he apparently decided that Wawatam's protection of his friend outweighed his participation in a cannibal feast, for the sentence appears in revised form in *A Week*. Amusingly, Thoreau was obviously more repelled by the "fire water," which he euphemistically refers to as "white man's milk," than by the "soup made of his English prisoners," which he revised to "human broth made of the trader's fellow-countrymen" (*W* 275).

The most significant change Thoreau made in his version of the Wawatam and Alexander Henry story was the addition of a description of their parting "after a long winter of undisturbed and happy intercourse." As Leslie Fiedler points out, Thoreau does not explain the reasons for their separation, "since making them clear would demand revealing that their association is not altogether voluntary."[25] Quoting Henry's final description of Wawatam, who "commenced an address to the Kichi Manito, beseeching him to take care of me, his brother, till we should next meet," he abruptly concludes, "We never hear of him again" (*W* 275). In the first draft their story is never-ending; in *A Week*, Wawatam and Henry are parted by hostile, mysterious forces. Their story thus illustrates a point Thoreau makes earlier in his discourse on friendship, where he notes, "Friendship is evanescent in every man's experience" (*W* 261). But it also illustrates a larger historical truth about Indian-white relations. The friend-

---

[25]Leslie Fiedler, *The Return of the Vanishing American* (New York: Stein and Day, 1968), p. 115. Fiedler discusses Thoreau's adjustments of Henry's account in detail, suggesting that Thoreau sought to evoke "a *Pagan* Paradise Regained . . . in the forests of the New World, a natural Eden lost when Christianity intervened—which means when woman intervened, when Hannah Duston appeared," pp. 115–16.

ship between Wawatam and Alexander Henry demonstrated that, for a season, an Indian and a white could meet without "coveting each other's scalps"; but the abrupt conclusion of their story, and the bloody scalps in the bottom of Hannah Duston's canoe in "Thursday," reveals how transitory that season had been.

The idyllic version of Henry's captivity contrasts sharply with Thoreau's account of Hannah Duston's captivity and escape, which he began to draft in 1847. Unlike Henry's obscure story, her tale had been told and retold, first by Cotton Mather in the *Magnalia Christi Americana*, then, in the nineteenth century, by Timothy Dwight, John Greenleaf Whittier, Nathaniel Hawthorne, and a host of lesser writers.[26] Thoreau may have been familiar with Hawthorne's account, which appeared in 1836, but his primary source was Benjamin L. Mirick's *History of Haverhill, Massachusetts*, which also provided a description of the first settlers of Concord earlier in "Thursday" (*W* 303). Although he does not refer to Mirick in his version of the Hannah Duston story in *A Week*, Thoreau in an early draft of the opening of the story briefly alluded to the history of Haverhill, even as he transformed Mirick's account:

> On the 31st day of March one hundred and forty two
> years before this, probably about this time in the
> afternoon, there were hurriedly paddling down this
> part of the river, which was rapid and swolen by the
> melting snow, between the pine woods which then
> fringed these banks, two white women & a boy, who
> had left an island at the mouth of the Contoocook
> before daybreak. They were slightly clad for the
> season, in the English fashion, and handled their
> paddles unskilfully but with nervous energy and
> determination, and at the bottom of their canoe lay the
> bleeding scalps of ten of the aborigines. They were
> Hannah Dustan, and her nurse Mary Neff, and an

[26]See Robert Arner, "The Story of Hannah Duston: Cotton Mather to Thoreau," *American Transcendental Quarterly* 18 (1973):19–23 (Thoreau spelled her last name "Dustan").

English boy named Samuel Lennardson, escaping
from captivity among the Indians. On the 15th of
March, about twenty Indians had come out of the
woods and made an attack on the outskirts of the
infant settlement of Haverhill, according to the history
of that town, and compelled Hannah Dustan to rise
from childbed, and half dressed, with one foot bare,
accompanied by her nurse, to commence an uncertain
march, in still inclement weather, through the snow
and the wilderness. She had seen her seven elder
children flee with their father, but knew not their
fate.— He on his horse, unable to choose which one
to save, hovered in the rear of this little band of
fugitives, returning the fire of the Indians and
checking their pursuit, and though overtaken by them,
by his courage and skilful conduct, at length got them
all off safely without a wound.— She had seen her
infant's brains dashed out against an apple tree, and
had left her own and her neighbors' dwellings in
ashes. The Indians at length retreated in small parties,
fearing pursuit, having burned nine houses and killed
twenty-seven settlers, carrying thirteen prisoners with
them; and as they went, they cut out the tongues of
oxen, and broiled and ate them, leaving the oxen alive.
When she reached the wigwam of her captor, situated
on an island in the Merrimack, she had been told that
she was soon . . . (HM 13195, "Thursday," 3, paged
389-90; cf. W 320-21)

Where Mirick began his account with the attack on Haverhill,
Thoreau begins with the trio's flight down the Merrimack. Unlike
the friendship between Wawatam and Alexander Henry, which
seems to exist outside of time, their flight is carefully placed in
time and history. Significantly, however, Thoreau does not initially
identify the trio. Instead, he describes them as alien presences
in the wilderness. After noting that they were "slightly clad for
the season, in the English fashion," he originally continued, "and
exhibited unusual marks of anxiety & fatigue." His revision, "and

handled their paddles unskilfully but with nervous energy and determination," underscores their lack of wilderness skills and makes them seem less fearful than purposeful. Their grim determination prepares for the carefully timed shock of "the bleeding scalps," later revised to "the still bleeding scalps of ten of the aborigines." Only then does Thoreau identify them and recount the events that led up to their flight down the river. The sympathy Hannah Duston's name might evoke is thus countered by the awe and terror her act inspires.

Thoreau's account of the Indian attack on Haverhill is intentionally sketchy. For example, in the manuscript he revised and compressed the opening of the fourth sentence to read, "On the 15th of March previous, she had been compelled to rise from childbed. . . ." He also deleted the description of her husband's heroic retreat and the gruesome details of the massacre and the Indians' withdrawal. In contrast, most historians stressed the Indians' savagery and dwelled upon her husband's heroic actions. Mirick, for example, began with a description of the Indians, "arrayed with all the terrors of a savage war-dress, with their muskets charged for the contest, their tomahawks drawn for the slaughter, and their scalping knives unsheathed and glittering in the sunbeams," and concluded with the long and edifying poem "The Father's Choice," which ends, "The sheltering roof is near'd, is gain'd,/All, all the dear ones safe!"[27] But Thoreau allows nothing to distract from the central drama. Moreover, while he merely alludes to the events—her abduction, the murder of her child, and the threat that she would be forced to run the gauntlet naked—that may have justified killing the Indians and taking their scalps, he describes the act in detail (W 321-22). We are not, however, asked to judge the act; rather, we are made to feel its consequences: "Early this morning this deed was performed, and now, perchance, these tired women and this boy, their clothes stained with blood, and their minds racked with alternate resolution and fear, are making a hasty meal of parched corn and moose-meat, while their canoe glides under these pine roots

[27]Benjamin L. Mirick, *The History of Haverhill, Massachusetts* (Haverhill: Thayer, 1832), pp. 86, 95.

whose stumps are still standing on the bank. They are thinking of the dead whom they have left behind on that solitary isle far up the stream, and of the relentless living warriors who are in pursuit. Every withered leaf which the winter has left seems to know their story, and in its rustling to repeat it and betray them" (*W* 322).

In contrast to the distant and detached tone of the opening of his account, Thoreau's recapitulation of the trio's flight is involved and immediate. Although it is still March, it is not with "one hundred and forty-two years before this," but with "this morning"—each person's morning—that he begins, suggesting that we are all heirs of her act and that she, like Captain Lovewell, is a primary source of New England's identity. Hannah and her party, first remembered because they made their escape "probably about this time in the afternoon . . . down this part of the river," suddenly and quite literally appear on the Merrimack, as "their canoe glides under *these* pine roots whose stumps are *still* standing on the bank." Shifting from the past to the present tense, Thoreau suspends time by using the present participle. Unlike Mirick, who blandly remarked that they commenced their journey "with cheerful hearts,"[28] he evokes the psychological terrors of their flight. Racked by guilt and anxiety, Hannah and her companions have fallen from nature, whose every withered leaf seems to betray them.

Thoreau links their fall from nature with a series of catastrophes. As he depicts them passing "an Indian grave . . . or the frame of the wigwam . . . or the withered stalks still rustling in the Indian's solitary cornfield," whose remains are described earlier in *A Week,* he suddenly exclaims, "These are the only traces of man,—a fabulous wild man to us" (*W* 323). Hannah Duston is implicated in the destruction of the Indian and of the frontier itself, "to the white man a drear and howling wilderness, but to the Indian a home, adapted to his nature, and cheerful as the smile of the Great Spirit" (*W* 323). Returning from a visit to Mount Washington, or Agiocochook, the home of the Great Spirit, the brothers silently watch as "the swift stream" bears Hannah's party

[28]Ibid., p. 91.

"onward to the settlements." As Robert Arner has remarked, Thoreau has turned the Merrimack into "a river of time, a stream of consciousness, bearing upon its spring freshets the detritus of the past and the driftwood of the present."[29] Breaking that visionary spell, Thoreau begins the final paragraph, "According to the historian," Hannah and her party "reached their homes in safety, with their trophies, for which the General Court paid them fifty pounds" (*W* 323). In fact, Mirick fastidiously noted that they received the fifty pounds "as a reward for their heroism."[30] Thoreau, however, once again calls attention to the scalps, for, even as he returns Hannah to history and to her family, he stresses the consequences of this bloody episode in the Indian wars, an episode he links to the Fall of Man. "The family of Hannah Dustan all assembled alive once more, except the infant whose brains were dashed out against the apple-tree," he concludes, reminding us of the savagery on both sides of the contest, "and there have been many who in later times have lived to say that they have eaten of the fruit of that apple-tree" (*W* 323-24).

The Hannah Duston story is followed by a brief disquisition on time and history. "This seems a long while ago," Thoreau remarks, "and yet it happened since Milton wrote his Paradise Lost." Implicitly, sometime after the epic was published in 1667, exactly thirty years before Hannah Duston's act, another paradise had been lost in America. He again stresses that our distance from the past is not one of time but of relation. The era when Penacooks and Pawtuckets roamed "these now cultivated shores" thus seems "more remote than the dark ages." He even includes a slightly revised version of the passage beginning, "On beholding a picture of a New England village" in "A Walk to Wachusett" (*Ex* 149; cf. *W* 324). But in "A Walk to Wachusett" the passage substituted for an account of Mary Rowlandson's captivity; in *A Week* it follows Hannah Duston's story, a demonstration that what seems remote is, in fact, everpresent and accessible to our imaginations. Although he asserts that the "age of the world is great enough for our imaginations, even according to the Mosaic account," and

[29]Arner, p. 22.
[30]Mirick, p. 92.

recounts the stages of that history, "a wearisome while," from "Adam and Eve . . . to—America," Thoreau also notes that the lives of sixty old women would span it. Stressing the short span of "Universal History," he concludes, "It will not take a very great grand-daughter of hers [Eve's] to be in at the death of Time" (*W* 325).

That cryptic reference to "the death of Time" foreshadows the meditation on Elisha's apple tree in "Friday," Thoreau's final excursion into colonial history in *A Week*. The story of a friendly Indian who was killed in one of the early wars between the races in New England is also one of the most obscure and, by conventional historical standards, one of the least significant episodes in the book. The story appears in none of his favorite sources, so Thoreau may, as he says, have heard it from an inhabitant of Tyngsborough. But he and John almost certainly did not hear it in 1839, as Thoreau implies, since the story was apparently not inserted in "Friday" until after his 1848 trip to New Hampshire, during which he and Ellery Channing passed through Tyngsborough. Wherever he unearthed the story (and he may have fabricated it), Thoreau made brilliant use of it in *A Week*, where it recalls his description of the Indian graves near Bedford in "Wednesday." There, he treats the graves as emblems of the Indian's death and continuing servitude to "new masters" (*W* 273); in "Friday" he uses Elisha's grave to suggest the possibility of rebirth.

Thoreau does so by removing the destruction of the Indians from white man's history and placing it in the context of natural history. In the manuscript of *A Week* Elisha's story followed "O River tell me what," a revised and compressed version of the poem entitled "Walden" in the 1838 Journal (*J* 1:47-48), and a paragraph describing the great freshets on the Merrimack (MH 15, U; cf. *W* 355-56). Thoreau, however, later omitted the poetical tribute to the river, whose "surging words," "flow of thought," and effort to express "truth" inspire his own verse. Perhaps he felt that such insistent personification diminished the natural force of the Merrimack, whose unbridled power is illustrated by the freshet of 1785, when the river rose nearly twenty feet. Following that apt preface, Thoreau in *A Week* continues: "The rev-

olutions of nature tell as fine tales, and make as interesting revelations, on this river's banks, as on the Euphrates or the Nile.
This apple-tree, which stands within a few rods of the river, is
called 'Elisha's apple-tree,' from a friendly Indian, who was anciently in the service of Jonathan Tyng, and, with one other man,
was killed here by his own race in one of the Indian wars" (*W*
356; cf. MH 15, P).

As his allusions to those biblical rivers and his emphasis on
revolutions-revelations suggest, Thoreau is less interested in historical facts than in natural and supernatural phenomena. Consequently, while his treatment of the historical episode is vague
and sketchy—Thoreau tells us who but not where, when, how,
or why—his description of its aftermath is almost pedantically
precise: "He was buried close by, no one knew exactly where,
but in the flood of 1785, so great a weight of water standing over
the grave, caused the earth to settle where it had once been disturbed, and when the flood went down, a sunken spot, exactly
of the form and size of the grave, revealed its locality; but this
was now lost again, and no future flood can detect it; yet, no
doubt, Nature will know how to point it out in due time, if it be
necessary, by methods yet more searching and unexpected" (*W*
356-57). The contrast between the beginning and end of that
long and intricate sentence is striking. At first Thoreau treats
nature as a phenomenon whose actions may be measured and
observed; by the end of the sentence he transforms nature into
a mysterious and enigmatic force, a participant in the Last Judgment whose methods are beyond our understanding. In the less
evocative manuscript version, he had written "by methods yet
more fine & searching in due time" and concluded: "Thus it seems
there is not only the crisis when the spirit ceases to inspire and
expand the body, marked by a fresh mound in the churchyard,
but there is also a crisis when the body crumbles and ceases to
take up room in nature, marked by a fainter depression in the
earth— Bodies displace earth, Spirits displace air. Every man
is destined to displace for a season his own bulk of earth. So long
perhaps his fame endures" (MH 15, P; cf. *W* 357).

Thoreau intensified the drama of these two crises. Deleting the
weak and evasive "it seems," he altered "crumbles and ceases,"

which suggests slow decay, to an abrupt "ceases." He also omitted the final three sentences, thus concluding with the stark vision of "a fainter depression in the earth" rather than with conventional sentiments about the transience of human life and fame. But those sentiments remind us that his meditation on Elisha's grave is related to his earlier remarks on tombstones and epitaphs, prompted by a glimpse of the Dunstable graveyard in "Monday," as well as to his elegiac description of the unmarked Indian graves in "Wednesday." Instead of contrasting the fate of the white set-tlers and the Indians or mourning the absence of memorials to the Indians, Thoreau in "Friday" depicts the fate of one Indian as the common fate of mankind. In that respect Elisha's grave is a powerful memento mori. Yet, like the grave of the prophet Elisha, into which a dead man was cast, "and when the man was let down, and touched the bones of Elisha, he revived, and stood up" (2 Kings 13:21), Elisha's grave seems to promise a resur-rection through the miraculous power of nature.

Like the larger narrative in which it plays so important a part, Thoreau's history of Indian-white relations ends on an optimistic note. Elisha's apple tree, he observes, bears "a native fruit, which was prized by the family" of the farmer who also raises "the blood peach," one fruit of which "makes an impression of paradisiacal fertility and luxury" (W 357-58). Flourishing on what was once a bloody battleground between the races, these rugged varieties thus offer a counterharvest to the apple tree in the Hannah Duston story, whose bitter fruits remind us of the Fall of Man. The ques-tion implicit in "Wednesday"—"Can these bones live?"—is finally answered in "Friday," as the brothers once again approach Wi-casuck Island, original point of departure for Thoreau's exploration of New England's dark past. Meditating there on a bit of local lore, "the particulars of which affair were told us on the spot" (W 356), he elevates those particulars of colonial history into the sta-tus of poetic truth and transforms the historical destruction of the Indians into a powerful scene in the drama of life, death, and rebirth in A Week.

5

The Literary Tradition

THOREAU'S PREOCCUPATION WITH the lost Indian past is closely related to his literary interests in *A Week*. As he embraced the figure of the noble savage, tragic victim of the advance of white civilization, so he clung to a version of literary history in which the advances of education and learning lead to the decline of imagination and creativity. Homer and Ossian, the primitive bards celebrated in "Sunday" and "Friday," thus share the vigor and simplicity of the American Indian. The destruction of the wilderness is consequently mirrored in the steady loss of spontaneity and naturalness from Homer through Anacreon to Aulus Persius Flaccus in the classical tradition, and, in the British tradition, from Ossian through Chaucer to poets of Thoreau's era. Like his depiction of the Indians and their world, Thoreau's primitivistic conception of literary history was deeply rooted in the late eighteenth century, especially in the view of the epic developed by Scottish defenders of Macpherson's so-called translations of Ossian and in the approach to medieval and Renaissance poetry sketched in works like Thomas Warton's *History of English Poetry*. But just as Thoreau appropriated the particulars of colonial history, he made the somewhat shopworn clichés of eighteenth-century criticism serve his own special purposes in *A Week*.

If he was slow to discover the uses of colonial history, Thoreau quickly learned the uses of the literary past, which strongly colored his own early career. At Harvard, where his literary habits and tastes developed, he began to read deeply in the classics of Continental and English poetry, works that continued to inspire his own literary efforts. Under Emerson's tutelage Thoreau began to assume the role of scholar-poet. His first contributions to the *Dial* were thus a critical article, "Aulus Persius Flaccus," and "Sympathy," first of a number of poems published there and later included in *A Week*. As his hopes to become a poet waned, he devoted more and more time to scholarly pursuits, especially to translations of Greek poetry and drama for the *Dial*. Between 1841 and 1844 he also worked sporadically on an anthology of English poetry. Though the project was never completed, his reading inspired "Sir Walter Raleigh" and "Homer. Ossian. Chaucer.," both of which later played a role in *A Week,* which also received many extracts from English poetry. That method of inserting poems, quotations, and digressions on literary matters was anticipated in essays like "Natural History of Massachusetts," "A Walk to Wachusett," and "A Winter Walk," which demonstrate the concord between Thoreau's early poetic and scholarly efforts and his growing interest in narrative prose, an interest that finally spurred him to begin *A Week* in 1844.

His literary interests provided the final thread in the increasingly complex weave of *A Week.* The first draft contained numerous poems and quotations, but only a few passages on literature. As Thoreau revised and expanded the manuscript, however, he gathered material on writers and writing from the early Journal and unpublished essays like "Sir Walter Raleigh." He also inserted a series of essays and translations originally published in the *Dial.* In fact, it appears that his latest additions to *A Week* included some of his earliest writings. Although he incorporated a good deal of material from the period of his literary apprenticeship, Thoreau arranged these materials in an intricate scheme in *A Week.* Through poems and translations, essays on writers, and digressions on books and style, he relates his own efforts in *A Week* to a long literary tradition. Early in the book he proclaims the dawning of a new literary era in Concord. In what amounts to a compressed history of western literature, Thoreau in later chapters expresses his ideals of writing and charts the decline of such writing from early epic poets to poets of more civilized eras. Finally, he asserts his own potential role in the creation of a native American literature, rooted in nature and bearing fruit in works like *A Week.*

Thoreau, like many more-recent graduates, complained about the quality of his college education, but Harvard helped prepare him for a literary career. The official curriculum stressed the classics of ancient and English literature, which play such an important part in his writings. His longest collegiate essay was a summary and review of *Introductions to the Study of the Greek*

Classic Poets, which Henry Nelson Coleridge intended "to enable the youthful student to form a more just and liberal judgment of the characters and merits of the Greek Poets" (*EEM* 50). As a supplement to his assigned work, Thoreau kept an "Index rerum," which contained reading lists, extracts from his reading, and book reviews written for a Harvard literary society. Without the means to buy many books, he also copied passages from volumes like Chalmers's *Works of the English Poets* into a notebook entitled "Miscellaneous Extracts," first of a series of commonplace books that provided many of the numerous quotations in his early essays and *A Week.*[1]

Harvard also inculcated a respect for the literary life. Asked to expound upon the "Privileges and Pleasures of a Literary Man," Thoreau in 1835 observed, "He holds sweet converse with the sages of antiquity, and gathers wisdom from their discourse—he enjoys the fruit of their labors—their knowledge is his knowledge—their wisdom his inheritance" (*EEM* 20). There, he defined a literary life in traditional scholarly terms, anticipating the numerous works of criticism and translation among his early writings. But in an essay on the topic "Advantages and disadvantages of foreign influence on American Literature," written a year later, he defined a different task for the American writer or scholar. Balancing his own admiration for the great English writers against his country's need for "a literature peculiarly its own," Thoreau faulted poets for singing "of skylarks and nightingales, perched on hedges, to the neglect of the homely robin-red-breast, and the straggling rail-fences of their own native land" (*EEM* 38, 41).

Emerson made similar points with far greater passion and eloquence in "The American Scholar," an address delivered before the Phi Beta Kappa Society at Thoreau's graduation in 1837. Thoreau had lamely observed, "Our literature though now dependent, in some measure, on that of the mother Country, must soon go alone" (*EEM* 39); Emerson ringingly announced, "Our

[1]This commonplace book, consisting mostly of extracts from English poetry, is in the Pierpont Morgan Library (MA 594). Thoreau's notes on Harvard reading and portions of the "Index rerum" (HM 945) are printed in *The Transcendentalists and Minerva,* I:130 ff.

day of dependence, our long apprenticeship to the learning of other lands, draws to a close" (*CW* I:52). He had already published *Nature,* so Emerson devoted the bulk of the address to the other great influences on the scholar, books and action. "Action is with the scholar subordinate, but it is essential," he declared. "Without it, he is not yet man" (*CW* I:59). But the greatest threat to self-reliant manhood, a danger amply illustrated by the imitative productions of American writers, was the overinfluence of books, which threatened to warp the scholar out of his own orbit, to make him "a satellite instead of a system" (*CW* I:56). Yet throughout the section Emerson's own luminous experience of books, "the best type of the influence of the past," shone through his argument. "We read the verses of one of the great English poets, of Chaucer, of Marvell, of Dryden, with the most modern joy," he exclaimed. "There is some awe mixed with the joy of our surprise, when this poet, who lived in some past world, two or three hundred years ago, says that which lies close to my own soul, that which I also had wellnigh thought and said" (*CW* I:57-58).

The interplay between writing and what Emerson defined as "creative reading," so important to his own early career, also became a crucial factor in Thoreau's earliest literary efforts. As the reference to "the great English poets" reminds us, during the winter of 1835-36 Emerson had delivered a lecture series on English literature, from the Anglo-Saxons through "Modern Aspects of Letters," with special attention to Chaucer, Shakespeare (two lectures), Bacon, and George Herbert, one of Emerson's favorites (Milton was absent only because Emerson had earlier dealt with him in a series entitled "Biography"). As Ralph Rusk has dryly remarked, the series "might have been very frankly entitled 'A Transcendentalist Looks at British Literature.' "[2] Thoreau, who jotted down mottoes from Herbert, Burton, and Marvell at the opening of the Journal, would later continue that examination.

[2]Ralph L. Rusk, *The Life of Ralph Waldo Emerson* (New York: Scribners, 1949), p. 239. The series is printed in *The Early Lectures of Ralph Waldo Emerson,* ed. Stephen E. Whicher et al., 3 vols. (Cambridge: Harvard Univ. Press, 1959–72), I:203–385.

But his earliest entries contained quotations from and comments on his own favorites, Virgil and Homer, in whom he discovered the same continuities between past and present as Emerson discovered in the English poets. The sense that a poet living hundreds of years earlier spoke directly to his own thoughts and experiences also underlies Thoreau's translations of Anacreon, begun in 1838. But, as Emerson had urged, such scholarship was but a part of Thoreau's own creative efforts, for by the time he began to translate Anacreon he had also begun to fill up pages in the Journal with his own verses. Thus, a poem, "Sympathy," drafted in June 1839, became the first of his works accepted for publication in the *Dial*.

To the chagrin of its more socially conscious contributors like Theodore Parker, the *Dial* was a very literary journal. In addition to "Sympathy," the first issue included poems by Christopher Pearse Cranch, John S. Dwight, Sarah Clarke, Ellen Hooper, Samuel Gray Ward, Margaret Fuller, and Emerson. In an introductory address to its readers, Emerson and Fuller stressed the importance of literature and literary criticism, and in "A Short Essay on Critics," which followed in the first issue, Fuller sought "to define the critical mission of writers in a country attempting to establish a new literature."[3] Indeed, as Perry Miller has observed, the editors were less sanguine about summoning a body of creative work from America than about their effort to promote criticism that might refine American taste.[4] Consequently, the first issue also contained articles on music, art, and literature, including Fuller's essay on the German romantic novelist Jean

[3]*Margaret Fuller,* p. 58. "The Editors to the Reader" is reprinted in *The Transcendentalists,* pp. 247–51. Perry Miller notes that it was drafted by Fuller but heavily revised by Emerson, who considered it his own. Other contributions to the journal are identified by Joel Myerson, "An Annotated List of Contributions to the Boston *Dial*," *Studies in Bibliography* 26 (1973):133–66. Myerson's excellent history, *The New England Transcendentalists and the Dial* (Rutherford, N.J.: Fairleigh Dickinson Univ. Press, 1980), contains brief biographies of the contributors to the journal.

[4]See his headnote to "A Short Essay on Critics," in *Margaret Fuller, American Romantic,* pp. 66–67.

Paul Richter and Thoreau's article on the Latin poet Aulus Persius Flaccus, in which he began to measure the poetic achievements of the past against an ideal of inspired, spontaneous, and natural verse. "Homer, and Shakespeare, and Milton, and Marvell, and Wordsworth, are but the rustling of leaves and crackling of twigs in the forest, and not yet the sound of any bird," he loftily observed. "The Muse has never lifted up her voice to sing" (*EEM* 122, *W* 308).

An effort to define—and to become—that ideal poet had a significant impact on Thoreau's account of the 1839 journey, which he was then beginning to plan. In the list of essay topics jotted down in 1840, he included "Horace" and "Greek Poetry" as well as "Memoirs of a Tour—A Chit-chat with Nature." Those critiques were never written, but the Journal of 1840-41 reveals his preoccupation with the problems of poetry, with its demands and rewards, with language, style, and form. "A great poet will write for his peers alone—and indite no line to an inferior," he reminded himself on August 28, 1841 (*J* 1:323). That entry, along with numerous others from the period, was later revised for *A Week* (*W* 341). The book would also receive his early publications in the *Dial,* including "Aulus Persius Flaccus," "Sympathy" (*W* 260-61), and his next three contributions, all poems: "Stanzas" in January 1841 (*W* 285); "Sic Vita" in July 1841 (*W* 383-84); and what Emerson called his "grand verses on Friendship" in October 1841 (*W* 287-89; see *L* II:242). On September 8, 1841, four days after he jotted down plans for the ambitious "poem to be called Concord" in the Journal (*J* 1:330), Thoreau wrote Lucy Brown, for whom he had composed "Sic Vita": "Just now I am in the mid-sea of verses, and they actually rustle around me as the leaves would round the head of Autumnus himself should he thrust it up through some vales which I know; but, alas! many of them are but crisped and yellow leaves like his, I fear, and will deserve no better fate than to make mould for new harvests. I see the stanzas rise around me, verse by verse, far and near, like the mountains from Agiocochook, not all having a terrestrial existence yet, even as some of them may be clouds; but I fancy I see the gleam of some Sebago Lake and Silver Cascade, at whose well I may drink one day" (*C* 46-47).

His imagery suggests that the trip to the White Mountains, which Thoreau included in the new list of essay topics drawn up that fall, was still very much on his mind. But he had more immediate plans and high hopes for his verses. In fact, despite his self-deprecating tone, Thoreau was obviously working toward publication, either in the *Dial* or as a collection of poetry. In either case he must have been keenly disappointed by Margaret Fuller's rejection of "With frontier strength ye stand your ground," which he had revised and submitted to the *Dial*. "I do not find the poem on the mountains improved by mere compression," she wrote on October 18, "through it might be by fusion and glow" (*C* 56). Fuller, never a fan of Thoreau or his work, was especially critical of the poem's "want of fluent music," which he himself had earlier defined as the chief requisite of great poetry. After Emerson assumed editorship of the *Dial* early in 1842, Thoreau published twelve additional poems there, eight of which he later inserted in *A Week*. Nonetheless, Fuller's sharp critique at least temporarily took the wind out of his sails, for whereas in September 1841 he was busily gathering together his own poems, that November he began work on a radically different collection of poetry.

Thoreau evidently planned to compile "an appreciative and critical collection of English poetry."[5] In preparation he spent two weeks from November 28 to December 10 or 12 working at the Harvard College Library. "When looking over the dry and dusty volumes of the English poets, I cannot believe that those fresh and fair creations I had imagined are contained in them," he noted in the Journal on November 30. "English poetry from Gower down collected into one alcove—and so from the library window compared with the commonest nature, seems very mean. Poetry cannot breath in the scholar's atmosphere" (*J* 1:337-38). His sour remarks, so different in tone from the expansive letter to Lucy Brown written two months earlier, recall "The American Scholar," where Emerson chastened bookworms, "the restorers of readings,

[5]Robert Sattelmeyer, "Thoreau's Projected Work on the English Poets," *Studies in the American Renaissance 1980,* ed. Joel Myerson (Boston: Twayne, 1980), p. 239. The article (pp. 239–57) contains a detailed description of this project and interesting insights into its place in Thoreau's literary career.

the emendators, the bibliomaniacs of all degrees," who value books "not as related to nature and the human constitution, but as making a sort of Third Estate with the world and the soul" (*CW* I:56). The Journal entry also anticipates Thoreau's dismissal of scholars and antiquarians in *A Week,* but he persevered with the onerous and distinctly un-Emersonian task, compiling a forty-page bibliography and copying out nearly three hundred pages of notes and extracts. For a second time he studied Chalmers's great collection. He possibly hoped to extend and expand Chalmers's selections from early British verse, for Thoreau also withdrew nearly twenty other volumes of poetry, including *Illustrations of Anglo-Saxon Poetry, The Canterbury Tales,* Headley's *Select Beauties of Ancient English Poetry,* and collections of early metrical romances, old ballads, and Renaissance lyrics compiled by scholars like Ritson, Hartshorne, Park, Edwards, and Jamieson.

Many of the volumes he consulted were a product of the revival of interest in early English poetry during the late eighteenth century among scholars in England and Scotland, whose critical writings had a marked impact on Thoreau. Among the four books he withdrew on his first day in Cambridge were Sharon Turner's *History of the Anglo-Saxons* and Thomas Warton's *History of English Poetry, from the Close of the 11th to the Commencement of the 18th Century* (1764-90), both of which Emerson had relied upon for factual information when preparing his lecture series on English literature six years earlier. Thoreau probably also found support for his own and Emerson's views in Warton's *History,* which inculcated the notion that learning and education conflict with imagination and creativity, and thus helped prepare for "the adoption of the primitivist view that simple manners foster poetry."[6] Nathaniel Hawthorne, who moved into the Old Manse in the summer of 1842, swiftly perceived Thoreau's primitivistic leanings. Stressing his love of nature, which "seems to adopt him

[6]René Wellek, *The Rise of English Literary History* (Chapel Hill: Univ. of North Carolina Press, 1941), p. 191. Thoreau withdrew all four volumes of a nineteenth-century edition of Warton's *History* (London, 1824), which probably served him as a bibliography and anthology of early English literature.

as her especial child," and his "great regard for the memory of
the Indian tribes, whose wild life would have suited him so well,"
Hawthorne continued, "With all this he has more than a tincture
of literature—a deep and true taste for poetry, especially the elder
poets, although more exclusive than is desirable, like all other
Transcendentalists, as far as I am acquainted with them."[7]

Although Thoreau continued to work on his anthology of English poetry until 1844, in 1842 his literary efforts took yet another
direction. But "Natural History of Massachusetts," written that
spring, and "A Walk to Wachusett," completed in the fall, also
reveal the continuity between his earlier scholarly and poetic interests and his evolving prose writings. In "Natural History of
Massachusetts," for example, he inserted more than one hundred
lines of poetry, including two of his translations of Anacreon.
Similarly, at the opening of "A Walk to Wachusett," he used the
poem "With frontier strength ye stand your ground," which Margaret Fuller had so sharply criticized a year earlier, and he quoted
lines from William Collins's *Oriental Eclogues,* printed in Chalmers, Wordsworth's *Peter Bell,* and Ritson's collection *Robin Hood*
in addition to Virgil's *Eclogues, Georgics,* and *Aeneid.*[8] Moreover,
following remarks on Virgil similar to those later incorporated in
A Week (FD 40, W 90), Thoreau in the earliest version of the
essay digressed on the value of the classics. "Reading the classics
and conversing with those old Greeks and Latins in their surviving
works," he observed, "is like walking amid the stars and constellations, a high and by way serene to travel." The passage,
which anticipates the meditation on literature and celestial phenomena in the final chapter of *A Week,* was omitted from the
published version of "A Walk to Wachusett." But Thoreau later
used it in an introduction to his translations of Anacreon, printed
in the April 1843 *Dial* and later inserted in *A Week* (W 225-31).

[7]Nathaniel Hawthorne, *The American Notebooks,* ed. Claude M.
Simpson (Columbus: Ohio State Univ. Press, 1972), p. 354 (Sept. 1,
1842).

[8]For the identification of Thoreau's sources I am indebted to Kevin P.
van Anglen's compilation "Quotations in the Princeton Edition of Henry
Thoreau's *Excursions"* (forthcoming).

An amusing example of his tendency to recycle material, the various uses of the passage also illustrate the congruity between his travels along the highways and byways of classical literature and his literary excursions through New England.

Thoreau's preoccupation with literary matters also provided a unifying thread in his diverse writings of 1843. In February he delivered the "Sir Walter Raleigh" lecture, the first fruit of his readings in English poetry. The biographical and critical study of Ralegh, portions of which he later revised for *A Week*, also reflected Thoreau's growing interest in Renaissance prose writers, who possessed "a greater vigor and naturalness than the more modern" (*EEM* 211, *W* 104). He sought to achieve similar qualities in "A Winter Walk," written in June, a few weeks after his arrival on Staten Island. But, although the essay depicted a withdrawal from the confinement of the village to nature, the inclusion of lines from Thomson's *The Seasons*, Milton's "L'Allegro," and Gavin Douglas's Scottish translation of the *Aeneid*, as well as his own translation of a passage from the *Iliad*, testified to the long hours Thoreau had spent—and continued to spend—in the library. "I have been translating some Greek, and reading English poetry," he wrote his mother on August 6 (*C* 132). By then he had completed a translation of Aeschylus' *Seven against Thebes*, a follow-up to his equally pedestrian translation of *Prometheus Bound* in the January 1843 *Dial*, and he had begun rather desultory work on Pindar's odes, which were later published in the *Dial* of January and April 1844.

Reading English and American poetry was far more satisfying to Thoreau. In response to the recent publication of the first volume of poems by his friend Ellery Channing, he observed on August 18: "He who is not touched by the poetry of Channing—Very—Emerson and the best pieces of Bryant may be sure he has not drunk deep of the Pierian spring. Channing's might very properly as has been suggested be called poetry for poets" (*J* 1:459). Thoreau's glowing remarks anticipate tributes to his friends in *A Week*, but he was even more engaged by early English poets, who would assume an equally important position in the book. The entry on Channing continues with brief remarks on Marlowe, who offers "food for poets," Quarles, "a true poet though not polished," Spenser, whose words are "sweet, and graceful, and full of hope," and Marvell (*J* 1:459-60), one of numerous commentaries on English poetry that dominate the Journal of the Staten Island period. From volumes he discovered in various libraries in New York, Thoreau took additional extracts for his projected anthology, many of which later found their way into *A Week*. Excited by his discovery of Quarles's *Divine Poems* and *Emblemes*, for example, he wrote Emerson in October: "He uses language sometimes as greatly as Shakspeare, and though there is not much straight grain in him, there is plenty of tough crooked timber. In an age when Herbert is revived, Quarles surely ought not to be forgotten" (*C* 144). Thoreau obviously hoped to revive Quarles in his anthology, for he took twenty pages of extracts (*TLN* 246-56, 279 ff.), later the source of a dozen scattered quotations in *A Week*. His greatest find, however, was Patrick MacGregor's *The Genuine Remains of Ossian*, which Thoreau borrowed from the Mercantile Library on November 1, 1843 (*C* 150).

Thoreau's excited discovery of Ossian coincided with an important shift in emphasis in his ongoing plans for *A Week*. Two weeks earlier he had jotted three brief paragraphs on the brothers' hike through the White Mountains, concluding: "Why should we take the reader who may be gentle and tender, through this rude tract. . . . Rude men and rough paths would he have to encounter—and many a cool blast over the mountain side" (*J* 1:476; cf. FD 77). Previously, he had tended to emphasize the idyllic and pastoral elements of the journey; he now began to stess the rugged and primitive aspects of New England, exemplified by his description of the autumn cattle show, which follows in the Journal (*J* 1:476-77). His earlier interest in the pastoral and his growing attraction to primitive poetry are indicated by his withdrawals from the Mercantile Library on November 1, when he borrowed M. J. Chapman's translations of *The Greek Pastoral Poets* in addition to MacGregor's edition of Ossian. But for Thoreau there was no contest between the rude poetry of Ossian, who "is like Homer & like the Indian," and pastoral poetry, which "belongs to a highly civilized and refined era" (*J* 1:487-88). Similarly, in a lecture entitled "The Ancient Poets," delivered during a trip home at

Thanksgiving and swiftly revised as "Homer. Ossian. Chaucer." for the Janury 1844 *Dial,* Thoreau contrasted Ossian with Chaucer and his heirs in English poetry, a decline later charted in "Friday," where the autumn cattle show is but one of many indications that the Celtic bard's primitive world survived in some measure in nineteenth-century New England.

By the time he began sustained work on the book in 1844, Thoreau had thus already amassed much of the material that could constitute one of its primary elements, but his early aspirations and literary concerns are only dimly reflected in the first draft. Like his earlier excursions, it contains a number of brief quotations from classical and English poets, as well as a substantial amount of Thoreau's own poetry, most of it concentrated in epigraphs to chapters, in the digression on friendship, and in "Friday." But, in contrast to the published version, the first draft contains little discussion of specific writers. Although he copied out some of the entries on English poets from the Journal of 1843 into the Long Book, Thoreau failed to include any of these entries in the first draft, where he limited himself to relatively brief and abstract comments on writing and books. Yet in these passages, from the digression on civilization and wildness in "Sunday," where he noted that "poets exhibit but a tame and civil side of nature" (FD 24; cf. *W* 56-57), to the final disquisition on sound and silence, where he described the function of a good book (FD 104, *W* 392-93), Thoreau set standards against which he would later measure a wide range of writers in *A Week.*

The growth of material on writers and writing in the book is partially explained by his literary activities at Walden Pond. Shortly after he completed the first draft, Thoreau began "Thomas Carlyle and His Works," his only extended evaluation of a contemporary writer. In it he compared the English writer to "our countryman Emerson, whose place and influence must ere long obtain a more distinct recognition" (*EEM* 251). The Journal of the Walden period also contains flattering observations on that "critic poet philosopher," especially Emerson's "personal influence upon young persons" (*J* 2:223-24), as well as somewhat more critical comments on the *Essays* (*J* 2:355-56), entries that anticipate Thoreau's oblique tribute to Emerson in *A Week* (*W* 100-

102). About the time Hawthorne moved away from the Old Manse, Thoreau in the summer of 1846 wrote a poem about the brothers' voyage along the shores of Concord, "where late/With soothed and patient ear we sat/Under our Hawthorne in the dale/ And listened to his Twice told Tale" (*J* 2:265; cf. *W* 19). The poem echoes Milton's "L'Allegro," but, as other entries in the Journal indicate, Thoreau was also once again absorbed in the Greek classics, the truest standard against which contemporary achievements might be measured.[9] Thus, in an even more exuberant mood, he had a few days earlier celebrated "the harvest of thought already yielded in this country," especially at the Concord Lyceum, "from which new eras will be dated as from the games of Greece" (*J* 2:261, *W* 99-100).

Thoreau's keen sense of the interplay between past and present—between the great tradition of Western literature and efforts to establish a native tradition in America—informed his additions to *A Week*. The aspiring poet was finally represented by more than fifty poems or fragments of poems, moments when Thoreau's recollections and more immediate impressions seem to inspire spontaneous song. The poetry of his friends Emerson and Ellery Channing is also represented, thus forming an American counterpoint to hundreds of lines of Greek, Latin, and, especially, English poetry, much of which Thoreau had originally gathered for his projected anthology. He also found use for his other critical and scholarly efforts during the early 1840s, both published and unpublished. In "Sunday," he used portions of the unpublished essay "Sir Walter Raleigh" and the section on Homer from "Homer. Ossian. Chaucer." in the *Dial*, the remainder of which he inserted in "Friday." Among the other *Dial* pieces in *A Week*, he added his translations of Anacreon to "Tuesday" and "Aulus Persius Flaccus" to "Thursday." The article on Persius, his first publication in the *Dial*, was added as late as 1848, by which time Thoreau had probably also added to "Thursday" a critique of Goethe he began to draft, apparently without reference to *A Week*, in the Journal at the end of 1846 (*J* 2:356 ff.). In the early Journal,

[9]Seybold, p. 51, notes that the Journal of the early Walden period "indicates that Greece and the classics were steadily in his thoughts."

he had treated Goethe as a paradigm of the writer as traveler. But a decade later, nearing the end of his own excursion, he used Goethe as a symbol of the decline of certain ideals of writing: simplicity, spontaneity, and primitive vigor, ideals that Thoreau implicitly sought to revivify in *A Week*.

His literary aspirations are revealed in "Concord River." In the first draft he associated it with the Mississippi, Nile, and Euphrates. He later added, "The murmurs of many a famous river on the other side of the globe reach even to us here, as to more distant dwellers on its banks; many a poet's stream floating the helms and shields of heroes on its bosom" (*W* 11). By associating the Concord River with the Xanthus, Scamander, and Simoïs, all mentioned in the *Iliad* and all "fed by the ever-flowing springs of fame," Thoreau extends the topography of *A Week* and prepares for the association of the Lyceum with the Olympic Games in "Sunday." To justify these associations, he quotes four lines from "Coopers Hill," which established the topographical poem in English poetry. With Denham, Thoreau insists that fame is not dependent on a place but rather on the poets who celebrate it (*W* 12).[10]

As Homer sang of the Trojan War, Concord poets sing of the Revolution. Following two stanzas from "Concord Hymn," which he and others in the choir sang at the dedication of the original monument at Old North Bridge on July 4, 1837, Thoreau early in "Saturday" includes "Ah, 't is in vain the peaceful din," his own paean to the heroes of the Revolution. In Thoreau's poem Emerson's "embattled farmers," who "fired the shot heard round

[10]Cf. his ideas for "a poem to be called Concord" (*J* 1:330). Examples of Thoreau's early experiments in topographical poetry, a genre largely outmoded by the romantic poets, include "When Winter fringes every bough," at various times entitled "Stanzas Written at Walden" and "Fair Haven" (*CP* 14–15), "The Assabet" (*CP* 113–15; cf. *W* 62, 179), and another "Fair Haven" (*CP* 383–84). Both *A Week* and *Walden* probably owe something to the tradition of topographical poetry, which Dr. Johnson defined as "*local poetry*, of which the fundamental subject is some particular landscape . . . with the addition of . . . historical retrospection or incidental meditation." See the *Princeton Encyclopedia of Poetry and Poetics* (Princeton: Princeton Univ. Press, 1965), p. 858.

the world," serve as analogues of ancient heroism and virtue: "Ye were the Grecian cities then,/The Romes of modern birth,/Where the New England husbandmen/Have shown a Roman worth" (*W* 18). Although the poem concerns the decline from the heroic stand at Lexington and Concord to the ignoble peace of the present town, in another poem that follows in "Saturday," compressed from the version in the 1846 Journal, Thoreau discovers signs of a modern renaissance in Concord.

The poem fuses Thoreau's elegiac and literary concerns in *A Week*. Like "Concord Hymn" and "Ah, 't is in vain the peaceful din," which are shot through with a sense of transience, the poem opens on a melancholy note: "But since we sailed/Some things have failed,/And many a dream/Gone down the stream" (*W* 18). Since their voyage, the river of time had carried away his brother and other inhabitants of Concord. In the second stanza Thoreau pays tribute to one of these men, the Reverend Ezra Ripley, "the aged pastor" who had died in 1841, a few months before John. The death of men like Ripley, an exemplar of older times, suggests a decline similar to that described in the preceding poems. But in the last stanza Thoreau observes, "Anon a youthful pastor came,/Whose crook was not unknown to fame" (*W* 19). As the remainder of the stanza indicates, this "youthful pastor" is Nathaniel Hawthorne, who moved into Ripley's house, the Old Manse, in 1842. Like Milton in "Lycidas," Thoreau associates the preacher and the writer. His use of pastoral conventions and of octosyllabic couplets in the last two stanzas also recalls "L'Allegro," echoed in the concluding lines: "Here was our Hawthorne in the dale,/And here the shepherd told his tale." Alluding to Milton's "And every Shepherd tells his tale/Under the Hawthorn in the dale," lines he had praised in an undergraduate essay (*EEM* 74), Thoreau transports the "ignoble town" of the preceding poem to a pastoral poetic realm. The heroes of an earlier generation had passed away, but their places had been taken by writers who were laying the groundwork for an even more glorious era in Concord.

Thoreau treats Ellery Channing's arrival as another sign of Concord's literary renaissance. In "On Ponkawtasset, since, we took our way," a poem that follows "But since we sailed" in "Saturday," he pays extravagant tribute to Channing, "whose fine ray/Doth often shine on Concord's twilight day" (*W* 19). Channing's poetry is given a prominent place in "Sunday," which opens with a stanza from "Boat Song" (*W* 43). Early in the chapter Thoreau also quotes seven lines from "The River," in which Channing, like Thoreau in "Saturday" and "Sunday," celebrates the glories of the Concord River (*W* 45). Emphasizing their shared experiences and poetic endeavors, Thoreau then juxtaposes another stanza from "Boat Song" and his own poem "Low in the eastern sky," both of which first appeared in the *Dial*. In "Boat Song" Channing describes a maiden who sailed with the poet; in "Low in the eastern sky" Thoreau metaphorically describes the stars as a maiden's eyes shedding their influence on the poet (*W* 46-48). The effect of these linked poems is akin to the poetic dialogues or contests in classical and Renaissance pastorals. But, as Thoreau well knew, Concord's chief claim to literary fame was not its two young and virtually unknown poets but Emerson, the "rare Contemporary" addressed later in "Sunday."

The apostrophe to Emerson mingles praise and criticism. Opening with an entry revised from the 1846 Journal, where he describes the birth of a native American literature, especially at "the peaceful games of the Lyceum," Thoreau hails the victor of this modern olympiad. But following a quasi-Pindaric ode to Emerson, the "Phaeton of our day," he launches upon a half-humorous critique of that "undisputed seer."[11] Most seriously, he faults Emerson's oracular utterances: "Let epic trade-winds blow, and cease this waltz of inspirations. Let us oftener feel even the gentle south-west wind upon our cheeks blowing from the Indian's heaven. What though we lose a thousand meteors from the sky, if skyey depths, if star-dust and undissolvable nebulae remain? What though we lose a thousand wise responses of the oracle, if we may have instead some natural acres of Ionian earth?" (*W* 101-2).

Thoreau's imagery implies the standards against which Emer-

---

[11]Joel Porte argues that "in the very act of lampooning Emerson's own comic literary tactics, Thoreau continues the Transcendental tradition of shrewd and effective self-parody learned from his mentor" ("Transcendental Antics," in *Veins of Humor,* ed. Harry Levin [Cambridge: Harvard Univ. Press, 1972], p. 182).

son is judged. Compared to "epic trade winds," Emerson's "waltz of inspirations" seems trivial and artificial. Even a gentle wind from the Indian's heaven is better, since that conception of paradise is at least rooted in the material world. The loss of a few meteors, bright but transient, is more than compensated by the less flashy but more enduring light of the fixed stars, associated in the first draft with Greek poetry and art (FD 95-96). He consequently pleads for "some natural acres of Ionian earth," something more substantial and physical than Emerson's abstract oracles. Although Thoreau concludes with a graceful tribute to his mentor, who evidences a literary renaissance in America similar to that in "Eliza's reign" (W 102), Emerson's works fall short of Thoreau's ideal, half-Indian and half-Greek, of writing rooted in nature and experience. He therefore placed the remarks on Emerson within an extended digression on poetry, books, and style, in which that ideal is developed in far greater detail.

Thoreau expanded the digression from fewer than a thousand words in the first draft to over six thousand words in *A Week*. In the first draft he introduced the digression with a reference to the *Gazetteer*, from whose "bald natural facts" the brothers "extracted the pleasures of poetry" (FD 32). He then briefly discussed two lines from Virgil's *Ecolgues* and described the uses of books. He later revised the discussion of Virgil, adding the section on Homer from "Homer. Ossian. Chaucer." in the *Dial* (W 90-95). He also expanded his remarks on the uses of books, which ends with the apostrophe to Emerson (W 95-102). Finally, he gathered passages from the Journal and "Sir Walter Raleigh" for a concluding discussion of prose style (W 102-9). He thus constructed a modified version of "The American Scholar": like Emerson, who described the scholar's education by nature, books, and action or experience, Thoreau first discusses the poet's relation to nature, then describes the uses of books, and finally stresses the connection between experience and style.

He uses the classics to demonstrate the poet's dependence on nature. In a related digression on civilization and wildness earlier in "Sunday," he observes, "There are other, savager, and more primeval aspects of nature than our poets have sung" (W 56). But Virgil, whose lines "were written while grass grew and water ran" (FD 33, W 90), and especially Homer, whose primitive poetry associates him with the American Indian, approach Thoreau's ideal. His emphasis on Homer's vigor and simplicity recalls mid-eighteenth-century Scottish critics, who maintained that "the greatest poetry is primitive, spontaneous, original, and natural," a definition that infiltrated Romantic criticism and helped establish "the distinction between 'natural' poetry and 'artificial' poetry."[12] Observing that the poet "needs such stimulus to sing only as plants to put forth leaves and blossoms," Thoreau remarks that in Homer "it is as if nature spoke" (*W* 91-92, *EEM* 154-55).

That primitivistic view of Homer dictated Thoreau's approach to the *Iliad*. He thus evaded formal questions about its coherence and artistry, primary concerns of neoclassic critics. He also ignored the controversy about whether the *Iliad* was composed by a single individual, a question he had discussed in some detail in his undergraduate essay "Greek Classic Poets" (*EEM* 53-58). He instead emphasized the richness of individual passages, in which Homer "conveys the least information, even the hour of the day, with such magnificence and vast expense of natural imagery, as if it were a message from the gods" (*W* 92, *EEM* 155). Appropriately, in a passage added to the section when he revised "Homer. Ossian. Chaucer." for *A Week,* he praised Homer's scenery, which "is always true, and never invented." As an illustration he quotes Homer's depiction of a march up the river Minyas from the sea to its sacred sources in the mountains, during which we constantly hear its "subdued murmuring" until we are finally cheered by "the gurgling fountains of Alpheus" (*W* 94), sounds that are reechoed in the account of the voyage up the Merrimack, whose course from the White Mountains to the sea is traced a few pages earlier in "Sunday" (*W* 83-89).

Thoreau's treatment of the *Iliad* diverged sharply from that of many contemporary critics.[13] Although scholarly interest in Greek

[12]Donald M. Foerster, *The Fortunes of Epic Poetry* (Catholic Univ. Press of America, 1962), p. 25.

[13]Ibid., pp. 107–8. This study contains only one paragraph on Thoreau, but Foerster's detailed discussion of attitudes toward the epic in nineteenth-century England and America in chaps. 2–4, from which much of the following paragraph, including the quotation from Godwin, is drawn, provides a useful background to Thoreau's approach to Homer. See especially pp. 35–40, 79–80, and 86–94.

civilization and literature had never been greater, the reputation of Homer and of the epic declined during the first half of the nineteenth century. Largely because of their conception of classical literature as objective and romantic literature as subjective, revealed in a marked preference for the lyric, the drama, and even the novel over the epic, numerous romantic poets and critics in England tended to disparage heroic poetry. In America the epic suffered from social and political as well as critical and aesthetic assumptions. Its reputation was damaged by its association with the derivative culture of the colonial period and with third-rate poems like Joel Barlow's *Columbiad*. Moreover, since the epic was thought to embody the values of aristocracy and social hierarchy, it was believed to be alien to democracy. It was also thought to be irrelevant to a people preoccupied with the practical concerns of life. As Parke Godwin observed in 1853, "A man who has his fields to clear, his house to build, his shoes and clothing to make, his ways of access to his neighbors to open, and above all, his government and social order to invent and institute . . . is not the man who constructs epics." Thoreau, of course, vigorously replied to that objection in the "Reading" chapter of *Walden,* published a year later. In the *Dial* and again in *A Week,* however, he challenged a different assumption: the deeply rooted American belief in the universal progress of mankind. To those sharing that assumption, primitive epics like the *Iliad* were outmoded, completely superseded by the products of an enlightened society in the New World. In contrast Thoreau asserts, "No modern joy or ecstasy of ours can lower its height, or dim its lustre, but there it lies in the east of literature, as it were at once the earliest and latest production of the mind" (*W* 94-95, *EEM* 156). Rooted in the permanent truths of nature and human life, the *Iliad* shares their permanence, unlike the transient books Thoreau discusses in the following section in "Sunday."

Like Emerson, he is concerned with both the abuses and uses of books. We should "read only the serenely true," Thoreau insists, "only great poems, and when they failed, read them again, *or perchance write more*" (*W* 95-96; emphasis added; cf. FD 33). Books, then, properly should inspire our own creative efforts. "What is the right use [of books]?" Emerson asked in "The American Scholar." "They are for nothing but to inspire" (*CW* I:56).

Thoreau observes that novels, "which afford us a cowering enjoyment," books of philosophy and natural history, "which do not in the least teach the divine view of nature, but the popular view," and other products of the modern press fail this severe test (*W* 96-97; cf. FD 33-34). With a further glance at his own book, he adds that readers gain most "from true, sincere, human books, from frank and honest biographies" (*W* 98). Although he hails the earlier appearance of "essays and poems," first signs of a native American literature, Thoreau implies that something is still lacking. Even Emerson, greatest of this new race of American writers, fails to achieve the vigor and naturalness of Homer's poetry or the prose of Sir Walter Ralegh, another writer whose style served as a model for the author of *A Week*.

Like the disquisition on books, the concluding discussion of style is an implicit defense of Thoreau's own life and writing. Denigrating "the charm of fluent writing," he praises Ralegh, whose "sentences are verdurous and blooming as evergreen and flowers, because they are rooted in fact and experience" (*W* 104, *EEM* 211). His emphasis on the relationship between writing and experience recalls "The American Scholar," in which Emerson also stressed the importance of action to the writer. But for Emerson action remained a secondary concern. Ellery Channing "says, that Writers never do any thing; they are passive observers," he recorded with apparent approval in 1843. Henry Thoreau "will never be a writer[;] he is active as a shoemaker" (*JMN* IX:45). In "Sir Walter Raleigh," drafted in 1843, and in extracts from the essay in "Sunday," Thoreau took issue with his friends. "The necessity of labor and conversation with many men and things, to the scholar is rarely well remembered," he observes; "steady labor with the hands, which engrosses the attention also, is unquestionably the best method of removing palaver and sentimentality out of one's style, both of speaking and writing" (*W* 105, *EEM* 212). Implicitly, his own steady labor, which included repairing a house for Channing and building a summer house for Emerson, bore a literary fruit that neither of Thoreau's less practical friends had anticipated.

He also calls attention to the link between a writer's style and experience on the one hand and his audience on the other. In

"Thomas Carlyle and His Works" Thoreau observed that Emerson, Carlyle, and other modern writers failed to speak to the condition of "the Man of the Age, come to be called working-man," because these writers were not in the working man's condition. "Like speaks to like only," he explained; "labor to labor, philosophy to philosophy, criticism to criticism, poetry to poetry, &c." (*EEM* 251-52). For all the poetry, criticism, and philosophy in his first book, Thoreau also sought to speak to labor in *A Week* as well as in *Walden*. Describing the "necessity of labor" in "Sunday," he continues, "Surely the writer is to address a world of laborers, and such therefore must be his own discipline" (*W* 106). Through labor and contact with laborers, whose homely, natural style Thoreau celebrates in the following paragraphs, the writer at once toughens his own style and opens his work to a hitherto neglected audience. Although he begins the digression on books and style by asserting the value of the classics, whose rays "struggle down to us, and mingle with the sunbeams of the recent day" (*W* 95, *EEM* 156), he concludes that there is always room for a true book, since "more rays will not interfere with the first" (*W* 109).

In "Sunday" Thoreau sets the standards against which other works are measured in *A Week*. Of all the various writings discussed in the following chapters, only the Hindu scriptures extolled in "Monday" match the elevation and sublimity of the *Iliad*. These ancient scriptures thus both serve as antipodes to Western philosophical and political traditions and antidotes to what Thoreau willfully viewed as the narrowness of Western culture. Blithely ignoring the spectacular growth and spread of interest in the language, literature, myth, and religion of ancient India during the late eighteenth century and the subsequent impact of that Indic Renaissance on writers in England, Germany, and France, he observes: "It is remarkable that Homer and a few Hebrews are the most Oriental names which modern Europe, whose literature has taken its rise since the decline of the Persian, has admitted to her list of Worthies" (*W* 143). In his digressions on European literature Thoreau thus charts a movement from east to west, the declension from Homer, through Anacreon in "Tuesday," to Aulus Persius Flaccus in "Thursday." He attributes that decline to the growth of society and civilization, the joint culprits identified in his critique of Goethe in "Thursday." In "Friday," he traces a similar descent from the rugged verses of Ossian, who resembles Homer, through Chaucer to poets of more civilized eras. In themselves, these individual digressions, most of which first appeared in the *Dial,* include some of the least effective material in *A Week.* But each takes its place in a coherent sequence, a compressed history of western literature that illuminates Thoreau's cultural background and literary debts as well as his own artistic goals in *A Week.*

Although he frequently assumes the role of literary excavator, the remains Thoreau describes in *A Week* had been unearthed and explored by hordes of earlier scholars and writers. When he began to translate Anacreon shortly after his graduation from Harvard, for example, Thoreau joined a long line of English admirers of the Teian poet whose odes (most of them now viewed as later Greek imitations) were first edited in 1554. From then on, Continental and English poets wrote imitations of Anacreon, though Abraham Cowley was apparently the first to use the term *Anacreontiques* (1656). The vogue for Anacreon reached even greater proportions during the eighteenth century, when poets wrote and composers set Anacreontic odes and when London had its Anacreontic Society and *Anacreontic Magazine.* In addition, ten translations of the odes appeared between 1650 and 1800, when a two-volume edition of the *Odes of Anacreon* was published by the Irish poet Thomas Moore, soon dubbed "Anacreon Moore," another young man fresh out of college and eager to gain a literary reputation. In prefatory remarks to his translation, which remained popular through the nineteenth century, Moore offered the conventional portrait of Anacreon, a man who retained his zest for wine, women, and song into old age, who died at eighty-five by choking on a grapestone, and whose odes diffuse "the seductive charm of sentiment over passions and propensities at which rigid morality must frown."[14] As Moore stressed, in the odes Anacreon is neither "wanton" nor "licentious," but rigid mo-

---

[14]"Remarks on Anacreon," *The Poetical Works of Thomas Moore,* 6 vols. in 3 (Boston: Houghton Mifflin, 1855), I:3 ff.

rality did indeed begin to frown on them during the nineteenth century.

In a brief introduction to his translations of eleven of the odes in "Tuesday," first published in the 1843 *Dial* (*D* III:484-90), Thoreau cast a radically different glance on the odes, insisting that "they are not gross, as has been presumed, but always elevated above the sensual" (*W* 227). He was far less interested in Anacreon's reputed frailties, however, than in the frail beauty of the odes themselves, which illustrate the decline of Homer's epic vigor in the Greek minor poets. He thus begins with a peroration on classical scholarship, that "highway down from Homer and Hesiod to Horace and Juvenal" (*W* 226). Charming as he finds the whole of that road, "more attractive than the Appian," he obviously sees it as sloping ever downward from its ancient peaks. In fact, although he knew that Anacreon lived in the sixth century B.C., probably not much more than a century or two after Homer and Hesiod, Thoreau does not mention that fact; instead, he observes that there "is something strangely modern about him," a rather backhanded compliment given Thoreau's view of modern poetry (*W* 226). In implied contrast to Homer's primitive simplicity, he compares Anacreon's odes to "gems of pure ivory" (*W* 226). Unlike the *Iliad*, which, "is brightest in the serenest days, and embodies still all the sunlight that fell on Asia Minor" (*W* 94, *EEM* 156), these odes "possess an ethereal and evanescent beauty like summer evenings" (*W* 226). Thoreau commends the "serenity," "flower-like beauty," and elevation of odes like "On His Lyre," which begins: "I wish to sing the Atridae,/And Cadmus I wish to sing;/But my lyre sounds/Only love with its chords" (*W* 227). As Lawrence Buell points out, these songs of love prepare for the digression on friendship in "Wednesday."[15] But Anacreon's inability to sing of the Atridae, Agamemnon and Menelaus, or of Cadmus, founder of Thebes, also reveals the failure of the epic impulse in later Greek poetry.

For Thoreau the declension of the classics reached the lowest point in Roman satirists like Aulus Persius Flaccus, subject of the *Dial* essay inserted in "Thursday" (*W* 307-13, *EEM* 122-27).

[15]Buell, p. 225.

"Here is none of the interior dignity of Virgil, nor the elegance and vivacity of Horace," he observes, "nor will any sybil be needed to remind you, that from those older Greek poets there is a sad descent to Persius" (*W* 307-8, *EEM* 122). The Roman satirist dramatizes the problems facing a poet in a corrupt society. In contrast to the frail beauty of Anacreon's odes, Persius' satires scarcely contain "one harmonious sound amid this unmusical bickering with the follies of men." Describing Juvenal and Persius as "measured fault-finders at best," Thoreau remarks that they "stand just outside the faults they condemn, and so are concerned rather about the monster they have escaped, than the fair prospect before them" (*W* 308, *EEM* 122). The comment illuminates the movement of *A Week* and *Walden*, in which Thoreau's attention shifts from the "monsters" described in "Economy" and in the digressions on church, state, and society in the early chapters of *A Week* to the fair prospects for man's life adumbrated in "Spring" and in "Friday." Obsessed with the corruption of society, the satirist is *"particeps criminis,"* a partner in the crimes he condemns (*W* 308, *EEM* 123), while the true poet frees himself from the transient manners of men in society to dwell in the timeless realm of nature.

The relationship between man, art, and nature is the central unifying theme in "Thursday." Following an epigraph from Emerson's "Woodnotes," Thoreau at the opening of the chapter asserts the superiority of the study of nature to the study of books. He thus reechoes "The American Scholar," where Emerson observed, "Books are for the scholar's idle times" (*CW* I:57). In "My books I'd fain cast off," Thoreau ebulliently announces, "Tell Shakspeare to attend some leisure hour,/For now I've business with this drop of dew" (*W* 301). As the brothers begin the return voyage from the wild and primitive precinct of Agiocochook, he meditates on the relationship between art and nature. In the digression, much of it drawn from the 1840-42 Journal, he initially stresses the interpenetration of art and nature. But he ends by emphasizing the limitations of man's art: "Nature is a greater and more perfect art, the art of God; though, referred to herself, she is genius" (*W* 318). Implicitly, the further works of art are removed from nature, the less perfect and divine they are, while the further a writer removes himself from nature, the less a genius he becomes. The observation looks back to Aulus Persius Flaccus, whose works fail because they are rooted in society instead of nature, and forward to Goethe, who fails the test of true genius because he moves from nature to society and civilization.

The digression near the end of "Thursday" reveals Thoreau's shifting attitude toward Goethe. He was initially influenced by Emerson, who encouraged him to read the German master. "Goethe the observor," Emerson exclaimed in 1836: "What sagacity! What industry of observation!" (*JMN* V:133). In remarks on *Italienische Reise* at the opening of the Journal, Thoreau in 1837 also praised Goethe's powers of observation. Extolling Goethe's ability to give "an exact description of things as they appeared to him, and their effect upon him" (*W* 326; cf. *J* 1:16), he revised and expanded the 1837 Journal entries in "Thursday." But in the midst of the admiring discussion of *Italienische Reise*, an early model of his own literary excursion, he inserted a sharp critique of Goethe based on a reading of volume two of John Henry Hopkins's translation of *Dictung und Wahrheit* (New York, 1846). Whereas he had earlier praised Goethe's truthful observations of man and nature, Thoreau now attacked Goethe's attachment to the artificial conventions of society and civilization.

To appreciate the significance of the critique in "Thursday," we must understand the reverence Goethe received from Thoreau's friends and contemporaries. Carlyle, who translated *Wilhelm Meister* and wrote a series of long articles on the German master, called Goethe "by far the notablest of all Literary Men" in the last hundred years.[16] Despite a certain uneasiness about his immorality, the cause of Goethe's unsavory reputation in America, the Transcendentalists celebrated him as a literary and cultural hero. Of all "the Transcendentalists' genuflections before Goethe,"[17] Margaret Fuller's article in the 1841 *Dial* and Emerson's chapter in *Representative Men* stand out. Describing her response to *Elective Affinities*, the most notorious of his works,

[16]Thomas Carlyle, *On Heroes, Hero-Worship, & The Heroic in History* (New York: D. Appleton, 1841), p. 181.

[17]*Margaret Fuller, American Romantic*, p. 78.

Fuller bravely asserted: "At last I understood that world within a world, the ripest fruit of human nature, which is called art. . . . I understood why Goethe was well content to be called Artist, and his works, works of Art, rather than revelations."[18]

For Emerson, who first lectured on him in 1846, Goethe represented "the power and duties of the scholar or writer" (*CE* IV:270). At once a poet, a philosopher, and a naturalist "who has said the best things about nature that ever were said" (*CE* IV:274), the Goethe portrayed in *Representative Men* is a cosmopolitan version of "The American Scholar." In the earlier address Emerson suggested that a revolution in men's lives was "to be wrought by the gradual domestication of the idea of Culture" (*CW* I:65). Although he regretted some of the moral and literary results of Goethe's "aim of culture," Emerson stressed its favorable aspects. "Goethe, coming into an over-civilized time and country, when original talent was oppressed under the load of books and mechanical auxiliaries and the distracting variety of claims," he observed in the penultimate paragraph of *Representative Men*, "taught men how to dispose of this mountainous miscellany and make it subservient" (*CE* IV:289).

Thoreau replied to Emerson and Margaret Fuller in "Thursday." "Goethe's whole education and life were those of the artist," he begins. "He lacks the unconsciousness of the poet" (*W* 327). Whereas Emerson argued that Goethe was not an artist, Thoreau adopted Fuller's terms "Art" and "Artist" to characterize Goethe. But he gave the terms a radically different twist. Thoreau "only hears the word Art in a sinister sense," an exasperated Emerson noted in his journal in 1844. "But I speak of instincts. . . . To me it is vegetation, the pullulation & universal budding of the plant man. Art is the path of the creator to his work" (*JMN* IX:71). Emerson's complaint is borne out by the critique in "Thursday," which illustrates Thoreau's divergent usage of the contended words. Asserting that the fault of Goethe's education was "its merely artistic completeness," he observes: "Nature is hindered, though she prevails at last in making an unusually catholic impression on the boy. It is the life of a city boy, whose toys are

---

[18]Ibid., p. 106.

pictures and works of art, whose wonders are the theatre and kingly processions and crownings. As the youth studied minutely the order and degrees in the imperial procession, and suffered none of its effect to be lost upon him; so the man aimed to secure a rank in society which would satisfy his notion of fitness and respectability" (W 327).

That interpretation of Goethe's life and education conflicts sharply with Emerson's views. Emerson applauded the German writer's rejection of social conventions and observed that Goethe was "easily able by his subtlety to pierce these and to draw his strength from nature, with which he lived in full communion (CE IV:271). Thoreau acknowledges that nature made an impression on the boy, but implies that even nature could not overcome Goethe's attraction to social and cultural institutions. Thoreau's list of the boy's diversions—museums, the theater, and royal processions—suggests a progressive withdrawal from nature to increasingly artificial interests and activities. In Emerson's view Goethe labored without the goad of "external popularity or provocation, drawing his motive and his plan from his own breast" (CE IV:289). In contrast Thoreau indicates that Goethe was primarily motivated by a desire "to secure rank in society." The construction of that sentence, "As the youth studied . . . so the man aimed," suggests that, instead of conflicting with his artistry, as Margaret Fuller had suggested, the failure of Goethe's character was a direct result of his education as an artist.

As it is portrayed in "Thursday," Goethe's education is a parable of man's fall from savage to civilized life. Thoreau knew that the word *savage* derived from the Latin *sylva,* "woods," while *civilized* meant "of cities."[19] He thus observes that, growing up in a city, Goethe "was defrauded of much which the savage boy enjoys (W 327). Although the boy absorbs culture, he loses the savage's closeness to and reverence for nature. In contrast to what nineteenth-century romantics conceived as the innocent eye, or unmediated vision, of children and primitive peoples, the young Goethe begins to view the world through the eyes of other artists. As an illustration Thoreau quotes Goethe's observation that, from

[19]Sayre, p. 8.

his early contacts with painters, he had accustomed himself "to look at objects, as they did, with reference to art" (*W* 328). As culture narrowed his vision of the world, society narrowed his experience of the world. "He says that he had no intercourse with the lowest class of his towns-boys," Thoreau observes. "The child should have the advantage of ignorance as well as of knowledge, and is fortunate if he gets his share of neglect and exposure" (*W* 328). In the digression on civilizaton and wildness in "Sunday," he describes the losses consequent upon civilization; similarly, in "Thursday" he suggests that Goethe became what Emerson called "the type of culture" only at the expense of the vigor, simplicity, and freedom of savage life.

These expenses are particularly costly to the writer. As he becomes estranged from nature and isolated from common humanity, the cultured writer loses touch with the deepest sources of his own originality and genius. Rather than a man of genius, "an originator, an inspired or demonic man, who produces a perfect work in obedience to laws yet unexplored," he becomes merely an artist, "who detects and applies the law from observation of the works of Genius, whether of man or nature," or, worse yet, merely an artisan or imitator (*W* 328; cf. *J* 1:169, *CC* 151). Calling attention to Thoreau's heavy revisions of this 1840 Journal entry, Perry Miller observed, "By such devious labor did the disguised Apollo ascertain the 'spontaneous' essence of his Genius!" (*CC* 152n).

Thoreau, however, was well aware that he, too, faced the dangers to which he felt Goethe and other artists had succumbed. Following the draft of the section in the Journal, he continued, "When I am stimulated by reading the biographies of literary men to adopt some method of educating myself and directing my studies—I can only resolve to keep unimpaired the freedom & wakefulness of my genius" (*J* 2:357). His harsh commentary on *Dictung und Wahrheit,* perhaps a spontaneous reaction in the Journal but surely a calculated strategy in *A Week,* may thus be understood as a kind of literary exorcism, an effort to insure that another writer's autobiography did not become his own biography. But at the end of the critique Thoreau hints that his remarks on Goethe might be applied to himself: "The talent of composition is very dangerous,—the striking out the heart of life at a blow, as the Indian takes off a scalp. I feel as if my life had grown more outward when I can express it" (W 329; cf. J 1:391).

By including those two sentences from the 1842 Journal, he subtly related his own vocation to that of both Goethe and Hannah Duston. He seems to use "talent" as a negative term, perhaps analogous to the deliberation with which Hannah Duston executed her task, described a few pages earlier in "Thursday." In Thoreau's terms, Hannah, like Goethe, is a type of the artist, since her deed was the result of observation and imitation.[20] As her act symbolizes the final destruction of the American Indian, the Fall of Man in history, Goethe's writing represents the final descent from the primitive poetry of Homer to the civilized art of modern Europe, the Fall of Man in literature. Thoreau earlier acknowledges Hannah Duston as a source of his own identity; he here recognizes that he is an heir to Goethe's dangerous talent. But in the concluding sentence he seeks to distinguish between the "talent of composition" and his own ideals of writing. To compose, to design and execute according to laws of proportion and harmony, is to strike out life; to express, to make known or exhibit, is to make life more outward. The former signifies the taking of life; the latter implies the giving of life. Following this brief paragraph in the Journal, where it formed part of an extended meditation on friendship, love, and charity, Thoreau asked, "What can I give—or what deny to another but myself?" (J 1:391). At its best, writing was an act of giving, an expression of genuine love and charity for other men.

Thoreau's preoccupation with his own vocation reemerges in a meditation on genius, poetry, and fame early in "Friday." Appropriately, as he nears the end of his first book, he is concerned with the writer's relationship with his audience. "To the rarest genius it is the most expensive to succumb and conform to the ways of the world," he observes. "Genius is the worst of lumber, if the poet would float upon the breeze of popularity" (W 339-40; cf. J 1:185). As we shall see in the following chapter, from the time he originally jotted down those sentiments in the 1840 Jour-

[20]Sayre, p. 53.

nal to the time he revised the entry for *A Week,* Thoreau himself gained little popularity or reputation, but he sustained himself by envisaging an entrance to a greater literary society: "Great men, unknown to their generation, have their fame among the great who have preceded them, and all true worldly fame subsides from their high estimate beyond the stars" (*W* 340; cf. *J* 1:264). As in his meditation on the Dunstable Graveyard in "Monday," Thoreau recalls "Lycidas" ("*Fame* is no plant that grows on mortal soil" [11. 78 ff.]). Like Milton, he implicitly hopes to take a place in a long literary tradition. That tradition, however, is not represented by a library, "a mere accumulated, and not truly cumulative treasure," but by a series of "immortal works" (*W* 341), many of which Thoreau quotes and discusses in *A Week.*

The remarks in "Friday" reveal his altered conception of himself as a writer. He initially seemed to suggest that only inspired poets could produce such "immortal works." In a heavily revised draft he interlined, "Nature does nothing in a prose mood but all her fruits are the product of enthusiasm" (MH 15, C). But he later deleted the comment and added the paragraph beginning, "Great prose, of equal elevation, commands our respect more than great verse" (*W* 342; cf. *J* 1:455). Significantly, that paragraph is a revised and expanded version of a Journal entry from April 1843, by which time Thoreau had abandoned his aspiration to become a poet and, with it, the view that poetry was the highest expression of the human spirit. Many of the fruits of his earlier poetic efforts are included in "Friday," where Thoreau inserted a dozen of his own epigrams and poems, including "Sic Vita," one of his earliest and finest poems, and "The Poet's Delay," a meditation on his own poetic efforts (*W* 383-84, 343). But the first great fruit of his literary career was *A Week,* a prose work that he hoped would bear comparison with the immortal works of the past in poetry or prose.

In "Friday" Thoreau's interest and inspiration shifts from Greece, Rome, and Europe to Britain and America. Throughout the chapter his own poems jostle against lines from his favorite Renaissance poets, including Spenser, Marlowe, Daniel, Donne, Fletcher, Davenant, and Quarles. Gathering together passages from the Long Book not used in the first draft, Thoreau also added a short digression on English poetry at the end of "Friday" (Appendix, no. 14). In it he briefly traced the course of English poetry from Gower through Shakespeare and his contemporaries, concluding, "But we are getting too near home for such a theme." He possibly omitted the leaf because he decided to insert portions of "Homer. Ossian. Chaucer." in "Friday." As he earlier charts the decline in European literature from Homer in "Sunday" through Anacreon in "Tuesday" to Persius and Goethe in "Thursday," he in "Friday" charts a similar decline from Ossian, the Celtic bard, through Chaucer, father of English poetry, to the civilized poets of nineteenth-century England and America.

Whatever doubts he may have had, Thoreau found it useful to accept James Macpherson's poems as "the genuine remains of Ossian" (W 343, EEM 157).[21] The authenticity of these so-called translations from the Gaelic of Ossian, son of Fingal, a bard of the third century A.D., had been questioned by English critics from the time the poems were published between 1760 and 1763. But such doubts did not undermine their impact on writers as diverse as Goethe, Blake, Byron, and Scott. In America the authenticity of the poems was debated up until the War of 1812. After that, there developed a growing skepticism about their genuineness. As an American reviewer observed in 1836, the poems had impressed earlier readers as "a voice from the depths of the ages, uttering the lofty inspirations of chivalry," but, when people became convinced that the poems were forgeries, "all these impressions vanished, like the wreaths of morning mist; the sound was full of sublimity so long as it was mistaken for the distant thunder, but became almost ludicrous, when it was believed to proceed from the rattling of the wagon on the pavement."[22] Nonetheless, the poems continued to cast a spell upon poets like Longfellow and Whitman. They also had a lasting impact on

[21]The reception and influence of Macpherson's poems is summarized in Foerster, Fortunes. See especially pp. 23–27, 57–59, 70–72, and 105–6. Foerster's only reference to Thoreau's views, however, is James Russell Lowell's remark that Thoreau "cited similes from Ossian as proof 'of the superiority of the old poetry to the new' " (p. 105).

[22]Quoted ibid., p. 106.

Thoreau, who praised Macpherson's translations in undergraduate essays (*EEM* 41, 76) and who later discovered Patrick Macgregor's edition of *The Genuine Remains of Ossian* in New York City in 1843.

If Thoreau was deceived, he was, in Swift's wonderful phrase, well deceived, since Ossian admirably suited Thoreau's philosophical and literary purposes. As John Macqueen has observed, "The Philosophical, as opposed to the antiquarian, justification of the poems is to be found in the doctrine of the Noble Savage who is more civilised than corrupt urban man."[23] For Thoreau, Ossian thus served as a compelling example of the natural epic poet, a British counterpart to Homer and the ancient Greeks. The connection between the two epic bards had been made again and again by Macpherson and his defenders. As one of them flatly stated, "Ossian was the Homer of the ancient Highlanders."[24] Recognizing that this similarity could be used as evidence that his translations were forgeries, Macpherson had argued that "the similarity must proceed from nature, the original from which both [Homer and Ossian] drew their ideas."[25] Thoreau gratefully embraced this argument, which enabled him to contrast such natural and inspired epics with the works of a later period, products of education and conscious literary imitation.

He thus emphasizes the primitive and pagan elements in Ossian's poems. "Ossian reminds us of the most refined and rudest eras, of Homer, Pindar, Isaiah, and the American Indian," he remarks. "In his poetry, as in Homer's, only the simplest and most enduring features of humanity are seen, such essential parts as Stonehenge exhibits of a temple" (*W* 344, *EEM* 158). The sim-

[23]*Poems of Ossian*, reprint of the 1805 edition with an introduction by John Macqueen (Edinburgh: James Thin, 1971), I, unpaged introduction.

[24]Quoted in Donald M. Foerster, *Homer in English Criticism* (New Haven: Yale Univ. Press, 1947), p. 53.

[25]Quoted in Macqueen. In his "Preliminary Dissertation," a vigorous 120–page defense of the authenticity of the poems, Macgregor made a similar point, remarking that it was hardly surprising that Ossian "observed several things which Homer observed" (*The Genuine Remains of Ossian* [London: Smith, Elder, 1841], p. 94).

plicity and vigor of primitive man are reflected in both poetry and religion. In fact, Thoreau apparently viewed the pagan religion of Ossian's poems as the best evidence of their authenticity. In a preliminary revision of the *Dial* article for *A Week,* he interlined: "It is remarkable that there is in Ossian no trace of the influence of Christianity. This is evidence enough, if any were needed, [to] prove the genuineness of these remains, for to omit thi[s in] a modern poem surpasses the cunning of man" (*EEM* TN 159.26). But he did not include these remarks in *A Week,* possibly because he did not wish to raise the issue of authenticity. Instead, he tacitly assumes Ossian's epic is an accurate portrait of a primitive era, compared with which "our civilized history appears the chronicle of debility, of fashion, and the arts of luxury" (*W* 345, *EEM* 159).

Although he accepted the eighteenth-century view of Ossian's heroes as noble savages, Thoreau flatly rejected the conventional sentimental view of Ossian's poetry. Since Ossian in old age relates the exploits of his youth and laments the passage of time and since for Macpherson and other late eighteenth-century poets the expression of natural feeling inevitably included melancholy, the conventional view was no doubt justified. Even Wordsworth, who thought the Scottish epics "a disgusting imposture," conceded that one's interest in Ossian was "connected with gray hours, infirmity, and privation."[26] Similarly, in *The Book of the Seasons,* subject of one of Thoreau's undergraduate essays, William Howitt began a chapter on "November" with a brief discussion of "melancholy" Ossian. "The harp of Ossian is truly a 'harp of sorrow,' " Howitt observed. "It breathes perpetually of melancholy tenderness. It is the voice of age lamenting over departing glory; over beauty and strength cut down in their prime."[27]

[26]Quoted in Foerster, *Fortunes,* pp. 71, 59.

[27]William Howitt, *The Book of the Seasons; or the Calendar of Nature* (Philadelphia: Carey & Lea, 1831), p. 288. Howitt acknowledged that the poems might be "a pleasant, modern fiction," but observed: "If this be true, it is wonderful; but I shall choose not to believe it true. I shall choose to think of Ossian as the ancient and veritable bard, and Macpherson as the fortunate fellow, who found his scattered lays, and who perhaps added links and *amendments* (to use the word in a parliamentary sense) of his own" (pp. 288–89).

Thoreau, who associated melancholy with weakness or lack of vigor, offers a radically different reading of the poems. In his comments on Howitt's chapter he developed the thesis that "there is nothing melancholy in Nature" (*EEM* 34). In "Friday," his own chapter on autumn, he insists that Ossian's poems, like the natural landscape, have nothing to do with transience or melancholy. Ossian's heroes "lead such a simple, dry, and everlasting life, as hardly needs depart with the flesh, but is transmitted entire from age to age" (*W* 344, *EEM* 158), Thoreau observes near the opening of the digression. Describing their expression of natural feeling, he later insists, "If Ossian's heroes weep, it is from excess of strength, and not from weakness, a sacrifice or libation of fertile natures" (*W* 347, *EEM* 161). These heroes thus serve as literary analogues to the signs of vigor and permanence in man and nature that Thoreau discovers throughout "Friday."

Chaucer, whom he discusses later in the chapter, stands poised between Ossian's epics and the polished poetry of more civilized eras. "What a contrast between the stern and desolate poetry of Ossian," Thoreau begins, "and that of Chaucer, and even of Shakspeare and Milton, much more of Dryden, and Pope, and Gray" (*W* 366-67, *EEM* 162). As a poet of a civilized era, Chaucer illustrates the loss of "the dignity and sacredness of [the bard's] office" and the decline from epic poetry to merely "pleasant" verse: "The poet has come within doors, and exchanged the forest and the crag for the fireside. . . . We see the comfortable fireside, and hear the crackling fagots in all the verse" (*W* 367, *EEM* 163). All the verse, of course, includes Chaucer and his modern successors in English and American poetry, including contemporary poets like Lowell, Whittier, Longfellow, and Holmes, who were already beginning to offer the warmth and security of the fireside to an increasingly grateful American audience. But whereas his successors are mere imitators, Chaucer was "the father of English poetry," the originator of a tradition now in decay. Describing him as "the Homer of the English poets," Thoreau continues, "He is so natural and cheerful, compared with later poets, that we might also regard him as the personification of spring" (*W* 368, *EEM* 163-64). He thus sketches two periods of decline: from Ossian to Chaucer and from Chaucer and his immediate heirs in the English Renaissance to the imitative poets of modern Eng-land and America.

Chaucer's poetry illuminates the failure of modern poets in English. His is "still the poetry of youth and life," since "though the moral vein is obvious and constant, it has not yet banished the sun and daylight from his verse" (*W* 368, *EEM* 164). In "pre-ferring his homely but vigorous Saxon tongue," Chaucer "ren-dered a similar service to his country to that which Dante rendered to Italy" (*W* 369, *EEM* 165). Implicitly, however, no poet had rendered a similar service to America, nor had any achieved Chaucer's special place in the hearts of his readers. In another implied contrast Thoreau commends Chaucer's "pure, and gen-uine, and childlike love of Nature" and "his familiar, yet innocent and reverent, manner of speaking of his God" (*W* 373, *EEM* 169). Acknowledging that the medieval poet lacked the taste and re-finement of more recent poets, Thoreau in a more general con-cluding section distinguishes between two kinds of writing, "one that of genius, or the inspired, the other of intellect and taste, in the intervals of inspiration" (*W* 375, *EEM* 171). As he notes, Goethe's works furnish examples of the latter, but Thoreau was clearly more inspired by the "rough-hewn" works of Homer, Os-sian, and Chaucer, whose "true finish" is the work of time and the elements (*W* 376-77, *EEM* 173).

Although his article on the ancient poets was written without reference to *A Week,* Thoreau carefully related the digressions on Ossian and Chaucer to the voyage down the Merrimack in "Friday." The weather changes from a "raw and gusty day," which reminds him of the "northern climes" of Ossian, to "the warmth of a summer afternoon," which prompts the remarks on Chaucer and "poets of a milder period" (*W* 343, 366). As the brothers float down the Merrimack, in imagination they float "further down the stream of time" from the ancient Celtic bard to modern poets. Their voyage carries them from the rude towns on the northern reaches of the Merrimack to Billerica, the civil and civilized town that occasions both the digression on civilization and wildness in "Sunday" and the remarks on Chaucer in "Friday." Finally, the progress of English poetry mirrors the seasonal progress from summer to autumn in *A Week.* As Thoreau observes at the opening of the digression on Chaucer, "Our summer of English poetry, like the Greek and Latin before it, seems well advanced toward its fall, and laden with the fruit and foliage of the season, with bright autumnal tints, but soon the winter will scatter its myriad clustering and shading leaves, and leave only a few desolate and fibrous boughs to sustain the snow and rime, and creak in the blasts of age" (W 367, EEM 162).

In the context of A Week Thoreau's depiction of the state of English poetry underscores the need to establish a native tradition in America. He implicitly associates English poetry with the beautiful but frail flowers described in "Saturday" rather than with the vigorous native wildflowers celebrated in "Friday." Like English poetry, which "seems well advanced toward its fall," the flowers along the banks of the Concord "showed by their faded tints that the season was verging towards the afternoon of the year" (W 20, FD 6). In contrast the flowers along the banks of the Merrimack achieve their true glory in autumn and even "abide with us the approach of winter" (W 355, FD 93). Winter will scatter the flowers and foliage of English poetry, leaving "only a few desolate and fibrous boughs to sustain the snow and rime," but it has little effect on rugged native plants like the witch hazel, which blooms "when other shrubs have lost their leaves, as well as blossoms" (W 355; cf. FD 94). These native wildflowers, which Thoreau initially used as a reassuring sign of nature's vigor and permanence, also came to serve him as a symbol of a vigorous, indigenous tradition in literature that might be achieved in America.

Despite his attention to the classics of Continental and British poetry, Thoreau stresses that a native tradition cannot be established through imitation. "The best poets, after all, exhibit only a tame and civil side of nature," he observed in the Journal in 1841, shortly before beginning work on the British poets. "It is only the white man's poetry—we want the Indian's report. Wordsworth is too tame for the Chippeway" (J 1:321). Revising the entry for A Week, he dropped the last two sentences and continued: "Homer and Ossian even can never revive in London or Boston. And yet behold how these cities are refreshed by the mere tradition, or the imperfectly transmitted flavor of these wild fruits.

If we could listen but for an instant to the chaunt of the Indian muse, we should understand why he will not exchange his savageness for civilization" (*W* 56). Homer and Ossian, the primitive bards celebrated in "Sunday" and "Friday," remain important sources of Thoreau's inspiration in *A Week*. But the works of even those ancient poets are fruits of the Old World, whose traditions finally offer no model for the writer in the New World. As Thoreau conceives it, a native tradition must savor of even wilder fruits, the indigenous growth of the America wilderness. Having tasted the fruits during the trip to Agiocochook and heard "the chaunt of the Indian muse" along the banks of the Merrimack, he thus returns to Concord refreshed and determined to transmit their flavor to posterity in *A Week*.

Thoreau uses nature's seasonal cycle as a paradigm for the writing of his book. "Nature, who is superior to all styles and ages, is now, with pensive face, composing her poem Autumn," he remarks in the paragraph following the digression on Chaucer, "with which no work of man will bear to be compared" (*W* 377). But the writer may at least emulate and participate in her seasonal process. Books "must themselves be the unconstrained and natural harvest of their author's lives," he declares in the digression on books and style in "Sunday" (*W* 98). In "Friday," following the eloquent disquisition on "a natural life," he remarks: "Thus thoughtfully we were rowing homeward to find some autumnal work to do, and help on the revolution of the seasons. Perhaps Nature would condescend to make use of us even without our knowledge, as when we help to scatter her seeds in our walks, and carry burrs and cockles on our clothes from field to field" (*W* 388-89). That "autumnal work" is the writing of *A Week*, at once the harvest of his early life and the first great fruit of his literary vocation. What was most important to Thoreau, however, was not the fruit itself but the seeds it contained. "Seeds! there are seeds enough," he proclaims in "Monday," "which need only to be stirred in with the soil where they lie, by an inspired voice or pen, to bear fruit of a divine flavor" (*W* 125; cf. *J* 1:49). The true test of *A Week* is whether its seeds will germinate in the lives of its readers.

The final digression in *A Week* concerns the relationship between a book and its readers. Originally drafted as part of an 1838 lecture on "Sound and Silence," recopied in the 1841 Journal transcripts, "Gleanings—Or What Time Has Not Reaped of My Journal," then in the Long Book, from which Thoreau excised the leaves for inclusion in the first draft in 1845, and finally revised and recopied once more in the second draft of 1846-47, the section serves as an apt coda to *A Week*. "We not unfrequently refer the interest which belongs to our own unwritten sequel, to the written and comparatively lifeless body of the work," Thoreau observes. "Of all books this sequel is the most indispensable part" (*W* 392-93, FD 104, *J* 1:64). He echoes "The American Scholar," where Emerson warned, "The sacredness which attaches to the act of creation,—the act of thought,—is instantly transferred to the record" (*CW* I:56). The proper function of books is to inspire. As Thoreau was inspired by books—by Homer and Virgil, by the great British poets, by the works of his friends and neighbors in Concord—so he hopes that his own first book will inspire others, thus establishing an ongoing cycle of creativity. Humbly accepting the reader's participation as a condition of his own vocation, in the penultimate paragraph he concludes, "Nevertheless, we will go on, like those Chinese cliff swallows, feathering our nests with froth, which may one day be bread of life to such as dwell by the seashore" (*W* 393, FD 105, *J* 1:64).

The final paragraph, drafted at the end of the transcriptions in the Long Book, ultimately proved even more effective in the published version than in the first draft of *A Week*. There, the elegy for John Thoreau concludes with an image of renewal and rebirth as the pair fasten their boat "to the little apple tree whose stem still bore the mark which its chain had worn—in the chafing of the spring freshets" (FD 105). As Thoreau wove other strands into his increasingly complex weave, the final action gained added resonance. Those "spring freshets," a promise of nature's seasonal renewal, resolve both his elegiac concerns and his concern for reform, which Thoreau also treated as a matter of life and death. His grief over the destruction of the Indians, implicitly associated with his brother, is also assuaged by this emblem of nature's power and permanence. Moreover, the apple tree came to echo Elisha's apple tree, which is visited by similar spring and autumn freshets.

Like that ancient tree on the banks of the Merrimack, the young apple tree in Concord, changed from a "little" one in the first draft to a "wild" one in the published version, produces a native fruit, an analogue to a native tradition in American literature which Thoreau, following in the footsteps of writers like Emerson and Hawthorne, hoped to establish with the publication of *A Week* in 1849.

6

"Whose Law Is Growth":
A WEEK and Thoreau's
Early Literary Career

AS THE ABOVE chapters indicate, the writing of *A Week* charts Thoreau's literary and intellectual development from his years at Harvard to its publication in 1849. But he was not simply becoming a mature artist during this period. He was also becoming a man, a frequently painful process that also had a marked impact upon *A Week*. "The changes which break up at short intervals the prosperity of men, are advertisements of a nature whose law is growth," Emerson observed in "Compensation," an essay that offers interesting insights into his own and Thoreau's early life. "Every soul is by this intrinsic necessity quitting its whole system of things, its friends, and home, and laws, and faith" (*CW* II:72). Thoreau, like Emerson before him, experienced precisely such "changes," a series of disappointments, failures, and losses, during the writing of *A Week*. He also enacted a series of what Emerson described as "revolutions," signing off from the church, refusing to pay the poll tax, and, in his move to Walden Pond, if not quitting at least putting some distance between himself and his family, friends, and neighbors in Concord. He moved to the pond, of course, on July 4, Independence Day. But genuine independence came more slowly, as gradually during the writing of *A Week* Thoreau began to resist the influence of those who had dominated his earlier literary career.

Foremost among these was Emerson himself, who was far more than a literary or philosophical influence. From the time Thoreau graduated from Harvard, Emerson took his young neighbor in hand, stimulating his reading, prompting him to begin a journal, overseeing his contributions to the *Dial*, and by example and advice directing his literary career. "If I feel overshadowed and outdone by great neighbors, I can yet love; I can still receive," Emerson eloquently affirmed in "Compensation"; "and he that loveth, maketh his own the grandeur he loves" (CW II:72). Emerson, of course, was not overshadowed by his neighbors, at least not those in Concord, where Thoreau constantly suffered an invidious comparison with the older man. Thoreau did love his friend, from whom he received a great deal, but he could hardly be satisfied by sharing Emerson's grandeur. Thoreau was instead determined to match it, especially in his first book, which both he and Emerson hoped would justify the master's faith in his disciple. In fact, disappointed in Thoreau's initial failure to live up to expectations, Emerson persistently sought to influence the direction and to arrange for the publication of *A Week*. Thoreau, however, was determined to chart his own course in *A Week*, which became a very different book from the one Emerson wanted him to write. Thus, as the foreground of *A Week* is dominated by the loving friendship between the brothers who made the trip (a friendship that had itself been strained by their rivalry over a young woman), so its background was dominated by the increasingly strained friendship between Emerson and Thoreau.

Similarly, where *A Week* reveals his struggle to come to terms with John's death, the book was also a product of Thoreau's long struggle to establish himself as a writer. Through Emerson he gained a small foothold in the narrow world of literary Transcendentalism, where he came into fruitful contact with writers like Margaret Fuller, Bronson Alcott, and Ellery Channing. In fact, his earliest plan for giving an account of the 1839 trip to the White Mountains was one of a number of projected works inspired by the establishment of the *Dial,* and Thoreau's first book cannot be fully understood without reference to his varied contributions to that "Magazine for Literature, Philosophy, and Religion," many of which later found their way into *A Week*. But, however valuable for his artistic growth, writing for the *Dial* offered Thoreau neither renumeration nor reputation. Nathaniel Hawthorne, who moved to Concord in 1842, helped him make contacts in Boston and, especially, in New York City, where Thoreau moved in 1843. There he became friends with Horace Greeley, editor of the *Tribune,* who later acted as an agent for his works. But Thoreau's efforts to find a place for himself in the New York literary world were futile. As it turned out, that failure and the collapse of the *Dial* in 1844, which might have combined to terminate his literary career, simply marked the end of his literary apprenticeship.

For the next five years Thoreau devoted most of his energies to books. During the fall of 1844, after deciding to move to Walden Pond, he began to gather material for the first draft of *A Week,* which he wrote in 1845. Events of 1846, especially his arrest that summer, profoundly influenced the direction of the second draft of the book, which Thoreau submitted to publishers in mid-1847, by which time he was also completing the first version of *Walden.* His failure to secure a publisher for *A Week* in 1847 had significant consequences for the ultimate shape and content of the book, which he temporarily laid aside in order to write lectures and essays, including "Ktaadn, and the Maine Woods," which Horace Greeley placed in the *Union Magazine.* Greeley, like Emerson, also offered a good deal of fatherly advice. But just as Thoreau resisted Emerson's ideas about the direction his writings should take, so he resisted Greeley's ideas about the direction his career should take. Thus, instead of writing short articles for the magazines, as Greeley urged, Thoreau during 1848 doggedly worked on *A Week* and *Walden,* which were crucial to his own strategy for becoming a self-supporting writer. Indeed, the failure of *A Week* is made all the more poignant by his great expectations, for by publishing the book at his own expense in 1849 he clearly hoped at once to free himself from the harsh necessities of the American literary marketplace and to step out from under Emerson's long shadow into the light of individual literary recognition.

Emerson began to cast that shadow even before he and Thoreau became friends.[1] In 1834 the older man moved to Concord, his ancestral village, where, in the Old Manse, he wrote his first book, *Nature.* Thoreau read and reread the volume in the spring of 1837, shortly before his graduation from Harvard. At the graduation ceremonies he perhaps heard Emerson deliver the Phi Beta Kappa address, "The American Scholar." A product of his own

[1]Additional details concerning the early Emerson-Thoreau relationship are given in *DHT,* especially pp. 59–73, and Rusk.

struggle with the problem of vocation, Emerson's address spoke to young men with a literary bent who were about to take their place in a country that offered few rewards to its writers.[2] Indeed, speaking in the midst of the panic of 1837, the worst economic depression the country had experienced, Emerson gave an unblinking assessment of the obstacles to a literary life—poverty, uncertainty, and the hostility of society, all of which Thoreau later experienced. Emerson, however, also described the scholar's compensations. "He is to find consolation in exercising the highest functions of human nature," he asserted. "He is one who raises himself from private considerations, and breathes and lives on public and illustrious thoughts" (CW I:62).

Emerson's inspirational ideas and presence in Concord had a profound impact on Thoreau. After a futile search for a teaching position, which was virtually impossible to find during the depression, Thoreau first founded a private school and then, in September 1838, took over the Concord Academy, which soon proved so popular that John left his position in Roxbury to join his brother in Concord. But Emerson, probably remembering his own frustrating years in his elder brother's English Classical School in Boston, where he had taught after graduating from Harvard, encouraged Thoreau's literary aspirations. It was no doubt Emerson who asked, "Do you keep a journal?" (J 1:5), the question that prompted him to make his first entry on October 22, 1837.[3] Early Journal entries record his reading of some of Emerson's favorite authors, especially Goethe, whose ideal of self-development and personal culture shaped each man's career. At

[2]See Henry Nash Smith, "Emerson's Problem of Vocation," in *Emerson: A Collection of Critical Essays*, ed. Milton Konowitz and Stephen Whicher (Englewood Cliffs, N.J.: Prentice-Hall, 1964), pp. 60–72. Merton Sealts, "Emerson on the Scholar, 1833–1837," *PMLA* 85 (1970):185–95, traces Emerson's shifting view of the scholar, while the national context of Emerson's address is sketched by Larzar Ziff, *Literary Democracy* (New York: Viking, 1981), pp. 18–23.

[3]For a discussion of the relationship between the Journal and Thoreau's early literary projects, see Robert Sattelmeyer's Historical Introduction to *Journal 1: 1837–1844* (J 1:592–613) and William Howarth, *The Book of Concord* (New York: Viking, 1982).

meetings of the Transcendental Club at Emerson's home, Thoreau participated in discussions that also strongly colored his ideas, which were further quickened by the inspiration of Emerson's lectures. On December 6, 1837, for example, he traveled to Boston to hear Emerson deliver the introduction to a new series, "Human Culture"; thereafter, he heard each of the lectures at private readings in Concord. He delivered his own first lecture, "Society," at the Concord Lyceum in April 1838. That summer Emerson delivered the "Divinity School Address," generating a controversy that hardened Thoreau's own growing opposition to the institutionalized church, which a decade later he would attack in *A Week*. Some of the material that would ultimately find its way into the book was paying more immediate dividends, however, for early in 1839 Emerson wrote Margaret Fuller that Thoreau, "my protester," had broken "into good poetry and better prose" (*L* II:182).

Although he took paternal pride in Thoreau's nascent literary abilities, Emerson was even more impressed by his young neighbor's practical attributes and knowledge of nature. After leaving the ministry in 1832, Emerson had initially planned to become a naturalist, so he had a keen interest in and a fairly secure grasp of modern science. But Thoreau's knowledge, he believed, had been gained directly through observation and experience, which Emerson valued more highly than book learning. "An education in things is not," he impatiently exclaimed after hearing an address by Horace Mann, the educational reformer, in September 1839. "We are shut up in schools & college recitation rooms for ten or fifteen years & come out at last with a bellyfull of words & do not know a thing." The complaint echoes "The American Scholar," where he had earlier emphasized the role of nature and experience in education. By 1839, however, Emerson had discovered a type of his ideal scholar. Thus, in contrast to "wordmen" like himself, who "do not know an edible root in the woods" and "cannot tell our course by the stars nor the hour of the day by the sun," Emerson offered the example of his "wise young neighbors," who had the day before returned from their voyage up the Merrimack, where they had lived "by their wits on the fish of the stream & the berries of the wood" (*JMN* VII:238). The outlines of his 1862 funeral oration, "Thoreau," eulogy of a writer who blended Emerson's own idealism and individualism with practical skills and an intimate knowledge of natural facts, had thus already begun to emerge.

Eager that Thoreau should have the opportunity to fulfill his early promise, Emerson helped establish the *Dial,* which he viewed as a golden opportunity for his young disciple. "We have a power of fine people who would write a few numbers of such book, who write nowhere else," he explained to his brother William on September 26, 1839, a week after he and other members of the Transcendental Club decided to found a new journal: "My Henry Thoreau will be a great poet for such a company, & one of these days for all companies" (*L* II:225). Emerson, however, had to elbow out a place for Thoreau in that company. Margaret Fuller had been named editor of the *Dial,* but he took the liberty of accepting Thoreau's poem "Elegy" ("Sympathy"), which Emerson had earlier hailed as the purest and loftiest strain "that has yet pealed from this unpoetic American forest" (*JMN* VII:230–31). When he read Thoreau's "fine critique on Persius" in March 1840, Emerson proclaimed it, too, "well worthy" of the *Dial* (*L* II:259). His letters suggest that, for various reasons, neither Thoreau nor Fuller was very enthusiastic about the prospect of publishing the article, but Emerson was determined. According to him, Thoreau had "too mean an opinion of 'Persius' or any of his pieces to care to revise them" (*L* II:280–81), so Emerson revised it for him. He also peppered Fuller with advance requests that she accept the article. As he prepared to send it to her, however, Emerson foresaw some objections. It had too much "manner" and not enough "method," and the piece was too long. "Yet it has always a spiritual meaning even when the literal does not hold," he asserted, "& has so much brilliancy & life in it that in our bold bible for The Young America, I think it ought to find a place" (*L* II:287). Although she apparently asked for further revisions, Fuller could hardly refuse to print "Aulus Persius Flaccus" in the first issue of the *Dial,* from which Thoreau later lifted it for inclusion in *A Week.*

Thoreau's earliest plan for giving an account of the 1839 trip
was but one of a number of writing projects occasioned by the
establishment of the *Dial*. Encouraged by the acceptance of his
first effort, he drew up a list of other essay topics: "Love," "Sound
& Silence," "Horace," "Greek Poetry," "The Brave man," "Memoirs
of a Tour—A Chit-chat with Nature," "Music," and "Hindoo
Scripture."[4] In retrospect, "Memoirs of a Tour," his first title for
a literary excursion, obviously strikes us as the most interesting
and significant topic. But the other topics on the list give a clearer
picture of his interests in 1840. Consequently, after making tentative efforts to reconstruct that "tour" in June, when he copied
his excursion notes into the Journal and drafted a few additional
passages, Thoreau turned his attention to one of the other topics,
"The Brave man."

The completed essay, which he sent to Margaret Fuller in July,
clearly reveals the influence of Emerson. Thoreau retitled it "The
Service," possibly to distinguish it from "Heroism," a lecture from
the "Human Culture" series Emerson was then revising for *Essays,* but the change hardly disguised their connections. In
"Heroism" Emerson remarked the absence of heroic traits in
modern literature and called for more "books of this tart cathartic
virtue," works that remind us of the need for "the arming of the
man," whose assumption of "a warlike attitude" affirms "his ability
to cope single-handed with the infinite array of enemies" (CW
II:147–48). In "The Service," with its imagery of fife and drums,
knights and crusaders, Thoreau assumed that warlike attitude
and so answered Emerson's call to arms. He was also recruited
by Emerson's literary methods, as Thoreau gathered together
scattered entries from the Journal into an essay on a single abstract topic, though the form such imitation took in "The Service"
hardly flattered the *Essays.* Consequently, the militant young
writer and his bellicose essay were vanquished by a tart critique
penned by Margaret Fuller, who—complaining that she could

---

[4]"Index rerum" (HM 945), p. 19. The list is undated, but Thoreau
probably wrote it in early 1840. The handwriting is characteristic of his
early period and all the topics except "Hindoo Scripture," in a different
ink and probably a later addition, are in his Journal of 1837–40.

still "hear the grating of tools on the mosaic" (*C* 42)—declined to print "The Service" in the *Dial.*

Thoreau was no luckier in love than in literature.[5] After sending off "The Service," he continued to jot passages for "Memoirs of a Tour" in the Journal, but by the summer of 1840 Thoreau must have had mixed feelings about his companion on that trip. A few weeks before their departure in 1839 the brothers had both met and fallen in love with Ellen Sewell, who stayed with their family during a two-week visit to Concord. Immediately after their return from the White Mountains, John visited Ellen at her home in Scituate. The success of that visit accounts for the mournful note in many of Thoreau's journal entries on love and friendship that fall. But he joined John in a visit to Scituate during Christmas vacation, and Thoreau saw more of her in June 1840, when Ellen again visited Concord. In fact, his recollections of the 1839 voyage, which he began to jot down at that time, were informed by the more immediate impressions of boating with Ellen on the Concord River. In an entry later revised for *A Week,* for example, Thoreau wrote on June 19, "The other day I rowed in my boat a free— even lovely young lady—and as I plied the oars she sat in the stern—and there was nothing but she between me and the sky" (*J* 1:132; cf. FD 21 and *W* 46).

But the idyll did not last. In July, John again visited Scituate where he proposed to Ellen, who first accepted but swiftly changed her mind. "I heard that an engagement was entered into between a certain youth and a maiden," Thoreau later observed in *A Week,* "and then I heard that it was broken off, but I did not know the reason in either case" (*W* 293). At the time, however, he was hardly as detached and dispassionate, for he himself proposed in a letter written to Ellen in early November. On November 9, after consulting her father, Ellen declined his proposal. Margaret Fuller, who asked him to pardon her long delay, rejected "The Service" in a letter dated December 1, 1840.

---

[5]For a more detailed account of his relationship with Ellen Sewell, see *DHT,* pp. 94–104, and Lebeaux, who stresses "the far-reaching implications of the rivalry" that developed between Henry and John for her affections (p. 116).

Emerson helped Thoreau weather this crisis in his life and career. Spurred by the organization of Brook Farm, Emerson decided to expand his household. He first approached the Alcotts, who had moved to Concord in 1840, but Mrs. Alcott wisely refused. But when John's failing health forced the brothers to close their school in the spring of 1841, Thoreau accepted an invitation to live with the Emersons, earning his room and board in return for work around the house and garden. The arrangement, however, was primarily intended to free Thoreau to work on his writing, especially the poetry Emerson praised so highly. "Thoreau is a scholar & a poet," he wrote his brother William on June 1, "& as full of buds of promise as a young apple tree" (*L* II:402). He pressed Margaret Fuller to accept the poem "Sic Vita" for the July 1841 issue of the *Dial* and prepared her to receive other of Thoreau's poems. In September, a week after Thoreau reported to his friend Lucy Brown that he was in "the mid-sea of verses" (*C* 46), Emerson exclaimed in a letter to Fuller, "H. T. is full of noble maddness lately, and I hope more highly of him than ever" (*L* II:447). Later in September, Emerson recommended his friend's poetry to Rufus Griswold, editor of *The Poets and Poetry of America,* but Griswold was evidently no more impressed by the poems Thoreau forwarded to him than Fuller was by Thoreau's efforts for the *Dial.*

He was clearly modeling his career on Emerson's. Emerson's interest in poetry, especially intense in 1840–41, when he published poems like "The Problem," "Woodnotes" numbers 1 and 2, "The Snow Storm," "The Sphinx," and "Fate" in the *Dial,* inspired Thoreau's ongoing efforts. Emerson also encouraged his plans for an anthology of English poetry, advancing Thoreau fifteen dollars to cover the expenses of his two-week stay in Cambridge in November–December 1841. In fact, Emerson, who someday hoped to publish his own commonplace book containing extracts from his favorite English poets, generously lent the notebook to Thoreau, who copied out twenty pages of extracts as a starting place for his own similar compilation.[6] But of all Emer-

---

[6]Sattelmeyer, "Thoreau's Projected Work on the English Poets," p. 242.

son's various literary activities, *Essays* was no doubt the most compelling example to Thoreau. Emerson began to work on the volume in earnest in the spring of 1840, about the time Thoreau drew up his first list of essay topics. *Essays* appeared in March 1841, shortly before Thoreau moved in with the Emersons, and its generally favorable and often enthusiastic reception no doubt had a profound impact on a young man struggling to articulate his own literary career. Consequently, in the fall of 1841, while he was transcribing portions of his early Journal, "Gleanings— Or What Time Has Not Reaped of My Journal," Thoreau drew up a new list of eleven essay topics, one fewer than *Essays:* "Merrimack & Musketaquid," "Sound and Silence," "Bravery," "Concord," "Friendship," "Books & style," "Seeing," "Obligation," "Dying," "Devil," and "Journal."[7]

Once again, his list was dominated by literary and philosophical topics à la Emerson. But, by placing "Merrimack and Musketaquid" at the head of the list, Thoreau signaled his growing interest in descriptive and narrative prose. Emerson had thought to call his volume "Forest Essays," perhaps in an effort to evoke their growth in a natural realm, but he dropped half of that title and began the volume with "History," which, "rather than nature, now appeared to be the best expositor of the divine mind."[8] In his plan for a similar volume Thoreau stuck with nature, obviously intending to introduce the reader to the withdrawn and unspoiled world of the rivers before embarking on more abstract meditations on topics like "Sound and Silence," "Bravery," "Friendship," "Books & style," and "Dying." The river voyage was not, of course, destined to introduce a book of essays on these topics; *A Week,* however, would provide a setting for digressions on many of these same subjects.

Thoreau's plan to write about the brothers' voyage probably served emotional as well as literary needs. In the postscript to a long letter criticizing his poem "With frontier strength ye stand your ground," later inserted in both "A Walk to Wachusett" and *A Week,* Margaret Fuller wrote on October 18, 1841: "The pen-

[7]"Index rerum" (HM 945), front endpaper [verso].
[8]Rusk, p. 278.

cilled paper Mr. E. put into my hands. I have taken the liberty
to copy it You expressed one day my own opinion that the moment
such a crisis is passed we may speak of it. . . .Thus you will not
be sorry that I have seen the paper. Will you not send me some
other records of the good week" (C 57). It is, of course, impossible
to say with any certainty exactly what that "pencilled paper" contained, but Fuller's closing words, "good week" (a phrase that
seems to have been used to describe any extended period of recreation), suggest that the paper may have been related to Thoreau's projected account of the 1839 voyage.[9] The "crisis" was
possibly occasioned by their loss of Ellen Sewell and, perhaps,
by Thoreau's guilt about having asked her to marry him after she
had rejected his brother. In any case, we may speculate that,
whatever its literary background and inspiration, Thoreau's plan
to give an account of the voyage was given added impetus by his
desire to reaffirm the bonds of friendship that had been strained
by the brothers' competition for the love of Ellen Sewell.

In addition to altering radically its scale and conception, John's
death in January 1842 dramatically raised the stakes riding on
that account. What Thoreau had for two years planned as an essay
would now become a book, at once a remembrance of and an
elegy for his brother. Indeed, like so many other nineteenth- and
twentieth-century artists, including Anthony Trollope, Vincent
Van Gogh (named after his dead brother), Gustav Mahler, James
M. Barrie, and Jack Kerouac, who insisted that his books were
written through him by his dead brother, Thoreau's mourning
took the form of art, while his art took the form of mourning in

---

[9]Pointing out that Fuller had visited the Emersons only a short time
earlier, between October 2 and October 8 or 9, when Thoreau had been
living there for six months, Thomas Blanding plausibly argues that the
"pencilled paper" contained records of her week-long visit, not records
of the trip depicted in A Week. For a full discussion of the issue see
Blanding's "Thoreau's A Week on the Concord and Merrimack Rivers
and Margaret Fuller's 'Good Week,' " Concord Saunterer 17, no. 1
(1984):6–9; and the author's response, "More on Thoreau's A Week on
the Concord and Merrimack Rivers and Margaret Fuller's 'Good
Week,' " Concord Saunterer 17, no. 3 (1984):17–20.

A Week.[10] But the book would carry an additional burden, one he had meditated upon nearly two years earlier. "On the death of a friend, we should consider that the fates through confidence have devolved on us the task of a double living," he wrote in the Journal on February 28, 1840; "we have henceforth to fulfil the promise of our friend's life also, in our own, to the world" (*J* 1:114). For Thoreau, that responsibility was made all the greater by the fact that John was by far the more popular and, to some at least, the more promising of the pair. *A Week* would consequently be informed by two powerful motives. First, it promised to satisfy his own growing hunger for literary recognition. Second, the book, which would be dominated by their shared interest in nature, in the American Indian, in religious reform, and in literature (at the Concord Academy, John had taught the English branches, while Henry handled Greek and Latin), offered an opportunity to fulfill both his own and his brother's promise to the world.

Though its writing was delayed, *A Week* would thus become what Emerson in "Compensation" called one of those "compensations of calamity," an unanticipated dividend of a seemingly unpayable loss. "The death of a dear friend, wife, brother, lover, which seemed nothing but privation, somewhat later assumes the aspect of a guide or genius," Emerson affirmed, alluding to a series of traumatic losses he had experienced; "for it commonly operates revolutions in our way of life, terminates an epoch of infancy or of youth which was waiting to be closed, breaks up a wonted occupation, or a household, or style of living, and allows the formation of new ones more friendly to the growth of character" (*CW* II:73). The death of Emerson's first wife in 1831 had done precisely that, spurring him to quit the Unitarian ministry, to move to Concord, and to begin his first book. John's death had less immediate and dramatic results, but it played an important role in closing out Thoreau's own youth and in inspiring his first book. But Thoreau, whose projected collection of the English

[10]In a review of Mary Lee Settle's *The Killing Ground*, Aaron Latham mentions various artists who have experienced such traumatic losses and describes the impact of the death of his sister on his own literary career (*New York Times Book Review*, July 11, 1982, p. 1).

poets had progressed no further than voluminous extracts and whose plan for a book of essays had faded when he was denied permission to build a hut at Flint's Pond, was in 1842 neither artistically nor financially secure enough to embark on a book-length excursion. During the next two years he therefore bided his time, occasionally jotting passages concerning the trip in the Journal and, perhaps more importantly, writing other works that would have a significant impact on the ultimate form and content of *A Week*.

In other ways as well 1842 represented a transitional period in Thoreau's career. In late March his prospects received a boost from Margaret Fuller's resignation as editor of the *Dial*. Emerson, who took charge, soon solicited an article from Thoreau, who had published only three poems in the *Dial* since the appearance of "Aulus Persius Flaccus" in the first issue. Significantly, however, Emerson did not ask for "The Service," the only portions of which to appear in Thoreau's lifetime were later revised for *A Week*, but instead put him onto a radically different topic. "I read a little lately in the 'Scientific Surveys' of Massachusetts," Emerson wrote Fuller on April 10, "and this day I have, as I hope, set Henry Thoreau on the good track of giving an account of them in the Dial, explaining to him the felicity of the subject for him as it admits of the narrative of all his woodcraft boatcraft & fishcraft" (*L* III:47). His suggestion proved crucial. In "Natural History of Massachusetts," his finest work to that time, Thoreau sharpened his descriptive prose and took a significant step toward the seasonal patterns of *A Week* and *Walden*.

Emerson, however, was disappointed in the piece. Partly as a consequence, his hopes for American literature began to shift from Thoreau to Ellery Channing, who moved to Concord in 1842, and Charles King Newcomb, a young poet and writer at Brook Farm whose allegorical story "Dolan" appeared along with "Natural History of Massachusetts" in the July issue of the *Dial*. In a letter written on July 19 to Fuller, then vacationing in the White Mountains, Emerson praised Newcomb and continued: "I am sorry that you, & the world after you, do not like my brave Henry any better. I do not like his piece very well, but I admire this perennial threatening attitude, just as we like to go under an overhanging precipice It is wholly his natural relation & no assumption at all. But I have now seen so many threats incarnated which 'delayed to strike' & finally never struck at all, that I begin to think our American subsoil must be lead or chalk or whatever represents in geology the phlegmatic" (*L* III:75).

Feeling that Thoreau had once again fallen short of expectations, Emerson for the first time acknowledged the possibility that his friend might never live up to his youthful promise. But others were more enthusiastic about "Natural History of Massachusetts." Bronson Alcott proclaimed it "worthy of Isaac Walton himself," observing that "the woods *[torn]* of Concord are classic now."[11] Somewhat more surprisingly, Nathaniel Hawthorne, who moved into the Old Manse in July 1842, also liked "Natural History of Massachusetts." Although he recognized Emerson's tendency to pick up "queer and clever young men . . . by way of a genius," as he observed of Ellery Channing, Hawthorne was impressed by Thoreau, who took him boating on Concord River and who, "being in want of money," sold him the *Musketaquid* (immediately rechristened the *Pond Lily*) for seven dollars. "He is a good writer," Hawthorne noted, "at least he has written one good article, a rambling disquisition on Natural History in the last Dial. . . . so true, minute, and literal in observation, yet giving the spirit as well as the letter of what he sees, even as the lake reflects its wooded banks, showing every leaf, yet giving the wild beauty of the whole scene." Hawthorne even found praise for Thoreau's "cloudy and dreamy metaphysics," and he especially liked the poems included in the essay, "passages where his thoughts seem to measure and attune themselves into spontaneous verse, as they rightfully may, since there is real poetry in him."[12]

[11]*The Letters of A. Bronson Alcott,* ed. Richard L. Herrnstadt (Ames: Iowa State Univ. Press, 1969), p. 89 (Aug. 2, 1842).

[12]*American Notebooks,* pp. 357, 355 (Sept. 1–2, [1842]). In the entry for Sept. 2, Hawthorne noted: "Ellery Channing called to see us, wishing to talk with me about the Boston Miscellany, of which he heard I was to be Editor, and to which he desired to contribute." Hawthorne was not to be its editor, but he evidently had some influence with the journal, where his "Virtuoso's Collection" had appeared in May 1842. For his other efforts on Thoreau's behalf, especially a letter on October 21, 1842, recommending Thoreau as a possible contributor to a new periodical edited by Epes Sargent, see *DHT*, pp. 139–40.

But by September 1, 1842, when Hawthorne jotted down these observations, Thoreau's poetic efforts had begun to wane. His early ardor had been partially cooled by Margaret Fuller's severe criticisms of many of the poems he had submitted to the *Dial*. After she stepped down as its editor, Emerson saw fit to print one of Thoreau's poems in the July 1841 issue and eight more in the October 1841 *Dial*. Emerson had evidently come to view these poems as crude but solid filler, for that fall he noted in his journal that the chief virtue of Thoreau's poetry was that "mass here as in other instances is some compensation for superior quality" (*JMN* VIII:257). Probably because of Emerson's strictures, Thoreau burned the manuscripts of many of his poems (*DHT* 117). Consequently, whereas in September 1841 he had found himself in "the mid-sea of verses," during the late summer and fall of 1842 Thoreau wrote "A Walk to Wachusett," which Hawthorne apparently encouraged him to submit to the *Boston Miscellany of Literature*, where it appeared in January 1843.

In retrospect the excursion seems like Thoreau's predestined form, but during 1843 he experimented with a number of formats that would also help shape *A Week*. Apparently planning "an article, lyceum lecture, or small book on subjects of central importance to him,"[13] Thoreau sometime in mid to late 1842 transcribed Journal entries on "Hindoo Scripture" and "Books & style," topics included in his early lists of potential writing projects. Before dropping the subject he drafted at least portions of an essay on the *Laws of Menu*, later revised for *A Week*. But Emerson, who had begun a series of extracts from Eastern scriptures in the July 1842 *Dial*, apparently found no use for the rather vaporous and abstract commentary, so Thoreau instead made some selections from the *Laws of Menu* for the January 1843 issue. That issue also contained his translation of *Prometheus Bound*, which Emerson also asked him to do, but none of his original poetry or prose. In contrast the April 1843 issue, which Thoreau edited, contained three of his poems (the last of them to be printed in the *Dial*), plus two pieces later inserted in *A Week*: "Dark Ages,"

[13]Kenneth Cameron, *Transcendental Climate*, 3 vols. (Hartford: Transcendental Books, 1963), III: 901. This volume contains a facsimile and transcript of the notebook, edited as "Transcripts, 1840–1842" in *J* 1:405–29.

the brief essay on history drawn from his 1842 transcripts, and his translations of Anacreon. *A Week* would also receive portions of the lecture "Sir Walter Raleigh," delivered in February, revised for the *Dial*, but apparently pigeonholed when Emerson returned to his editorial duties. In fact, Emerson found little to celebrate in any of Thoreau's writings. "Young men like H. T. owe us a new world & they have not acquitted the debt," he dispiritedly observed in his journal in late March, as Thoreau was preparing to move to Staten Island; "for the most part, such die young, & so dodge the fulfilment" (*JMN* VIII:375).

But Thoreau and others had high hopes for the Staten Island venture, which marked his most serious effort to become a self-supporting writer. Emerson, who helped arrange for him to earn his room and board plus one hundred dollars a year as a tutor to William Emerson's son, reported that Thoreau also hoped to earn a little extra money by doing clerical work for William or some other lawyer. A decade later a writer who in 1843 was polishing brass and standing watch aboard the American man-of-war *United States* would imagine just how deadly the life of a scrivener in a New York law office might be. Thoreau, however, viewed such part-time work as a temporary expedient, "pending the time when he shall procure for himself literary labor from some quarter in New York," and other members of the Emerson household were "charmed with the project" (*L* III:158). Hawthorne also felt the change would do him good. Noting that he would miss the companionship of the younger man, whose combination of "wild freedom" and "high and classic cultivation" Hawthorne found so stimulating, he sympathetically observed: "I am glad, on Mr. Thoreau's own account, that he is going away; as he is physically out of health, and, morally and intellectually, seems not to have found exactly the guiding clue; and in all these respects, he may be benefitted by his removal;—also it is one step towards a circumstantial position in the world."[14]

---

[14]*American Notebooks*, p. 369. The following day Hawthorne and Emerson had a long talk, during which they discussed Channing's poems, which Emerson praised as "poetry for poets," and Thoreau's departure, about which the two "agreed pretty well," though Hawtorne observed that "Mr. Emerson appears to have suffered some inconveniency from his experience of Mr. Thoreau as an inmate" (p. 371).

Although he made a few contacts, Thoreau found that "circumstantial position" in the literary world elusive. In New York City, which was beginning to eclipse Boston as the center of American publishing, he renewed his acquaintance with Horace Greeley, the New England farm boy who, only six years older than Thoreau, had in the course of the previous decade worked his way up from journeyman printer to editor of his own newspaper, the successful *New-York Daily Tribune*. Greeley would later act as an agent for his works, but in 1843 Thoreau peddled his own wares. He thus contacted J. L. O'Sullivan, editor of the *Democratic Review*, to whom Hawthorne had introduced him when O'Sullivan visited Concord the previous January. Thoreau offered him a review of J. A. Etzler's Fourierist tract *The Paradise within Reach of All Men*, a review Emerson wanted for the *Dial*, but O'Sullivan instead asked for "some of those extracts from your Journal, reporting some of your private interviews with nature, with which I have been so much pleased" (C 130). Thoreau, evidently eager not to be typecast, declined.

He had even less success with publishers. "I have tried sundry methods of earning money in the city of late but without success," he wrote his mother on August 29. "Among others I conversed with the Harpers—to see if they might not find me useful to them—but they say they are making fifty thousand dollars annually, and their motto is to let well alone" (C 135). Emerson, who heard of Thoreau's experiences in "the limbo of the false booksellers" from friends in New York, was sympathetic. "I could heartily wish that this country, which seems all opportunity, did actually offer more distinct and just rewards of labor to that unhappy class of men who have more reason and conscience than strength of back and of arm," he wrote on September 8; "but the experience of the few cases that I have lately seen looks, I confess, more like crowded England and indigent Germany than like rich and roomy Nature. But the few cases are deceptive; and though Homer should starve in the highway, Homer will know and proclaim that bounteous Nature has bread for all her boys. To-morrow our arms will be stronger; to-morrow the wall before which we sat will open of itself and show the new way" (C 136–37).

Emerson's inspirational tone recalls "The American Scholar."

But the pep talk must have sounded like cant and complacency to Thoreau, who was confronting obstacles familiar to most nineteenth-century American writers. Indeed, those "few cases" of indigent and starving writers, his own included, were all too illustrative of the harsh conditions on America's Grub Street. "Literature comes to a poor market here," he replied to Emerson on September 14, "and even the little that I write is more than will sell" (C 139). He reported that O'Sullivan had accepted his revised review of Etzler's book, "Paradise (to be) Regained," for the *Democratic Review,* in which "The Landlord," his experiment in the "familiar essay or sketch so popular in mid-nineteenth-century periodicals" (*DHT* 141), would also appear in 1843. As he told Emerson, however, Thoreau had discovered that most periodicals, "overwhelmed with contributions which cost nothing, and are worth no more," did not pay for contributions. He had therefore been forced into the desperate and equally unsuccessful expedient of selling subscriptions to the *American Agriculturist,* founded the year before and published in New York City (C 139). Though he stayed on in New York through the autumn, the wall never opened. Thus, despite his effort to break out of the circumscribed literary world of the Transcendentalists, Thoreau remained dependent on the *Dial.*

His final submissions to the *Dial* reflect the range of Thoreau's interests, interests that were to give *A Week* its eclectic quality. While in New York he responded to Emerson's request for a contribution with a batch of poems and a translation of *Seven against Thebes,* neither of which Emerson used, plus his second literary excursion, "A Winter Walk," an essay that revealed his distaste for the city and his yearning for Concord. Ellery Channing "admired the piece loudly and long," but Emerson, who appreciated its "faithful observation," objected to its "mannerism," the trick of calling "a cold place sultry, a solitude public, a wilderness *domestic* (a favorite word), and in the woods to insult over cities, whilst the woods, again, are dignified by comparing them to cities, armies, etc." (C 137). Nonetheless, after making "pretty free omissions," Emerson included "A Winter Walk" in the October 1843 issue of the *Dial.* Returning home for a brief visit, Thoreau in November delivered the lecture entitled "The Ancient Poets," which he soon revised as "Homer. Ossian. Chaucer." for the *Dial*. The essay, later revised again for *A Week*, first appeared in the January 1844 issue, which also contained his translations of Pindar, sixteen lines of which he later quoted in *A Week* (*W* 244). The April 1844 issue contained more Pindar plus his enthusiastic notice of Nathaniel Rogers's *Herald of Freedom*, a review that he later recast for *A Week*. There, he would also seek to find a place for portions of his 1844 lecture on the conservative and the reformer, which Thoreau had probably originally hoped to publish in the *Dial*. But the April issue was the last, so he no longer had a dependable outlet for his diverse writings.

Thoreau's failure to establish himself as a writer by 1844, nearly five years after the establishment of the *Dial*, must have been made all the more painful by the current successes of his friends and associates. Disappointed in Thoreau, who he had hoped would become "a great poet . . . for all companies," Emerson had increasingly turned his attention to Ellery Channing, whose first book, *Poems*, was published in 1843. Emerson, who had earlier favored Channing by making him the only writer paid for his contributions to the *Dial*, also uncharacteristically agreed to review the volume for the September issue of the *Democratic Review*, where his fulsome praise of Channing's *Poems*, echoed by Thoreau in the Journal, formed an ironic prelude to Thoreau's meager contributions to the periodical later that fall (*L* III:197–98n; cf. *J* 1:459). Ellery "puts all poets & especially all prophets far far in the background," Emerson exclaimed in a letter to Margaret Fuller on December 17, 1843 (*L* III:230). That day Thoreau returned for good from his abortive literary venture in New York to Concord, where he began work in his father's pencil factory, making tools for other writers. By then Margaret Fuller was also working on the book about her recent trip west, published as *Summer on the Lakes* in June 1844. Emerson called it "a very good & entertaining book" (*L* III:255), and Horace Greeley liked it so much that he hired her as his assistant on the *Tribune*. Before joining the paper, she revised and expanded her *Dial* article "Great Lawsuit" as *Woman in the Nineteenth Century*, whose publication in February 1845, combined with her prominent role in the *Tribune*, made Fuller one of the most celebrated social and literary critics in the country. Meanwhile, in 1844 Emerson was busy working on *Essays: Second Series,* published at the end of October, which proved to be his best-received volume to date. To Thoreau, the message must have seemed clear: genuine literary recognition depended on books.

However inauspicious they seemed at the time, his circumstances in 1844 set the stage for *A Week.* Although he had failed to become Emerson's long-awaited Transcendental bard, he had become a prose writer of considerable promise.[15] Moreover, like John's death in 1842, a loss that inspired the book, Thoreau's literary failures and disappointments during 1843 and 1844 helped spark a revolution in his life and writings, determining him to grasp the first opportunity to begin *A Week.* Thus, after a walking tour of the Berkshires and Catskills with Ellery Channing, Thoreau in August declined his friend Isaac Hecker's invitation to undertake a similar tour of Europe, observing, "I cannot so decidedly postpone exploring the *Farther Indies,* which are to be reached you know by other routs and other methods of travel" (*C* 156). The opportunity to embark on both an inward and a literary exploration presented itself when Emerson purchased Wyman Field on the shore of Walden Pond in September. The purchase marked a crucial turning point in Thoreau's life and writings. Three years earlier he had been denied permission to build a hut at Flint's Pond, where he had hoped to write a book of essays, including "Merrimack & Musketaquid"; he now received Emerson's blessing to build at Walden Pond, where Thoreau would finally gain the solitude and independence he needed to write *A Week on the Concord and Merrimack Rivers.*

In anticipation of his move to Walden Pond, he gathered material for *A Week,* a process informed by his memories of John Thoreau. On the first page of the Long Book he inscribed its opening epigraph, concluding: "Be thou my muse, my Brother" (*J* 2:3, *W* 3). By invoking his brother, Thoreau reaffirmed their

---

[15]For a detailed discussion of Thoreau's early stylistic development, see Charles R. Anderson, "Thoreau and the *Dial:* The Apprentice Years," in *Essays Mostly on Periodical Publishing in America,* ed. James Woodress (Durham, N.C.: Duke Univ. Press, 1973), pp. 92–120.

joint aspiration ard endeavor: as John inspired the writing of the book, so its completion might fulfill the early promise both young men had displayed. Moreover, the initial transcripts in the Long Book are divided between descriptions of the voyage plus other passages on sailing from the early Journal and numerous entries on friendship, topic of the longest digression in the first draft and the published version of A Week. The theme of fellowship was further developed in various incidents he jotted down in the Long Book, from their friendly meetings with lockmen and boatmen to Thoreau's encounter with Rice, an innkeeper he had met during his trip to the Berkshires and Catskills in 1844. As he sifted through the Journal of 1837–44, Thoreau also revised and recopied material that revealed the brothers' mutual love of nature and literature as well as their shared fascination with the American Indian, including passages on Indian relics, quotations from and estimates of various writers, examples of Thoreau's own poetry, and entries on flowers and birds, natural phenomena that he closely associated with his lost brother. He then wrote a lecture on the fish of Concord River, drafted in the Long Book and delivered at the Concord Lyceum March 25, 1845. With his preparations nearly complete, he gathered a few more scattered entries from the Journal, adding the exquisite description of water lilies used in "Saturday." Finally, just before numbering each passage in the Long Book according to its designated chapter in the first draft, he wrote the final paragraph of A Week, with its resonant depiction of the brothers' return to Concord.

That triumphant note of fulfillment and expectancy must have echoed Thoreau's feelings as he completed preparations for his first book and began preparations for his new life at Walden Pond. Some of his friends in Concord, however, were dubious about both ventures. "These things go together," Emerson grumpily noted in his journal in 1845. "Cultivated people cannot live in a shanty, nor sleep at night as the poor do in a bag" (JMN IX:195–96). At the other end of town Hawthorne, who had earlier been so supportive, had now begun to doubt that Thoreau would ever fulfill his youthful promise. Planning a new series of books for Wiley and Putnam, a New York publisher, Evert Duyckinck in the summer of 1845 asked Hawthorne to contribute a volume and solicited the names of other potential contributors to the American Library. Since Duyckinck, who was born the same year as Thoreau, was especially interested in new talent, "young men with fresh material, with truly American styles,"[16] Thoreau might have seemed tailor-made for the series. Indeed, in "The Old Manse," the prefatory essay to his own contribution to the series the American Library, *Mosses from an Old Manse* (1846), Hawthorne would soon describe Concord and its river in ways that testified to his fruitful association with Thoreau. Yet Hawthorne was hardly encouraging. "As for Thoreau, there is one chance in a thousand that he might write a most excellent and readable book; but I should be sorry to take the responsibility, either towards you or him, of stirring him up to write anything," he wrote on July 1, 1845. "The only way, however, in which he could ever approach the popular mind, would be by writing a book of simple observation of nature, somewhat in the vein of White's *History of Selborne*" (*DHT* 243–44), a reference to Gilbert White's *The Natural History and Antiquities of Selborne* (1793), a work almost exclusively concerned with the natural phenomena, especially the animals and birds, of a secluded region of England, and one that consequently made few references to its villagers and none to cultural, social, or political developments in the world around it. Since Duyckinck, a city man deeply involved in contemporary affairs, already distrusted the Transcendentalists and strongly opposed the cult of the rural, Hawthorne's comments were hardly likely to fire the editor with zeal to sign up Thoreau for the American Library.

Ironically, Thoreau probably soon began the first draft of *A Week*, which promised to be far more than "a book of simple observation of nature." But he had not yet overcome the problems associated with writing an extended narrative. He gathered material and wrote the first draft in 1844–45, roughly half-way between the essay conceived in 1840 and the book published in 1849. Its intermediate position is revealed by the length of the first draft, which—despite its ambitious design and numerous

[16]Perry Miller, *The Raven and the Whale* (New York: Harcourt, Brace, 1956), p. 114.

digressions—is closer to that of an extended essay than to that of the published version. Although he established the rhythm of *A Week,* with its alternating flow of action and meditation, advance and withdrawal, he had failed to achieve a completely coherent narrative structure. For example, in addition to the untitled introduction, later called "Concord River," the first draft contained eight chapters, one for each day the brothers had spent upon the rivers, including both Thursday, September 5, and Thursday, September 12, indicating that Thoreau had not yet discerned the symbolic and structural advantages of playing upon the Creation in his own account of the brothers' recreation. Moreover, his depiction of the voyage was frequently sketchy, while his introduction of digressions was sometimes rather awkward and forced. Finally, the first draft merely hinted at the concerns, notably reform, Indian-white relations, and literary history, that would account for the rapid growth of *A Week* during the following years.

Some of those concerns are more clearly evident in Thoreau's other writings during 1845. After he finished gathering materials for the first draft, he wrote "Wendell Phillips before Concord Lyceum," drafted in the Long Book and swiftly published in Garrison's *Liberator* on March 28. Thoreau's growing involvement in the debates over slavery and the annexation of Texas had obviously softened his attitude toward reformers, "those earnest reprovers of the age," as he called them elsewhere in the Long Book (*J* 2:117). But he sought to put controversy behind him when he moved to Walden Pond, where Thoreau devoted himself to aesthetic pursuits. He immediately began jotting down Journal passages destined for *Walden,* which he seems to have planned from the beginning of his sojourn there, and writing *A Week.* When he completed the first draft, probably in the fall of 1845, he began the lecture on Thomas Carlyle, a topic that indicated his persistent interest in writers and writing. After he delivered the lecture before the Concord Lyceum on February 4, 1846, he began to revise and expand *A Week.*

Though relatively brief, the additions to the first draft offer revealing glimpses of Thoreau's interests and methods of composition. Having included two leaves from the 1842 essay on Manu in the first draft, he began to quarry other unpublished writings.

To a brief digression on music in "Monday" he added passages from his 1840 essay on bravery, "The Service." Margaret Fuller had criticized its crude mosaic method, so it is ironic that Thoreau sought to use bits and pieces of "The Service" in the far more ambitious mosaic of *A Week*. But by 1846 he had learned to muffle his tools. Indeed, since heroism is a strong theme in *A Week*, his depiction of the brothers' exuberant response to a drummer near Nashua seems far more appropriate here than in "The Service," where Thoreau failed to locate that response in specific circumstances. Heroism had also been an important theme in "Sir Walter Raleigh," from which he copied out two pages of extracts for addition to the first draft of *A Week*. Although he later skimmed the essay for the discussion of literary style in "Monday," at first Thoreau adopted only a few passages about Ralegh's *History of the World*. "For the most part an author only *writes* history, treating it as a dead subject," he observed, "but Raleigh tells it like a fresh story" (MH 19). Thoreau's own effort to vivify history is illustrated by another addition to the first draft, a two-page account of an Indian ambuscade of a group of soldiers near Thornton's Ferry, germ of a longer more extended re-creation of that incident in *A Week*.

By the summer of 1846 he was ready to read portions of the manuscript to friends. In a diary entry headed *Thoreau's Book*, Alcott on Sunday, July 12, reported: "Read some parables to the children at *Emersons*. Dined there. And after much conversation and hearing some of his late verses, we walked to Thoreaus who read some passages upon his '*Concord and Merrimac Rivers*' a pastoral Book now ready for the Press."[17] A few days after that round of Transcendental walks, talks, and readings, Emerson began excitedly to spread the news. "In a short time, if Wiley & Putnam smile, you shall have Henry Thoreau's 'Excursion on

[17]"Diary for 1846," Houghton Library MS*59M-308 (15), pp. 190–91. In the same diary, Alcott on December 31, 1846, recorded: "Passed the afternoon and evening with Thoreau at his Hermitage on Walden. He read me many passages from his Concord and Merrimac Rivers—A Week" (p. 350). The entry suggests that Thoreau had by then changed the tentative title of the book, though, as indicated below, Emerson continued to refer to it as an "Excursion" until August 1847.

Concord & Merrimack rivers,' a seven days' voyage in as many chapters, pastoral as Isaak Walton, spicy as flagroot, broad & deep as Menu," Emerson on July 16 wrote Charles King Newcomb, who had asked advice about a trip to the White Mountains. "He read me some of it under an oak on the river bank the other afternoon, and invigorated me" (*L* III:338).

The immediate effect of Thoreau's work on *A Week,* then called an "Excursion," was thus to rekindle Emerson's flagging enthusiasm. Sitting on the bank of the stream and listening to the opening chapters, with their depiction of the flora and fauna of the rivers, Emerson must have thought that Thoreau had finally hit upon his proper metier. Here at last, Emerson's imagery suggests, was a subject that brought into play Thoreau's intimate knowledge of nature, a knowledge given an added dimension by the serene philosophizing both men valued in the *Laws of Menu* and other Eastern scriptures. In fact, the letter hearkens all the way back to Emerson's 1839 Journal, where he applauded his "wise young neighbors" for their mode of travel to the White Mountains. Congratulating Newcomb in advance on "the good week" before him, Emerson offered conventional advice about railroad and stage routes, but he clearly felt that Thoreau's excursion would offer a fresh and far more original approach to the White Mountains.

Emerson, who was arranging for the publication of a number of books in 1846, pressed for the swift publication of the "Excursion," but despite Thoreau's assurances the book was evidently far from ready for submission. Earlier that year Emerson had struck a bargain with James Munroe and Company of Boston for the publication of his *Poems* and for a smaller edition of the second series of Ellery Channing's poems, for both of which Emerson bore the cost of printing. When he wrote Newcomb in July, Emerson was negotiating for the reprint of some of Carlyle's works by Wiley and Putnam, the publisher of the American Library, which he hoped would soon include Thoreau's book. Thoreau, however, was then revising his Carlyle lecture, which he sent off to Horace Greeley in August. Greeley's gloomy remarks about "writing to sell," the one thing "calculated to make a scoundrel of an honest man" (*C* 170), probably had little effect on Thoreau, who obviously hoped the obstacles confronting articles like "Thomas Carlyle and His Works" would be overcome by his version of a travel book, a far more popular format. But unless he had begun a second draft of his book, which is possible but unlikely, Thoreau read to Emerson from the untidy and heavily revised first draft, from which he would have to prepare fair copy before submission to a publisher. Moreover, Thoreau's entries in the Journal during the summer of 1846 indicate that he planned substantial additions before preparing a final copy.

The nature of those additions and the direction of *A Week* were profoundly influenced by his arrest that summer. About the time he read portions of the manuscript to Emerson and Alcott in July, Thoreau was drafting in the Journal extended passages apparently intended for the digression on Hindu scripture in "Monday." He also ironically suggested that a comparison of "the God of New Englanders with the god of the Greeks" would be useful (*J* 2:260), but in general his tone was contemplative rather than combative. In sharp contrast, alluding to his arrest on July 23 or 24, he savagely denounced "dead institutions"—the church and the state (*J* 2:262). Emerson, who described the state as "a poor beast who means the best: it means friendly," disapproved of Thoreau's stand and its consequences. "Don't run amuck against the world," Emerson pleaded (I did not "run 'amok' against society," Thoreau replied in *Walden;* "I preferred that society should run 'amok' against me, it being the desperate party" [*Wa* 171]). Contrasting Thoreau to the abolitionists, "hot headed partialists," Emerson desperately exhorted his young friend, "Reserve yourself for your own work" (*JMN* IX: 446). If he had then realized the full impact of the arrest and its aftermath on Thoreau's work, especially on the invigorating book Emerson had praised so highly a week earlier, he no doubt would have been even more upset and depressed. In the first draft of *A Week* Thoreau had extolled the simplicity of the Greek poetry and the elevation of Hindu scripture, literary and spiritual analogues to the natural world celebrated in *A Week*. He now began to underscore the conflict between Christianity, later a target of his harsh critique in "Sunday," and the pagan

religions celebrated in *A Week,* a dichotomy that was to prove far
more controversial than his assault on the state in "Monday,"
which the 1846 Journal entry on "dead institutions" also anticipated.

Thoreau's trip to Maine at the end of the summer of 1846 had
a more subtle impact on *A Week.* In the first draft he had devoted
only three brief paragraphs to the week he and John had spent
in the White Mountains. But, perhaps in anticipation of his ascent
of Mount Katahdin, Thoreau in late August drafted an account
of the 1839 walking tour through the White Mountains to link
the two "Thursday" chapters in the first draft of *A Week.* After
his trip to Maine, which began on August 31, the same day he
and John had begun their journey seven years earlier, mountains
were again much in Thoreau's thoughts. During the fall of 1846
he drafted in the Journal a detailed account of his experiences
in Maine, culminating in the ascent of Katahdin, that home of
"Chaos and Old Night" (*MW* 70), an incident that also influenced
his treatment of various ascents in *A Week.* He decided to omit
the reminiscences of the walking tour through the White Mountains, a section that might have tended to domesticate Agiocochook, or Mount Washington, which stands remote and mysterious in "Thursday." But he revised portions of "A Walk to
Wachusett" for inclusion in "Monday" and greatly expanded the
account of his ascent of Saddleback Mountain in "Tuesday,"
which he had only briefly described in the first draft. These twin
ascents thus anticipate the final climb to "the summit of AGIO-
COCHOOK" (*W* 314), tallest of the peaks that came to jut above
the slowly formed alluvial plain of *A Week.*

As he worked on *A Week* and *Walden* during the winter of 1846–
47, Thoreau received conflicting advice about the direction his
literary career should take. On February 5 Horace Greeley informed him of the final arrangements to print "Thomas Carlyle
and His Works" and invited him to follow it up with similar articles
on Emerson, Hawthorne, and others. Probably thinking of Margaret Fuller's *Papers on Literature and Art,* a collection of her
Tribune articles published in the American Library in 1846,
Greeley assured Thoreau: "In a year or two, if you take care not

to write faster than you think, you will have the material of a volume worth publishing, and then we will see what can be done. There is a text somewhere in St. Paul . . . which says 'Look not back to the things which are behind, but rather to these which are before,' &c." (C 174). Thoreau, no doubt eager to catch up with Emerson and Channing, whose volumes of poetry had recently appeared, as well as with his old foe Margaret Fuller, was indeed looking ahead, but not to a collection of literary profiles. By then he had completed part of the first version of *Walden,* which he read as "A History of Myself" before the Concord Lyceum on February 10. He was also forging ahead with the second draft of *A Week.*

In contrast to Greeley, Emerson considered these books, and especially *A Week,* as far more crucial to Thoreau's literary career than works like "Thomas Carlyle and His Works." Announcing the publication of that article in *Graham's Magazine,* Emerson on February 27 wrote Carlyle, "You are yet to read a good American book made by this Thoreau."[18] In a letter to Margaret Fuller written the following day, he told her that Thoreau's "Excursion" would "soon be ready" and continued: "Admirable, though Ellery rejects it altogether. Mrs. Ripley & other members of the opposition came down the other night to hear Henry's Account of his housekeeping at Walden Pond, which he read as a lecture, and were charmed with the witty wisdom which ran through it all" (L III:377-78). For different reasons from those of communitarians like the Ripleys and others from the Fourierist community at Brook Farm, Emerson had never really approved of Thoreau's "housekeeping," but he, too, was apparently won over by the lecture, germ of "Economy" in *Walden.* He was, however, far more interested in *A Week.* Thus, at the end of a letter written on March 12 to Evert Duyckinck of Wiley and Putnam, to whom he inquired about printing the book, Emerson noted that Thoreau had published the article on Carlyle and a number of pieces in the *Dial,*

[18]*The Correspondence of Emerson and Carlyle,* ed. Joseph Slater (New York: Columbia Univ. Press, 1964), p. 415.

"but he has done nothing half so good as his new book" (*L* III:384).

The letter to Duyckinck indicates that both *A Week* and Emerson's view of it had changed significantly since Thoreau had first read portions of it to him in 1846. Describing it as "a book of extraordinary merit," Emerson observed, "It purports to be the account of 'An Excursion on the Concord & Merrimack Rivers,' which he made some time ago in company with his brother, in a boat built by themselves." In contrast to his letter to Newcomb in July 1846, when Emerson described that excursion as "a seven days' voyage in as many chapters," to Duyckinck he indicated that it *purported* to be such an excursion. Reading the manuscript, which Emerson estimated to be as long as Dickens's *Pictures of Italy,* that is, about seventy thousand words or nearly twice its first-draft length, had clearly revealed it to be very different from the travel narrative Emerson had earlier believed Thoreau was writing. In 1846 he described the book as a combination of Isaak Walton and Manu; in 1847 he omitted the reference to Manu, which would hardly have been a selling point to Duyckinck, a staunch Episcopalian who had little patience with the Transcendentalists' embrace of the East. Moreover, although he once again invoked Walton (Thoreau rarely escaped that comparison), Emerson now described a book that sounded as if it had been written by a Walton who had at various times forsaken his angling equipment, put on spectacles, and joined Sir Thomas Browne in the library: "This book has many merits. It will be as attractive to *lovers of nature,* in every sense, that is, to naturalists, and to poets, as Isaak Walton. It will be attractive to scholars for its excellent literature, & to all thoughtful persons for its originality & profoundness. The narrative of the little voyage, though faithful, is a very slender thread for such big beads & ingots as are strung on it. It is really a book of the results of the studies of years" (*L* III:384).

Only fragments of the second draft have survived, so it is impossible to say with any certainty exactly what those "studies of years" then included. But Bronson Alcott, to whom Thoreau read additional portions of the manuscript on March 13, offers further hints about the nature and contents of the book early in 1847.[19] Emphasizing the figurative meaning of Thoreau's title, Alcott observed, "The symbol [of the rivers] is well chosen, and serves him admirably. These streams flowing as gracefully through the continents and defining so the banks of his Nature, while his genius glides so meditatively and descriptively along its currents, with senses the freshest and most healthful, and eye direct on nature the while." Like Emerson, he stressed the book's value to naturalists, but Alcott also recognized Thoreau's characteristic fusion of natural fact, pastoral imagery, and classical allusion: "It is Virgil, and Gilbert White of Selbourne, and Izaak Walton, and Yankee settler all, singing his prose poems with remembrances of his readings and experiences in the woods and road-paths." At the same time, Alcott insisted that it was a "purely American" book, "fragrant with the lives of New England woods and streams, and could have been written nowhere else."

Alcott was, however, sensitive to the elegiac overtones of Thoreau's depiction of New England. The book explores "the remoter haunts of the simplest-mannered of our beasts and birds, the fishes, and the natural mankind surviving still in our farm houses, and on the hillsides and plains, with their rustic speech, manners, and arts." But these loving depictions of primitive men and of primeval nature did not blur the author's "perception of the ill turns she is put to here in New England, and by the simplest too, and least vitiated of the population." Indeed, in Thoreau "the rocks, and animals, and woods, and the green earth" had at last found an author "to whom they could decare their grief and shame at the bereavement of their red brethren, and the wrongs these

[19]Portions of Alcott's extended commentary on *A Week* appear in *The Journals of Bronson Alcott*, ed. Odell Shepard (Boston: Little, Brown, 1938), pp. 213–14. The complete text has been edited by Walter Hesford, "Alcott's Criticism of *A Week*," *Resources for American Literary Scholarship* 6 (1976): 81–84, from which all of the following quotations are taken. As Hesford notes, Alcott recopied the passage into his journal of 1849 after reading both the published version and reviews of *A Week*, so he may have revised and expanded his original impressions accordingly.

have endured from their oppressors the whites." Thoreau had clearly begun to establish the link between the exploitation of nature and the destruction of the Indians, one of the most significant changes between the first and second drafts of *A Week*. By the time he read portions of the manuscript to Alcott on March 16, however, Thoreau had not yet fully developed that theme, for sometime after April 8 he began to draft the Hannah Duston story for "Thursday," where it served as a brilliant conclusion to the story of Indian-white relations in *A Week*.

Alcott's commentary suggests that Thoreau had also begun to incorporate a good deal of the material that was to give the final version its distinctly literary flavor. "It has the merit, moreover, that, somehow, despite all presumption to the contrary, the sod, and sap, and fibre, and flavor of New England have found at last, a clear relation to the literature of other and classic lands," he explained, "and we drink off here the significance also of the literature the oldest and freshest; Egypt, India, Greece, England, from the poet's hands, as he scoops the waters for us from the rivers." Through quotations, extracts, and, possibly, translations like those of Anacreon in "Tuesday," Thoreau had clearly begun to mingle the waters of the Concord and Merrimack with the deepest sources of his own inspiration. As in the first draft of *Walden*, he evidently also inserted a large number of his early verses in the second draft of *A Week*. "Poems are here, also, vigorous and rugged enough to defy Quarles or Donne, and as sound and seasonable as theirs," Alcott remarked. Like the translations of Anacreon, many of these poems had no doubt first appeared in the *Dial*, which Thoreau quarried for additional material. "Criticisms, too, we have of the like radical quality and toughness," he continued: "Homer, Hesiod, Eschylus, and Chaucer, have got some one to look a little into their merits now and modernize and make them indiginous and home-felt once in Concord and abroad aside[?] the translator's genius." Thoreau had praised Aeschylus in the early Journal (*J* 1:82 ff.), and he may have used portions of either his translation of *Prometheus Bound* from the *Dial* or his unpublished translation of *Seven against Thebes* in the second draft of *A Week*, though none of this material appears in the published version, which contains no references to the Greek dramatist and only two lines from Hesiod's *Works and Days* (*W* 63). But Alcott's reference indicates that Thoreau had already incorporated "Homer. Ossian. Chaucer." from the *Dial* in "Sunday" (Homer) and "Friday" (Ossian and Chaucer), thus providing a frame for a growing number of digressions on writers and writing in *A Week*.

Alcott vigorously defended what was to become the most controversial digression in *A Week*, an attack on the Christian church that Thoreau had at least begun to mount by early 1847. "And if Jerusalem is wakened by an Arab's warble here," he asserted, "it seems but a trial of spies, and we delight the rather in the audacity, feeling that the Holy City even, has no good right to detain, nor aught to bestow that can quicken the healthful morning spirits of our traveller; and are all the more disposed to hope, he will provoke alike Hebrew, pagan, and Christian too, still lingering on, to overtake him if they can, as he goes blest and bright over the Magian mountains in the distance." That dense and allusive remark resists complete penetration, but Alcott's general meaning seems clear. Others might view the critique of the church in "Sunday," that "Arab's warble," as simply profane and blasphemous, a threatening prelude to an assault on the Holy City itself. But Alcott, whose love of the *Pilgrim's Progress* had spurred Thoreau's interest in the book, saw the critique in the context of a larger spiritual quest in *A Week*, a quest that prompted Thoreau to explore the various streams of man's spiritual heritage as the brothers charted the course of the Concord and the Merrimack. Indeed, as Alcott shrewdly perceived, Thoreau's goal was audaciously to provoke his readers to undertake a spiritual journey similar to that figured by the various journeys in *A Week*, with its ascents of Wachusett, Saddleback, Agiocochook, and other "mountains in the distance." Thus, among his friends in Concord, Thoreau's strategy in *A Week* was well understood, but it is doubtful that Evert Duyckinck proved to be as sympathetic and understanding.

Although Emerson told Duyckinck on March 12 that the manuscript was "quite ready," Thoreau continued to revise and expand *A Week* during the spring and summer of 1847. Alcott on March 16 simply noted that his friend planned to print the book "some day," perhaps indicating that Thoreau had not authorized Emerson to approach Duyckinck, who announced in the *Literary World*: "Henry D. Thoreau, Esq., whose elaborate paper on Carlyle, now publishing in Graham's Magazine, is attracting considerable attention, has now completed a new work of which reports speak highly. It will probably be soon given to the public."[20] Thoreau, however, did not send the manuscript to Duyckinck until May 28. "I should not have delayed sending you my manuscript so long," he explained, "if I had not known that delay would be no inconvenience to you, and advantage to the sender" (C 181). If his other revisions and additions compared in style and force to the Hannah Duston story, written during the two and a half months between Emerson's inquiry and Thoreau's submission, the delay had indeed been advantageous. But in other ways it was costly, since by May, Duyckinck, whose aggressive literary nationalism disturbed his employers, had been dismissed as editor of the *Literary World* and had lost influence with Wiley and Putnam, the major backers of that journal and the publishers of the American Library.[21]

As he waited impatiently for Duyckinck's answer, Thoreau worked on *A Week* and *Walden*. On June 14 he again wrote Duyckinck, telling him that he would wait two weeks for an answer, and asking him to return the manuscript for "corrections" (C 173). He had possibly also decided to make further additions and to shift some material from the manuscript of *A Week* to the first version of *Walden*, which he completed that summer. In any case, he resubmitted the manuscript of *A Week* to Duyckinck on

[20]*Literary World*, Mar. 27, 1847. Quoted in *The Raven and the Whale*, p. 192.

[21]The circumstances surrounding Duyckinck's dismissal, which Perry Miller calls "the major crisis of his career" (p. 209), are described in *The Raven and the Whale*, pp. 186–202. *A Week* apparently did not make much of an impression on Duyckinck, who made no mention of receiving or reading the manuscript in a fairly detailed diary of his reading and other activities during 1847. See Donald Yanella and Kathleen Malone Yanella, "Evert A. Duyckinck's 'Diary: May 29–November 8, 1847,' " *Studies in the American Renaissance 1978*, ed. Joel Myerson (Boston: Twayne, 1978), pp. 207–58.

July 3. Thoreau must have received a negative answer between July 27, when he sent an inquiry to Duyckinck (*C* 184), and August 6, when Emerson approached his longtime friend William Henry Furness about the possibility of finding a publisher for *A Week* in Philadelphia:

> I write because Henry D. Thoreau has a book to print. Henry D. Thoreau is a great man in Concord, a man of original genius & character, who knows Greek, & knows Indian also,—not the language quite as well as John Eliot—but the history monuments & genius of the Sachems, being a pretty good Sachem himself, master of all woodcraft, & an intimate associate of the birds, beasts, & fishes, of this region. I could tell you many a good story of his forest life.—He has written what he calls "A week on the Concord and Merrimack Rivers," which is an account of an excursion made by himself & his brother (in a boat which he built) some time ago, from Concord, Mass., down the Concord river & up the Merrimack, to Concord, N. H.—I think it a book of wonderful merit, which is to go far & last long. It will remind you of Izaak Walton, and, if it have not all his sweetness, it is rich, as he is not, in profound thought.—Thoreau sent the manuscript lately to Duyckinck . . . who examined it, & "gave a favorable opinion of it to W. & P." They have however declined to publish it. (*RLF* 60–61)

This description of the book differs markedly from that contained in Emerson's letter to Duyckinck five months earlier. To Duyckinck, Emerson had noted that it "purports" to be an account of an excursion but that the narrative of the voyage was "a very slender thread for such big beads & ingots as are strung on it." Indeed, Thoreau possibly altered the title from "An Excursion" to "A Week" to de-emphasize the travel motif. But to Furness, Emerson characterized it as primarily a travel book, once again extolling the originality and self-sufficiency of the brothers' voyage. Moreover, whereas he alluded to Thoreau's knowledge of

Greek—probably one of those "studies of years" he had cited in the letter to Duyckinck—Emerson gave far greater prominence to his friend's knowledge of "the history monuments & genius" of the Indians, an element of *A Week* that Thoreau had reinforced as he revised and expanded it during the spring and summer of 1847. But for Emerson, Thoreau remained most notable as a "master of all woodcraft, & an intimate associate of the birds, beasts, & fishes," a characterization that recalls Emerson's reason for asking Thoreau in 1842 to review the scientific surveys, a subject that had also admitted of "the narrative of all his woodcraft boatcraft & fishcraft" (*L* II:47). "Natural History of Massachusetts" had disappointed Emerson, probably for many of the same reasons he would finally be disappointed by *A Week*. In fact, although he no doubt tailored his descriptions of Thoreau's book to suit different auditors, one strongly suspects that Emerson would have liked *A Week* better if it had turned out to be more like the relatively simple narrative he described to Furness and less like the compound volume he had described to Duyckinck.

Emerson's letter to Furness also offers interesting sidelights about Thoreau's hopes and plans for the publication of *A Week*. Near the end of the letter he observed, "I have promised Thoreau that I would inquire a little in N. Y. & Philadelphia before we begin to set our own types" (*RLF* 61). Three years earlier, in April 1844, when Emerson was seeking a publisher for Fuller's *Summer on the Lakes,* he had written her that "Henry Thoreau has been showing me triumphantly how much cheaper & every way wiser it would be to publish the book ourselves paying the booksellers only a simple commission for vending it & conducting personally the correspondence with distant booksellers" (*L* III:250). Given his experience in manufacturing and marketing pencils, Thoreau may also have contemplated such an entrepreneurial method of publishing his own book, but Emerson was probably bluffing. He told Furness that *A Week* would be about as long as his own *Essays,* an estimate Thoreau also gave in a letter to a Boston publisher on August 28 (*C* 185). If that estimate is accurate, either the earlier estimate was low or the second draft had expanded from roughly seventy thousand to nearly ninety thousand words since Emerson had approached Duyckinck five months earlier, indicating just how rigorously Thoreau had worked over the manuscript during the spring and summer of 1847. Finally, Emerson noted that Thoreau, who was willing to accept "any reasonable terms," was "mainly bent on having it printed in a cheap format for a large circulation" (*RLF* 61). Thus Thoreau, who in "Thomas Carlyle and His Works" had faulted both the English writer and Emerson for directing themselves to a narrow audience of intellectuals, was himself clearly determined to speak to what he had there described as "the Man of the Age, come to be called working-man" (*EEM* 251).

A Week, however, was not destined to be printed in any format in 1847. In response to Emerson's letter Furness replied that he would contact publishers but that he was "doubtful of success" (*RLF* 63). Emerson wrote Margaret Fuller on August 29 that Thoreau was "on the point of concluding the contract" for *A Week* (*L* III:413), but the manuscript was still making the rounds of publishers when Thoreau left Walden Pond on September 6 to move in with the Emersons. On September 19 Furness wrote that he had talked to a friend in Philadelphia about Thoreau's book, but that the publisher was not interested. "He is run down, he says, with applications to print" (*RLF* 66). Ten days later William Emerson, who also acted on Thoreau's behalf, wrote that he was waiting for an answer from Harpers, but apparently none came before Emerson sailed for England on October 5. Finally, on November 14, Thoreau wrote him: "I suppose you will like to hear of my book, though I have nothing worth writing about it. Indeed, for the last month or two I have forgotten it, but shall certainly remember it again. Wiley & Putnam, Munroe, the Harpers, and Crosby & Nichols have all declined printing it with the least risk to themselves; but Wiley & Putnam will print it in their series, and any of them, anywhere, at *my* risk. If I liked the book well enough, I should not delay; but for the present I am indifferent. I believe this is, after all, the course you advised,—to let it lie" (*C* 191).

Thoreau's indifference may have been defensive, for Emerson strongly opposed any delay. "I am not of opinion that your book should be delayed a month," he responded. "I should print it at once, nor do I think that you would incur any risk in doing so

that you cannot well afford. It is very certain to have readers &
debtors here as well as there" (*C* 195). Thoreau obviously did not
wish to pursue the subject, for in a chatty reply to Emerson's
letter he neither responded to the advice nor mentioned *A Week*
(*C* 199–201). But on December 27, in a letter to James Munroe
and Company concerning some other matters Emerson asked him
to attend to, he firmly stated, "I may as well inform you that I do
not intend to print *my book* anywhere immediately" (*C* 198).

The failure to find a publisher for *A Week* in 1847 influenced
both his writings and his views of writing as a trade. Thoreau
was not exaggerating when he told Emerson that he had not
looked at *A Week* for "a month or two," since during the fall and
winter of 1847 he wrote two lectures, "Ktaadn" and "The Relation
of the Individual to the State," both delivered before the Concord
Lyceum early in 1848. In a letter to James Elliot Cabot, who had
inquired about Emerson's itinerary in England and, apparently,
about *A Week*, Thoreau replied on March 8, "My book, fortunately,
did not find a publisher ready to undertake it, and you can imagine
the effect of delay on an author's estimate of his own work." But,
noting that he liked the book "well enough to mend it" after he
had "dispatched" his lectures, written "mainly for my own pleasure and advantage," he continued: "I esteem it a rare happiness
to be able to *write* anthing, but there (if I ever get there) my
concern for it is apt to end. Time & Co. are, after all, the only
quite honest and trustworthy publishers that we know" (*C* 210).

Despite his emerging view of writing as an end in itself, Thoreau
still needed money, and he continued to work toward the more
immediate publication of *A Week*. In the letter to Cabot, coeditor
of the *Massachusetts Quarterly Review*, founded in 1847 as the
successor to the *Dial*, he inquired, "Is your journal able to pay
anything, provided it likes an article well enough?" Apparently
the answer was no, for at the end of March he sent a revised
version of "Ktaadn" to Horace Greeley, who paid him $25. Thoreau
then turned to *A Week*. He initially did not plan to make major
revisions, however, for on April 16 Alcott reported that "Thoreau
has a Book nearly off his hands."[22] But on May 19, declining a

---

[22]*The Letters of A. Bronson Alcott*, p. 137.

request for short articles that Greeley might sell "readily and advantageously" (*C* 223), Thoreau explained, "My book is swelling again under my hands" (*C* 225).

A Week was indeed "swelling" during the early months of 1848. As early as January 12 Thoreau told Emerson that, in addition to "Ktaadn," he had written "what will do for a lecture on Friendship" (*C* 204), presumably yet another and even longer version of the extended digression in the first and second drafts of *A Week*. Those earlier versions contained numerous Journal entries from the late 1830s and early 1840s, when his friendship with Emerson had been flourishing. That the two men remained close is revealed by their letters during Emerson's tour of England during 1847–48, in one of which Thoreau sent along "The good how can we trust?," his recent verses "on that universal theme—your's as well as mine, & several other people's," a poem that soon found its way into the essay on friendship in *A Week* (*C* 200, *W* 281). But other additions in the 1848 version of the essay, which Alcott pronounced "superior to anything" he had heard, bear witness to a certain awkwardness between Thoreau and Emerson.[23] Apparently alluding to Emerson's departure for Europe a few months earlier, for example, Thoreau wrote: "Suppose you go to bid farewell to your Friend who is setting out on a journey. . . . Have you any *last* words? Alas, it is only the word of words, which you have so long sought and found not; *you* have not a *first* word yet" (*W* 273).

Thoreau, however, soon received a reminder of Emerson's early help and encouragement. In March 1848 H. G. O. Blake, a teacher from Worcester, reread "Aulus Persius Flaccus" in the 1840 *Dial* and wrote that he found in it "pure depth and solidity of thought" (*C* 214n). Thoreau replied that he had not read the article in years and "had to look at that page again, to learn what was the tenor of my thoughts then" (*C* 214). Pleased with the early effort and possibly also remembering Emerson's enthusiasm about it, he later inserted a corrected version of "Aulus

---

[23]Quoted in F. B. Sanborn, *Henry D. Thoreau* (Boston: Houghton Mifflin, 1882), p. 304.

Persius Flaccus" in "Thursday," from which he omitted another *Dial* article, "Herald of Freedom."

The omission of the tribute to Nathaniel Rogers and other material from "Thursday" illuminates significant shifts in emphasis as Thoreau revised *A Week*. His initial determination to avoid polemics had been shaken by his arrest in 1846, after which he began to use *A Week* to express a wide variety of social, political, and religious concerns. Some of this material, including extracts from the unpublished lecture on the conservative and the reformer and brief satires of clothing and fashion, was shifted to the first version of *Walden*, but other digressions in *A Week*, notably the extended critique of the Christian church in "Sunday" and the attack on the state in "Monday," testified to his growing militancy. His hostility to church and state was intensified by the ignoble conclusion of the Mexican War in the summer of 1847, when he was probably further embittered by his failure to find a publisher for *A Week*. As he read *A Collection from the Newspaper Writings of Nathaniel Rogers*, published that summer, Thoreau no doubt responded strongly to the abolitionist's comments on slavery, the military, and the bankruptcy of American institutions, issues he dealt with in the 1848 lecture "The Relation of the Individual to the State." Probably in late 1847 or early 1848 he also revised "Herald of Freedom" for insertion in "Thursday," where it joined a revised version of the unpublished 1843 essay "Conversation," his somewhat labored effort at social satire, and his account of the desperate journey undertaken by the "poor wretch" from New York, a dark parable informed by Thoreau's own futile efforts to find work in New York City during 1843. Together, these sections underscored the moral, social, and economic failures of New England, also the theme of "Economy" in *Walden*. By omitting these sections from "Thursday" in 1848, Thoreau in *A Week* as in *Walden* thus shifted attention from the failures of New England life, depicted in the opening chapters, to the promise of life in New England, a promise that underlies his celebration of the autumnal landscape in "Friday" and his ecstatic vision of "Spring," then the concluding section of *Walden*.

To fill the gaps left by the late omissions from "Thursday," Thoreau introduced additional material on colonial history and

European literature, his other central concerns as he revised and expanded *A Week* during 1847 and 1848. In place of "Herald of Freedom," tribute to the editor of a newspaper in Concord, New Hampshire, Thoreau in 1848 added a passage on the early settlement of that town from Benjamin L. Mirick's *History of Haverhill, Massachusetts,* which he had also consulted when drafting the Hannah Duston story in 1847. But, in contrast to her story, final scene in a tragic drama of destruction in *A Week,* the passage on the settlement of Concord occasioned an optimistic meditation on the possibility of living a true frontier life despite the destruction of Indians and the wilderness. "The frontiers are not east or west, north or south, but wherever a man *fronts* a fact," Thoreau affirmed (W 304), thus forging an additional link between the preliminary voyage of discovery in *A Week* and his efforts to apply those lessons in *Walden,* the record of his various efforts to "stand right fronting & face to face to a fact" (S 157, Wa 98).

Other additions to "Thursday" also played a role in a narrative of decline, fall, and renewal. The article "Aulus Persius Flaccus" helped chart the decline in European literature from Homer in "Sunday" to Anacreon in "Tuesday" through the works of the Roman satirist, representative of the decay of the Greco-Roman tradition. To "Thursday" Thoreau also added a critique of Goethe, at least partly in response to Emerson's tribute to the German master in "Representative Men," a series of lectures already well known in England and the United States. As Hannah Duston represented the Fall of Man in history, so Goethe, another imitator, represented the Fall of Man in literature, the final loss of the originality and spontaneity of the early Greeks. But as the destruction of the wilderness by civilization might be reversed by leading a true frontier life, so the collapse of European literature into artificiality might be overcome by establishing a native American tradition, a program that informs Thoreau's various digressions on writers and writing in *A Week.*

He made similar adjustments in the treatment of another crucial issue. His elegiac concerns, which had determined Thoreau to write *A Week,* provided a central unifying thread for its various strands, from his digressions on reform, defined as a matter of life and death, to his explorations of New England's dark colonial past, scene of the destruction of the Indians and their world, to his meditations on writers and literary immortality. Other passages, however, seemed incongruous in a book conceived of as an elegy for his brother, whom Thoreau associated with the unspoiled and enduring natural realm celebrated in *A Week*. He therefore canceled descriptions of fishing and hunting, the digression on guns, the most vituperative portions of his meditation on graveyards, and his rather strident defense of mercy killing. He also omitted the attack on museums, "the catacombs of nature," which appeared before the description of autumn flowers in "Friday." "Men have a strange taste for death who prefer to behold the cast-off garments of life," he observed, "rather than life itself" (Appendix, no. 13). Thoreau apparently realized that such passages blurred his own focus on "life itself," a vital drama of growth, fruition, death, and rebirth in *A Week*.

As he put the finishing touches on *A Week*, he also began to revise *Walden* with an eye to early publication. The first version of *Walden* was only slightly longer than the first draft of *A Week*, but Thoreau did not expand it significantly in 1848. Instead, he worked on improving its style. He wrote a second version, revised it, and wrote a third version "so close upon II that they seem almost one piece" (S 28). Thoreau clearly hoped to see *Walden* published soon after *A Week*, which he continued to revise and expand. Following a walking tour through southern New Hampshire with Ellery Channing in the late summer of 1848, Thoreau added numerous bits of local lore and descriptive passages to shore up the book's narrative elements. But he also added to its contemplative sections, jotting entries that autumn in the Journal on reformers, Christianity, Greece and Rome, and the East, many of which entered the pages of *A Week*.

Emerson, who had returned from Europe in July, was far less pleased with some of Thoreau's late additions to *A Week* than with "Ktaadn, and the Maine Woods," which was published serially from July through November 1848. In October, after reading a critique of the *Bhagavad-Gita* added to the discussion of Hindu scripture in "Monday," Emerson impatiently remarked in his journal: "I owed,—my friend & I,—owed a magnificent day to the Bhagavat Geeta. . . . Let us not now go back & apply a minute criticism to it, but cherish the venerable oracle" (*JMN* X:360). He had, of course, earlier first encouraged Thoreau to read and then to gather extracts from various Eastern scriptures for the *Dial,* but Emerson now clearly felt that his friend's continuing awkward embrace of the East was misguided and regressive. In sharp contrast, after reading the final installment of "Ktaadn" in the *Union Magazine,* Emerson a few weeks later exclaimed: "We have not had since ten years a pamphlet which I have saved to bind! and here at last is Bushnell's; and now, Henry Thoreau's Ascent of Katahdin" (*JMN* XI:20). The entry, headed "American Literature," could not have linked more dissimilar works than Horace Bushnell's *An Argument for "Discourses on Christian Nature"* and Thoreau's narrative of his 1846 trip to Maine. Implicitly, however, Emerson felt that each writer was contributing to American literature by engaging a subject that suited his peculiar interests and talents. Moreover, despite the complex issues raised in "Ktaadn," in which he was profoundly concerned with man's relation to and place in nature, Thoreau's spare account was almost purely narrative and descriptive, "a woodsy, outdoors essay filled with the odor of pine trees and the rushing waters of mountain streams" (*DHT* 229). That is, it was precisely the kind of work Emerson had thought *A Week* would be until he discovered that Thoreau had radically different ideas abut his first book.

For different reasons Horace Greeley was also troubled by the direction Thoreau's works were taking. Having placed "Ktaadn," the editor also wrote an enthusiastic introduction to some extracts from the essay published in the *Tribune.* But he kept urging Thoreau to write shorter articles, suggesting "an essay on 'The Literary Life' " (*C* 229). Thoreau declined, citing his work on *A Week* and *Walden.* "You must write for the magazines in order to let the public know who and what you are," Greeley replied on October 28. "Ten years hence will do for publishing books" (*C* 232). Thoreau evidently replied that he had no intention of waiting ten years to publish his books, for Greeley on November 19 kindly offered to place passages from either of the books in magazines in advance of publication, adding the warning: "You may write with an angel's pen, yet your writings have no mercantile, money value till you are known and talked of as an author. Mr. Emerson would have been twice as much known and read if he had written for the magazines a little, just to let common people know of his existence" (*C* 232). He was no doubt amused by Greeley's witty paraphrase of Paul's admonition to the Corinthians, but Thoreau, understandably eager to declare his independence from Greeley as well as Emerson, ignored the offer and the warning.

Even if he had been considering Greeley's advice to write for the magazines, the appearance of James Russell Lowell's *Fable for Critics* probably would have determined Thoreau to publish his books as soon as possible. Pairing Thoreau and Ellery Channing, Lowell in the poem wickedly satirized them as imitators of Emerson:

> There comes ———, for instance; to see him's rare sport,
> Tread in Emerson's tracks with legs painfully short;
> How he jumps, how he strains, and gets red in the face,
> To keep step with the mystagogue's natural pace!
> He follows as close as a stick to a rocket,
> His fingers exploring the prophet's each pocket.
> Fie, for shame, brother bard; with good fruit of your own,
> Can't you let neighbor Emerson's orchards alone?
> Besides, 'tis no use, you'll not find e'en a core,—
> ——— has picked up all the windfalls before.[24]

Lowell's charge was hardly new, but it must have been particularly galling to Thoreau in 1848. As early as August 1840, after visiting Emerson in Concord, Theodore Parker wrote in his journal: "In our walk E expressed to me his admiration of Thoreau, & his foolish article on '*Aulus Persius Flaccus*' in the Dial. He said it was full of life. But alas the life is Emersons, not Thoreau's, & so it had been lived before" (*L* II:324n). But, as Emerson replied, Thoreau was then "but a boy," at best a somewhat promising apprentice writer. During the years of the *Dial* he continued

[24]James Russell Lowell, *A Fable for Critics* (New York: Putnam, 1848), p. 30. After a visit to Concord in the late 1830s, "Lowell wrote a friend that Thoreau so imitated Emerson's tone and manner that with his eyes shut he wouldn't know them apart" (*DHT* 66).

to follow in Emerson's footsteps, but Thoreau also began to branch out on his own. After the failure of the *Dial* in 1844 he was increasingly independent of Emerson, whose example and advice Thoreau often ignored. Emerson was put off by his refusal to pay the poll tax, a stand Thoreau vigorously defended in the 1848 lecture soon to be published as "Resistance to Civil Government." Initially, at least, Emerson also disapproved of Thoreau's life at the pond, celebrated in *Walden*. Nor had Emerson's influence altered the direction taken by *A Week*, whose publication Thoreau no doubt hoped would finally still charges that he was a mere imitator of Emerson.

By February 1849, having completed *A Week* and preparing to make a fair copy of *Walden*, Thoreau was again ready to approach publishers, this time on his own. He first sent *A Week* to Ticknor and Company, apparently with an advance inquiry about *Walden*. On February 8 they proposed to publish *Walden*—which had gained a certain notoriety from puffs in Greeley's *Tribune* and through Thoreau's lectures in Salem, Gloucester, and Concord that fall and winter—allowing him 10 percent on the retail price (*C* 236). *A Week* did not fare as well; on the sixteenth they agreed to publish it only at his expense, after a down payment of $450 (*C* 237–38). Thoreau refused both offers, either because *A Week* was in more finished form or because he believed it should precede *Walden*. He next sent *A Week* to Emerson's publisher, James Munroe and Company, who offered to let Thoreau pay costs out of expected sales, as long as he guaranteed full reimbursement to the publisher. *Walden* was to follow publication of *A Week*. He agreed to those terms, despite the worries and warnings of his family. His mother feared that he was "putting things into his book that never ought to be put there," while his Aunt Maria thought parts of *A Week* were blasphemous and darkly prophesied it would not sell enough copies to pay the publishing costs (*DHT* 246). As it turned out, she was right, but Thoreau's literary friends were more encouraging. "Mr. Alcott delighted my wife and me . . . by announcing that you had a book in prep," Hawthorne wrote him. "I rejoice at it, and nothing doubt of such success as will be worth having" (*C* 238).

Thoreau soon discovered the woes of having "a book in prep."

"I am glad to know of your interest in my book," he gracefully replied to Hawthorne, "for I have thought of you as a reader while writing it."[25] That was probably a reference to their shared experience aboard the *Musketaquid,* or *Pond Lily,* but the experience of seeing *A Week* into print may well have reminded him of the Preacher's gloomy admonition: "Of the making of books *there is* no end; and much study *is* a weariness of the flesh." In the note to Hawthorne, dated February 20, Thoreau remarked that he had not yet convinced the printer to take the manuscript, which he must have begun to send off in batches soon after that. In his rush to complete two books, however, Thoreau had not made fair copy of the second draft of *A Week,* which he had heavily revised and expanded since sending it around to publishers in 1847. Consequently, when he began to receive proof sheets in March, he found that the printer was having difficulty reading the manuscript, which would constitute a larger and costlier book than anticipated. To Elizabeth Peabody, who requested a copy of his essay "Resistance to Civil Government" for the first volume of *Aesthetic Papers,* a harried Thoreau responded on April 5, "I have so much writing to do at present, with the printers in the rear of me, that I have almost no time left, but for bodily exercise" (*C* 242). The remark suggests that he was revising later portions of the text even as he corrected proofs of earlier sections, an awkward procedure that caused him to overlook numerous errors. Even so, by the time he sent back the last of the proofs on April 30, he had made more than a thousand corrections, many of which the printer ignored.

Added to his concern for his elder sister Helen, who was dying of tuberculosis, these complications must have dampened the ex-

[25]The letter, dated February 20, 1849, is printed in Kenneth Walter Cameron, *Companion to Thoreau's Correspondence* (Hartford: Transcendental Books, 1964), p. 184. Hawthorne later had kind words for *A Week* and *Walden,* both of which he included in a list of six "good American books" he asked his publisher to send to his friend Monckton Milnes, noting "that these books must not be merely good, but must be original, with American characteristics, and not generally known in England" (Edward C. Peple, Jr., "Hawthorne on Thoreau: 1853–1857," *Thoreau Society Bulletin* 120 [Spring 1972]:1–3).

citement Thoreau felt as publication of his first book approached. Moreover, Emerson, who since 1846 had put increasing pressure on him to complete and publish *A Week,* was now considerably less enthusiastic about the project. On May 22 he wrote friends in England that he had "nothing very good to tell you of the people here, no books, no poets, no artists," later adding as an afterthought, "I ought to say, however, that my friend Thoreau is shortly to print a book . . . which, I think, will win the best readers abroad & at home" (*L* IV:145). Bronson Alcott, however, was more generous. "Today comes Henry Thoreau to town and gives me a copy of his book," he noted on May 26, after Thoreau returned from Boston with advance copies. "An American book, worthy to stand beside Emerson's Essays on my shelves."[26] Finally, nine years and nine months after Henry and John Thoreau had embarked from Concord on August 31, 1839, *A Week on the Concord and Merrimack Rivers* was officially published on May 30, 1849. Despite the book's long gestation, Thoreau was still only thirty-one, five years younger than Emerson had been when *Essays* appeared in 1841.

[26]*The Journals of Bronson Alcott,* p. 209.

Epilogue:
An American Book

AS ALCOTT RECOGNIZED, *A Week* was distinctly an American book, the work in which Thoreau most clearly defined and defended his vocation as an American writer. Indeed, a strongly nationalistic thread runs through each of its various strands. In his depiction of an excursion to the White Mountains, he celebrates the American landscape, at once a source of inspiration and an emblem of the untapped spiritual resources of the New World. Like Milton in "Lycidas," Thoreau in his elegy for his brother naturalizes the classical pastoral elegy on native soil. In his comments on reform he implicitly plays off an ideal of American society against outmoded traditions of the European past. By exploring America's own colonial past, he consequently seeks to discover a more meaningful relationship between past and present. For it was his own time that most concerned Thoreau, an age in which he hoped writers would cease to imitate the European masters and begin to create an indigenous American literature. His conception of that task is illuminated by a passage omitted from *A Week* on traveling "through the kingdoms and empires of Europe," a favorite pastime of educated Americans. Stressing the financial and spiritual costs of such a trip, which "threatens to take all the youth and nerve out of a man & make his after life pathetic" (cf. *W* 306), Thoreau argued:

> Comparatively speaking I do not much prize the inspiration to be derived from studying the works of European art—and the history of those antiquated states— It will never make men fit to inhabit this new world. Such is not our beginning life it is the old world life a dying in us. I think that we young Americans need some experience still & forever in the great but simple & aboriginal arts of life—to make us wise—to use simpler & not more complex modes of

living—practice still—though our orators deny it—
more than science or literature—and experience
genuine & sincere more than speculation &
philosophy. As Americans we have not yet begun to be.
In fulfilling our destiny—whatever that may be—it will
not avail us to stand on the shoulders of Europe—we
have got to down into the dirt & grope amid the
elements of things for a root-hold among the nations.[1]

Thoreau views the infatuation with the Old World as a sign
that his countrymen have not yet begun to live in the New World.
In contrast to the journey depicted in *A Week,* a life-giving voyage
to the primitive sources of originality and inspiration, European
travel leads to imitation and stagnation. His use of the word *derived* in the opening sentence is strategic, for the inspiration Europe offers Americans is *derivative,* something transmitted or ed-
uced rather than something radical and fundamental. Old World
culture cannot make men "fit to inhabit" the New World because
Europe's rigid forms and conventions have nothing to do with an
expansive, experimental America. Indications of the persistence
of European culture in America are therefore signs of death rather
than rebirth. Such a renaissance demands a sharp break with
the European past, a return to those "simple & aboriginal arts of
life," precisely those arts depicted in *Walden,* which Thoreau
consciously designed to "fit" his countrymen (*Wa* 4).

By stressing those fundamental arts of life, however, Thoreau
was not rejecting science, philosophy, and literature. Instead, he
suggests that these flowers of culture will bloom only when a
people develop their embryonic roots, or radicals, striking them
deep in their native soil. Americans have "not yet begun to be,"
have not truly fulfilled their "destiny" (as distinct from the su-

---

[1]The leaf, paged 139–[140] in the second draft of *A Week,* is in the
Berg Collection of the New York Public Library (*LMHDT,* D8g). Thoreau
heavily revised the passage before omitting the leaf from the manuscript.
He possibly intended the last sentence, canceled during the revision, to
read "dig down into the dirt."

perficial claims of Manifest Destiny), because they own the land but they are not *of* the land. He alludes to Robert Burton's famous observation that "a dwarf standing on the shoulders of a giant may see farther than the giant himself," but Thoreau draws a different lesson from such a relationship between America and Europe. He implies that by standing on the shoulders of Europe, Americans, like Antaeus, lose the strength whose renewal depends on touching the ground. Only when its people begin to delve into their native soil will America gain "a root-hold among the nations." By extension, only when his countrymen actually become Americans will American literature take its place on an equal footing with the national literatures of Europe.

Thoreau's agenda for Americans was an implicit defense of his own life and vocation, so different from those of his contemporaries in Concord. We recall that in the summer of 1844 Isaac Hecker invited Thoreau to join him on a walking tour of Europe. Thoreau, having just returned from an excursion to the Berkshires and Catskills with Ellery Channing and about to begin gathering material for *A Week,* replied that he was strongly tempted but that he could not "postpone exploring the *Farther Indies,* which are to be reached you know by other routs and other methods of travel" (*C* 156). As he also remarked, Channing wondered how he could resist the invitation, a reaction that anticipated the poet's trip to Europe two years later. "Ellery Channing has suddenly found out that he must see Europe, that he must see it now,— nay, that it is a matter of life & death that he should set out for Havre & Italy on the first of March," Emerson wrote Samuel Gray Ward in 1846, a few months before his other young friend read him portions of *A Week.* "He thinks it indispensable that he should see buildings, & pictures, & mountains, & peasantries, part of his poetic education—never was poet who did not see them— that he has seen this country through—there is no hope for him but in the excitement of that. Art, Art alone is his object. &c, &c. He talks well enough about it and I can see well enough that it is all in his system, truly enough" (*L* III:327).

Despite his amused tone, Emerson arranged and helped subsidize Channing's tour of Italy, partly out of kindness and partly because Europe exerted a similarly strong pull on him. In "Self-

Reliance," Emerson had denigrated "the superstition of Travelling, whose idols are Italy, England, Egypt," and asserted, "They who made England, Italy, or Greece venerable in the imagination, did so by sticking fast where they were, like an axis of the earth" (*CW* II:46). But Emerson was ambivalent about Europe, which he first visited in 1833, when, "to his own surprise, he was startled and ensnared by Old World culture."[2] His desire for a return visit was probably spurred by Channing's trip and by letters from Margaret Fuller, who embarked for Europe in August 1846. Thus, during 1846–47, as Thoreau worked on the second draft of *A Week,* Emerson slowly succumbed to Carlyle's urging that he undertake an extended lecture tour of Britain.

By midsummer of 1847, shortly after the publication of Channing's prose work *Conversations in Rome,* Emerson had completed arrangements for the lecture tour. Describing his plans to Margaret Fuller, then in Rome, Emerson on August 29 wryly remarked: "America the great listless dumb lifeless America has urgent claims on her children, which, as yet are all unanswered. If by staying at home, or returning home,—they could be any nearer to a satisfaction!" (*L* III:413). Appropriately enough, Emerson On October 5 boarded the packet *Washington Irving* bound for Liverpool and a triumphal tour out of which grew his book *English Traits* (1856). Thoreau left Walden Pond to stay with Emerson's family during his absence, when Emerson wrote his wife Lidian: "My reception here is really a premium often on authorship, & if Henry Thoreau means one day to come to England let him not delay another day to print his book. Or if he do not, let him print it" (*L* IV:16). That book was *A Week,* which had failed to interest a publisher in 1847. But, as indicated by his remarks on foreign travel and influence, probably jotted down sometime between Channing's return in 1846 and Emerson's departure in 1847, Thoreau emphatically did *not* hope one reward of his first book would be the reception accorded in Europe to writers like Irving, Cooper, and Emerson.

Thoreau's remarks also underscore his links to nationalistic lit-

[2]*Literary History of the United States,* ed. Robert Spiller et al., 3d ed. rev. (New York: Macmillan, 1974), p. 367.

erary movements of the 1840s. The *Dial,* which Emerson described as "our bold bible for The Young America" (*L* II:287), formed a somewhat isolated branch of the most vocal movement, which was rooted in New York.[3] Partly for that reason Thoreau's contributions to it were minimal. In 1842 he sent Rufus Griswold some of his poems, but none of them appeared in Griswold's anthology *The Poets and Poetry of America,* an early assertion of nationalism in American literature. During Thoreau's stay on Staten Island in 1843 he published two articles in the *United States Magazine and Democratic Review,* whose editor, John Louis O'Sullivan, was close to both Hawthorne, then living in Concord, and Evert Duyckinck, the leader of the Young America movement in New York. As Thoreau's reference to "we young Americans" suggests, he shared many of the literary aspirations and ideals (though not the jingoistic politics) of Young America, which, unbeknownst to those in New York, found one of its staunchest champions in Concord. Thus, while Emerson was in England, Thoreau wrote of his companionship with Emerson's son Edward, proclaiming: "I am glad that we are all natives of Concord—It is *Young Concord*—Look out—World" (*C* 200). It is therefore all the sadder that *A Week* was not included in Wiley and Putnam's American Library, which Duyckinck hoped would counter the overwhelming dominaton of English books in the American market and in which *A Week* would have taken its rightful place alongside Poe's *Tales,* Hawthorne's *Mosses from an Old Manse,* and Melville's *Typee* and *Omoo.*

Although Thoreau's Boston publisher, James Munroe, made almost no effort on behalf of *A Week,* in which it had little financial interest, the book received fairly wide notice, especially in New York.[4] Predictably, the first review appeared on the front page of

---

[3]See *The Raven and the Whale.*

[4]For a detailed treatment of the reception of *A Week* and additional bibliographical information concerning the reviews cited in the following paragraphs, see my Historical Introduction to the Princeton edition (*W* 433 ff.). There, I also discuss Thoreau's efforts on behalf of *A Week* after the publication of the first edition in 1849, the arrangements his friends made for the publication of a "new and revised edition" in 1868, and its critical fortunes during the nineteenth and twentieth centuries.

Greeley's *Tribune* on June 13, 1849, less than two weeks after the publication of *A Week*. The anonymous reviewer (Thoreau thought it was Greeley; others have ascribed it to George Ripley, who joined the staff of the *Tribune* in 1849, two years after the failure of Brook Farm) praised Thoreau's observations of nature and "scholastic treasures," but he strongly objected to the "misplaced Pantheistic attack on the Christian faith" in "Sunday." That issue distracted the attention of a number of reviewers, including Evert Duyckinck, who had purchased the *Literary World* in 1848. In a review published there on September 22, 1849, Duyckinck also applauded Thoreau's love of nature and of good books but censured the "flippant style" of Thoreau's approach to "what civilized men are accustomed to hold the most sacred of all" questions. "The author, we perceive, announces another book, 'Walden, or Life in the Woods,' " Duyckinck observed in the final paragraph of his review: "We are not so rash or uninformed in the ways of the world as to presume to give counsel to a transcendentalist, so we offer no advice; but we may remark as a curious matter of speculation to be solved in the future—the probability or improbability of Mr. Thoreau's ever approaching nearer to the common sense or common wisdom of mankind. He deprecates churches and preachers. Will he allow us to uphold them? or does he belong to the family of Malvolios, whose conceit was so engrossing that it threatened to deprive the world of cakes and ale."

Duyckinck's comments had serious literary implications. With the powerful example of Dickens, that magnificent provider of cakes and ale, before them, Duyckinck and his adherents in the Young America movement strongly believed that such a common touch would also characterize a truly indigenous native literature. In fact, Duyckinck later scolded his friend Melville for a similar violation of "the most sacred associations of life" in his "piratical running down of creeds and opinions" in *Moby-Dick*, another book that ran afoul of its potential audience's religious beliefs and literary expectations.[5] Thus, though it was couched in the language of outraged orthodoxy, Duyckinck's review of *A Week* also cast a

---

[5]Quoted in *The Raven and the Whale*, p. 299.

good deal of doubt on Thoreau's role in the creation of an American literature.

Some others expressed doubts about Thoreau's originality, as critics on both sides of the Atlantic invoked the names of Emerson and Carlyle. "Mr. T. writes in their vein and to some extent in their dialect," one reviewer remarked, "yet he is not a servile imitator . . . having his own sphere in which to move, and his own mission to consummate." The reviewer for *Holden's Dollar Magazine* (July 1849) made a similar point, hailing *A Week* as "a rare work in American literature" and observing: "Some people have compared it with Emerson's essays, but the only points of resemblance between Emerson and Thoreau, that we have discovered, are that they are both pantheistic in their philosophy, both are ardent lovers of Nature, both follow out their own instincts, and both are residents of the town of Concord. In style and habits of thought they are quite unlike, and we think that Mr. Thoreau may be safely judged, in reference to his own merits, without comparing his name with Emerson's." But an English reviewer in the *Athenaeum* (October 27, 1849), which had earlier blasted Emerson's *Essays*, described Thoreau's "manner" as "that of the worst offshoots of Carlyle and Emerson" and dismissed portions of *A Week* as "imitations of an imitation."

The issue of originality made James Russell Lowell's review of *A Week* all the more interesting and significant. A year earlier the poet had satirized Thoreau as an imitator of Emerson in *A Fable for Critics*. Moreover, Lowell was asked to write the notice for the December 1849 issue of the *Massachusetts Quarterly Review* only after Emerson declined, explaining to Theodore Parker that he and Thoreau were "of the same clan and parish" (*L* IV:151). That position had not deterred him from reviewing Ellery Channing's first book of poems six years earlier, but his refusal probably had little impact on the fate of *A Week*, since Lowell's mixed review turned out to be very much like what Emerson himself might well have written, or at least like what he had avoided the necessity of writing. Lowell was critical of the poetry in *A Week*, and he vigorously objected to its long digressions. Although he discriminated between the admirable disquisitions on books and friendship and the less valuable commentaries on

Eastern scriptures, Anacreon, and Aulus Persius Flaccus, Lowell insisted that all of the digressions were "out of proportion and out of place" in a book that he, like Emerson, valued primarily for its narrative and descriptive elements.

But the sympathetic and poetic depictions of nature in *A Week* convinced Lowell that Thoreau was a distinctive and original, if somewhat limited, talent. "Since we cannot have back the old class of voyagers, the next best thing we can do is send poets out a-travelling," he observed. "Mr. Thoreau is clearly the man we want." Lowell thus praised what Emerson had most admired, Thoreau's knowledge of boatcraft, woodcraft, and fishcraft. "He might be Mr. Bird, Mr. Fish, Mr. Rivers, Mr. Brook, Mr. Wood, Mr. Stone, or Mr. Flower, as well as Mr. Thoreau." Lowell was so taken with the descriptions of the fish of the Concord River that he expressed regret that Thoreau had not been asked "to make the report of the Ichthyology of Massachusetts," a reference to one of the volumes Emerson had asked Thoreau to review in "Natural History of Massachusetts," the article in the 1842 *Dial* that had first begun to typecast him as a poet-naturalist. "One would say that this is the work of some bream Homer," Lowell exclaimed. 'Melville's pictures of life in Typee have no attraction beside it."

Thoreau had, in fact, probably dreamed of equaling the phenomenal success of Melville's first book, which had appeared three years earlier. But the success of an even more apposite work provided the most ironic counterpoint to the critical and commercial fortunes of *A Week*. In June 1850, after a gestation period of nearly seventeen years, Tennyson finally published *In Memoriam*, his ambitious elegy for the scholar and poet Arthur Hallam, whose sudden death in 1833 at the age of twenty-two had as profound an impact on Tennyson as John's death had on Thoreau. Their works had other things in common as well. Tennyson wrote the earliest of the long sequence of lyrics without, in his term, any idea of "weaving" them together; and, like *A Week, In Memoriam* achieved its unity through the interplay of its underlying patterns rather than by a strict adherence to a predetermined plan. Indeed, what Robert Martin has characterized as "Tennyson's wonderful amalgam of forms, ideas, sources, and viewpoints" might also describe Thoreau's luxuriant book, since, while each is at heart a lament and a celebration of friendship, both works reveal a wide range of other concerns, including poetry, history, the state of society, the relation of man to nature, and theology.[6]

There, however, the two works—and the public response to them—diverged dramatically. Although Emerson dismissed *In Memoriam* as the "the commonplaces of condolence among good unitarians in the first weeks of mourning," he recognized its great "advantage," that Tennyson "is never for a moment too high for his audience" (*JMN* XI:322). Just how directly and powerfully the poem spoke to that audience was revealed by the reviews, which were almost unanimously favorable. A few churchmen grumbled about its theology, but critics in the literary journals hailed its "true religion" and its "pure" Christianity. "Blessed it is to find the most cunning poet of our day able to combine the complicated rhythm and melody of modern times with the old truths which give heart to the martyrs at the stake," Charles Kingsley exulted in *Fraser's Magazine,* "to see in the science and history of the nineteenth century new and living fulfillments of the words which we learned at our mothers' knee."[7] Thoreau, who attacked those "old truths" with such gusto in *A Week*, paid the price for his temerity with the predominantly conservative reviewers and readers of the time.

In further sharp contrast to *A Week, In Memoriam* vividly illustrated what a book could do for an author's reputation. Before its publication, Tennyson had been a promising poet, admired by other writers but with little public recognition. Six months after the appearance of *In Memoriam,* he was invited to succeed Wordsworth, who had died in April 1850, as poet laureate, and Tennyson's fame among writers of any kind in England was sec-

[6]Robert Bernard Martin, *Tennyson: The Unquiet Heart* (New York: Oxford Univ. Press, 1980), p. 343. My comments on the writing, form, and impact of *In Memoriam* are greatly indebted to Martin's biography, which also contains some interesting observations about the relationship between the poem and Victorian literary and artistic taste.

[7]Quoted in Edgar Finley Shannon, Jr., *Tennyson and the Reviewers* (Cambridge: Harvard Univ. Press, 1952), p. 149.

ond only to that of Dickens. In fact, the extraordinary critical and commercial success of the volume, which sold vigorously in England and America, apparently intensified Tennyson's ambivalence about having claimed public notice with an expression of private grief, an ambivalence Thoreau may also have experienced when he published *A Week*.[8] Ironically, however, he had veiled its elegiac purpose so effectively that no reviewer discerned it, so his memorial to John remained a private one. *A Week* remained private in another sense as well, for, despite its modest critical successes, by the time the last notices appeared six months after publication Thoreau knew that it would never sell even enough copies to pay the costs of publication.

That cruel disappointment brought his relationship with Emerson to a crisis. "The fruit of partiality is enmity," Thoreau bitterly noted in the Journal in September 1849: "I had a friend, I wrote a book, I asked my friend's criticism, I never got but praise for what was good in it;—my friend became estranged from me and then I got blame for all that was bad, & so I got at last the criticism which I wanted" (*J* 3). Exactly what that criticism amounted to (it is described in the following paragraph of the Journal as "shot" at him "on a poisoned arrow") is unclear. But any stricture from Emerson, who had earlier so strongly encouraged him to publish *A Week*, must have been a painful wound for Thoreau to endure, especially at a time when Emerson was solidifying his own reputation with *Nature; Addresses, and Lectures*, published that September, a new edition of *Essays: Second Series*, and *Representative Men*, whose appearance in January 1850 prompted wide and generally favorable comment on both sides of the Atlantic.

Given the tensions inherent in their unequal relationship, a breach with Emerson was probably inevitable, but it is sadly ironic that the publication of *A Week*, a book inspired by the death of a friend, should have led to the death of Thoreau's other closest

[8]The relationship between the public and private aspects of the poem is discussed by Michael Mason, "The Timing of *In Memoriam*," in *Studies in Tennyson*, ed. Hallam Tennyson (London: Macmillan, 1981), pp. 155–68.

friendship. "We lose our friends when they cease to be friends, not when they die," he observed in the Journal early in 1850, eight years after John's death: "Then they depart;—then we are sad & go into mourning for them. Death is no separation compared with that which takes place when we cease to have confidence in one with whom we have walked in confidence" (*J* 3). By the time the two got together for a talk that October, "the first in a long time," they met "with malice prepense," as Emerson noted in *his* journal, and argued about "America & England," which, appropriately, had come to symbolize their divergent personalities and positions, and especially about "American & English scholars." Citing the example of Ellery Channing and Charles King Newcomb, but obviously also struggling to come to terms with his own condition in 1850, Thoreau insisted that, because they were "obscure," American scholars were "in a more natural, healthful & independent condition" (*JMN* XI:283–84). Like America and England following the trauma of the Revolution, after the crisis passed, Emerson and Thoreau once again became close acquaintances on an increasingly equal footing, but the ties that had earlier bound the two had been irrevocably sundered.

The failure of *A Week* also radically altered Thoreau's hopes for a literary career. Because of its wretched sales, Munroe declined to publish *Walden,* leaving Thoreau with a debt for $290, more than his total earnings from writing during the 1840s. Failing to meet the debt by lecturing, which, as he wrote a friend in 1853, "has not offered to pay for that book which I printed," he earned a dollar a day surveying. "I have not only cheap hours, but cheap weeks and months," he punningly remarked, "i.e. weeks which are brought at the rate I have named" (*C* 295). The debt was not quite paid off by October 1853, when the unsold copies were returned to Thoreau, who wittily observed of them in the Journal: "They are something more substantial than fame, as my back knows, which has borne them up two flights of stairs to a place similar to that to which they trace their origin. . . . I have now a library of nearly nine hundred volumes, over seven hundred of which I wrote myself."[9] Of the first edition of a thou-

---

[9]*The Journal of Henry D. Thoreau,* V:459.

sand, *A Week* had sold roughly 200 copies (75 copies had been sent to various literary figures in England and America), though it was rumored in Concord that Thoreau "had written a book no copy of which had ever been sold" (*DHT* 225).

Denied a popular audience, Thoreau increasingly wrote for himself or for an idealized audience in the Journal. Thus, alluding to the failure of *A Week,* that "basket of a delicate texture," in the parable of his literary vocation in *Walden,* finally published in 1854, he asserted, "Instead of studying how to make it worth men's while to buy my baskets, I studied rather how to avoid the necessity of selling them" (*Wa* 19). After the relatively greater success of *Walden,* however, Thoreau asked his new publisher, Ticknor and Fields, to reissue the remaining copies of the 1849 edition of *A Week.* He obviously hoped to recoup some of his losses, but even after the publisher declined Thoreau continued to revise *A Week* during the 1850s. He had little reason to anticipate the early publication or the commercial success of a revised edition, which did not appear until 1868, six years after his death; but Thoreau possibly hoped that, in time, some new readers might recognize the value of his first book and its important place in the emergent literature of the United States.

As it was, another writer at the fringes of Young America gave even fuller expression to Thoreau's literary nationalism. Speaking of European travel and the study of the masterpieces of European art, he had insisted, "Such is not our beginning life it is the old world life a dying in us." Walt Whitman, who absorbed the spirit of Young America from across the river in Brooklyn, also forecast the death of European culture in American life. America, he announced in the opening paragraph of the Preface to *Leaves of Grass,* "perceives that the corpse is slowly borne from the eating and sleeping rooms of the house . . . perceives that it waits a little while in the door . . . that it was fittest for its days . . . that its action has descended to the stalwart and wellshaped heir who approaches . . . and that he shall be fittest for his days." In both Thoreau and Whitman the reports of the death of European influence were a bit premature. Yet, at least in retrospect, the publication of *A Week* in 1849 may be seen as both a culmination of literary movements in the 1840s and a herald of that long-awaited birth of American literature signaled by the swift succession of masterpieces in the early 1850s: *The Scarlet Letter* (1850), *Moby-Dick* (1851), *Walden* (1854), and *Leaves of Grass* (1855).

Like Emerson, Thoreau hailed the appearance of Whitman's volume. "On the whole it sounds to me very brave & American," Thoreau observed after the publication of the second edition in 1856. Echoing his earlier statement that "we young Americans need some experience still & forever in the great but simple & aboriginal arts of life," he continued, "Though rude & sometimes ineffectual, it is a great primitive poem,—an alarum or trumpet-note ringing through the American camp" (*C* 445). Those notes should have been familiar to Thoreau, who, like Whitman, had first heard them in Emerson's early writings and who had sounded similar notes first in *A Week* and then in chanticleer's full-throated cry in *Walden*.

PART TWO

The First Draft of
*A Week on the Concord
and Merrimack Rivers*

Introduction

1. The Sequence of Manuscripts

The surviving manuscripts of *A Week* have created some confusion about exactly when and how Thoreau wrote his first book. In 1905, F. B. Sanborn printed what he described as portions of two drafts of *A Week,* including a "fragment" of "the earliest diary of the voyage noted down in 1839, in the boat or tent and afterwards more fully in the Concord home."[1] However, as Carl Hovde later observed, this "fragment," now in the Henry E. Huntington Library, contains Journal entries from as late as 1844, and therefore it could not have been written in 1839.[2] Describing the manuscripts as "few in number" and "chaotic in their lack of sustained coverage for even small parts of the work," Hovde concluded: "My belief is that individual sections, often on sheets of paper written several years apart, made up the text, and would be revised and recopied part by part over long periods of time, individual sheets and sections being rejected from the draft as they were recopied in more finished form."[3] More recently, William Howarth identified and described Thoreau's surviving manuscripts in *The Literary Manuscripts of Henry David Thoreau.* "Once a unified and orderly set of papers," he notes, "Thoreau's manuscripts are now widely scattered across the

[1]*The First and Last Journeys of Thoreau,* ed. F. B. Sanborn, 2 vols. (Boston: Bibliophile Society, 1905), I: xi–xii. This "fragment" and most of the other manuscripts of *A Week* Sanborn printed are portions of the first draft. He also had access to at least two leaves now missing from the first draft (see FD 64.28–66.3 and TN).

[2]Hovde, "The Writing of *A Week,*" pp. 137–38.

[3]Ibid., pp. x, 130.

length and breadth of America."[4] Howarth's descriptions greatly facilitate the study of the seemingly chaotic manuscripts of *A Week,* and comparisons of their paper types, ink, handwriting, and revision states indicate that Thoreau was not responsible for the confusion.

When they are arranged in chronological order, the surviving manuscripts reveal a coherent sequence of composition that may be divided into three distinct stages:

I. 1839–44

A. Excursion notes "Copied from pencil" in the Journal in June 1840 when Thoreau began to draft additional entries for a projected lecture or essay about the excursion (*J* 1:124 ff.)

B. Surviving Journal entries from the fall of 1842 to 1844 for a projected book about the excursion (*J* 1:445, 466, 476)

II. 1844–46

A. Transcriptions of Journal entries, November 1837–summer, 1844, plus original passages drafted in the Long Book, ca. 1844–45 (see below, section 2)

B. First draft of *A Week,* ca. 1845 (see below, section 3)

C. Additions to the first draft (ca. 1846), including revised portions of unpublished early essays such as "The Service" and "Sir Walter Raleigh"

III. 1846–49

A. Preliminary drafts for, plus revised and omitted portions of, the second draft (ca. 1846–49)

B. Corrected page proofs of the 1849 edition[5]

As this outline indicates, Thoreau did most of the work on *A Week* between 1844–1849. Although he began drafting passages about the 1839 excursion as early as June 1840, he did not gather his materials for a book until the fall and winter of 1844–45, when he transcribed entries from the Journal, 1837–44, into a large

[4]*LMHDT,* pp. xxviii–xxix. The manuscripts of *A Week,* arranged by chapter and location, are described on pages 180–209.

[5]The page proofs are in the Huntington Library (PB 110229). For a detailed discussion of Thoreau's post-1849 reivsions, see the Textual Introduction to the Princeton edition of *A Week* (*W* 501 ff.).

notebook he referred to as the "long book."[6] Between 1845 and 1847 he wrote two separate drafts of *A Week*. The first was written in 1845, set aside, and then revised and expanded in 1846, when Thoreau began work on the second draft. The earliest version of the second draft was probably completed by the end of February 1847, when Emerson, describing Thoreau's manuscript as "quite ready," wrote Evert Duyckinck about the possibility of publishing *A Week* (*L* III:384). Evidence gleaned from surviving manuscripts also suggests that Thoreau completed the draft early in 1847. As noted above, he began to write the Hannah Duston story in the Journal that April (*J* 2:377). By then he apparently had a complete, paginated draft of *A Week*, for between the paragraphs of a leaf paged 356–57 he later jotted, "On the 31st day of March &c" (MH 15, G), a penciled note indicating that the Hannah Duston story was to be inserted at that point in "Thursday." The leaf containing the opening of the story is paged 389–90 (HM 13195, "Thursday," 3; see ill. 5), while other leaves were renumbered, including one from "Friday" that was originally paged 379–80 and later paged 428–29 (MH 15, E). Thoreau had therefore added about fifty pages of material by the time he renumbered the draft, probably before sending it to Duyckinck on May 28, 1847. After failing to find a publisher that summer, he continued to revise and expand the second draft, but he probably did not renumber it again until shortly before sending it to the printer in 1849.

Although the corrected page proofs of the 1849 edition have survived, Munroe, as was customary at the time, did not return the printer's copy to Thoreau. Consequently, the only surviving manuscripts of the second draft are leaves containing preliminary versions of passages, passages from the draft he later revised and recopied, or passages he omitted as he worked on the draft during 1846–49. (The bulk of those leaves are in the Huntington Library and the Houghton Library, Harvard University.) Most of the earlier manuscripts have survived, however, including the Long Book and all but a few leaves of the first draft of *A Week*.

---

[6]Thoreau refers to MA 1303 as "long book" in his cross references to the notebook in his revised copy of "Natural History of Massachusetts" in the *Dial,* now in the Southern Illinois University Library.

2. The Long Book

Thoreau's Long Book, a bound notebook designated MA 1303 in the Pierpont Morgan Library, contains preliminary versions of most of the paragraphs in the first draft of A Week. Written in ink with numerous iterlineations in ink and pencil, the large-format notebook originally contained 132 leaves measuring 31.9 × 19.5 cm. Thoreau paginated the leaves in pencil on the recto, using odd numbers only, from 1 to 201 and from 221 to 237. Pages 240–41 are numbered in ink; pages 202–12, 217–20, 238–39, and 242–64 are unnumbered; pages 253–64 are blank. Thoreau removed twenty-six leaves (one of them a half leaf) from the notebook, incorporating nineteen leaves in the first draft of A Week and placing four leaves in a preliminary draft of Walden. Three leaves, pages 213–16 and 251–52, are missing.[7]
   A brief outline of the contents of the Long Book follows:

Pages 1–160	Primarily transcriptions, in approximate chronological order, from the Journal, November 1837 to the summer of 1844 (J 2:3–91)
Pages 161–77	Miscellaneous poems, transcriptions, and drafts of passages for A Week (J 2:92–103).
Pages 178–91	Draft of the lecture "Concord River," delivered March 25, 1845 (J 2:103–12)
Pages 192–99	Miscellaneous poems, transcriptions, and drafts of passages for A Week (J 2:112–17)
Pages 199–[203]	Drafts of passages on reformers and literary style, probably for A Week (J 2:117–20)
Pages [203–11]	Draft of "Wendell Phillips before Concord Lyceum," published March 28, 1845 (J 2:120–24)

[7]Thomas Blanding located the leaves removed from the Long Book. Those incorporated in the first draft of A Week are identified in the following section. The others, plus one Thoreau transferred from the first draft, are in the Huntington Library (HM 924, Before A). For a more detailed physical description of the notebook see J 2:470–71.

Pages [211–50]   Drafts of passages for *A Week, Walden,* and
the lecture on Thomas Carlyle, delivered
February 4, 1846 (*J* 2:124–52)[8]

Although it is clear that Thoreau completed his transcriptions
from the Journal of 1837–44 by the spring of 1845, it is not certain
when he began to gather the material for *A Week* in the Long
Book. The opening pages of the notebook contain two dated
entries: September 12, 1842, on page 16, and July 28, 1842, on
page 18 (*J* 2:9, 10–11). Except for his 1839 excursion notes, all
other dated entries among the Journal transcriptions in the Long
Book are also from 1842: September 29, page 95; October 7, page
96; October 21, page 100; October 26, page 101; and October
30, page 102 (*J* 2:50 ff.). The original Journal for these dates is
missing, so Robert Sattelmeyer, one of the editors of the Princeton
edition of the Journal, conjectured that, with the exception of the
passage dated July 28, the dated passages from 1842 were current
entries Thoreau jotted in the Long Book instead of in the Journal.[9]
In my Historical Introduction to the Princeton edition of *A Week*
I therefore suggested that Thoreau began his transcriptions in
the Long Book in the fall of 1842, worked on them on and off
during 1843–44, and completed them early in 1845 (see *W* 446
ff.).

Since he began to plan a book sometime after his brother's
death in January 1842, Thoreau may have begun work on the
Long Book that fall. But I now strongly believe that the passages
on pages 1–160 of the notebook, including the dated entries from
1842, are later transcriptions from the Journal of 1837–44, made
during the fall and winter of 1844–45. First, if Thoreau began
work on the Long Book in the fall of 1842, as the dated passages

[8]An entry dated "March 13th 1846" near the end of the Long Book (*J*
2:149) suggests that Thoreau used it as a Journal-notebook during the
winter of 1845–46, when he was concurrently drafting similar material
in the notebooks designated Walden 1 and Walden 2 (*J* 2:153–229). The
first entry in the Berg Journal of 1846 in dated April 17 (*J* 2:233).

[9]See Sattelmeyer's Historical Introduction to *Journal 2: 1842–1848* (*J*
2:449 ff.). If Thoreau did not begin to gather material in the Long Book
until 1844, the second volume of the Princeton edition of the Journal
should have been dated 1844–1848.

might suggest, there should be marked differences between the ink and handwriting of these early entries and the later transcriptions in the notebook, written nearly two and a half years apart. The notebook, however, reveals no such differences. Second, although the Journal for those specific dates from 1842 in the Long Book is missing, surviving fragments of the 1842 Journal include entries later transcribed in the Long Book. For example, on November 16, 1842, Thoreau began an entry in the Journal, "In many parts the merrimack is as fresh and natural as ever" (*J* 1:445). Without dating it, he transcribed this entry on page 105 of the Long Book, only three pages after the passage he dated October 30, 1842 (*J* 2:56). If by then he had already begun to gather material for *A Week* into the Long Book, it seems unlikely that he would have first drafted a description of the Merrimack in the Journal and later recopied it in the Long Book. It is more probable that both the dated and undated passages from the 1842 Journal in the Long Book are later transcriptions, probably begun after September 1844 when Emerson bought some land at Walden Pond and Thoreau began to make plans to move there and to write *A Week*.

The reason Thoreau dated only a few of the transcriptions in the Long Book is related to his method of transcription and to his process of composition. At first he arranged some entries in the Long Book by topic or by chapter. For example, on page 8 he transcribed an entry on friendship from the Journal of April 8, 1841 (*J* 1:298) and added four related entries from the Journal of 1839–40 (*J* 1:98–99, 110, 117) on pages 9–10 (*J* 2:6–7). Similarly, on pages 11–18 he interspersed the two dated entries from the summer of 1842 with a description of the brothers' preparations and departure from the Journal of June 1840 (*J* 1:124–26), adding his excursion notes to complete a miniature draft of "Saturday" (*J* 2:7–15). But the brothers left Concord on August 31; the descriptions of summer flowers from the 1842 Journal are dated September 12, two weeks later, and July 28, more than a month earlier. Thoreau probably dated these transcriptions in the Long Book as a reminder that he would need to revise them accordingly for *A Week*.

After experimenting with the rather arduous topical arrangement of entries, Thoreau transcribed entries from 1840–

44 in chronological order in the Long Book, arriving at the dated passages from late September and October 1842 on pages 95–102 (*J* 2:50 ff.). He probably dated these entries for the same reason he dated the two earlier entries from 1842. Like the entries on summer flowers, each entry from the fall of 1842 concerns a natural phenomenon that occurs at a specific time of the year: the migrations of birds (September 29 and October 7); the light and atmosphere of autumn (October 21); and the changing foliage (October 26 and October 30). In order to place these passages in an accurate sequence in his meditation on the autumnal landscape in "Friday," Thoreau dated them in the Long Book. For example, the passage dated October 30, 1842, concerns the witch hazel "which is now in bloom" (*J* 2:54). Using the date as a guide, Thoreau in the first draft revised the entry to read "the witch-hazle which blossoms late in October or in November (FD 93). The dates from 1842 in the Long Book are thus probably not indications that those entries were current or that he began his transcriptions that fall, but are rather illustrations of the care and integrity he brought to his work when he began to gather material for *A Week* in the fall of 1844.

By adding poems, miscellaneous transcripts, and drafts to the transcriptions from the Journal of 1837–44, Thoreau compiled nearly 200 pages of passages in the Long Book by March 1845. With a few exceptions, he then numbered each passage in pencil to indicate its projected location in the first draft:

1. Saturday, August 31, 1839
2. Sunday, September 1st
3. Monday, September 2nd
4. Tuesday, September 3d
5. Wednesday, September 4th
6. Thursday, September 5th
7. Thursday, September 12th
8. Friday, September 13th[10]

---

[10]Thoreau assigned these numbers to his dated excursion notes copied on pages 24–28 of the Long Book (*J* 2:13–16).

The last numbered passage, on page 197 of the Long Book, is an early version of the final paragraph of *A Week* (J 2:116). Although he possibly intended the poems on page 198 and the prose passages on pages 199–[203] for *A Week*, they do not appear in the first draft, nor do any of the passages in the remainder of the notebook. Indeed, most of the pages that follow "Wendell Phillips before Concord Lyceum" appear to date from the winter of 1845–46. After completing the first draft, probably sometime in the fall of 1845, Thoreau then made further use of the notebook, drafting passages for his lecture on Thomas Carlyle and for *Walden* plus some additional material for *A Week*, including the poem "I am bound, I am bound" and a description of the Concord meadows (J 2:126–27). Since both the description and the poem were intended for the beginning of *A Week*, he may have begun to revise and expand the first draft chapter by chapter.

3. The First Draft

The first draft consisted of seven pinned and/or stitched gatherings:

1. Untitled introduction and "Sat Aug 31 1839." (19 leaves stitched together with red thread)
2. "Sept 1st 1839" (18 leaves stitched together with white thread)
3. "Sept 2nd" (12 leaves, one torn in half, pinned together)
4. "Tuesday Sept. 3d" (17 leaves pinned together)
5. Untitled Wednesday Sept. 4th (at least 21 leaves pinned together)
6. "Thursday Sept. 5th" (1 leaf) pinned to "Thursday sept. 12th" (4 leaves stitched together with white thread)
7. "Friday sept. 13th" (17 leaves pinned together plus 2 leaves in the Long Book)

Except for the fifth and seventh gatherings, these groups have survived virtually intact. Although some leaves were later numbered, apparently by F. B. Sanborn among others, Thoreau did not paginate either individual groups or the draft as a whole, which consisted of at least 111 leaves or fragments of leaves. Of these, 107 leaves have survived and at least four are missing.

The draft, which Thoreau apparently wrote chapter by chapter, contains three different types of paper. Most of the draft is written on 35 folio leaves (each folio inscribed as four pages of writing on two conjugate leaves) of an inexpensive grade of white wove paper measuring 24.7 × 19.7 cm and bearing an AMES stationer's mark.[11] The draft also contains 14 single leaves (each half an original folio leaf) or fragments of the same paper. Two of these leaves are surviving portions of original folio leaves of which the second part is missing. Seven others were inserted in the draft later, but before Thoreau pinned and/or stitched together the various groups of leaves. These seven leaves, including the final leaf in "Sept 2nd," recopied from the first leaf in "Tuesday Sept. 3d," originally had blank versos; all other Ames leaves are written on both sides except the final leaf in Wednesday Sept. 4th and "Thursday sept. 12th." The draft also contains two leaves of light blue wove paper measuring 24.7 × 20.2 cm from a draft essay on Hindu scripture (ca. 1842) and nineteen leaves excised from the Long Book. Thoreau incorporated these leaves to avoid recopying extended passages. Two leaves remaining in the Long Book constitute the final two leaves of the draft. Thoreau probably did not excise these leaves from the notebook because they also contain unrelated material he planned to use elsewhere.

Of all Thoreau's surviving manuscripts, the first draft of *A Week* is among the most illegible. The ink tended to bleed into the coarse Ames paper, whose imperfections also led to numerous slips and blots. Moreover, by 1845 Thoreau's handwriting, so legible in earlier manuscripts, had degenerated. Replying to one of the Thoreau's letters, Ellery Channing on March 5, 1845, remarked, "The hand writing of your letter is so miserable, that I am not sure I have made it out" (*C* 161). That miserable handwriting is

---

[11]The AMES paper is designated "white wove 11" in *LMHDT*. Howarth indicates that the latest Thoreau used the paper was 1844. But the first draft was written the following year, and additions to the draft were written on AMES paper as late as 1846, when Thoreau finally exhausted his large supply.

illustrated by the first draft, especially in the later chapters, where Thoreau apparently worked with increasing haste. Having decided that it was simply a rough draft, Thoreau also heavily revised the manuscript in pen (ca. 1845) and, later, in pencil (ca. 1846).

The table that follows is a chapter by chapter reconstruction of the first draft, with each leaf listed in its probable original order. I have identified two leaves torn out of "Sept 1st 1839," probably by Thoreau. I have reconstructed Wednesday Sept. 4th and "Friday sept. 13th" by comparing the paper types, handwriting, and contents of scattered leaves. I have also matched pinholes and followed the order indicated by Thoreau's cross references such as "v[ide] n[ext] p[age]." The table contains the following information:

Leaf. I have assigned each of the 107 surviving leaves and four missing leaves a number within one of Thoreau's seven gatherings. Numbers assigned to missing leaves are enclosed by square brackets. Titles, blank pages, and other significant textual matters are recorded in the space following the assigned number, where I employ the abbreviations r (recto), v (verso), and MS. (manuscript).

Paper. I indicate paper types by AMES (one of two conjugate leaves), AMES s. (a single leaf), LB (a leaf from the Long Book followed by Thoreau's page numbers), and HS (a leaf from the draft essay on Hindu scripture followed by Thoreau's page numbers). Dimensions of these leaves are given above. Dimensions of fragments are recorded in centimeters in the table. Conjectured paper types of missing leaves are enclosed by square brackets.

Manuscript/Foliation. I identify the location of each leaf by manuscript number or collection. When the manuscript is foliated, I also give the page number of each leaf, although these are not Thoreau's numbers. For example, the manuscript in the Berg Collection contains 20 leaves, paged 1–40, but only 19 of these leaves are part of Thoreau's stitched gathering. The remaining leaf, Berg, 29–30, is therefore not included in the table.

Similarly, the eighth leaf in in Wednesday, Sept. 4th, is now bound in with Thoreau's gatherings of "Sept 2nd" and "Tuesday Sept. 3d" (HM 956), in which the leaf is numbered 14. When a manuscript is not foliated, but the leaves are arranged in a set order, I enclose the number in square brackets. HM 924, HM 956, HM 13188v, HM 13194, and HM 13195 are in the Henry E. Huntington Library. Other manuscripts are in the following collections:

Abernethy   "Fragments" in the Abernethy Library of American Literature, Middlebury College
Berg   The Berg Collection of the New York Public Library
Houghton   bMS Am 278.5 (by folder number) in the Houghton Library, Harvard University
Morgan   The Long Book (MA 1303) in the Pierpont Morgan Library
Thomas   The Collection of W. S. Thomas, Rochester, New York

Text. For each chapter as a whole I give page and line references to the edited text. I also give page and line references for individual leaves or groups of leaves Thoreau incorporated or inserted in, or later removed from, the manuscript, all of which are discussed in the textual notes.

The First Draft Manuscript

Leaf	Paper	Manuscript/Foliation	Text
1	AMES	Berg 1–2	1.1–
2 (v originally blank)	AMES s.	Berg 3–4	2.1–19
3	AMES	Berg 5–6	
4 (r)	AMES	Berg 7	–3.28
4 (v) "Sat Aug 31 1839."		Berg 8	4.1–
5	AMES	Berg 9–10	
6	AMES	Berg 11–12	
7	AMES	Berg 13–14	
8	AMES	Berg 15–16	
9	AMES	Berg 17–18	
10	AMES	Berg 19–20	
11	AMES	Berg 21–22	
12	AMES	Berg 23–24	
13	AMES	Berg 25–26	
14	AMES	Berg 27–28	
15	AMES	Berg 31–32	
16	AMES	Berg 33–34	
17	AMES	Berg 35–36	
18	AMES	Berg 37–38	
19	AMES	Berg 39–40	18.12

Leaf	Paper	Manuscript/Foliation	Text
1 (r) "Sept 1st 1839"	AMES	HM 13195, "Sunday" [1]	19.1–
2 (v blank)	AMES s.	HM 13195, "Sunday" [2]	20.1–15
3	AMES	HM 13195, "Sunday" [3]	
4 (torn out of MS.)	AMES s.	Houghton, 15,B	21.18–22.20
5	AMES	HM 13195, "Sunday" [4]	
6	AMES	HM 13195, "Sunday" [5]	
7	AMES	HM 13195, "Sunday" [6]	
8	LB, 131–32	HM 13195, "Sunday" [7]	25.35–
9 (torn out of MS.)	LB, 133–34	HM 924, Before A	27.30
10	AMES	HM 13195, "Sunday" [8]	
11 (v blank)	AMES s.	HM 13195̃, "Sunday" [9]	28.28–29.6
12	AMES	HM 13195, "Sunday" [10]	
13	AMES	HM 13195, "Sunday" [11]	
14	AMES	HM 13195, "Sunday" [12]	
15	AMES	HM 13195, "Sunday" [13]	
16	AMES s.	HM 13195, "Sunday" [14]	
17	AMES	HM 13195, "Sunday" [15]	
18	AMES	HM 13195, "Sunday" [16]	–36.8

Leaf	Paper	Manuscript/Foliation	Text
1 (r) "Sept 2nd"	AMES	HM 956:1	37.1–
2	AMES	HM 956:2	
3	AMES	HM 956:3	
4	AMES	HM 956:4	
5 (left margin trimmed)	AMES s.	HM 956:5	
6	HS, 7–8	HM 956:6	42.13–43.13
7 (torn in half)	HS, 9–10	HM 956:7 (top) & 10 (bottom)	and 46.3–29
8	AMES	HM 956:8	
9	AMES	HM 956:9	
10	AMES	HM 956:11	
11	AMES	HM 956:12	
12 (v blank)	AMS s. fragment (12.8 × 19.4)	HM 956:13	–48.23
1 (r) Recopied on 12 (r) in "Sept 2nd"	AMES	HM 956:15	
1 (v) "Tuesday Sept. 3d"			49.1–
2	AMES	HM 956:16	
3 (v blank)	AMES s. fragment (16.2 × 19.2)	HM 956:17	50.27–51.5
4	AMES	HM 956:18	
5	AMES	HM 956:19	

Leaf	Paper	Manuscript/Foliation	Text
6	LB, 165–66	HM 956:20	53.4–
7	LB, 167–68	HM 956:21	
8	LB, 169–70	HM 956:22	
9	LB, 171–72	HM 956:23	
10	LB, 173–74	HM 956:24	57.21
11	AMES	HM 956:25	
12	AMES	HM 956:26	
[13]	[AMES]		[One leaf missing]
14 (v blank)	AMES s. fragment (15.5 × 19.3)	HM 956:27	59.22–32
15	AMES s. [originally AMES]	HM 956:28	
16	AMES	HM 956:29	
17 (v blank)	AMES	HM 956:30	–63.5

Wednesday Sept. 4th

Leaf	Paper	Manuscript/Foliation	Text
1	LB, 129–30	HM 13194: [1]	64.1–
[2–3?]	[AMES folio?]	Missing: ed. F.B. Sanborn	64.3–26
4	AMES	HM 13195, "Wednesday," 7[1r-v]	64.28–66.3
5	AMES	HM 13195, "Wednesday," 7[2r-v]	
6	AMES s.	HM 13195, "Wednesday," 8	67.33–68.27
7	AMES	HM 13194: [2]	
8	LB, 91–92	HM 956: 14	69.29–70.33

Leaf	Paper	Manuscript/Foliation	Text
9	AMES fragment (8.0 × 19.6)	HM 13194: [3]	69.31–70.5
10	AMES	Houghton, 15, T	
11	AMES	Houghton, 15, T	
12	AMES	Houghton, 15, T	
13	AMES	Houghton, 15, T	
14	LB, 163–64	HM 13188v	74.22–75.25
15	AMES	Houghton, 15, T	
16 (v blank)	AMES s.	Houghton, 15, T	76.6–11
17	AMES	Houghton, 15, T	
[18]	[AMES]		[One leaf missing]
19	AMES s. [originally AMES]	Houghton, 15, T	
20	AMES	Houghton, 15, T	
21 (v blank)	AMES	Houghton, 15, T	–81.12
1 (r) "Thursday Sept. 5th"	AMES s.	HM 13195, "Thursday": [1]	82.1–83.9
2 (r) "Thursday sept. 12th"	AMES	HM 13195, "Thursday": [2]	84.1–
3	AMES	HM 13195, "Thursday": [2]	88.8
4	AMES	HM 13195, "Thursday": [2]	85.12–35 and
5 (v blank)	AMES	HM 13195, "Thursday": [2]	86.17–87.34

Leaf	Paper	Manuscript/Foliation	Text
1 (r) "Friday sept. 13th"	AMES	Abernethy	89.1–
2	AMES	Abernethy	
3	LB, 143–44	Thomas	91.1–
4	LB, 145–46	Thomas	
5	LB, 147–48 (bottom half)	Thomas	92.33
6	AMES	Thomas	
7	LB, 101–2	Thomas	93.35–94.21
8	AMES	Thomas	
9	AMES	Thomas	
10	LB, 43–44	Thomas	96.17–25 and 97.7–27
11	AMES	Thomas	
12	AMES	Abernethy	
13	LB, 103–4	Thomas	99.34–100.20
14	AMES	Abernethy	
15	LB, 87–88	Thomas	101.15–102.9
16	LB, 191–92	Thomas	102.35–
17	LB, 193–94	Thomas	
18	LB, 195–96	Morgan	105.7
19	LB, 197–98	Morgan	105.9–16

June 11ᵗʰ—40

We had appointed Saturday, Aug.
31ˢᵗ 1839 for the commencement of
our White Mountain expedition—
We awoke to a warm drizzling rain
which threatens delay to our plans, but at
length the leaves and grass are dried,
and it comes out a mild afternoon of
such a sober serenity and freshness
that nature herself seems maturing
some greater scheme of her own.
All things wear the aspect of a fertile
idleness — It is the eventide of the soul.
After this long dripping and oozing from
every pore — nature begins to respire again
more healthily than ever. So with a
rejoicing shore we launch our boat
from the bank, while the flags and
bulrushes curtsy a God-speed, and
drop silently down the stream. And if
we had landed our bark on the sluggish current of our thoughts, and
are bound nowhither.
   Gradually the village murmur subsides — as when one falls into a placid
dream and on its Lethe tide is

A page from Thoreau's Journal (transcribed ca. 1841),
containing his first jottings about the journey. (By permission
of The Pierpont Morgan Library)

The first page of the Long Book *(ca. 1844), containing the dedicatory verse to John Thoreau. (By permission of* The Pierpont Morgan Library)

The first page of "Friday" in the first draft (ca. 1845). (By permission of the Abernethy Library of American Literature, Middlebury College)

A page from "Sunday" in the second draft (ca. 1846–47), containing the omitted passage on the two Yankee priests. (By permission of the Houghton Library)

On the ~~31st~~ thirty first day of March one
hundred and forty two years before
this, probably about this time
in the afternoon, there were hurriedly
paddling down this part of the
river, which was rapid and swollen
by the melting snow, between the pine
woods which then fringed these banks
two white women & a boy, who had
left an island at the mouth of
the Contoocook before daybreak.
They were slightly clad for the season, in the English fashion, and
~~exhibited~~ unusual marks of ~~marriage &~~
~~fatigue~~ handled their paddles
unskilfully but with nervous energy
and determination, and at the bottom
of their canoe lay the still bleeding scalps
of ten of the Aborigines. They were
Hannah Duston, and her nurse
Mary Neff, and an English boy
named Samuel Lennardson, escaping from captivity among the Indians. On the 15th of March about
twenty Indians had come out of the
woods and made an attack on
the outskirts of the ~~settle-~~
ment of Haverhill ~~eighteen miles~~ and compelled
Hannah Duston to rise from child-

*A page from "Thursday" in the expanded second draft (ca.
1847), containing the opening of the Hannah Duston story,
later revised. (By permission of The Huntington Library, San
Marino, Calif., HM 13195)*

Note on the Text

What follows is a clear-text edition of the untitled first draft of *A Week,* which Thoreau began in 1845, probably after moving to Walden Pond on July 4. The manuscript, described in detail in section 3 above, consisted of at least 111 leaves divided into seven pinned and/or stitched gatherings. At least four leaves are missing, but I have reprinted a portion of the missing text from *The First and Last Journeys of Thoreau,* edited by F. B. Sanborn, who apparently had access to two missing leaves (see 64.28–66.3 and note). References to other missing leaves appear within square brackets in the text.

Most of the 107 surviving leaves were written seriatim. But as Thoreau wrote the draft, he incorporated over twenty leaves written earlier. Either as he wrote or soon afterwards, but before pinning and/or stitching together the seven gatherings, he also inserted seven other leaves, one containing a recopied passage and six others containing additional passages. When he incorporated or inserted a passage written on a separate leaf or leaves and its place in the narrative was not obvious, he indicated its intended position by jotting a marginal note such as "v[ide] s[heet]." Where he did so, I print the passage in the position indicated and discuss his note and the corresponding leaf or leaves in a textual note keyed to the page and line numbers of the passage in the text.

The manuscript is heavily revised in pen and pencil. Consequently, in an editor's version of the Judgment of Paris, I faced a choice among three possible copy-texts: (1) an unrevised manuscript; (2) a manuscript revised in pen; (3) a manuscript revised in pen and pencil. For a number of reasons, I have chosen the second of these alternatives, establishing the manuscript revised in pen as copy-text for this edition.

My copy-text policy is similar to those adopted in J. Lyndon Shanley's edition of the first version of *Walden* and in the Princeton edition of Thoreau's Journal. The editors of the latter chose Thoreau's "earliest stage of composition" as copy-text, arguing that his "final intentions are often indeterminate" and that his "revisions were in many cases made for preliminary or intermediate stages of other, separate literary works" (*J* 1:628). As explained below, I have excluded Thoreau's pencil revisions in the first draft of *A Week* for similar reasons. His ink revisions, however, are a very different matter. Shanley's edition of the first version of *Walden* incorporates only a few corrections and interlineations, "only those which, on the basis of handwriting and ink and context, Thoreau certainly made as he was writing this version" (S 104). But the same physical and contextual evidence indicates that many of the numerous ink revisions in the first draft of *A Week* fall into such a category. In fact, the concept of an original, or unrevised, manuscript is largely meaningless when applied to the first draft, since, instead of first writing and then revising it in pen, Thoreau heavily revised as he wrote, canceling and interlining material, adding longer passages in the margins, and inserting leaves into the draft. He no doubt made additional revisions in pen soon after he finished writing, probably in the fall of 1845, but his ink revisions were almost certainly completed by the time he pinned and/or stitched together the seven gatherings that constituted the first draft. His ink revisions were thus part of a discrete phase of the composition of that draft, so they also form part of the copy-text for this edition.

In contrast, Thoreau's pencil revisions represent distinctly different phases of composition, of both *A Week* and other literary works. The earliest of the pencil revisions were probably made in 1846, when Thoreau began to revise and expand the first draft with an eye to a second draft of *A Week*. In fact, many of the pencil revisions are in the nature of rough notes, jotted in the draft about the same time Thoreau added additional leaves to the previously pinned and/or stitched gatherings. Moreover, he later used portions of the first draft for other purposes, revising at least one leaf in pencil for use in *Walden* (see "Sept 1st 1839," leaf 9), and, as late as 1848, evidently revising other leaves in pencil for a lecture on Friendship (see Wednesday Sept. 4th, leaves 10–21). Thoreau's pencil revisions in the first draft thus constitute part of either a later, intermediate stage of *A Week* or a preliminary stage of other, separate literary works, so they are excluded from my copy-text.

But my copy-text policy is designed to be flexible. In a few instances where Thoreau corrected an obvious error or omission, I have followed his pencil revisions, reporting them as alterations in the textual notes. I have followed all his ink revisions, including indications to transpose or rearrange portions of the text, except where his revision is incomplete or his intention is doubtful. Where Thoreau made no initial choice between the original and an alternate reading (i.e., a word or phrase interlined above an uncanceled word or phrase), I follow the original reading, even if he later canceled it in pencil. Similarly, where he placed a portion of the text in parentheses, an indication that he considered omitting it, I follow the original reading, even if he later canceled it in pencil. In those two cases, cancelations in pencil are recorded in the textual notes, as are a few other alterations in pencil that clarify Thoreau's earlier intentions. All of his substanative alterations in pen, including parentheses, alternate readings, and all ink revisions, whether or not they are followed in the text, are reported in the textual notes. The only alterations in pen not reported are Thoreau's corrections of handwriting where he merely reformed or retraced the same letters, and false starts, like a canceled "ol" preceding "only." Where the canceled letters indicate that Thoreau had begun to write another word, however, I report the alteration in the textual notes.

The text is conservatively emended, thus preserving many idiosyncratic features of the draft, which Thoreau, of course, did not prepare for publication. I follow his word divisions, and I reproduce words hyphenated at the end of lines according to his usual practice elsewhere in the draft. In the case of words like *farewell,* which Thoreau at various points wrote *fare-well* and *farewell,* I have recorded my resolution of an end-of-line hyphenation in the textual notes. I have retained his abbreviations and his spelling of words like *bad* (8.2), the archaic past tense of *bid,* and his use of other obsolete forms like *skolars* (92.4) and *crede* (94.10), as well as his inconsistent spelling of certain words, for example *sailed* and *saild.* I have also retained incorrect spellings like *boyantly,* where he obviously intended a wordplay, *amoenities* (23.33), where he played upon the Latin root of a word, and other incorrect spellings where the exact meaning of the word remains clear, including *junglle* (19.28), *floted* (71.1) and *propitios* (97.31). But I have emended incorrect spellings in eleven instances where what I judged to be Thoreau's inadvertent reversal, substitution, or omission of letters strongly affected the pronunciation of the word or the meaning of the passage, for example, where he wrote *lenght* for *length* (54.20), *brink* for *bring* (72.1), and *folled* for *followed* (82.35). I have supplied the title of Wednesday, Sept. 4th, and in five instances I have supplied a word he inadvertently omitted. I have also corrected his inadvertent duplications. All emendations are recorded in the textual notes, where they are marked by an asterisk.

I have also adopted a conservative policy of emending Thoreau's puncutation and capitalization. Where he omitted punctuation with an interlineation or at the end of a line in the draft, I have supplied a comma or a dash in eight instances where I judged that its omission would be misleading or confusing. Where he canceled the first word of a sentence, added a word or phrase to the beginning of a sentence, or interlined & to connect two sentences, I have altered his puncutation and capitalization accordingly. Thoreau frequently continued a sentence after a period. When he added a dash, I have retained both the period and the dash. (Such dashes are treated like other dashes used as internal punctuation, which are printed as a closed one-em dash: *word—word.*) When he added a comma after the period, I have emended to a comma. When he added no additional punctuation, I have either altered the period to a comma or shifted the period to the end of the completed sentence. Where Thoreau inadvertently ended a sentence with a comma, I have emended the comma to a period, but I have not otherwise supplied terminal punctuation. His irregular spacing of sentence endings is normalized as follows: an en space for the norm (*river. We*); an em space if the sentence ends with a dash *(river—   We)*, if the first word of the next sentence is not capitalized *(river.   we)*, or if the sentence has no end mark but the next sentence begins with a capital *(river   We)*; a 2-em space if the sentence has no end mark and the first word of the next sentence is uncapitalized *(river   we)*.

I have followed Thoreau's paragraphing. But he often left a blank space between paragraphs in the draft, usually because he expected to add material at a later date. Where he left the space blank or later made an addition in pencil, I have represented the blank space in the manuscript by an additional line space between paragraphs in the text, all of which are indented whether or not Thoreau indented them. When he added additional material in the blank space in ink, I have incorporated the addition into the text and reported the alteration in the textual notes, inserting an additional line space in the text only where I judged that he had originally left the space blank for a different purpose, for example to indicate divisions within chapters or to set off verse extracts, all of which are set off by additional line spaces in the text. I have also inserted an additional line space before and after sections of the text written on leaves Thoreau incorporated or inserted into the draft. A line space coincides with the bottom of pages 1, 5, 6, 11, 13, 21, 32, 37, 46, 62, 73, 90, 92, and 95 in the text.

The text is printed with a ragged right-hand margin to avoid hyphenating compound words at the end of a line. All words so hyphenated in the text are also hyphenated in those instances in the draft. Except for dashes at the ends of paragraphs, all dashes that fall at the end of a line in the text should be construed as closed dashes.

Text of the
First Draft

Were it the will of Heaven, an osier bough
Were vessel safe enough the seas to plough.

The village of Concord is situated on Concord river, about 15
miles from where it empties into the Merrimack. This town too
lies under the skies, a port of entry and departure for human
souls. The Musketaquid or 'Grass-ground' river—the original
name, it is conjectured, being "formed of two Indian words,
moskeht, signifying 'grass', and ohkeit, signifying 'ground' "—
though as old as the Euphrates or the Nile, did not begin to
have a place in civilized history, until the fame of its grassy
meadows, and its fish, attracted settlers out of England in
1635—when it received the other kindred name of Concord
from the quiet and peaceable lives of these men, both with one
another and with the Indians— According to the faithful
historian of the town. "One branch of it rises in the south part
of Hopkinton; and another from a pond and a large cedar-
swamp in Westborough," and running into Hopkinton, forms
the boundary line between that town and Southborough.
Thence in a northerly direction it passes through Framington,
and forms the boundary line between Sudbury & East-Sudbury
(where it is sometimes called Sudbury River), and enters
Concord at the south part of the town. While? passing through
it in a diagonal direction, it receives the North River, and
going out at the north east part between Bedford and Carlisle
and through Billerica, empties into the Merrimack at Lowell. It
is remarkable for the gentleness of its current, which is
scarcely perceptible to the eye. "At low water it is from 4 to 15
feet deep, and from 100 to 300 feet wide.— In times when
the river is highest, it overflows its banks, and is in many
places more than a mile wide."
The North or Assabeth River, which has its source a little
farther to the north and west, and is neither so wide nor so
long as the former, joins it near the middle of the town, and
thenceforth their united currents bear the name of the
Concord.
Its general course is from S.W. to N.E., and its length about
50 miles.

The current is so slow that the story is current that the only bridge ever carried aways by it within the limits of the town was floated up stream by the wind. It creeps through broad meadows, for the most part, interspersed with oaks—where the cranberry is found in abundance covering the ground like a moss bed, a fruit peculiar to America now so important an article of commerce, with English hay being the most valuable acres—a barrel of which when sent to London many years ago by one of our farmers as a present—is said to have been duly acknowledged by his friend—though he regretted to say they had soured in the passage— A row of sunken drawf willows on one or both sides borders the river—while the meadow is skirted by maples & alders and other fluviatile trees—usually over run with the grape vine bearing fruits in their season—purple fox—red—& white—

Of huckle-berries—blue berries & blackberries the still more distant hills and secluded swamps furnish an abundant supply—of the huckle-berry alone we have the black—blue—white and red—beside some other varieties

Consider the phenomenon of a river—a huge volume of matter ceaselessly rolling through the fields and meadows of the substantial earth, making haste from the high levels of the globe by the stable dwellings of men, to its ancient reservoir — The Mississippi—the Nile—the Ganges have they not a personal interest in the annals of the world?— These journeying atoms—from the Andes and Himmaleh and Mountains of the moon—by villas, villages—and marts—with the moccasined tread of an Indian warrior.— The heavens are not yet drained over their sources. The Mountains of the moon still send their annual tribute to the Pacha without fail, as they did to Pharaoh, though he must collect the rest of his revenue at the point of the sword.

Rivers must have been the guides which conducted the footsteps of the first travellers, they are the constant lure when they flow by our doors to distant enterprise and adventure. By a natural impulse the dwellers on their banks, would at length accompany their currents to the lowlands of the globe, or explore with their guidance the interior of the continents.

They are the natural highways of all nations, not only levelling the ground and removing obstacles from the path of the traveller, quenching his thirst, and bearing him on their bosom, but conducting him through the most interesting scenery, the most populous portions of the globe, and where the animal and vegetable kingdoms attain their greatest perfection

Many a time had I stood on the banks of the stream, watching the lapse of the current, an apt emblem of all progress, following the same law with the system, with time, with all that is made. The weeds at the bottom gently bending down the stream, shaken by the watery wind, still planted where their seeds had sunk, but ere long to die and go down the stream. The shining pebbles at the bottom, not anxious to better their condition. The chips and weeds and occasional logs and stems of trees that floated past, fulfilling their fate— these were objects of singular interest to me—   And at length I had resolved to launch myself on its current, and float like them whither it might bear me.

This great but silent traveller which had so long been moving past my door, at three miles an hour—might I not put myself under its escort.

> I was born upon thy banks, River,
> My blood flows in thy stream,
> And thou meanderest forever
> At the bottom of my dream.

Sat Aug 31st 1839.

A warm drizzling rain obscured the morning and threatened
to delay our voyage, but at length the leaves and grass were
dried, and it came out a mild afternoon, as serene and fresh, as
if nature were maturing some greater scheme of her own.
After this long dripping and oozing from every pore, she began
to respire again more healthily than ever. So with a vigorous
shove we launched our boat from the bank, while the flags and
bullrushes curtsey'd a God-speed, and dropped silently down
the stream.

The boat had been loaded at the door the evening before,
half a mile from the river, and furnished with wheels against
emergencies, but with the bulky cargo we had stowed in it,
proved but an indifferent land carriage. There was a store of
melons from our patch, and chests and spare spars, and sails
and tent, and guns and ammunition enough to stock a
galleon—and as we pushed it through the meadows to the
river's bank, we stepped lightly about it, as if a portion of our
own bulk and burden were stowed in its hold, with scarcely
independent force enough to push or pull effectively.

It was what the fishermen call a dory—15 feet long by 3 in
breadth at the widest part, a little forward of the centre, and
had cost us a week's labor in the spring. It was green below
with a border of blue, out of courtesy to the green sea and the
blue heavens. Stout and servicable, but consequently heavy
and difficult to be dragged over shallow places or carried
around falls

A boat rightly made and launched upon its element acquires
a sort of life. It is a kind of amphibious animal, a creature of 2
elements—a fish to swim & a bird to fly—related by one half
its structure to some swift and shapely fish, and by the other,
to some strong-winged and graceful bird. The fins of the fish
direct where to set the oars, and the tail gives some hint for
the form and position of the rudder—   And so we may learn

where there should be the greatest breadth of beam & depth in the hold.— The bird shows how to rig and trim the sails, and what form to give to the prow that it may balance the boat and divide the air and water best.

In the present case our boat took readily to the water, since from of old there had been a tacit league struck between them, and now it gladly availed itself of the law that the heavier shall float the lighter. The wood which was grown upon this river's brink had already learned to float upon its current.

One of our masts served for a tent-pole at night, and we had other long and slender poles for shoving in shallow places. A buffalo skin was our bed at night, and a tent of twilled cotton our roof.

Some of our neighbors stood in a recess of the shore, the last inhabitants of Ithaca, to whom we waved a farewell salute, and consigned the welfare of the state.

Gradually the village murmur subsided, and we seemed to be embarked upon the placid current of our dreams, floating from past to future, as silently as we awake to fresh morning or evening thoughts.

We glided noiselessly down the stream occasionally driving a pickerel from the covert of the pads, or a bream from her nest, and the small green bittern now and then sailed away on sluggish wings from some recess in the shore. By its patient study by rocks and sandy capes had it wrested the whole of her secret from nature yet? What a rich experience must be its—standing on one leg and looking out from its dull eye for so long, on sunshine and rain, moon and stars! What could it tell of stagnant pools, and reeds, and damp night fogs. It would be worth while to look into the eye which has been open and seeing at such hours and in such solitudes. I would fain lay my eye side by side with its. When I behold its dull yellowish green, I wonder if my own soul is not a bright invisible green.

The tortoises rapidly dropt into the water as our boat ruffled the surface amid the willows breaking the reflections of the trees.

The banks of the river had perhaps passed the height of their beauty, and some of the brighter flowers showed by their faded tints that the season was verging toward the afternoon of the year, but this circumstance enhanced their sincerity, and in the still unabated heat, they seemed like the mossy brink of some cool well.

The narrow leaved willow lay along the surface of the water, in masses of bright green foliage, interspersed with the large white balls of the button bush.

The rose colored polygonum raised its head proudly above the water on either hand, and flowering at this season and in these localities, in the midst of dense fields of the white species which skirt the sides of the stream, its little streak of red looked very rare and precious.

The pure white blossoms of the arrow-head stood in the shallow parts, and a few Cardinals on the margin still proudly surveyed themselves reflected in the water, though the latter as well as the Pickerel weed, was now nearly out of blossom.

The snake-Head (Chelone Glabra) grew close to the shore. A kind of coreopsis turning its brazen face to the sun—full and rank—and a tall dull red flower like the milk weed—formed the rear rank of the fluvial array.

The bright blue (purple?) flowers of the Soapwort Gentian, were sprinkled here and there in the meadows, like flowers which Proserpine might have dropped—while above the last— still farther in the fields and higher in the bank, and in the adjacent low grounds were seen the Virginian Rhexia—and Drooping Neottia, or Ladies' Traces.

And from the more distant waysides which we occasionally passed and banks where the sun had lodged was reflected a dull yellow beam—from the ranks of tansy now in its prime.

Indeed nature seemed to have attired herself for our departure, with a profusion of fringes and curls, reflected in the water—

But we missed the white water lily—which is the queen of river flowers—notwithstanding the pretensions of the Cardinal—its reign being over for this season— He makes his voyage too late perhaps by a true water clock—who delays so long— Many of this species lead their pure and innocent lives in our Concord water— I have passed down the river before sunrise on a summer morning, between fields of lilies still shut in sleep, and when at length the flakes of sun light from over the bank fell upon the surface of the water, whole fields of white blossoms seemed to flash open before me as I sailed along, like the unfolding of a banner. So sensible is the flower to the influence of the sun's rays. So forward is purity to greet its Lord.

As we were floating through the last of those familiar meadows—we passed the large and conspicuous flowers of the hibiscus—covering the dwarf willows, and peering through the leaves of the grape. And we wished to inform our nature-loving-friends whom we had left behind of the locality of this somewhat rare and inaccessible flower before it was too late, but we were just gliding out of sight of the village spire when it occurred to us, that the farmer in the adjacent meadow, would wend to church on the morrow, and carry the news for us, and by the monday while we should be floating on the bosom of the Merrimack the flower's-friend would be reaching to pluck this blossom over the brink of the Concord.

After a pause at Ball's hill—the St Anne's of Concord voyageurs, not indeed to say any prayer for the success of our voyage but to gather the few berries which were still left on the hills—hanging by very slender threads, we set sail again and were soon out of sight of our native village.

The land seemed to grow fairer as we withdrew from it — Far away to the south west lay the quiet village left alone under its elms and button woods in mid afternoon. And the hills notwithstanding their blue etherial face, seemed to cast a

saddened eye on their old play-fellows.   but turning short to
the north we bad adieu to their familiar outlines, and
addressed ourselves to new scenes and adventures.

Nought was familiar but the heavens, from under whose
roof the traveller never passes, but with their countenance and
the acquaintance we had with river and wood we trusted to
fare-well under any circumstances.
From this point the river runs perfectly straight for a mile or
more to Carlisle bridge, which consists of 20 piers, and in the
distance its surface looked like a cobweb gleaming in the sun.
It is broad—deep—and tranquil—with a muddy bottom—
bordered with willows beyond which are broad lagoons covered
with pads bullrushes and flags.

We passed a man on the shore fishing with a long birch pole
its silvery bark left on and a dog at his side.—so near as to
agitate his cork with our oars, and drive away his luck for a
season, and when we had rowed a mile as straight as an
arrow—with our faces turned toward him—our wake still
visible on the tranquil surface—there stood the fisher still with
his dog like caryatides under the other side of the heavens
without having moved, the only objects to relieve the eye in
the extended meadow—   And there would he stand abiding
his luck, till he took his way home at evening with his fish. He
and his dog—may they farewell. I trust we shall meet
again   They were no chimera or vision to me.

The pursuit and pleasure of my earliest youth has become
the inheritance of other men—   And that Scythia in the
geography looks strange to me. This man is still a fisher
though I have wandered on, by other ways. Perchance he is
not confounded by many knowledges, and has not sought out
many inventions, but how to take many fish before the sun
sets, with his slender birchen pole and hempen lines—that is
invention enough for him. To him nature is still natural—
while he finds his account in this—I will not say sport, since it

is the most serious and deliberate employment to which the mind can herd itself— And he is still natural to nature.

It is good to be a fisherman in summer and in winter. Some men are judges these august days and serve the state, sitting on benches, even till the court rises. They sit judging in their ermine between the seasons and between meals, leading a civil politic life, arbitrating in the case of Spaulding *versus* Cummings—from highest noon till the red vesper sinks into the west.— The fisherman meanwhile stands in 3 feet of water under the same summer's sun, arbitrating in other cases between muck-worm and shiner, scenting the fragrance of water-lilies mint and pontederia. Leading his life many rods from the dry land—within a pole's length of where the larger fishes swim. Human life is to him very much like a river—

'aie renning downward to the see.'

He was the first to observe this. His Honor made a great discovery in bailments.

How many young finny contemporaries have I in this water— And methinks it will not be forgotten by *some* memory that we *were* contemporaries.

There is the Fresh Water Sun Fish—Bream—or Ruff (Pomotis Vulgaris) the most common of all, seen on every urchins string. A most simple and inoffensive fish, whose nests are seen all along the shore, hollowed in the sand, over which it is steadily poised through the summer hours on waving fin.— It is a perfect jewel of the river—the green—red— coppery—and golden reflections of its mottled sides—being the concentration of such rays as struggle through the floating pads and flowers to the sandy bottom—in harmony with the sun-lit brown and yellow pebbles.
Behind its watery shield hove far from many accidents inevitable to human life— It enhances the grand security and

serenity of nature, to watch the still undisturbed economy, and content even of the fishes of this century.—their happiness a constant fruit of the summer—   The Fresh Water Sun Fish— one and the same—as it were without ancestry—without posterity—still represents the Fresh Water Sun Fish in nature.

The common Perch (Perca flavescens) which name describes so well the bright gleaming golden reflections of its scales as it is drawn out of the water—its red gills standing out in vain in the thin element, is the handsomest and most regularly formed of all—and at such a moment as this reminds us of the fish in the picture which wished to be restored to its native element, until it had grown larger—and indeed most of this species that are caught are not half grown. In the ponds they swim in schools of many hundreds in company with the Shiner (Leuciscus Crysoleucas) averaging not more than six or 8 inches in length—while only a few larger specimens are found in the deepest water, which probably prey upon their weaker brethren.

It is a tough and heedless fish—biting from impulse without nibbling—and from impulse refraining to bite, and sculling indifferently past—defended by a tough coat of scales—which covers also as fine a flesh—well known to epicures—   It rather prefers the clear water and sandy bottoms, though here it has not much choice.

It is a true fish—such as the angler loves to put into his basket or hang at the top of his willow twig—in shady afternoons along the banks of the stream—   So many unquestionable fishes he counts—and so many shiners which he counts and then throws away.

The chivin is always an unexpected prize—which however any angler is glad to hook for its rarity—   It is a name that smacks of many an unsuccessful ramble by swift streams— when the wind rose to disappoint the fisher. It is a silvery soft-scaled fish—but of slender scholar like look—with a comical aspect like many a picture in an English book and bites

inadvertently, yet not without appetite for the bait. It loves a
swift current and a sandy bottom. The minnows are used as
bait for pickerel in the winter.

The Shiner (Leuciscus Crysoleucas)—a slight—soft-scaled—
tender fish—timid and sprightly. Found in all places deep and
shallow—clear and turbid—picking up an uncertain
subsistence. The victim of its stronger neighbors. Generally the
first nibbler at the bait, but with its small mouth and
propensity to nibble, not easily taken. It is simple enough, but
with a grain of cunning and suspicious guiltiness. It is a gold
or silver bit—that passes current in the river its limber tail
dimpling the surface in sport or flight. I have seen the young
fry when frightened by some thing thrown into the water, leap
out by dozens and wreck themselves upon a floating plank.
This little light-infant of the river with body armor of gold or
silver spangles—slipping sliding its life through with a quirk of
the tail. It is a tolerably firm fish in the spring, but too soft to
be edible in mid summer.

The Pickerel (Esox Reticulatus) is very common along the
shallow and weedy sides of the river. It is a solemn stately
ruminant fish—lurking under the shadow of a pad at noon—
with still circumspect voracious eye—motionless as a jewel set
in water.—or moving slowly along to take up its position.
Darting from time to time at some unlucky fish—or frog or
insect that comes within its range, and swallowing it at a gulp.
It is exceedingly ravenous—a sort of fresh water shark. I have
caught one which had swallowed a brother pickerel half as
large as himself—the tail still visible in his mouth, while the
head was already digested in his stomach. They are frequently
caught by being entangled in the line the moment it is
cast   They are the swiftest and wariest of fishes.
The Brook pickerel is a shorter & thicker fish than the
former—and is not found quite so large.

The Horned Pout (Pimelodus Nebulosus) is a dull
blundering fellow—like the eel vespertinal in his habits, and
fond of the mud. It bites slowly and deliberately as if about its
business, and is much prized by epicures. They are taken at
night with a light to attract them, and a mess of worms strung
on a thread which catches in their teeth. Sometimes 3 or 4 are
pulled out at once with an eel. They are extremely tenacious
opening and shutting their mouths for an hour after their
heads have been cut off. I have seen the young fry not an inch
long darkening the shore with their myriads.

The suckers in schools of a hundred or more—stemming the
current in the sun on their mysterious migrations.—and
sucking on the bait which the fisherman suffers to float toward
them—   Though they are hardly known to the mere angler
while the spearer brings home many a mess in the spring. To
our village eyes these schools have a most foreign and
imposing aspect—realizing the fertility of the seas. They are
perhaps on an average the largest of our fishes   They are
altogether a peculiar fish getting their living by suction with
mouths wide open—and indifferent selection.

The Common Eel too (Muraena Bostoniensis) a slimy
squirming creature informed of mud—still squirming in the
pan. Speared and hooked up with various success. Methinks it
too occurs in picture left after the deluge, in many a meadow
high and dry.

In the shallow parts of the river, where the current is rapid
& the bottom pebbly you may sometimes see the curious
circular nests of the Lamprey Eel (Petromyzon Americanus)—
as large as a cart wheel, a foot high & dishing with-in. They
are said to collect these stones of the size of a hen's egg and
larger as their name implies with their mouths, and fashion
them into circles with their tails.
   It is doubtful whether they still frequent this part of the river
on account the dams.
   Their nests which still remain—look more like art than

anything in the river.

Salmon Shad and Alewives were formerly abundant in this
river & taken with weirs by the Indians who taught this
method to the white settlers, who used them as food and as
manure, until the dam and afterward the canal at Billerica,
and the factories at Lowell put an end to their migrations
hitherward.

Perchance after a few thousands of years if the fishes will be
patient, and pass their summers in other creeks meanwhile—
nature will have levelled the Billerica dam, and the Lowell
factories, and the "Grass-ground" river run clear again, to be
explored by new migratory schools even as far as the
Hopkinton pond and Westborough swamp.

One would like to know more of that race now extinct,
whose seines lie rotting in the garrets of their children, who
openly professed the trade of fishermen and even fed their
townsmen to their credit, not skulking through the meadows
to a rainy afternoon sport. But alas no record of their lives
remains, unless it be one brief page of hard but
unquestionable history which occurs in Day Book no 4 of an
old trader long since dead, which shows pretty plainly what
constituted a fisherman's stock in trade in those days.

It purports to be a Fisherman's account current probably for
the fishing season for the year 1805   During which months
he purchased daily rum & sugar—sugar & rum—NE & W.I.,
'one cod line'—'one brown mug'—and 'a line for the sein'—
rum & sugar sugar & rum 'good loaf sugar' or 'good brown'
W.I. & NE.—all carried out in pounds shillings & pence from
March 25th to June 5th, and settled promptly by receiving
cash in full at the last date. But perhaps not so settled
altogether.

With Salmon Shad and Alewife, fresh and pickled, he was
thereafter independent on the groceries. Rather a
preponderance of the fluid elements one would say yet such is
the fishermans nature.—   As the poet says;

"Soon could my sad imagination find
A parallel to this half world of flood,
An ocean by my walls of earth confined,
And rivers in the channels of my blood;
Discovering man, unhappy man, to be
Of this great frame Heaven's epitome."

And still he lived and settled his account for these were the necessaries of life in those days.

Truly the gods are kind. Though natures laws are more immutable than any despots yet to our daily life they rarely seem rigid, but permit us to relax with license in summer weather. We are not often nor harshly reminded of the things we may not do. I am often astonished to see how long and often after what manifold infringements of the natural laws some men maintain life. She certainly does not deny them quarter, they do not die without priest—   And what does she care, in any case they are sure not to depart out of her demesnes.—   It would seem as if consistency were the secret of health. How many a pure man—striving to live a pure life pines and dies after a life of sickness, and his friends wonder if nature is not pitiless. While the confirmed and consistent sinner, who is content with the rank life he leads, a mass of corruption still dozes comfortably under a hedge. Nature is very kind and liberal to all persons of vicious habits, and does not exhaust them with many excesses.

Shad are still taken in the basin of Concord River at Lowell, where on account of the warmth of the water they are said to be a month earlier, and readily distinguished from the Merrimack shad. Still patiently almost pathetically, with instinct not to be discouraged, not to be *reasoned* with, revisiting their old haunts as if their stern Fates would relent, and still met by the Corporation dam.

Poor Shad—when nature gave thee instinct, gave she thee the heart to bear they fate? Where is thy redress? Still wandering the sea in thy scaly armor to inquire humbly at the mouths of rivers, if man has perchance left them free for thee to enter. By countless schools loitering uncertain meanwhile, merely stemming the tide there, in danger from sea foes, in spite of thy bright armor, awaiting new instructions—until the sands until the water itself tell thee if it be so or not. Thus by whole migratory nations—full of instinct which is thy faith, in this backward spring to be turned adrift, and perchance knowest not where men do *not* dwell, where there are *not* factories in these days. Armed with no sword—no electric shock—but mere shad—armed only with innocence and a just cause—with tender dumb mouth only forward, and scales easy to be detached. Not despairing utterly when whole myriads have gone to feed those sea monsters, during thy suspense, but still brave, indifferent, on easy fin there, like shad reserved for higher destinies. Willing to be decimated for man's behoof—not demanding protective law even game law—   I for one am with thee, and who knows what may avail a crow bar against that Billerica dam!

Away with the superficial and selfish philanthropy of men—who knows what admirable virtue of fishes may be below low-water mark, bearing up against a hard destiny, not admired by that one who alone of fellow creatures could appreciate it. But thy dumb instinctive interrests are mighty. The time is not far off when thou shalt have thy way up the rivers, up all the rivers of the globe, If I am not mistaken, and thy nature prevail. If it were not so but thou were to be over looked at first *and* at last—then would not *I* take their heaven.

Verily that was a long pull from Balls hill to Carlisle bridge— and so it was—sitting with our faces to the south—and a slight breeze rising from the north.   but nevertheless water still runs, and grass grows   For now having passed the bridge between Carlisle and Bedford—we see men haying far off in the meadow, their heads moving like the grass which they cut. In the distance the wind seemed to bend all alike.

As the night stole over such a freshness was wafted across the meadow that every blade of cut grass seemed to teem with life.

Faint purple clouds began to be reflected in the water and the cow bells tinkled louder along the banks, while like sly water rats we stole along nearer the shore looking out for a place to pitch our camp.

At length when we had made 7 miles, as far as Billerica, we moored our boat on the west side of a little rising ground, which in the spring forms an island in the river. The sun was setting on the one hand, while our eminence was contributing its shadow to the night on the other. Here we found huckleberries still hanging on the bushes, which seemed to have slowly ripened for our especial use and with gratitude partook of this unlooked for repast. It seemed insensibly to grow lighter as the night shut in, and a distant and solitary hamlet was revealed which before might have lurked in the shadows of the noon.

A little bread and sugar and cocoa boiled in river water made our repast, and as we had drank in the fluvial prospect all day so now we took a draught of the water with our evening meal—to propitiate the river gods and whet our vision for the sights it was to behold.

When we had pitched our tent on the hill-side a few rods from the shore, we sat looking through its triangular door in the twilight, at our lonely mast on the shore, just seen above the alders. The first encroachment of commerce on this land. There was our port—our Ostia— It was the harbor of Tyre. That straight geometrical line against the water stood for the last refinements of civilized life. Whatever of sublimity there is in history was there symbolized.

For the most part there seemed to be no recognition of human life in the night—no human breathing was heard— only the wind was alive and stirring. And as we sat up kept awake by the novelty of the situation we heard at intervals foxes stepping about over the dead leaves, and brushing the

dewy grass close to our tent—and once a musquash fumbling
among the potatoes and melons in our boat, but when we
hastened to the shore to reconnoitre, we could detect only a
ripple in the water ruffling the disk of a star. We heard
occasionally the song of a dreaming sparrow and the startling
throttled cry of an owl.

After each sound which near at hand broke the stillness of
the night each crackling of twigs or rustling among the leaves,
there seemed to be a sudden pause and deeper and more
conscious silence, as if the intruder were aware that no life
was rightfully abroad at that hour.

To be reminded of the presence of man in nature as well as
of the inferior orders, we heard the sound of a distant alarm
bell born to these woods, not far from midnight, from the town
of Lowell—and could see the light in the northern horizon.

But the most constant and memorable sound of a summer
night—which we did not fail to hear every night afterward,
though at no time so incessantly and with so much interest as
now—was the barking of the house dogs.— From the loudest
and hoarsest growl to the faintest aerial palpitation under the
roof of heaven, from the patient but anxious mastiff—to the
timid and wakeful terrier—wow—wow—ow—w—w—w Even
in a retired and uninhabited district like this it was a
sufficiency of sound for the vast ear of night—and more
impressive than any human music. And there seemed to be
reason in Shakspeare's line

> "I had rather be a dog and bay the moon"

I have heard the voice of a hound just before daylight, while
the stars were still shining, from over the woods and river far
in the horizon, when it sounded as sweet and melodious as an
instrument.

The hounding of a dog pursuing a fox in the horizon seems
naturally to have suggested the harmonious notes of the
hunting horn, to alternate with and relieve the lungs of the
dog. How long this natural bugle must have rung in the woods
of Attica and Latinum before the horn was invented.

The night is equally indebted to the shrill clarion of the cock—with wakeful hope—even from the very setting of the sun—prematurely ushering in the dawn.

All these sounds—the crowing of cocks—the baying of dogs—and the hum of insects at noon—are the evidence of nature's health and *sound* state—   Such is the never failing beauty and accuracy of language—

At length the antepenultimate and drowsy hours drew on— and we remembered the saying

> Who sleeps by day and walks by night
> Will meet no spirit but some sprite.

Sept 1st 1839

> In each dew drop of the morning
> Lies the promise of a day.

>   Morning
> Thou unconverted Saint
> Early Christian without taint—
> Heathen without reproach
> Who dost upon the evil day encroach,
> Who ever since thy birth
> Hast trod the outskirts of the earth.
> Strict anchorite who dost simply feast
> On freshest dews—I'll be thy guest,
> And daily bend my steps to east
> While the late risen world goes west.

In the morning the whole river and adjacent country was covered with a dense fog—through which the smoke of our fire curled up like a subtler mist. But before we had rowed many rods the sun arose, and the fog dispersed as by magic and a slight steam was left to curl along the surface of the water. The morning broke for us two alone as for a thousand more, and with such serenity as if it too observed the sabbath which man had appointed. As we passed the various islands or what were islands in the spring, we gave them names as the brothers or the sisters—   And one fine densely wooded island surrounded by deep water a junglle of Maples and alders overrun with grape vines which drooped in the water so as to form an inaccessible imbowered canal around it we named Grape Island. It was a no-mans land & piece of unexplored America

We named the island where we had camped Fox island

From Balls Hill to Billerica Meeting H. the river is twice or three times as wide as in Concord. A still deeper darker and more dead stream flowing between gentle hills & occasional cliffs, and well wooded all the way. It is an long woodland lake bordered with willows, and for long reaches there is no house in sight hardly any cultivated field.

It was a natural sunday. As we dipt our way along between fresh masses of foliage, overrun with the grape and other small flowering vines, the surface was so calm and both air and water so transparent that the swift flight of a king-fisher or robin over the river, was as distinctly seen reflected in the water below as in the air above, and it was hard to tell whether the water floated the land or the land held the water in its bosom. The heavens were of so pure and vivid a blue that we saw how vain it would be for the painter to copy them—that only nature could exaggerate herself. The dead limbs of the willow were rounded and adorned with the climbing Mikania (Mikania scandens) which filled every crevice in the leafy bank, contrasting agreeably with the gray bark of its supporter, and the balls of the button bush.

There was not the least vestige of any haze but the air was as elastic and crystalline as if it were a glass to the picture of the world, & explained the artifice of the picture dealer who does not regard his picture as finished until it is glassed.

In this bright and chaste light the world seemed like a pavilion made for holidays and washed in light. The ocean might be a summer's lake, and the land a smooth lawn for disport, into which the course of our lives was seen winding like a country road. While in the horizon the sun fell upon walled towns and villas.

It was like the landscape seen through the bottom of a tumbler in my youth, clothed in a mild quiet light, in which the barns and fences chequer and partition it with new regularity, and rough and uneven fields stretch away with lawn-like smoothness to the horizon. The clouds finely distinct—and picturesque—the light blue of the sky contrasting with their feathery softness.—so light and etherial, that they seem a fit drapery to hang over Persia—and the smiths shop resting in the Greek light seems worthy to stand beside the Parthenon. The potato and grain fields are such as he imagines who has schemes of ornamental husbandry.

Not only has the foreground of a picture its glass of transparent crystal spread over it, but the picture itself must be

a glass to a remoter background. We demand chiefly of all
pictures whether actual or painted that they be perspicuous
in this sense—and the laws of perspective duly observed,
that so we may see through them to the reality, or thing
painted.

It is not the oasis in the foreground of the desert—but the
infinite level and roomy horizon—where the sky meets the
sand, and into which leads the path of the pilgrim, that detains
the eye and the imagination.

Such a back ground do all our lives want—and such
character always secures to itself.

For the most part only the life of the anchorite will bear to
be considered but all our motions should be as impressive as
objects in the desert—a broken shaft or crumbling mound
against a limitless horizon.

All character is unrelated and of distinct outline. On this
same river a young maiden once sailed in my boat thus solitary
and unattended, but by invisible spirits. As she sat in the prow
there was nothing but herself between me and the sky, so that
her form and character was marked and as picturesque to my
eye as rocks and trees. She was no man's child. No priest was
keeper of her soul, nor guardian of her free thoughts.

Nothing is so attractive and unceasingly curious as
character. It is genius settled. There is no plant that needs
such tender treatment, there is none that will endure so rough.
It is at once the violet and the oak. It is most easily & most
hardly dealt with.—

> Methinks that by a strict behavior
> I could elicit back the brightest star
> That lurks behind a cloud

It has no acquaintance nor companion, but goes silent and
unobserved longer than any planet in space, and when at
length it does show itself, it is like the flowering of all the
world, and its before unseen orbit is lit up like the path of a
meteor.

It is what we mean let us say what we will. We hear no good news but some trait of noble character. After years of vain familiarity, some distant gesture or unconscious behavior speaks to us with more emphasis than the wisest or kindest words.

It goes hence to make itself more known by distance, and though the world may be very busy while the bud is unfolding yet when the flower is seen, all this forwardness is as it were put back and defeated.

> Oft in my passage through this star-lit clime
> I have come near some other spirit's path,
> And felt its purer influence on my mass
> But always was I doomed to learn alas
> I had scarce changed its siderial time.

For amusement we watched the flight of the robins & blackbirds which at this season may be seen flying directly and high in the air especially over rivers—constantly passing and repassing in the early part of the day. As it waxed later the cattle stood up to their bellies in the water, and made us think of Rembrandt who had never seen his pictures.

The reflection in still water shows that for every oak and birch too growing on the hill top, as well as for elms and willows there is a graceful etherial Tree making down from the roots—an ideal for every actual.—   It suggests the mystery of all picture—   What is that which is satisfied with this equally with the substance?

I have heard a landscape painter of no great genius advised to make ripples on the surface of his water to avoid difficulty—where nature had suggested innumerable deep reflections.

As we sailed along we occasionally heard the song sparrow, whose voice is one of the first heard in the spring, still singing as from a greater depth in the summer, as it were behind the notes of other birds.

The clear whistle of the oriole is occasionally heard among

the elms as late as the middle of aug., as if he sung out of a
perennial near-lying spring. This sound harmonizes with the
aftermath springing under our feet. This bird resumes its
strain as if it were still the love season and he had paused a
moment to secure his prey.

Two men, whom we passed, in a skiff, floating boyantly
without a ripple amid the reflections of the trees like a feather
in mid air, or a leaf wafted to the surface of the water without
once turning over or wetting its upper side, seemed still in
their element so silently and delicately had they followed their
instinct without interrogating the natural laws, or any noise of
invention or experiment. But as birds fly and fishes swim so
these men walk & sail. It reminded us how noble and natural
the whole life of man might be—as fair actually as at this
distance it seems

When we were opposite to the middle of Billerica, the fields
on either hand had occasionally a soft and cultivated English
aspect—whether owing to the quality of the atmosphere or
some peculiarity in the scenery—the village spire being seen
over the copses which skirted the river—and occasional
orchards sweeping down to the waterside. It seemed as if one
could lead a quiet and civil life there.

In such a scenery the inhabitants are plainly cultivators of
the earth, and live under an organized political government.
The school house stood with a meek aspect entreating a long
truce to war and savage life. Even the cultivators are the
cultivated.

Every one finds by his own experience, as he reads a
history, that the era in which men cultivate the apple and the
amoenities of the garden, is essentially different from that of
the hunter's and forest life. And neither can displace the other
without loss.

I too have my *day* dreams, but as for farming I am
convinced it is too tame for me, and my genius dates from an
older era than the agricultural. I would at least strike my spade

into the earth with such careless freedom but accuracy, as the woodpecker his bill into a tree.

Gardening is civil and social, but it wants the vigor and freedom of the forest and the outlaw. We talk of civilizing the Indian—but by his wary independence and aloofness he is admitted to a refinement in his untrimmed mistress, which is like the distant but permanent light of the stars, compared with tapers. There are the innocent pleasures of country life, but the heroic paths are rugged and retired in another sense, and he who treads them studies his plots and parterres in the stars, and gathers nuts and berries by the way—and orchard fruits with such heedlessness as berries.

The gardiner conciliates—soothes—tames nature. He breaks the horse and the ox.—but the Indian rides the horse wild, and chases the buffalo, and worships them both as his gods. His intercourse with nature is such as admits of the greatest independence of each.

The gardiner takes plants out of the forest and sets them in his garden, but the true child of nature finds them in his garden already wherever they grow, and does not have to transplant them.

If the Indian is somewhat of a stranger in nature, the gardiner is too much of a familiar. There is something vulgar and foul in the latter's closeness to his mistress, something noble and cleanly in the former's distance.

Ah, the poet knows uses of plants which are not easily reported, though he cultivates no parterre. See how the sun smiles on him, while he walks in the gardiner's aisles rather than on the gardiner.

In civilization as in a southern latitude man degenerates at length, and yields to the incursion of more northern tribes—

> "Some nation yet shut in
> With hills of ice."

The poets exhibit but a tame and civil side of nature. They have not gone west of the mountains. There are sterner

savager and more primeval aspects than they have sung. It is
only white man's poetry we have read. If we could get a clear
report from the Indian no doubt it would be essentially
different—   And we should do him more justice and
understand better why he will not exchange his savageness for
civilization.

We must not accuse him of wilfullness—for steel and
blankets are strong temptations. But death is the result.

Scholars have for the most part a diseased, or at least a partial
way of looking at the world. They mean only a few cities, and
unhappy assemblies of men and women—who might all be hid
in the grass of the prairie. They describe the world as old or
new—diseased or healthy, according as there is more or less
dust on the shelves of their libraries. When I go abroad from
under the roof I find several things which they have not
considered—and their conclusions seem imperfect. Homer is
almost the only poet who seems in any degree to have looked
over the whole world in sunshine and in shade.

After sitting in my chamber many days reading the poets, I
have been out early on a foggy morning in July and heard the
cry of an owl in a neighboring wood, as from a nature behind
the common.

None of the feathered race has yet realized my youthful
conception of the woodland depths. I had seen the red election
bird on my comrad's string brought from the recesses—
gleaming like a coal of fire amid the pines, and fancied that
their plumage would assume stronger and more dazzling
colors—like the brighter tints of evening, in proportion as I
advanced farther into the darkness and solitude of the forest.

And I have not seen such bright and far-fetched tints on any
poet's string.

These modern ingenious sciences and arts do not affect me
as do those more venerable arts of hunting and fishing and
perhaps of husbandry   As ancient and honorable trades as
those which the sun and the moon and winds pursue—coeval
with the faculties of man—and invented when hands were

invented.— We do not know their John Gutenberg and
Richard Arkwright. Though the poet would make them to have
been gradually learned and taught—

According to Gower

And Iadahel as saith the boke,
Firste made nette, and fishes toke.
   Of huntyng eke he fonde the chace,
Which nowe is knowe in many place.
A tent of clothe with corde and stake
He sette up first, and did it make.

also Lydgate says

Jason first sayled, in story it is tolde,
Toward Colchos to wynne the flees of golde,
Ceres the Goddes fond first the tilthe of londe;

. . .

Also Aristeus, fonde first the usage
Of mylke, and cruddis, and of hony swote;
Peryodes, for grete avauntage,
From flyntes smote fuyre, daryng in the roote;

   This carries us back indeed to those days—or rather that
morning twilight, when men went groping about to find the
simple gifts which the gods had dropt—and one found this and
another that. May be even at this day some less indispensable
one is discovered fallen into some crevice or pool—first
bestowed by divine hand. The gifts of Ceres and Minerva have
been long known & prized by men—but the potatoe which
sprang from a goodwill as ancient and divine as this is a recent
discovery   "The boat was invented upon crossing pieces of
water which were difficult to pass; the lamp upon the
approach of darkness; the fan, upon a defect of wind; and
injuries, to gratify the pride of men blinded by intoxication! In
short, there is not anything in the world, wherein the idea of
invention was not suggested by Providence."
   It was even a lucky thought perchance of some early

wight—the taking shelter in caves from sun and rain—a first
doubtful step—uncertain whether of instinct or reason—a
great deal better than the old way, which yet was not without
its conveniences. After long experience of pelting storms on
the bare skin, and the alteration of sunshine and shade, some
inspired wit did discover how to use nature as a shield against
herself, and doubtfully at first—yet impelled by the idea, crept
into a cavity in the rock. And then some remote descendent of
inventive genius pitying the hard fate of men, who were
obliged to forego as yet, the fair plains and fertile vallies visible
afar, and restrict their wandering to the porous hill country
—   Some genius (I say) nicely discriminating what was
essential in the cave and what adventitious—invented the
roof—the cave above ground—the portable cave invented to
stand under a palm tree—to extend palm leaves over head—
impermeable to sun and rain—an effectual protection—the
record of which remains yet in all languages. In the Latin
tectum in English shelter or roof—   And in course of ages the
slow conviction was forced upon all men—that the roof was
good, and should prevail—nor would the gods be displeased
thereby. And lo! the plains and valleys too were populated, and
the dingy cramped and misinformed families of men were
dispersed into nimble and spreading nations.

And this invention has been patented in sun and rain to this
day—roofs of palm leaves with flickering sun beams
instreaming, and dates dropping upon table—of bark or
boughs—of grass and stubble—of linen woven and stretched—
of stone and tiles—of boards and shingles.—

And hence it may be this fair-complexioned Caucasian
race—so many ages in advance of its sun burnt brothers.

Just before it reaches the canal the river contracts very
much and becomes swifter and shallower with a yellow pebbly
bottom—hardly passable for a canal boat, leaving the broader
deeper and more stagnant portion of its current above—like a
turn among the hills   But think not that we have been
becalmed all this while, for we arrived at the Billerica falls,
before noon. As we have said before the Concord is a dead

stream, but its scenery is the more suggestive to the
contemplative traveller—   And this day its water was fuller of
reflections than our pages can ever hope to be.

We here left the river for the canal, which runs six miles
through the woods to the Merrimack at Middlesex. As we did
not care to loiter in this part of our voyage, while one ran along
the tow path drawing the boat by a cord, the other kept it off
from the shore with a pole, so that we accomplished the whole
distance in little more than an hour.

This canal which is the oldest in the country—and has even
an ancient and classical look beside our modern Yankee
railroads—is fed by the Concord—so that we were still on that
familiar water. It is so much water which the river lets for the
advantage of commerce.

There is some abruptness and want of harmony in its
scenery—since the canal is not of equal date with the forest
and meadows through which it runs, or rather is led. You miss
the conciliatory influence of time on land and water. In the
lapse of ages no doubt nature will recover and indemnify
herself. Gradually fit shrubs and flowers will be planted along
the borders. Already the king-fisher sits on a pine over the
water—and the bream and pickerel swim below. Her own fish-
hawks hover over our fish ponds. All works pass directly out of
the hands of the architect into the hands of nature, and
though he has bungled she will perfect them at last.

The people were coming out of church in crowds—and
passing over the bridge as we floated under. They were
probably Congregationalists who are still as formerly the most
numerous denomination in these parts, according to the
historian of N.H.

"In the town of Portsmouth," he says, "there is a society of
Sandemanians and another of Universalists;"—and it is still
true that "The people in general throughout the State are
professors of the christian religion in some form or other.
There is, however, a sort of *wise men,* who pretend to reject it;
but they have not yet been able to substitute a better in its

the revolutions of nature will confirm and strengthen not obliterate them.

The *Merrimack* or as its name signifies the *Sturgeon* River is the main artery of New Hampshire though this state should have a mountain boundary on the west and east instead of a river which divides it against itself and makes it face both ways. It is formed by the confluence of the Pemigewasset, which rises near the Notch of the White Mountains, and the Winnepisiogee, which drains the lake of the same name, at Plymouth from which place it runs south 78 miles to Massachusetts, and thence east 35 to the sea. Rising at an equal height with the Connecticut, it reaches the sea by a course only one half so long, and hence has no leisure to form broad & fertile meadows like the former—but is hurried along rapids and down numerous falls—without long delay. The banks are steep and high for the most part and bordered by a strip of high interval land formerly levelled by water which is never overflowed at present reaching back to the hills which is most valuable to the farmers. The Nashua railroad has taken advantage of this level bank and the general directness of the river—

The Pemigewasset has been known to rise 25 feet in a freshet

A small steam boat recently plied upon this river between Lowell & Nashua before the rail road was completed. It is navigable for vessels of burden about 20 miles—and for boats, by means of locks, as far as Concord about 75 miles from the mouth. For small boats to Plymouth. Unlike the Concord it has a swift current—a clayey bottom, almost no weeds, and but few fishes, in this part of its course.

Shad and alewives are abundant—but salmon though at one time more numerous than shad are now rare. Bass also are taken occasionally.

The shad make their appearance early in May at the same time with the blossoms of the Pyrus, one of the most conspicuous early flowers, which is for that reason called the shad-blossom. A troublesome insect called the shad-fly also appears at the same time covering the houses and fences. Their greatest run is said to be "when the apple trees are in full blossom" The old are said to come down the river in August and the young 3 or 4 inches long in September.

A rather picturesque or at least luxurious mode of fishing was formerly practised in the Connecticut at Bellow's falls where a large rock divides the stream. "On the steep sides of the island rock hang several arm chairs, fastened to ladders, and secured by a counterpoise, in which fishermen sit to catch salmon and shad with dipping nets." On the Winipiseogee the remains made of large stones of Indian weirs are still to be seen.

It cannot but affect our philosophy favorably to know of these schools of migratory fishes, of Salmon, shad alewives swiss-bankers &c which penetrate up the innumerable rivers of our coast in the spring—some even to the interior lakes, and again of the young fry which in still greater numbers wend their way downward to the sea.

On the sandy shore opposite to Tyngsboro we discovered the harebell of the poets—which is common to both hemispheres, growing close to the water.

As we rested in the shade or rowed leisurely along we had rcourse from time to time to the gazeteer, which was our Navigator. And from its bald natural facts extracted the pleasure of poetry. Beaver river comes in a little lower down draining the meadows of Pelham Windham and Londonderry, the Irish settlers of which latter town according to this authority were the first to introduce the potatoe into NE. Every thing that is printed and called a book contains some echo at least of the best that is in literature. (Literature must be a fine thing which has so broad a representation and such a prestige everywhere.) And even the best books have a use above and sometimes beneath? themselves, which is the final reason of their existence—like sticks and stones, which the dedication does not cover nor the appendix conclude I should read Virgil if only to be reminded of the identity of human life in all ages. I am pleased even with such still lines as

—"jam laeto turgent in palmite gemmae"

or

"strata jacent passim sua quaeque sub arbore poma"

In ancient and dead languages any recognition of still living nature attracts us. Such sentences were written while grass grew and water ran.

Mere unobstructed sunshine or daylight are a severe test by which to try a book.

I have thought sometimes when walking in the woods, through a certain retired dell, bordered with shrub oaks and pines far from the village, and affording a glimpse of the mountains through an opening, how my life might pass there as it were in my native country, simple and true and natural, and how many things would be impossible to be done there. How under such circumstances I should select my reading.
—   Might read only henceforth *serene truth*—never statistics—nor news—nor reports—nor periodicals, only great poems, and when they failed read them *again,* or write more.

Scholars are wont to sell this birthright for a mess of learning. Is it necessary to know of Greek art and Philosophy—of Hindoo wisdom—or German criticism? Does the sun shine to light us to these things?

All that are printed and bound are not *Books,* they belong not of course to letters, but are often to be ranked with the other luxuries and conveniences of civilized life. There are new and patented inventions in this shape purporting to be for the elevation of the race—which many a pure scholar and genius who has learned to read is deceived by, and finds himself reading a horse rake or spinning jenny—or steam power press, or kitchen range—who was seeking serene truths as from Zoroaster.

Alas! paper is cheap and authors do not now have to erase one book before they write another, as anciently.

Books are for the most part wilfully written, and as part of a system—the common school system, it is, as methods to a

method, and do not teach the divine view of nature but the
popular view—and conduct the persevering pupil to that
dilemma in which the professors always stand. They teach the
elements of ignorance for strictly speaking there can be no
elementary knowledge. There is always a chasm between
knowledge and ignorance which the arches of Science can
never span.

A book should contain pure discoveries, and not the skilful
work of the author. And children should be encouraged to
study not man's view of nature—but nature.

At least let us have healthy books—even a stout horse
rake—and a kitchen range which is not cracked. Let not the
poet shed tears only for the public weal. The writer should be
as vigorous as a sugar maple with sap enough to maintain his
own verdure beside what runs into the troughs—but for the
most part he is like a vine pruned late in the spring which
bleeds to death in the endeavor to heal its wounds.

The poet is he that hath fat enough like bears and marmots
to suck his claws all winter. He hibernates in this world and
feeds on his own marrow. I love to think in winter as I walk
over the snowy pastures of those happy dreamers that lie
under the sod, of dormice and all that race of dormant
creatures, which have such a superfluity of life, enveloped in
thick folds of fur, impervious to winter. The poet is a sort of
dormouse, that early in autumn goes into winter quarters of
deep and serene thoughts,—and insensible to surrounding
circumstances—his words are the relation of his oldest and
finest memory—a wisdom drawn from the remotest
experience.

But most men lead a starved existence meanwhile like
hawks that would fain keep on the wing, and trust to pick up a
sparrow now and then.

As we rowed along near to the shore, to avoid the current,
we glanced up many a pleasant ravine, with its farm house in
the distance, or where some contributing stream came in—the

site of a saw mill, with a few forsaken eel pots at its mouth.
Two men, travellers who had been way laid by the sabbath,
called out to us from the steep and wooded banks to be taken
as far as Nashua—but we were too deeply laden. As we glided
away with even sweeps, while the fates scattered oil in our
course, the sun sinking behind the willows on the distant
shore, we could see them far off over the water running along
the shore and climbing over the rocks and fallen trees like
ants, the unsympathizing river ever flowing in the other
direction till they reached a spot where a broader stream
poured its placid tribute into the Merrimack—and when nearly
a mile distant—we could see them stripping off their clothes
and preparing to ford the stream. But whether they got safely
through or went round by the source we never learned.

Thus does nature put the busiest merchant to pilgrim's
shifts, and soon drives him to staff and scrip and scallop shell.

We camped this night under some oaks on the east bank
still in Tyngsboro, just below the ferry. And instead of the
Scythian vastness of the Billerica night, and its wild musical
sounds, we were kept awake by the boisterous sport of some
Irish laborers on the railroad—wafted to us over the water—
still unwearied and unresting on this 7th day—who would not
have done, with speeding up and down the track with ever
increasing velocity, and still reviving shouts—till late in the
night.

But at length nature prevailed with her unwearied hist-st—
and they rested.

One of the buffaloes which had been cured by the Indians
was soft and pliable and much more comfortable than the
other— They are said to prepare them by stretching the skin
over a smoky fire and incessantly beating and kneeding it.

Having reached a retired part of the river, we pitched our
tent upon the gently sloping grassy bank with the door to the
water—so that we should need no pillow for our heads and
spreading a buffaloe first on the ground—each had a blanket
for his covering— Such of our stores as were required were

transferred from the boat to the tent—a lantern was suspended
to the tent pole just over the small round table through which
it passed—while our fire blazed merrily before the door so near
that we could tend it without going outside—   And when we
had eaten our supper—we put out the fire—closed the
entrance of the tent—and sat up to read the gazetteer and
write the journal of our voyage, or listened to the wind or the
rippling of the river till sleep over took us.

Sept 2nd

Early this morning we were again on our way—steering
through a fog as before—   The country men recruited by their
day of rest were already awake, and passengers had begun to
cross the ferry on the business of the week—   The fog soon
dispersed and again we rowed leisurely along under a clear
sky—and in a mild atmosphere—under favorable auspices—
leaving the habitations of men behind.—between the territories
of Dunstable and Nashua on the one hand and Hudson on the
other.

It was from the former place it will be remembered, then a
frontier town, that the valiant Capt. Lovewell with his
company marched in pursuit of Paugus on the 18th of April,
1725. He was the son of "an ensign in the army of Oliver
Cromwell, who came to this country and settled at Dunstable,
where he died at the great age of 120 years." In the words of
the old nursery tale written about a hundred years ago—

>   full wide,
> He and his valiant soldiers, did range the woods
> And hardships they endured to quell the Indian's pride.

The incidents and exploits of that march would furnish
materials for one book of the Iliad at least. In this shaggy pine
forest of Pigwacket they met the 'rebel Indians' and conquered
them, and a remnant returned home to enjoy the fruits of their
victory in the township granted them by the state.

> Of all our valiant English, there were but 34,
> And of the rebel Indians, there were about fourscore.
> And sixteen of our English did safely home return,
> The rest were kill'd and wounded, for which we all must mourn

> Our worthy Capt. Lovewell among them there did die,
> They killed Lieut. Robbins, and wounded good young Frye,
> Who was our English Chaplain; he many Indians slew,
> And some of them he scalp'd when bullets round him flew.

Alas our brave forefathers have exterminated all the Indians, and their degenerate children no longer dwell in garrisoned houses, nor hear any war whoop in their path, but rust in disgraceful peace perchance, while enemies as active are still in the field. It would be well perchance if many an 'English Chaplain' in these days could exhibit trophies of his valor as unquestionable as did 'good young Frye.'

And braving many dangers and hardships in the way,
They safe arriv'd at Dunstable the 13th day of May.

2 of the 7 who marched from Concord who were wounded— were fourteen days in the wilderness creeping toward the frontiers. One of them cut his moccasins into strings and with a hook caught fish in a pond—but the fish and cranberries which they ate are said to have come out through their wounds

Meanwhile we were advancing farther into the country and into the day—which last proved almost as golden as the preceding—the slight bustle and activity of a monday being added to the sundayness of nature. Now and then we had to muster all our energy to get round a point where the river broke rippling over rocks and the maples trailed their branches in the stream   There is generally a backwater on the sides of the stream which the boatman takes advantage of. Occasionally one would run along the shore for a change examining the country, and visiting the nearest farm-houses, while the other followed the winding of the river alone—from time to time scaring up a king-fisher—or a summer duck—to meet his companion at some distant point and hear the report of his adventures. How the farmer praised the coolness of his well—and his wife offered the stranger a draught of milk. For though the country was so new and unexplored by us—shut in between the steep banks that still & sunny day—we did not have to travel far to find where men inhabited like wild bees, and had sunk wells in the loose sand and loam. There dwelt the subject of the Hebrew scriptures and the Esprit des Lois, where a thin vaporous smoke curled up through the noon.

All that is told of that mankind—of the inhabitants of the
upper Nile—and the Sunderbunds and Timbuctoo—and the
Orinoko—is experience here.

While we were engaged in these reflections—and thought
ourselves the only navigators of this sea, suddenly a canal boat
like some huge river beast with its large sail set, glided round
a point before us and changed the scene in an instant—   And
then another and another glided into sight, and we found
ourselves in the current of commerce once more

At length we were fairly delivered from this fleet of junks—
and possessed the river in solitude once more—   In the
middle of the day we rested us under a willow or maple which
hung over the water, and drew forth a melon for our repast.
Contemplating at our leisure the lapse of the river and of
human life. As that current with its floating twigs and leaves,
so did all things pass in review before us, while far away in
cities and marts on this very stream the old routine was
proceeding still. All was river that we saw or thought.
It seemed that there was indeed a tide in the affairs of men,
as the poet says—and yet that the ebb always balanced the
flow, and the shores were unchanged but in longer periods
than we can measure.
The hardest material obeys the same law with the most
fluid. Trees are but rivers of sap and woody fibre flowing from
the atmosphere and emptying into the earth by their trunks, as
their roots on the other hand flow upward to the surface. And
in the heavens there are rivers of stars and milky ways. There
are rivers of rock in the surface and rivers of ore in the bowels
of the earth. And our thoughts flow and circulate—and
seasons lapse into the current year.
But as things flow they circulate and all streams are but
tributary to the ocean, which itself does not stream.
There are moments when all anxiety and practical desires
must be becalmed in the infinite leisure and repose of nature.
Laborers must have their nooning undisturbed. The sailor in a
sultry day stretched on the deck of his craft and drifting with
the sluggish water, is even more of a philosopher than a

reformer—   So when we have ceased to row against the
stream, and float or sail upon the tide of life—rock—tree—
kine—knoll—and all the panorama of the shore—assuming
new and varying positions as wind and current shift the scene,
invite this liquid undulating lapse of thought.

When I go into the museum and see the mummies wrapped
in their linen bandages, I see that the times began to need
reform as long ago as when they walked the earth—   I go out
into the streets and meet men who declare that other times
and other dynasties are now at hand.—   But still I know that
as man stood in Thebes so does he stand in Dunstable today.
   The sap of all noble schemes drieth up and the schemers
return again and again in despair to "common sense and
labor" but to return is not the right way, nor will it be the last.
   Such is the testimony of the past—and time seems longer
than eternity.   but there are secret articles which the historian
can never know.
   As often in the treaties of states there are secret articles
inserted which are of more importance than all the rest—so is
it in our treaties with the gods the faintest and most secret
articles are ever the most vital.

All things teach man to be calm & patient. The language of
excitement is only picturesque—but you must be calm to utter
oracles—not such as the Delphic priestess did. Enthusiasm is
a supernatural serenity. Such is the oldest history.   mankind
seem anciently to have exercised the passive virtues—and all
these active Saxon qualities seem modern
   While lying on our oars under these willows in the heat of
the day our boat being held by an osier put through the staple
in its prow, and slicing the melons which are the fruit of the
east—our thoughts reverted to Arabia—Persia and Hindostan,
the lands of contemplation, and dwelling places of the
ruminant nations.—   And in the experience of this noon-tide
we found apology for the instinct of the opium—betel and
tobacco chewers. Mount Sabér, according to the French
traveller and naturalist Botta, is celebrated for producing the

Kát tree, of which "The soft tops of the twigs and tender leaves are eaten," says his reviewer, "and produce an agreeable soothing excitement, restoring from fatigue, bannishing sleep, and disposing to the enjoyment of conversation."

What a dignified oriental life might be lived along this stream, browsing the tree tops—and chewing mallows, and apple tree buds, like the camelopards, rabbits & partridges!

I have sometimes wished to go away and live by some river or pond side, and have had no other reason to give my friends than that so I might have a fair opportunity to hear the wind whispering among the reeds, and see the spring come in.

But sometimes man's blood seems to circulate farther than the currents of the universe—and he has his morning while she has her noon. Eternity is merely long—and the tune unchangeable.

One wonders if setting hens are troubled with ennui those long march days setting on and on in the crevice of a hay-loft with no active employment.

At length we threw our rinds into the water for the fishes to nibble, and added our breath to the life of living men. Our melons lay at home on the sandy bottom of the Merrimack and our potatoes in the sun and water in the bottom of our boat looked like a fruit of the country.

Again we rowed steadily upward saxon-wise as it were against the currents of nature from time to time scaring up a king-fisher or a summer duck.— The former flying rather by vigorous impulses than by steady and patient steering with that short rudder of his—sounding his rattle along the fluvial street. And anon another scow hove in sight creeping down the river—and hailing it we attached ourselves to its side and floated back in company chatting with the boatmen—and obtaining a draught of cooler water from their jug— they appeared to be green hands from far among the hills—who had taken this means to get to the sea-bord and see the world, and would probably visit the Falkland isles—and the China

seas before they again saw the waters of the Merrimack or
perhaps not return this way forever. They had already
embarked the private interests of the landsman in the larger
venture of the race and were ready to mix with mankind—
reserving only the till of a chest to themselves.

But still the noon prevailed and we turned the prow ashore
to spend the remainder of it under the oaks of a retired pasture
slooping to the waters edge—and bordered with hazles—   Still
had India the better part of our thoughts, and that old noontide philosophy.

We will not inquire into the antiquity of this scripture. One
might as well investigate the chronology of light and heat. Let
the sun shine. Menu understood this matter best when he said
"Those persons best know the divisions of days and nights,
who understand that the day of Brahmá, which endures to the
end of a thousand such ages, gives rise to virtuous exertions;
and that his night endures as long as his day." The true India
is neither now nor then—east nor west. Who has not lived
under the Mussalman and Tartar dynasty. You will not have to
pierce far into the summer day to come to these. In the New
England noontide are more materials for oriental history than
the Sanscrit contains. In every man's brain is the sanscrit. Was
not Asia mapped there before it was in any geography? The
Védas and their Angas are not so ancient as serene
contemplation—   The mind contemplates them as Brahmá his
scribe.
Why will we be imposed on by antiquity—   Is the babe
young?—   When I behold it it seems more ancient than
Nestor or the Sybil, and bears the wrinkles of Saturn himself.
It is more venerable than the oldest man—and does not soon
learn to attend to these new things. And do we live but in the
present? How broad a line is that? I sit now on a stump whose
rings number centuries of growth. If I look around I see that
the soil is composed of the remains of just such stumps
ancestors to this. The earth is covered with mould—   I thrust
this stick many aeons deep in its surface. With my heel I make

a deeper furrow than the elements have ploughed here for a
thousand years, and unearth walnuts and acorns which were
buried before the Védas were written. If I listen I hear the
peeping of frogs which is older than the slime of Egypt, or the
distant drumming of a partridge on a log—as if it were the
pulse beat of the summer air. I raise my fairest and freshest
flowers in the old mould. Why what we would fain call new is
not skin deep—the earth is not yet stained by it. It is not the
fertile ground we walk upon but the leaves that flutter over our
heads. When we dig up the soil from a thousand feet below
the surface—we call it new, and the plants which spring from
it. When our vision pierces deeper into space and detects a
remoter star we call that new also.

Suddenly a boatman's horn was heard echoing from shore to
shore to give notice of his approach to the farmer's wife with
whom he was to take his dinner, though in that retired place
only the muskrats and king fishers seemed to hear.
Proceeding on our way in the afternoon the banks became
lower, or receded farther from the channel—leaving a few
trees to fringe the waters edge—among which were the
maple—birch—and bass   The last—also called the lime or
linden—the white-wood of the mechanics—overhangs the
water with its broad leaf affording a grateful shade to the
sailor. The inner bark of this genus affords the material of the
fisherman's matting, of which the Russians make so much
use. The peasants use the same material for shoes.

In the wildest scenery is the raw material of the most
refined life. Here is bast for our shoes and for matting—and
rushes for our light—and no doubt there is papyrus by this
river's side—while the goose only flies over head.

The bass was a new tree to us—with a new leaf—but still
like those we knew. What an impulse was given some time or
other to vegetation that now nothing can stay it—but every
where it is nature's business constantly to create new leaves
and repeat this type in many materials—   One who travelled

hastily through her territories would say that she was a vast manufactory of leaves.— The leaf is her constant cypher. It is grass in the field—the garment she wears—it flutters on the oak—it springs in the mould upon a jar—and in animal, vegetable, & mineral—in fluids and in crystals—plain or variegated—fresh or decayed it acts how large a part in the economy of the universe.

The flower is the colored leaf—and the trunk the leaf stalk or as it were folded leaves—and in the bare tree stalk in the winter is seen—the naked fibres and outline of the leaf which in the spring will be filled up with vegetable pulp. And layers of leaves make the soil itself—in which new forests are planted.

Whatever Coleridge thought of Tasso's having chosen the last remaining topic for an epic poem in the Delivery of Jerusalem—I think his critic was right who thought one could write an epic to be called the leaf.

In all her various products nature only developes her simplest germs—and whether it be tangled and weathered vines—or cedar or oak forests or stretching grain fields—all are to be referred to one—all belong to one head like the curls of a maiden's hair— It seems to have been no great stretch of invention to have created birds— The hawk perchance which now takes its flight over the top of the wood was at first only a leaf which fluttered in its aisles. From rustling leaves she came in the course of ages to the loftier flight and clear carol of the bird.— Look up at the tree tops and see how finely she finishes off her work there as if she would never have done. See how the pines spire without end higher and higher, and give a graceful fringe to the earth. And who shall count the finer cob-webs that soar and float away from their utmost tops, and the myriad insects that dodge between them.—

Salmon Brook comes in from the west—under the rail-road, but we saild up far enough into the meadows which border it to learn its piscatorial history from a haymaker on its banks. He told us that the silver eel was formerly abundant here and pointed to some sunken creels at its mouth. Pennichook forms

the northern boundary of Nashua—and we expected to reach
this before night. In these fair meadows where the hayer
rested on his rake and told us all his fishy lore, we never trod,
and yet our eyes ranged over them contentedly and we
touched their edges with our hands—and made a pleasant and
memorable acquaintance that afternoon—

But we could not afford to loiter in this pleasant roadsted
and so stood out to sea again.

> Salmon Brook,
> Pennichook,
> Ye sweet waters of my brain,
> When shall I look,
> Or cast the hook,
> In your waves again?

> Silver eels
> Wooden creels
> These the baits that still allure,
> And dragon fly
> That floated by,
> May they still endure?

We soon after passed the village of Nashua upon the river of
the same name—where a stately covered bridge spans the
Merrimack. While one threaded the town his companion rowed
steadily on to meet him above at a pine wooded Island at the
mouth of the Nashua, where a few sheep, the only inhabitants,
who were reposing in the shade upon its summit—reminded
us of Colchos and the argo. The nashua one of the largest
tributaries which is so pleasant a stream where it winds
unobstructed through the meadows of Lancaster and Groton—
was here so obstructed by falls and factories—that we did not
delay to explore it.

We rowed slowly on before sunset looking for a retired place
for our camp—a few red clouds beginning to be reflected in
the yellowish water— Soon the village was out of sight—and
the woods were gained again—and so calm was the surface that

the muskrats were easily detected by the dimples in the stream.

Here the woodcutters have felled an ancient pine forest and brought to light to these distant hills a fair lake in the south west. It is not wholly a disservice they have done. One wonders if the very bare earth did not experience emotion at beholding so fair a prospect. This gleam reflected by the evening sky will sow flowers here of various hues with its slanted rays. That fair water lies there in the sun revealed to these distant hills, as if it needed not to be seen. Its beauty seems yet lonely—sufficient to itself, and quite superior to observation. And now in an instant and distinctly, it is shown to these woods, as if its rays had travelled hither from eternity. So are these old truths like serene lakes in the horizon—at length revealed to us, which have so long been reflecting our own sky in their bosom. And thus serene is antiquity always—like the horizon in which the wind never blows.

When I revolve it again in my mind gazing into the west at evening whether these ordinances of the Hindoos are to be passed by as the whims of an Asiatic brain—I seem to see the divine Brahmá himself sitting in the angle of a cloud, and revealing himself to his scribe Menu—and this fair modern world is only a reprint of The Laws of Menu with the Gloss of Culluca. Tried by a New England eye—or the more practical wisdom of modern times, they are simply the oracles of a race already in its dotage, but held up to the sky, which is the only impartial and incorruptible ordeal, they are of a piece with its depth and serenity, and I am assured that they will have a place and significance as long as there is a sky to test them by.

We camped this night on the confines of Nashua on the west bank by a deep ravine—under the skirts of a pine wood — The dead pine needles were our carpet—and their tawny boughs stretched protecting arms over us.

The building a fire and spreading our buffalo skins was too frank an advance to be resisted. The fire and smoke seemed to tame the scene. The rocks consented to be our walls and the pines our roof.

A forest is in all mythologies a sacred place, as the oaks among the Druids, and the grove of Egeria—and what is Robin Hood without his Barnsdale and Sherwood. It is the life that is lived in the unexplored scenery of the wood that charms us.

There is something indescribably wild and beautiful in the aspect of the forest skirting and occasionally jutting into the midst of new towns, which like the yellow sand heaps of fresh fox boroughs have sprung up in their midst. The uprightness of the pine and maples assert the ancient—& everlasting rectitude and vigor of nature, & our lives need the relief of such a back-ground—where the pine flourishes and the jay still screams.

So near us is the forest of undreamed of exploits—and the whole genii of untamed & winged thoughts.

I shall not soon forget the sounds which we heard when falling asleep this night on the banks of the Merrimack. Far into night we heard some tyro beating a drum incessantly in preparation for a country muster, in Compton as we learned, and thought of the line

"When the drum beat at dead of night."

The very firmament echoed his beat and we could have assured him that it would be answered and the forces be mustered. Fear not thou drummer of the night—we too will be there.

And still he drummed on alone in the silence and the dark.

This stray sound from a far off sphere came to our ears from time to time to remind us of those fabulous Aeolian notes we had almost forgotten. It was as if our shoulders jogged the stars.

When we hear any musical sound in nature—it is as if it were a bell ringing, and we feel that we are not belated, but in season wholly, and enjoy a prime and leisure hour.

Occasionally we hear a remote sound with so unprejudiced a sense, far—sweet—and significant—that we seem for the first time to have heard at all. And thus the cheapest sound has a larger meaning & a wider undulation than we knew.

What a fine and beautiful communication from age to age of the fairest and noblest thoughts—the aspirations of ancient men—even such as were never communicated by speech—is music. It is the flower of language. Thought colored and curved—tinged and wreathed—fluent & flexible   Its crystal fountain tinged with the sun's rays—and its purling ripples reflecting the green grass and the red clouds.

It teaches us again and again to trust the remotest and finest as the divinest instinct—and makes a dream our only real experience.

There was a high wind this night which we afterwards learned had been still more violent elsewhere, and had done much injury to the corn-fields far and near. But we only heard it sigh occasionally that it could not shake the foundations of our tent, and laid our ears closer to the ground with a sense of security, while the blast swept on to alarm other men.

The pines murmured the water rippled, and the tent rocked a little, and before sunrise we were ready to pursue our voyage as usual.

Tuesday Sept. 3d

By three o'clock we had completed our preparations and were ready to pursue our voyage anticipating another pleasant day. We preferred to take time by the fire and loiter in the heat of the day.

Buonaparte said that the 3 o clock in the morning courage was the rarest. But methinks fear does not awake so early. Few men are so degenerate as to baulk nature by not beginning the day well. We could excuse them for not fighting to prolong their afternoons.

The fog this morning was thick & fragrant and though we were enveloped in it, we trusted that it was confined to this river and that a bright day lurked behind it. Dr Belknap the historian of NH. says that. "In the neighborhood of fresh rivers and ponds, a whitish fog in the morning, lying over the water, is a sure indication of fair weather for that day; and when no fog is seen, rain is expected before night." That which seemed to invest the world to us—was probably but a narrow and shallow wreath of vapor stretched over the channel of the Merrimack, though it might be from the sea-board to the mountains. I once saw the day break from the top of Saddle back mountain in Massachusetts when the whole earth was invested with clouds and not a crevice was left through which the state of Massachusetts—or New York—or Vermont—or the state of the lower world could be seen—while I still inhaled the pure atmosphere of a July morning. At length the sun arose over this world of clouds, and around me was spread for a hundred miles and as far as the eye could reach an undulating country of vapor—answering in the varied swell and fantastic features of its surface to the terrestrial world it veiled. There were snowy pastures apparently as firm as smooth shaven lawns—gleaming in the sun—and shady vales between the vaporous mountains—and far in the horizon I could see where some luxuriant timber jutted into the prairie—and trace the windings of some water course from the far sea-board till it was lost in the west—by the misty—but sunlit—trees upon its brink—

And I remained there till noon—when the clouds had risen
& enveloped me also and the rain began to fall around me—
and I descended into the neighboring vallies, where it was
inserted in the meteorological journals the whole of that day
was cloudy.

Such morning experiences methinks should not be lost upon
an cloudy philosophy.

Fog.

Thou drifting meadow of the air,
Where bloom the dasied banks and violets,
And in whose fenny labyrinth
The bittern booms and heron wades;
Low anchored cloud,
Newfoundland air,
Fountain head and source of rivers,
Ocean branch that flowest to the sun,
Diluvian spirit—or Deucaleon shroud,
Dew cloth—dream drapery,
And napkin spread by fays.
Spirit of lakes and seas and rivers
Sea fowl that with the east wind
Seek'st the shore, groping thy way inland,
Bear only perfumes and the scent
Of healing herbs to just men's fields.

The same pleasant & observant historian whom we quoted
above says that "In the mountainous parts of the country, the
ascent of vapors, and their formations into clouds, is a curious
and entertaining object. The vapors are seen rising in small
columns, like smoke from many chimneys. When risen to a
certain height, they spread meet, condense, and are attracted
to the mountains, where they either distil in gentle dews, and
replenish the springs, or descend in showers, accompanied
with thunder. After short intermissions, the process is repeated
many times, in the course of a summer day, affording to
travellers a lively illustration of what is observed in the book of
Job, 'They are wet with the showers of the mountains.' "

Thus is the Bible illustrated by natures cheap lithograph and wood cuts.

Our tent was generally so wet with the dew that it had to be spread in the

[Bottom third of leaf missing]

We passed a canal boat before sunrise, and though we could not distinguish it for the fog the few dull sounds we heard, carried with them a sense of weight, and irresistible motion— which was quite impressive.

The trees were dripping with dew and the springs seemed to trickle colder from the moist banks.

> "And now the taller suns (whom Titan warms)
> Of unshorn mountains blown with easy winds,
> Dandled the morning's childhood in their arms,
> And, if they chanced to slip the prouder pines,
> The under corylets did catch the shines,
> To gild their leaves;"—   Giles Fletcher

Streaks of sun light struggled through the fog—and the pines on the shore—to the river—

The river becomes swifter and the scenery more pleasing   The banks of the Merrimack are steep and clayey for the most part, and trickling with water, and where a spring oozes out a few feet above the river, the boatmen cut a trough out of a slab with their axes and place it so as to receive the water, and fill their jugs conveniently. Bursting out from under a pine or a rock, sometimes this purer and cooler water is collected into a little basin close to the edge of and level with the river—a fountain head of the Merrimack.

So near along life's stream *lie* the fountains of innocence and youth making fertile its sandy margin. And the voyageur will do well to replenish his vessels at these uncontaminated sources. Some youthful spring perchance still empties with tinkling music into the oldest river, even when it is falling into the sea, and we imagine that its music is distinguished by the river gods from the general lapse of the stream, and falls sweeter upon their ears in proportion as it is nearer to the ocean.

As thus the evaporations of the river feed these unsuspected springs which filter through its banks, so our aspirations fall back again in springs upon the margin of life's stream to refresh and purify it.

Our course this morning lay between the territories of Merrimack and Litchfield once called Brenton's Farm, and the Indian Natticott. We passed the first falls we had met with by means of locks and soon afterwards some others and did not have to use our wheels. And it now became a pleasant change after rowing for many hours to lock ourselves through—in some retired part of the river—one sitting in the boat while the other with no small labor and heave yo ing opened and shut the gates—waiting patiently to see the locks fill up with river water—   Taking advantage of the eddy or back water we were sometimes floated up to the locks almost in the face of the falls—without any effort. Any floating timber is carried round in a circle and repeatedly drawn into the rapids before it goes down the stream. These old grey structures with their giant arms stretched over the river in the sun, seemed like natural objects in the scenery—where the king fisher and the sand piper alighted as readily as on stakes or rocks.

When we reached the first falls there were several boats passing through the locks, for whom we waited—and in the forward part of one stood a brawny N Hampshire man— leaning upon his pole—bare headed and in simple shirt and trowsers—a rude apollo of a man coming down from that "vast uplandish country" to the main—of nameless age, with flaxen hair and vigorous weather-bleached countenance in whose wrinkles the sun still lodged.

An undressed—unkempt—uncivil man with whom we parleyed for awhile—not without a sincere interest in one another.

All his humanity was instinctive and therein resided the
man—but his rudeness was a manner

There is reason in the distinction of civil and uncivil. The
manners are sometimes so rough a rind that we doubt whether
they conceal any sap wood—or core at all. We sometimes meet
uncivil men—children of Amazons, who dwell by mountain
paths, and are said to be inhospitable to strangers, whose
salutation is as rude as the grasp of their brawny hands, and
who naturally deal with men as unceremoniously as they are
accustomed to deal with the elements. They have only to
extend their clearings and let in more sun light, to seek out
the southern slopes of the hills from which they may look
down upon the civil plain or ocean, and temper their diet duly
with cereal fruits, consuming less wild meat and acorns, to
become like the inhabitants of cities.

I was once travelling in a distant and mountainous part of
the country, along the banks of a stream whose course I had
followed for several days, when I reached a succession of
shady vallies, sunken deep among the hills—with a few mild
and hospitable inhabitants—who informed me that on either
hand—high up on the level tops of the mountains dwelt a less
polished race of settlers who had but little intercourse with
themselves—so near indeed though directly inaccessible that
they could occasionally hear the bleating of their flocks—
As the day was not yet spent and I was anxious to improve
the light though my path was gradually rising to these higher
levels my kind hosts directed me to the dwelling of the nearest
of these settlers whose name was Rice, who they said was a
rude and inhospitable man.
"What is a foreign country to those who have science? What
is a stranger to those who have the habit of speaking kindly?"
At length as the sun was setting behind the mountains in a
still darker and more solitary valley, where the shaggy woods
almost joined their tops over the torrent I reached his dwelling.
I observed as I drew near to his abode that he was less rude
than I had anticipated, for he kept many cattle and dogs to
watch them, and I saw where he had made maple sugar on

the sides of the mountains, and more than all detected the voices of children mingling with the murmur of the torrent before the door.

As I passed his stable I met one whom I took to be a hired man attending to his cattle, and inquired if they entertained travellers at that house.— "Some times we do"—he answered gruffly, and immediately went to the farthest stall from me — And I perceived that it was Rice himself whom I had addressed. But pardoning this incivility to the wildness of the surrounding scenery—I bent my steps to the house— There was no sign post before it nor any invitation to the traveller though I saw by the road that many went and came there— but the owner's name only was fastened to the outside—a sort of implied and sullen invitation, as I thought.

I passed from room to room without meeting any one, at first, till I came to what seemed the guests apartment, which was neat and even had an air of refinement about it, and I was glad to find a map on the wall which would direct me upon my journey on the morrow.

At length I heard a step in a distant apartment which was the first I had entered, and went to see if the master of the house had come in, but it proved to be only a child, one of those whose voices I had heard, probably his son, and between him and me stood in the door way a large watch dog, which growled upon me and looked as if he would presently spring, but the boy did not speak to him nor seem to observe the danger. And when I asked him for a glass of water he briefly said "It runs in the corner." So I took a mug and went out doors again—and searched round the corners of the house, but I could find no well nor spring, nor any water, but the stream I have mentioned—which ran all along the front   I came back therefore and set down the empty mug—thinking to ask if the stream was good to drink—saying I could not find it— whereupon the child seized the mug and going to the corner of the room where a cool spring trickled through a pipe into the apartment, filled it and drank, and gave it to me empty again—and calling to the dog rushed out of the room, leaving me alone.

This spring was cool and pure and seemed to issue from the mountain behind the house, and was conducted through it in pipes, and thence flowed into the stream in front.

At length some of the men came in and drank at the spring and washed and combed their hair. And some of them sat down, as if weary; and fell asleep, without having spoken.

All the while I saw no females, but sometimes heard a bustle in that part of the house, from which the spring came and whither the child had gone.

At length Rice himself came in with an ox whip in his hand, breathing hard, and going to a corner drank some kind of liquor.

He sat down not far from me and when I asked if he could give me a bed, he said there was one ready, but in such a tone as if I ought to have known it, and the less said about that the better.

I observed that it was a wild and rugged country which he inhabited and worth coming many miles to visit—"not so very rough neither," said he, and appealed to his men to bear witness to the breadth and smoothness of his fields, and the size of his crops, "And if we have some hills, there's no better pasturage any where."

I then asked if this place was not the one I heard of, calling it by the name I had seen on the map—or if it was a certain other, and he answered gruffly—that it was neither the one nor the other—that he had settled it—and cultivated it—and made it what it was—and I could know nothing about it—

To tell the truth I was very much pleased with my host's residence, and inclined even to exaggerate the grandeur of the scenery—and sought in many ways to make known my content.

Observing some guns and other implements of hunting on the wall, and his hounds now sleeping on the floor, I took occasion to change the discourse, and inquired if there was much game in that country—and he answered this question more graciously for he was evidently fond of the chace—but

when I asked if there were many bears, he answered
somewhat impatiently that he did not loose more sheep than
his neighbors—he had tamed and civilized that region.

After a pause, thinking of my journey on the morrow, and
the few hours of day-light in that hollow and mountainous
country, which would require me to be on my way betimes, I
remarked that the daylight must be shorter by an hour there
than in the neighboring plains, at which he gruffly asked what
I knew about it. And affirmed that he had as much day-light
as his neighbors—he ventured to say the days were longer
there than where I lived as I should find if I stayed—that some
how or rather as I could'nt understand the sun came over the
mountains a half an hour earlier and stayed half an hour later,
than elsewhere.

Without regarding his rudeness I said with a little less
familiarity that he was a fortunate man, and I trusted he was
grateful for so much light—and rising said I would take a
light, and I would pay him then for my lodging, for I expected
to commence my journey on the morrow, even as early as the
sun rose in his country, but he answered somewhat more
civilly as I thought that I should not fail to find some of his
household stirring however early, for they were no sluggards,
and I could take my breakfast with them before I started if I
chose, and as he lighted the lamp I could see a gleam of true
hospitality and ancient civility—a beam of pure and even
gentle humanity, from his bleared and moist eyes, for the
effect of the liquor had in some measure passed off—   And he
led the way to my apartment stepping over the limbs of his
men who were asleep on the floor, and showed me a clean and
comfortable bed. But I arose by star light the next morning as
usual, before my host or his men or even his dogs were awake,
and having left a ninepence on the counter, was already half
way over the mountain with the sun, before they had broken
their fast.

But before I had quite left the country of my host, while the
first rays of the sun slanted over the mountains, as I had

stopped by the wayside to gather some wild berries, a very old man came along with a milking pail in his hand, and turning aside also began to pluck the berries near me, but when I inquired the way he answered in a low rough voice without looking up, or seeming to take any notice of me.—which I imputed to his years—and presently mutturing to himself he proceeded to collect his cows in a neighboring pasture, and when he had again returned near to the wayside, he suddenly stopped while his cows went on before, and uncovering his head prayed aloud to God for his daily bread, and also that he who letteth his rain fall on the just and on the unjust, and without whom not a sparrow falleth to the ground—would not neglect the stranger—meaning me—

And when he had done praying I made bold to ask him—if he had any cheese in his hut which he would sell me, but he answered without looking up and as gruffly as before—that they did'nt make any—and went to milking.

"The stranger who turneth away from a house with disappointed hopes, leaveth there his own offences, and departeth, taking with him all the good actions of the owner."

The routine of these boatmen's lives suggests to me how indifferent all employments are and how any may be made infinitely noble and poetic to the eyes of men, if pursued with sufficient innocence and freedom. Given pleasant weather and scenery and the simplest occupation is alluring which detains us in the neighborhood.

For the most part they carry down wood and bring back stores for the country, piling the wood so as to leave a little shelter in one part, where they may sleep or retire from the rain if they choose.

I can hardly imagine a more healthy employment—or more favorable to contemplation or the observation of nature—for unlike the mariner they have the constant panorama of the shore to relieve the monotony of their labor. In no weather subject to great exposure, as the lumberers of Maine, and in summer inhaling the healthfullest breezes. But slightly encumbered with clothing—frequently with the head and feet bare—   And met at noon as they were leisurely descending the river—their busy commerce looked not like toil—but some ancient oriental game still played—like chess—handed down to this generation.

From morning till night the boatman—walks backwards and forwards on the side of his boat—now stooping with his shoulder to the pole—then drawing it back slowly to set it again.—   Meanwhile moving steadily and majestically forward through an endless valley, & an ever changing scenery—now distinguishing his course for a mile or two—and now shut in by a sudden turn of the river in a small woodland lake.

All the phenomena which surround him are simple and grand. There is something impressive and stately in the motion which he assists—which is communicated to his own character—and he feels the slow irresistible motion under him with pride as if it were his own energy.

It was pleasant to hail these sailors of the river and learn the news which circulates with them. Their breath is strong and windy, as if they fed on open air and their lungs were as familiar with the breeze, as the leaves that rustle on shore. Their privatest thoughts are broad and public as the Merrimack and the sun which shines on them

At intervals when there was a suitable reach in the river, we caught sight of the Goffstown mountain, the Indians Un-can-nu-nuc rising before us on the west of the river. And it was a pretty victory to conquer these distances and dimensions so easily with our eyes which it would take our feet so-long to traverse.

About noon we passed the village of Merrimack (where there is a ferry?) near to which some carpenters were at work mending a scow on the bank. The strokes of their mallets echoed from shore to shore and up and down the river, and their tools gleamed in the sun a quarter of a mile from us — And we realized that boat building was as ancient and

honorable an art as agriculture—and how there might be a
naval as well as a pastoral life—

The whole history of commerce was made plain in this scow
turned bottom upward on the shore. Thus did men begin to go
down upon the sea in ships. There was Iolchos and the
launching of the argo. We thought how noble it would be for
the traveller to build his boat on the banks of the stream
instead of finding a ferry or a bridge.

As we glided past at a distance these out-door workmen,
seemed to have added some dignity to their labor by its
publickness—it seemed a part of the industry of nature like
the work of hornets and mud wasps.

> The waves slowly beat
> Just to keep the noon sweet,
> And no sound is floated oer
> Save the mallet on shore,
> Which echoing on high
> Seems a caulking the sky.

Sometimes the routine which is manifest in the sunshine &
the finest days, as that which has conquered and prevailed,
commends itself to us by its very antiquity, and apparent
solidity and necessity. Our weakness needs it, and our strength
uses it. We cannot draw on our boots without bracing
ourselves against it. During the many hours we spend in this
waking sleep the hand stands still on the face of the clock, and
we grow like corn in the genial darkness of the night.

Men seem as busy as flowers or bees, and postpone every
thing to their business, as carpenters discuss politics between
the strokes of the hammer, while they are shingling a roof.

According to the Gazetteer
"The first house in this town was erected on the margin of
the river for a house of traffic with the Indians. For some time
one Cromwell carried on a lucrative trade with the Indians,

weighing their furs with his foot, till, enraged at his supposed or real deception, they formed the resolution to murder him. This intention

[One leaf missing]

We landed upon a large island near the mouth of this river to rest us during the heat of the day—with steep banks, and scattered oaks and pastured by a herd of cattle. There was a sufficient channel for canal boats on both sides—though at this time they chose the narrower.

When we made our fire on the banks of the Merrimack at noon to boil some rice for our dinner the fine grey smoke went silently up and sealed the treaty we had made with nature. The flames of our fire spreading amid the dry grass, and its smoke casting grotesque shadows on the ground, seemed a phenomenon of the yellow noon. And we sat like Indians on the banks bound upward through the summer. Our adventure seemed in harmony with the operations of nature, and we progressed up the stream without effort as naturally as the wind and tide went down, not outraging the calm days by unworthy bustle or impatience.

The woods upon the neighboring shore were alive with pigeons, which were now moving south looking for mast—like ourselves spending their noon in the shade. We could hear the slight wiry winnowing sound of their wings, as they changed their roosts from time to time and their gentle tremulous cooing. You will frequently discover a single pair sitting upon the lower branches of a white pine in the depths of the wood, at noon; so silent and solitary, and with such a hermit-like appearance, as if they had never strayed beyond its skirts— while the acorn which was gathered in the forests of Maine is still undigested in their crops.

We raised our sail for the first time this afternoon and for a short hour the south west wind was our efficient ally—   This the warmest of summer winds and is sometimes said to be accompanied with a serene sky—whence the tradition of the Indians that heaven is situated in the S.W.   but it did not please heaven to abet us with its wind very long. With one sail raised and a light wind we crept slowly up the side of the stream steering clear of the rocks—while from the top of a high hill which formed the opposite bank lumberers were rolling down timber—to be rafted down the stream. The logs came down with a dust and rumbling sound, which was reverberated through the woods beyond us on the other side of the river like the roar of artillery—   We could see their axes & levers gleaming in the sun—   But the Zephyr soon took us out of sight & hearing of this commerce & we soon had recourse to our oars again & we went on our way, driving the small sand-piper before us, passing another ferry and more falls—

This country was once famous for the manufacture of straw bonnets of the leghorn kind—and occasionally some industrious damsel tripped down to the water's edge to put her straw asoak—and stood awhile to watch the retreating voyageurs, and catch the fragment of a boat-song wafted over the water.

Occasionally we rowed near enough to a cottage to see the sun flowers before the door, and the seed vessels of the poppy like small goblets filled with the waters of Lethe, but without disturbing the sluggish household behind.

Toward the end of summer when the reign of sunshine is drawing to a close, and the earth has absorbed enough of golden rays, the flowers of the sun begin to bloom. On every hill side, and in every valley, stand countless asters, coriopses, tansies, golden-rods, and the whole race of yellow flowers, like Brahminical devotees, turning steadily with their luminary from morning till night. The Pythagoreans attached much importance to this "circular dance" of the sun flower imagining "that if any one could hear the pulsation made by its circuit in the air, he would perceive" a hymn to be composed "in honor of its king, such as a plant is capable of framing"   It is the floral solstice—a little after midsummer. As if the particles of golden light—the sun-dust, had fallen like seeds upon the earth and produced these blossoms.

As in the bones of man are found the various earths which entered into their composition, so, no doubt, some finer soils are found in which the most delicate flowers grow, and the oxids and other coloring matter which impart to them their hues. This is in harmony with the instinct which we call love of flowers, by which they answer a certain etherial utility to our higher nature. All nations make flowers express sentiments and finer qualities of the character.

The human eye is the first of flowers and one of fairest hue. Its perennial & unfading colors attest its superiority. It is in young and old the unwrinkled feature like the soul which abides behind it.

The hard avaricious man is not more conscious of the fair azure or hazel blossom which he bears, than of those which spot the fields. So is every flower in the field an eye—to those who are apt to detect character—with its seer perhaps not so near nor so directly behind it.

Late in the afternoon we reached some more falls in the town of Bedford, where were some masons employed in repairing the locks, in a wild and solitary part of the river, who expressed an interest in our adventures. Especially one young man of our own age, who had inquired if we were bound up to "Skieg," who when he had heard our story and examined our out-fit, still asked us other questions as it were reluctantly and always turning to his work again—as if it had become his duty. As he looked casually up the river many a distant forest and wooded shore seemed reflected in his eye   When we were ready he left his work and helpt us through the locks with quiet enthusiasm telling us we were at Coos falls—and we could still distinguish the strokes of his chisel for some sweeps after we had left him.

We wished to camp this night on a large flat rock in the middle of the stream just above these falls but the want of fuel and the difficulty of fixing our tent firmly—prevented.—   So we made our bed upon the main-land on the west bank in the town of Bedford.

Wednesday Sept. 4th

We made our way slowly up the river, through the fog—till at length the sun's rays began to struggle through the mist— and showed the pines dripping with dew.

The small green bittern—the genius of the shore—stood probing the mud for its food, a melancholy contemplative bird, with ever an eye upon us though so demurely at work, or was running along over the wet stones like a wrecker in his storm coat, looking out for wrecks of snails and cockles. Then away it goes with a limping flight uncertain where it will alight, until a rod of clear sand amid the alders invites its feet. But now our steady approach compels it to seek a new retreat. It is a bird of the oldest Thalesian school and no doubt believes in the priority of water to the other elements. When the world was made from water was he made—when the earth subsided from the waters was he left on the shore. A relic perhaps of some slimy antediluvian age, which yet inhabits these bright American rivers with us Yankees. He is of my kindred after all then—and I have a lingering respect for my unreclaimed brother. There is something venerable in this race of birds, which might have trodden the earth while yet in a slimy and imperfect state. What second advent does he look forward to— meanwhile bravely supporting his fate—without sympathy from proud man.

We passed in the late forenoon a large and densely wooded island, which would have been an addition to a nobleman's estate. We fancied we could see the deer glancing between the stems of the trees. It was a perfect San Salvador or Bahama isle; and if it had been at evening or nearer nightfall we should have occupied and taken possession of it in the name of our majesties; but we passed on, like Americus Vespucius, flattering ourselves that we should discover a mainland. We soon after saw the Piscataquoag emptying on our left, and heard the Falls of Amoskeag above.

It was here, according to tradition, that the sachem Wonolancet resided; and when at war with the Mohawks, his tribe are said to have concealed their provisions in the cavities of the rocks in the upper part of these Falls.

The future reader of history will associate this generation with the red man in his thoughts, and give it credit for some sympathy with his race. Our history will have some copper tints and reflections at least, and be read as through an Indian-summer haze. But such are not our associations. The Indian has vanished as completely as if trodden into the earth; absolutely forgotten but by a few persevering poets. The white man has commenced a new era. Instead of Philip and Logan, there are Webster and Crockett on the plains; instead of the Council House is the Legislature. What do our anniversaries commemorate but white men's exploits? For Indian deeds there must be an Indian memory; the white man will remember only his own. The foeman is dead or dying. We have forgotten their hostility as well as friendship. This oldest race, a venerable and hospitable nation, gave us liberty to settle and plow these fields. Who can realize that, within the memory of this generation, the remnant of an ancient and dusky race of warriors now, like Ossian's heroes, no more resident on this earth, furnished a company to the war, on condition only, as they wrote to the General Court, that they should not be expected to train or fight white man's fashion, but Indian fashion. And occasionally their wigwams are seen on the banks of this very stream, still solitary and withdrawn, like the cabins of the muskrats in the meadow.

They seem like a race who have exhausted the secrets of Nature; tanned with age, while this younger and still fair Saxon race, on whom the sun has not long shone, is but commencing its career. Their memory is in harmony with the russet hue of the fall of the year. And yet they did not always retreat before the ravages of time,—more than before the arrows of their foes. These relics in the fields, which have preserved their rugged forms so long, are evidence of the vital energy of the people that made them. Wherever I go, I am still on the track of the Indian. The light sandy soil which the first settlers cultivated were the Indian corn-fields, and with every fresh plowing the surface is strewn with their relics.

Arrow heads—spear heads—tomahawks, axes—chisels gouges—pestles—mortars—hoes—pipes of soapstone, ornaments for the neck & breast, and other curious implements of war and of the chace, attract the transient attention of the farmer. I have collected some hundreds myself. One is as surely guided to their localities, as to the berry fields in autumn. Unlike the modern farmer they selected the light and sandy plains and rising grounds near to ponds and streams, which the squaws could easily cultivate with their rude hoes.

And where these fields have been harrowed and rolled for grain in the fall, their surface yields its annual crop of arrow heads and other relics, as regularly as of grain. And the circles of burnt stones on which their fires were built are seen dispersed by the plow on every side.

These arrow heads are of every color and of various forms and material, though commonly made of a stone which has a conchoidal fracture. Many small ones of white quartz are found, which are mere equilateral triangles, with one side slightly convex. These were probably small shot for birds & squirrels. The chips which were broken off in making them are also found in large quantities, wherever a lodge has stood for a length of time. And these slivers are the surest indication of Indian ground, since the geologists tell us that the stone of which they are principally made does not occur in this manner—nor in many neighborhoods where they are found.

The spear heads are of the same form and material, only larger.

Some are found as perfect and sharp as ever, for time has not the effect of blunting them, but when they are broken they preserve a ragged and cutting edge still. Yet they are so brittle that they can hardly be carried in the pocket without being broken.

It is a matter of wonder how the Indians manufactured even

these rude implements without iron or steel tools. It is doubtful whether one of our mechanics, with all the aids of Yankee ingenuity, could soon learn to copy one of the thousands under his feet. It is well known that the art of making flint, with a cold chisel, as practised in the continent of Europe requires long practice and a knack in the operator, but the arrowhead is of much more irregular form, and like the flint such is the nature of the stone, must be struck out by a succession of skilful blows.

An Indian to whom I once exhibited some arrow heads, to whom they were the objects of as much curiosity as to myself, suggested that as many white men have but one blacksmith—so the Indians had but one arrow-head maker for many families. But there are marks of too many forges—unless they were like travelling cobblers, to admit of this supposition.

I have seen arrowheads from the South seas precisely similar to those found here

So necessary and so little whimsical the form of this little tool—   So has the steel hatchet its prototype in the stone one of the Indian, as the stone hatchet in the necessities of man.

Venerable are these ancient arts whose history is lost in that of the race itself.

Here too are the pestle and mortar—those ancient forms and symbols older than the plow or the spade.

The invention of the plow which now turns these up marks the era of their burial. An era which can never have its history—which is older, or more primitive, than history itself.

These are relics of an era older than modern civilization—compared with which Greece and Rome and Egypt—are modern. And still the savage retreats and the white man advances.

Some of these implements deserve notice for the constancy with which they occur and their uniformity wherever found —   They are part of the history of the Indian and identified with his race. These slowly wrought—durable and widely dispersed forms in stone mark some prevalent peculiarities and permanent customs

Many of them are symbols which cannot be interpreted at this day

A race has swept over this portion of the earth—and like drift has left these seams in the rocks—   The life of those men wore itself then into the stones

Spherical stones of various sizes with a groove run quite round them—whose use can only be conjectured.

A small pearshaped implement—of stone 2 or three inches long with a short neck is found every where whose use is unknown—

Sometimes the surface of a cornfield ploughed in an unusually dry and windy season has been blown away to the depth of several feet exposing the foundations of an Indian village the site of the several wigwams distinctly marked—and interspersed with relics of every description.

The bodies of warriors of other centuries are dug up in our gardens—with their soap stone pipes still unbroken—the arrow and spear head released from their shafts again lying loose in the dust by his side—the deer horns which were his trophy and his amulet—are the record in stone of the scalps he had taken.

I am interested by the sight of these arrowheads and spear heads without their shafts—still pointed and sharp—and undying as the Indian's revenge.

These rudest implements will still be respectable beside the latest improvements of art.

The Indians who hid their provisions in these holes, and affirmed "that God had cut them out for that purpose"—seem to have understood their philosophy better than the royal society—which has declared in their philosophical transactions formerly that "they seem plainly to be artificial."

I have seen many beautiful white basins of this kind formed in the limestone rock at Shelburne fall on Deerfield river— from 1 foot to 5 or six feet in diameter and as many in depth—

with smooth and delicately curved brims like goblets— The origin is apparent to the most careless observer. Some stone which the current has washed down—meeting with some obstacles in front revolves as on a pivot where it lies— gradually sinking in the course of ages deeper and deeper into the rock—and in new freshets receiving the assistance of fresh stones drawn into this trap and doomed to revolve for limitless periods—doing Sysiphus like pennance for stony sins until it wears through the bottom of its prison or is redeemed by some gradual or sudden revolution of nature There lay the stones of various sizes from a pebble to a foot in diameter and in one instance near the edge of the fall they had finally worn quite through the rock—so that a portion of the river leaked through and anticipated the fall.

But the most remarkable instance of this kind is the well known Basin on the head waters of this stream—by the roadside in the town of Lincoln—where a mere brook which may be passed at a stride falling upon a rock has worn a basin from 30 to 40 feet in diameter—and proportionally deep—and passes out probably after one revolution or more when it is swolen—by a deep channel scarcely more than a foot in width cut directly opposite to its entrance. It has a rounded brim of glassy smoothness and is filled with cold transparent greenish water.

These holes may be observed at the flume also on the head waters of this stream—at Bellows Falls—and more or less generally I presume about all falls.

The manchester manufacturing company have constructed a canal here about 1 mile long—through which we passed.

Above Amoskeag the river spreads out into a broad lake reaching a mile or two without a bend. There were many canal boats here bound up to Hooksett about 8 miles—and as they were going up empty with a fair wind one boatman offered to take us in tow—if we would wait for them. But when we came along side we found that they meant to take us on board, but as our boat was too heavy to be lifted, we pursued our way up the stream while the lumbermen were at their dinner and came to anchor at length under the alders on the opposite shore—where we could take our lunch. Though far to one side—every sound was wafted over from the opposite shore and we could see every thing that passed—

Presently came several canal boats at intervals of a quarter of a mile standing up to Hooksett with a light breeze, and one by one disappeared round a point above. Their broad sails set they moved slowly up the stream in the sluggish and fitful breeze—as if impelled by some mysterious counter current— like Antediluvian birds. A grand motion so slow and steady. It reminded us of the beauty of the expression—"standing out"— applied to a vessel—expressing its gradual and steady progress as it were by mere rectitude and disposition without shuffling. Their sails which stood so still in the air were like chips cast into the current of the air to show which way the current set.

At length came the boat we have mentioned, keeping the middle of the stream with a fair wind and when within speaking distance the steers man called out ironically if we would come along side now he would take us in tow. But not heeding their taunts we made no haste to give chase. But when the last had disappeared round the point with flapping sail—for the wind had sunk to a zephyr and they were anxiously measuring the volume of each puff of wind in suspense whether to resume their poles or not, putting up our two little sails—and plying our four oars, we shot swiftly up the stream after our friends, and one after another we overtook them vainly invoking Aeolus to their aid—and as we glided close under the side of our acquaintances whose sail was heard panting for a breath of air, we quietly promised if they would throw us a rope that we would take them in tow.

And then we gradually overhauled each boat in succession, until we had the river to ourselves again.

While we sail here we can remember without reserve & without interruption the friends who dwell far away on that tributary to this stream—who people the world for us.

Though we have floted down that river and reached through many rapids this different level—still a subtler tide rises in our breasts to our equal height—. Hearts put in circulation a finer blood than Lavoisier has discovered the laws of.

Like the stars our thoughts rise up in their horizon still.

We are sometimes made aware of a kindness which may have long since been shown, which reflects its light long after its heat, & realize that there have been times when our friends thoughts of us have been of such lofty humanity? that they passed over us like the winds of heaven unnoticed. They have loved us not for what we were—but for what we aspired to be. There has just reached us perchance the kindness of some acts—not to be forgotten—not to be remembered, and we shudder to think how it had fallen upon us cold, though in some true but tardy hour we wipe off these scores at midnight, in moments of insight and gratitude.

> My friends, my noble friends, know ye—
> That in my waking hours I think of ye
> Ever a godlike bond uncompromised & free

My friend is not of some other race or family of men, but flesh of my flesh bone of my bone. Have not the fates associated us in many ways. Water from the same fountain— lime from the same quarry—grain from the same field, compose our bodies. And our elements but reassert their ancient kindredship. Is it of no significance that we have so long partaken of the same loaf, breathed the same air, summer and winter, felt the same heat and cold, that the same fruits of summer have been pleased to refesh us both, and we have never had a thought of different fibre, the one from the other.

Friends are the ancient and honorable of the earth. The oldest men did not begin this league. It is older than Hindostan and the Chinese empire.— So long has it been cultivated. It is a natural and durable league. Warm serene days like this only bring it out to the surface. There is a friendliness between the sun and the earth in pleasant weather—& the grey content of the land is its color.

There is one principle at the bottom of all affinities. The magnet cultivates a steady friendship with the pole, and all bodies with all others. The friendliness of nature is some goddess Ceres perchance who presides over every sowing and harvest.—and we bless the same in sun and rain. The seed in the ground tarries for a season with its genial friends there— all the earth and minerals & gasses, are its hosts who entertain it hospitably—and plenteous crops are the result.

This principle is not only at the bottom of all romance and chivalry, but of all rural—pastoral—poetical life. Only lovers understand nature and use her aright   The moon shines for some Endymion—   Smooth pastures and mild airs are for some Coridon and Phyllis—   Plato's republic is the scene of Platonic love, and Paradise is the garden of Adam and Eve.

Consider how much the sun and the summer—the buds of spring, and the sered leaves of autumn—are related to the cabins of these settlers along the shore. How all the rays which paint this landscape radiate from them, & the flight of the crane, and the gyrations of the hawk have reference to their roofs.

And who dwell there but friends or lovers?

Yet without any outrage to the tenderest ties which exist, compared with his dreams, one is ever ready to say, that friendship is unrealized. It is slight and evanescent in every man's experience like the fluttering of a leaf over his head—& remembered like heat lightening in past summers.

But it is hard to know rocks, they are crude and inaccessible to our nature. We have not enough of the stoney element in us.

It is hard to know men by rumor only. But to stand near somewhat living and conscious—who would not sail through mutiny and storm to reach the fabulous retreating shores of some continent man.

There may be curtesy, there may be good-will, even temper—wit, and talent, and sparkling conversation, and yet the highest faculties pine for exercise. But ignorance & bungling with love are better than wisdom and skill without. Our life without love is like coke and ashes. Men may be pure as alabaster and Parian marble, elegant as a Tuscan villa, sublime as Terni, and yet if there is no milk mingled with the wine at their entertainments better is the hospitality of Goths and Vandals.— Comparatively speaking I care not for the man or his designs who would make the highest use of me short of an all-adventuring friendship.

Who does not walk upon the plain as amid the columns of Tadmore of the desert?

There is in the earth no institution which friendship has established. It has no temple—nor even a solitary column. It governs no where—it is worshipped no where—but is as a thing unheard of. It is not taught by any religion.

He seeking a friend walks on and on through the crowds of men as if in a straight line without stopping.

There goes a rumor that the earth is inhabited, but he has not seen a foot print on the shore. The hunter has found only fragments of pottery and mounds of inhabitants.

> I walk in nature still alone
>   And know no one.
> Discern no lineament nor feature
>   Of any creature.
>
> Though all the firmament
>   Is oer me bent,
> Yet still I miss the grace
> Of an intelligent and kindred face.

I still must seek the friend
Who does with nature blend,
Who is the person in her mask,
He is the man I ask.

Who is the expression of her meaning,
Who is the uprightness of her leaning,
Who is the grown child of her weaning

The centre of this world,
The face of nature,
The site of human life,
Some sure foundation
And nucleus of a nation—
At least a private station.

We twain would walk together
Through every weather,
And see this aged nature,
Go with a bending stature.

The Friend.
The great friend
Dwells at the land's end,
There lives he
Next to the sea.
Fleets come and go,
Carrying commerce to and fro,
But still sits he on the sand
And maketh firm that headland.
Mariners steer them by his light
Safely in the darkest night,
He holds no visible communion
For his friendship is a union.
Many men dwell far inland,
But he alone sits on the strand,
Whether he ponders men or books
Ever still he seaward looks,

Feels the sea-breeze on his cheek,
At each word the landsmen speak;
From some distant port he hears
Of the ventures of past years
In the sullen ocean's roar
Of wrecks upon a distant shore;
In every companions eye
A sailing vessel doth descry;
Marine news he ever reads
And the slightest glances heeds.

Near is India to him
Though his native shore is dim,
But the bark which long was due,
Never—never—heaves in view,
Which shall put an end to commerce
And bring back what it took from us,
(Which shall make Siberia free
Of the climes beyond the sea)
Fetch the Indies in its hold,
All their spices and their gold,
And men sail the sea no more
The sea itself become a shore,
To a broader deeper sea,
A profounder mystery.

None was ever party to a secure and settled friendship
— For it is no more a constant phenomenon—than meteors
and lightning. But a war of positions, of silent tactics.

The friend is some fair floating isle of palms, cheering the
mariner in the pacific sea near whose coast he in vain stands
off and on sounding for some safe entrance within its coral
reef.

The friend is forever uncertain of his friend— But I know
of no rule which holds so true as that we are always paid for
our suspicions by finding what we suspect. Our suspicions
exercise a demoniacal power over the subject of them, & by

some obscure law of influence when we are unconsciously the subject of another's suspicion, we feel a strong impulse, even though it is contrary to our nature, to do that which he expects but reprobates.

Some wilful behavior—even the best *behavior,* is ever the bane of this intercourse. But my friend is not chiefly wise or beautiful or noble at least it is not for me to know it. He has no visible form nor appreciable character. I can never praise him, nor esteem him praise worthy—   He needs no such rewards of merit from my judgment or good will. Let him not think he can please me by any behavior, or even treat me well enough. None remembers that his worth and influence is the result of his *entire* character, as well that which is superior, as that which is subject to his understanding—   And what he really means or intends, it is not in his power to explain or apologize for.

Must not our whole lives go unexplained without regard to us, notwithstanding a few flourishes of ours—which themselves need explanation.

A friend does not afford us cheap contrasts or encounters. He forbears to ask explanations but doubts and surmises with full faith, as we silently ponder our fates. For he is vested with full powers—plenipotentiary.

My friend can only be in any degree my foe, because he is fundamentally my friend—for every thing is after all more nearly what it should rightfully be, than that which it is simply by failing to be something else.

"Although friendship between good men be interrupted, still their principles remain unaltered. The stalk of the lotus may be broken, and the fibres remain connected."

Yet we wend not asunder—our courses do not diverge;—but as the web of destiny is woven it is fulled and we are cast more and more into the centre. Our fates at least are social.

All exhibition of emotion or affection seems premature—like the buds which push out and unfold themselves in warm days near the end of winter, before the frosts are gone.

But the thrifty native plants survive this disappointment & can afford thus to anticipate the summer. Nor is this any

infraction of the universal law, & the intercourse of friends is
regulated by the same constant and beneficent natural laws—
like the rest of the universe.

Yet friendship—if we consider what climates are necessary
to mature it, is essentially a fruit of the temperate zone
—   The balance of extremes   The subsidence of all emotions.

The friend is simply a *necessarius* such is the accuracy of
language—and will meet his friend on the homely ground of
necessity,—not on carpets and cushions—but on the ground
and rocks will they sit—obeying the simplest primitive laws.

All those abuses which are the subject of reform with the
philanthropist—the statesman & the housekeeper, are
unconsciously amended in this intercourse.

As with two eyes we see and with two ears we hear, with
the like advantage is man added to man—making no
complaint—offering no encouragement—one human being is
made aware of the neighboring and contemporaneous
existence of another. Such is the tenderness of friendship.
"Metals unite from fluxility; birds and beasts from motives of
convenience; fools from fear & stupidity; and just men at
sight."

There is a persevering and serene reserve in friendship
which implies such qualities as the warrior prizes. The simple
but determined friendship which Wawatam testified for Henry
the fur-trader—so almost bare and leafless, yet not blossomless
nor fruitless—the reader remembers with satisfaction and
security.

The stern imperturbable man comes to his lodge, and
affirms that he is the white brother whom he saw in his
dream, and adopts him henceforth. And they practise not
hostility but friendship thereafter as children of one father.
Having a welcome always ready for each other. Wawatam
buries the hatchet as it regards his friend, and they feast and
hunt together, no longer coveting each other's scalps.

My friend meets me face to face while others if not
indifferent only venture to meet me under the shield of

another's authority backed by an invisible corps du reserve of wise friends and relations or interpret me by hearsay—that is what others say—while I am myself talking or silent. To such I say fare well we cannot dwell alone in this world.

I would have such remember that it takes a valor to open the hearts of men—superior to that which opens the gates of cities. Only lovers know the value of magnanimity and truth.

If ever an idea of a friend is realized it will be in some broad and generous natural person—as frank as the day-light—in whose presence our behavior will be as simple and unconstrained as is the wanderer's amid the recesses of the hills.

And we shall meet while standing on the level of our actual lives, with our eyes raised and as it were by the coincidence

[One leaf missing]

the atmosphere like electricity. It is as far from pity as from contempt. I should hesitate even to call it the highest sympathy since the word is of suspicious origin, and implies more of suffering than of joy.

Kindness, which has so good a reputation elsewhere, can least of all consist with it, & no such affront can be offered as a conscious good will, a friendliness which is not a necessity of the friend's nature. That is infidelity and a rupture of the treaty. Its foundations must be surer than those of the globe itself—secure from whim or passion, and the laws of truth and magnanimity have their root and abiding place therein.

Without any slander we may call it an essentially Heathenish pastime—free and irresponsible in its nature, & practising all the virtues gratuitously.

It was established before religion—for men are not friends in religion, but over and through it—and it records no apostacy or repentance—but has a certain divine and innocent and perennial health about it.

In friendship we worship moral beauty without the formality of religion.

A certain disregard of the Christian duties and humanities
consists with its perfect integrity. For it is rather a society than
a sympathy—as it were a fragmentary and god like intercourse
of ancient date still kept up at intervals—which remembering
itself does not hesitate to neglect the humbler rights and
charities of humanity. Other religions teach tolerance and
loving-kindness but Friendship requires immaculate and godlike qualities—full grown, & exists at all only by
condescension and anticipation of the remotest future   Its
charity is generosity—its virtue nobleness, its bravery
trust   While other trades and indeed all professions have their
living by close calculation and exaction—this is maintained by
boundless trust. We come nearer to friendship with flowers
and inanimate objects than with merely affectionate and loving
men. It is not for the friend to be just even, but to be only a
larger and freer existence representative of humanity—its
general court—admirable to us as the heavenly bodies, but like
them affording rather a summer heat and day-light—the light
& fire of sunshine & stars—than the intense heats and
splendors which our weakness sometimes requires.

As for the numbers to be admitted to this league, it is at any
rate a society to be begun with one, the noblest and greatest of
mankind—and whether the world will ever carry it further
remains to be seen.
It remains to be proved whether

> "There be mo sterres in the skie than a pair"

In a promiscuous company we always address ourselves to
that person who can understand us best—and cannot get him
out of our minds, even when conversing with another—   So
our whole life is in some sense addressed to that one among
men whom we most esteem—and who is most able to interpret
it.

No doubt by a pleasing sad wisdom we shall find ourselves
carried beyond all counsel and sympathy, and our friends'

words will not reach us—but then we shall only forsake our
false friends to find our true friend.

This to my cis Alpine & cis Atlantic friends.

And also to those more distant & stranger nations with
whom I may have intercourse or commerce in times to come
as I have had in times past I would submit this word of
entreaty & advice especially to the large and powerful nation of
Acquaintances beyond the sea—Greeting.

If ye cannot be my most serene and irresponsible friends,
then I pray you let us find some other ground than
ceremony—even of broad humanity to stand on—and see that
we have the whole advantage of one another—we will be to
each other at least useful if not admirable.—   Strike boldly at
head or heart or any vital part—so you may possibly hit. And
hold on your own tack—as if your companion were so
insignificant that it did not signify, and so important that it did
not import.

Depend upon it the timber is well seasoned and tough, and
will bear rough usage, and if it should crack there is plenty
more where it came from. I am no piece of China ware that
cannot be jostled against my neighbor without danger of
rupture from the collision, and must needs sing a scrannel
strain to the end of my days when once I am cracked, but
rather one of the old fashioned wooden trenchers, which one
while stands at the head of the table, and another is a milking
stool, and another a seat for children, and finally goes down to
its grave not unadorned with honorable scars, and does not die
till it is worn out.

Use me, for I am useful in my way, and stand as one of
many petitioners from toadstool and henbane up to Dahlia and
violet supplicating to be put to my use, if by any means ye may
find me servicable; whether for a medicated drink or bath, as
balm & lavender, or for fragrance, as verbenum and geranium,
or for sight, as Cactus, or for thoughts as pansy.

Let me at least serve these humblest if not those highest uses.

Commonly we use life, which is only the sum of its nobler qualities, sparingly, we husband it as if it were scarce, and admit the right of prudence, but occasionally we see how ample and inexhaustible is the stock from which we so scantily draw, and learn that we need not be prudent.—that we may be prodigal, and all expenses will be met

Thus we saild between the territories of Manchester & Goffstown.

Thursday Sept. 5th

When we awoke this morning we heard the ominous still deliberate sound of rain drops on our cotton roof—

The rain had pattered all night, and now the whole country wept—the drops falling in the river, and on the alders—and in the pastures—but instead of any bow in the heavens—there was the trill of the tree sparrow—all the morning— The cheery faith of this little bird atoned for the silence of the whole woodland quire.

We learned afterwards that we had pitched our camp upon the very spot which a few summers before had been occupied by a roving party of Penobscots—as if we had at length been lead by our Indian instinct. We could see rising before us a dark conical eminence called Hooksett pinnacle a landmark to boatmen.

It was a cloudy drizzling day with occasional brightenings in the mist when the trill of the tree sparrow seemed to be ushering in sunny hours.

This was the utmost limit of our voyage—for a few hours more in the rain would have taken us to the last of the locks— and our boat was too heavy to be dragged around the long and numerous rapids that would occur.

On foot indeed we continued up along the banks—feeling our way with a stick through the showery and foggy day—and climbing over the slippery logs in our path—still with as much pleasure and boyancy as in brightest sunshine   Still pushing on whither our path lead through the genial drenching rain— & cheered by the tones of invisible waterfalls—scenting the fragrance of the pines and the wet clay under our feet—with visions of toad stools and wandering frogs—and festoons of moss hanging from the spruce trees—and thrushes flitting silent under the leaves— The road still holding together through that wettest weather like faith—and reaching to distant points—while the travellers confidently followed its lead.

And in fair days as well as foul we walked on up the country—until from Merrimack it became the Pemigewassett

that leaped by our side—and when we had passed its fountain-
head the wild Ammonusuck whose puny channel we crossed
at a stride guiding us to its distant source among the
mountains until without its guidance we reached the summit
of agiocochook.

But why should we take the reader who may have been
tenderly nurtured—through that rude country—where the
crags are steep and the inns none of the best, and many a
rude blast would have to be encountered on the mountain side.

Thursday sept. 12th

Finding our boat safe in its harbor under the Un-can-nu-nuc mountain—with a fair wind & the current in our favor we commenced our return voyage at noon, sitting at our ease and conversing, or in silence watching for the last sign of each reach in the river, as a bend concealed it from view. As the season was now further advanced the wind blew steadily from the north—and we were enabled to lie upon our oars without much loss which pleased us. The lumbermen throwing down wood from the top of the high bank 30 or 40 feet above the water, that it might be sent down the river—paused in their work to watch our retreating sail.—   And by this time indeed we had become known as a strange craft upon the river—and had acquired the nick-name of the Revenue Cutter.—

In many parts the Merrimack is as wild and natural as ever, and the shore and surrounding scenery exhibit only the revolutions of nature. The pine stands up erect on its brink, and the alders and willows fringe its edge, only the beaver and the red man have departed.

The sound of this timber rolled down the steep banks—or the vision of a distant scow just heaving in sight round a headland—enhances the majestic silence and vastness of nature. They are the primeval and natural echoes that are awakened.

Through the Din and desultoriness even of a Byzantium noon is seen the fresh and primitive and savage nature in which Scythians and Ethiopians dwell. What is echo—what are light & shade—day and night, ocean & stars, earthquake and eclipse there? The works of men—which we call art—are swallowed up in immensity.

The savage will find his Ontario is the AEgean sea

On the other hand there is all the refinement of civilized life—in the woods under a sylvan garb. The wildest scenes even have an air of domesticity and homeliness to the citizen, and when the flicker's cackle is heard in the clearings he is reminded that civilization has imported nothing into them.

Science is welcome to their deepest recesses for there too nature obeys the same old civil laws.

The little red bug on the stump of a pine—for him the wind shifts and the sun breaks through the clouds.

With this propitious breeze and the additional help of our oars we soon reached the falls of Amoskeag—and the mouth of the Piscataquoag   And recognized as we passed rapidly by many a fair bank and islet upon which our thoughts had rested in the upward passage.

Our boat was like that which Chaucer describes in his Dream in which the Knight took his departure from the island.

> To journey for his marriage,
> And return with such an host,
> That wedded might be least & most—
> . . . .
> Which barge was as a man's thought,
> After his pleasure to him brought,
> The queene her selfe accustomed aye
> In the same barge to play,
> It needed neither mast ne rother,
> I have not heard of such another,
> No maister for the governaunce,
> Hie sayled by thought and pleasaunce,
> Without labour east and west,
> All was one, calme or tempest,

So we sailed this afternoon.

"It is beautiful, therefore," said Pythagoras, "when prosperity is present with intellect, & when sailing as it were with a prosperous wind, actions are performed looking to virtue; just as a pilot looks to the motions of the stars."

All the world reposes in beauty to him who preserves equipoise in his life—and moves serenely on his path without resistance—as he who sails down a stream—he has only to steer—keeping his boat in the middle of the stream—and carry it around the portages—

Without any design or effort of ours the ripples curled away in the wake of our boat, like ringlets from the head of a child, while we went serenely on our way. And so always when we are performing our proper work well—the forms of beauty fall naturally around our path—like the curled shavings which drop from the plane or the borings from his auger, and our work makes no rubbish or dust.

How much gracefulness we learn from the ripples and curves of running water—and the form & motions of trees on the shore—grace truly is undulatory—and the sailor derives some suppleness from his element even through the planks of his ship.

Nature is a greater and more perfect art. When the overhanging pine drops into the water by the action of the sun—and the wind rubbing it against the shore, its boughs are worn white and smooth, and take fantastic forms as if turned by a lathe.

Nature has perfected herself by an eternity of practice. Consider the—evening stealing over the fields—the stars come to bathe in retired waters—the shadows of the trees creeping farther & farther into the meadows and a myriad phenomena beside

She supplies inexhaustible means to the most frugal methods. Having carefully determined the extent of her charity, she establishes it forever; her almsgiving is an annuity.—   She supplies to the bee only so much wax as is necessary for its cell, so that no poverty could stint it more, but the little economist which fed the Evangelist in the desert, still keeps in advance of the immigrant, and fills the cavities of the forest for his repast.

It is wholesome to contemplate the natural laws—gravity— heat—light—moisture—dryness. Though to the indifferent and casual observer they are mere science—to the enlightened and spiritual they are not only facts but actions—the purest morality—or modes of divine life—   And all nature invites to further acquaintance and abets the efforts of the honest inquirer—for by the visible form or shell truth is simply contained not withheld.—as one of the 3 circles on the cocoa nut is always so soft that it may be pierced with a thorn, and the traveller is grateful for the thick shell which held the liquor so faithfully. Science must have love & reverence & imagination from her pioneers and counsellors as well as sturdy & patient husbandmen to complete & fence and settle her clearings. Degerando said justly that "Plato gives science sublime counsels, directs her toward the regions of the ideal; Aristotle gives her positive & severe laws, and directs her toward a practical end." Only in this study let not the higher faculties interfere with the lower. Let the mind reside steadily in the labyrinth of the brain—let the affections not misplaced have their constant residence in the heart—and not interfere with the hands and feet—more than with birds and monkies and other parts of nature.

Facts must be learned directly and personally—   The collector of facts possesses a perfect physical organization —   Principles may be deduced from information—   The philosopher possesses a perfect intellectual one—   But in the poet they are so fairly—but mysteriously balanced—that however frail he may be—that he can use the results of both— and generalizes even the widest deductions of philosophy.— seed—stalk—flower—for as yet the fruit eludes our grasp—and whether he had best eat it or plant it is uncertain—   At any rate when it is mature it drops to the ground and if it is not disturbed springs again. Some dig up the root—some sever the stalk some pluck the flower—some gather the kernel, but all equally interrupt the order of nature. The wise incline always to make an innocent use of all—and to them all are but the phases of one flower.

We passed in broad daylight the scene of our nights encampments—and Coos falls   And at length pitched our tent on the west bank in the Northern part of Merrimack opposite to the large island on which we had spent a noon in our way up the river.

When we looked out from under our tent this evening the trees were seen dimly through the mist like spectres, and a cool dew hung upon the grass—which seemed to rejoice in the night.

In the damp air we seemed to inhale a solid fragrance.

Friday sept. 13th

As we lay awake long before day light listening to the sound
of the current and of the wind—we already suspected before
we had looked abroad by the fresh wind that was blowing, the
rustling of the leaves—and the rippling of the water, that there
was a change in the weather.

The wind in the woods sounded like an incessant waterfall,
dashing and roaring among rocks. One cannot but be
encouraged by this blithe activity in the elements in these
degenerate days. Who hears the rippling of rivers will not
utterly despair.

When at length we struck our tent and committed ourselves
to the current before sunrise—the face of nature seemed to
have undergone a change. We heard the sigh of the first
Autumnal wind, and even the water seemed to have got a
greyer hue— We soon passed the mouth of the Souhegan
and the village of Merrimack. And as the mist gradually rolled
away and we were relieved from the trouble of watching for
rocks—we saw by the flitting clouds—by the first russet tinge
on the hills—by the rushing river, and the lights in the
cottages on shore—and later in the day by the grape vine—the
goldfinch in the willow—the flickers flying in flocks and the
piping plover—and when we passed near enough to the shore
by the faces of men—that the fall had commenced. Cottages
looked more snug and comfortable.

"For summer being ended," said the pilgrims, "all things
stand in appearance with a weather beaten face, and the whole
country full of woods and thickets represented a wild and
savage hue."

> "And now the cold autumnal dews are seen
>   To cobweb ev'ry green;
> And by the low-shorn rowens doth appear
>   The fast declining year."

The woods & fields begin to assume the brighter tints of
autumn about the middle of september. The sumach—grape &

maple, are among the first to change. The milk-weed turns to
a very deep rich yellow.

The banks of retired roadsides are covered with asters,
hazles—brakes—and huckle berry bushes, emitting a dry ripe
scent.

Dense flocks of bobolinks russet and rustling as if they were
the seeds of the meadow grass floating on the wind, rise before
us in our walk—like ripe grain threshed out by the wind.
—   Each tuft gives up its bird.

The lark sings again down in the meadow—and the robin
peeps—and the blue birds old and young revisit their boxes
and hollow trees—as if they would fain repeat the summer,
without the intervention of winter, if nature would let them.

The purple finch or American linnet is seen early in october
moving south in straggling flocks—and alighting on the apple
trees—   Reminding one of the pine and spruce—Juniper and
Cedar—on whose berries it feeds. Its plumage has the crimson
hues of october evenings—as if it had caught and preserved
some of their beams. Many a serene evening lies snugly
packed under its wing—   We know it chiefly as a traveller.

By the beginning of October especially if the frosts have not
come on too gradually but are sudden & severe—the woods are
in the height of their beauty and the leaves fairly ripened for
the fall. They are not the dry and sere leaves of the poets—not
the tints of decay but of maturity—more lively than the
green   Not a withering but a ripening. A fresh and lively
gloss—with full veins   The maples stripped of their leaves
among the earliest, stand like a wreath of smoke along the
meadows.

As I pass along the streets of our village on the day of our
Annual Cattle show, when it usually happens that the leaves of
the elms & button-woods begin first to strew the ground under
the breath of the October wind, the lively spirit in their sap
seems to mount as high as any plough-boys let loose that day.
It leads my thought away to the rustling woods where they are
preparing for their winter campaign.

The low of the cattle in the street sounds like a low
symphony or running base to the hurry scurry of the leaves.
    The wind goes hurrying down the country, gleaning every
loose straw that is left in the fields—while every farmers lad
too seems to scud before it—having donned his best pea-jacket
and pepper and salt waistcoat—his as yet unbent trowsers—
outstanding rigging of duck or kersymere, or corduroy—and
his furry hat withal—to county fairs and Cattle-shows—to this
Rome amid the villages where the treasures of the year are
gathered.—   All the land over they go leaping the fences with
their tough idle palms which have not yet learned to hang by
their sides, amid the low of calves and the bleating of sheep.
— Amos—abner—Elnathan Elbridge.

"From steep pine bearing mountains to the plain."

I love these sons of earth—every mothers' son of them—with
their great hearty hearts rushing tumultuously in herds—from
spectacle to spectacle, as if fearful that there should not be
time between sun and sun to see them all.—   And the sun
does not wait more than in haying time.

"wise Nature's darlings, they live in the world
Perplexing not themselves how it is hurl'd."

    They may bring their fattest cattle and their fairest fruits—
but they are all eclipsed by the show of men.
    These are stirring autumn days when men sweep by in
crowds amid the rustle of leaves, like migrating finches
—   This is the true harvest of the year when the air is but the
breath of men—and the rustling of leaves is as the trampling
of the crowd.
    We read now adays of the ancient festivals games and
processions of the Greeks and Etruscans with a little
incredulity—or at least want of sympathy—but how childlike—
how natural and irrepressible must be in all people some
hearty palpable greeting of nature. The Corybantes the
Bachannals—the rude primitive tragedians with their
procession and goat song and the whole paraphernalia of the

Panathenaea—which seem so antiquated and peculiar are easily parralleled now. The husbandman is always a better Greek than the scholar is prepared to understand—and the old custom still survives while antiquarians & skolars grow grey in commemorating it

The farmers crowd to the fair today—in obedience to the same ancient law of the race—which Solon or Lycurgus did not enact—as naturally as bees swarm and follow their queen.— I love to see the herd of men feeding heartily on coarse succulent pleasures—as cattle feed on the husk and stalks of vegetables   Many of them it is true are crooked and crabbed specimens of humanity, run all to thorn and rind and crowded out of shape by adverse circumstances like the third chestnut in the bur—yet fear not that the race will fail or waver in them—like the crabs which grow in hedges they furnish the stocks of sweet and thrifty fruits still—   Thus is nature recruited from age to age while the fair and palatable varieties are dying out and have their period.

This is that mankind.

How cheap must be the material of which so many men are made—   And where is that quarry in the earth from which these thousands were dug up?

Running hither and thither with appetite for the coarse pastimes of the day—now with boisterous speed at the heels of the inspired negro—from whose larynx the melodies of all Congo and Guinea coast had brook loose into our streets.

— Now to see the procession of a hundred yoke of oxen all as august and grave as osiris—or the droves of neat cattle or milch cows as unspotted as Isis or Io. Such as had no love for nature before

"Went lovers home from this great festival."

I mark the summers swift decline
The spinning sward its grave clothes weaves
Where rustling woods the gales confine
The aged year turns on its couch of leaves.

Oh could I catch the sounds remote
Could I but tell to human ear—
The strains which on the breezes float
And sing the requiem of the dying year.

It proved a cool and breezy Autumn day, and by the time we
reached Nashua we were obliged to sit muffled in our cloaks,
while the wind and current carried us along—   The
inhabitants left their houses to gaze at us from the banks.

We glided past the mouth of the Nashua—and not long after
of Salmon brook without more pause than the wind—but not
without a passing regret—

The places where we had camped or spent the noon had
already a slight historical and familiar interest—
Many upward days were unravelled in this rapid downward
voyage.
So rapidly we sped along with sail and oar that when one
landed for a change he soon found himself falling behind his
companion by a mile or two—and was obliged to take
advantage of the curves and ford the brooks and ravines in
haste, to recover his ground.

In Autumn what may be termed the dry colors
preponderate—   In summer the moist. The asters and golden
rods are the livery which nature wears at present. The latter
alone seem to express all the ripeness of the autumn—and
shed their mellower lustre over the fields, as if the now
declining summers sun had bequeathed its hues to it. Asters
everywhere spot the fields like so many fallen stars.

There is a peculiar interest belonging to the latest flowers—
those which abide with us the approach of winter

There is something witch-like in the appearance of the
witch-hazle which blossoms late in October or in
November. Its irregular—angular stem, and petals like
Furies' hair, or small ribbon streamers. Its blossoming too at

this irregular period, when other shrubs have lost their leaves
even, looks a little like witches' craft. Surely it blooms in no
garden of man's   There is a whole fairy land on the hillside
where they grow.

Every little flower that grows by some remote dingle or pond
side, has virtues medicinal to heal our spirits which do not
have to be distilled from its roots, but by its simply growing
and blooming thus our lives are constantly related to the
healthy and true. No crede or theory can be true which will
not bear to be contrasted with these simple and cheerful
aspects of nature. No greatness can afford to bustle past the
humblest flower or blade under its feet. Even the tiny
blossoms of the cryptogamous plants bloom yet in silent
reproach to the imposing theories of the philosopher—which
have overlooked their existence
   I feel that I draw nearest to understanding the great secret
of my life in my closest intercourse with nature. There is a
reality and health in present nature, which cannot be
contemplated in antiquity—   I suppose that what in other
men is religion is in me love of nature.

We skimmed lightly over the water before a smacking
breeze, with all sails set—passing rapidly by Hudson
Dunstable & Tyngsboro. The wind in the horizon seemed to
roll in a flood over valley and plain, and every tree bent to the
blast—and the mountains like school boys turned their cheeks
to the blast.
   The flowing sail—the running stream—the waving tree—the
roving wind—are all great & current motions.
   We sailed along as gently and steadily as the clouds over our
head, watching the receding shores and the motions of our
sails   The north wind stepped readily into the harness we had
provided, and pulled us along with good will—   We were not
tired of watching the motions of our sail—so thin & yet so full
of life—so noiseless when it labored hardest, so noisy and
impatient when least effective. Now bending to some generous

impulse of the breeze, and then fluttering and flapping with a kind of human suspense. We watched the play of its pulse as if it were our own blood beating there.

It was the scale on which the varying temperature of distant atmospheres was graduated— And it was some attraction for us that the breeze it played with had been out of doors so long— Our lives are much like a sail, alternately steady and fluttering and always the sport of the breeze.

The air already showed a finer and sharper grain—seen against the russet pastures and meadows—than when we had ascended the river.— It was somewhat cleanzed of the summers impurities— And this subsidence goes on steadily until the winter solstice.

In october the air is really the fine element the poets describe.—wafting a dry and temperate odor from the fields. There is something in this refined and elastic air which reminds us of works of art—of a verse of Anacreon or a tragedy of Eschylus

The atmosphere is so dry and transparent and as it were inflammable—at that season, that the lights in the windows at evening have a starry and dazzling splendor as if fed by the atmosphere—and a candle set in the grass shines white and dazzling and purer and brighter—the farther off it is. The ancients were more than poetically true when they called fire Vulcan's flower. Its heat seems to have been extracted and only its harmless refulgent light left. It is a star dropt down—

The stars are now akin to the tapers of men.

It suggests the difference between the severe beauty of Greek art and the luxury of modern taste, as felt in the contrast between his expressions Το καλον—& *beau ideal*

The former is a chaste and reserved beauty—the ideal *beau ideal*—a pure core of light—and reminds us of the line

"Her beauty twinkleth like a star within the frosty night."

It leaves behind our grosser duller conceptions as the nucleus of a comet its lurid train. Φοιβος Απολλωγ, Ροδοδακτυλολgos εωs

The latter is low—lurid—and flitting—light like the will-o-the-wisp—a midsummer night lamp—a student's taper—a meadowy boggy light.

Light is somewhat almost moral— All plants and creatures turn toward it. The most intense—as the fixed stars and sun— have an unquestionable preeminence in the system. It guides to the first rudiments of life—for at a certain stage in the generation of all life—no doubt light like heat, is developed. Indeed is not heat an intense light

Among the quiet splendors of that season the Harvest and Hunters moons are not to be forgotten.

I never tire of the beauty of certain epithets which the ages have slowly bestowed as the Harvest and Hunters moon — There is something pleasing in the fact that the irregularity in the rising of these two moons, and their continuing to rise nearly at the same time for several nights should have been observed by the husbandman, before it attracted the attention of Science.

All great laws are really known to the simple necessities of men before they become the subject of science.

Thompson—who was a true lover of nature, in whom we look for such simple cheer as the almanack furnishes, who is so deservedly popular, and seems to have needed only a deeper human experience, to have taken a more vigorous and lofty flight—has well sung the glories of the Autumnal moon.

> her spotted disk,
> Where mountains rise, umbrageous vales descend,

> ———

> ———

> —gives us his blaze again,
> Void of its flame, and sheds a softer day.

Now through the passing cloud she seems to stoop,
Now up the pure cerulean sides sublime.

———

The whole air whitens with a boundless tide
Of silver radiance, travelling round the world.

What an impartial and instructed teacher is nature
— Spreading no crude opinions—flattering none. The moonlight so civil yet so savage—because equally above and
indifferent to all sublunary conditions.

The moon shines with a pale, historical light,—and hence is
best suited to ruins. In this light there are no fresh colors—but
only light & shade—and the new is confounded with the old.

It is therefore the best restorer of antiquity. Of a mild night
when the moon shines full—the houses in our village have a
classical elegance— And our half finished wooden church
has at such an hour reminded me of whatever is most famous
and excellent in art. So serene it stood like a living creature,
under the dews of night, intercepting the stars with its
rafters.— Whatever architect it may have had by day—it
acknowledged only Vitruvius at night— The architectural
beauty of its bare rafters—and its irregular staging built
around it—told of an old master It had an unintentional
flowing grace. The stageing which the workmen erect for their
convenience is for the most our only genuine native
architecture—and deserves to stand longer than the building it
surrounds.

When we reached the great bend just above Middlesex—
whence the river runs eastward 35 miles to the sea—we bade
adieu to the propitios wind—contriving how ever to make one
long judicious tack carry us nearly to the locks of the canal—

We were here locked through at noon—by our old friend the
'lover of the higher mathematics'—but we endeavored in vain
to persuade the wind to plow this long corridor of the canal—
and were obliged to revert to our old expedient of drawing by a
cord. And when at length we reached the Concord—we were
forced to row in good earnest with neither wind nor current in

our favor. But by this time the rawness of the day had
disappeared and we experienced the warmth of a summer
afternoon.

In summer I live out of doors and have only impulses and
feelings which are all for action, and must wait for the quiet
and stillness of and longer nights of autumn and winter, before
my thoughts will subside.

> On fields oer which the reaper's hand has passed,
> Lit by the autumn sun & harvest moon,
> My thoughts like stubble floating in the wind,
> And of such fineness as October airs,
> There after harvest could I glean my life,
> A richer harvest reaping without toil,
> And weaving gorgeous fancies at my will
> In subtler webs than finest summer haze.

There is a depth in Autumn which no poetry has fathomed.
Behind the rustling leaves, and the stacks of grain, and the
bare clusters of the grape—I am sensible of a wholly new life,
which no man has lived. My faith is fed by the yellow leaf.
Who can hear the wind in october rustling the wood without
believing that this earth was made for more mysterious and
nobler inhabitants that Fauns and Satyrs—Elves and Fairies.
In the fading hues of sunset we see the portal to the other
mansions of our father's house.

> I am the autumnal sun,
> With autumn gales my race is run.
> When will the hazel put forth its flowers,
> And the grape ripen under my bowers?
> When will the harvest and hunters moon
> Turn my mid night into mid-noon?
>   I am all sere and yellow
>   And to my core mellow.
> The mast is dropping within my woods
> The winter is lurking within my moods,

And the rustling of the withered leaf
Is the constant music of my grief,
   My gay colored grief,
   My autumnal relief.

The moon no longer reflects the day
But rises to her absolute rule,
And the husbandman and hunter
Acknowledge her for their mistress.
Asters and golden rods reign along the way
And the life-everlasting withers not.
The fields are reaped and shorne of their pride
But an inward verdure still crowns them.
The thistle scatters its down on the pool
And yellow leaves clothe the vine—
And nought disturbs the serious life of men.
But behind the sheaves and under the sod
There lurks a ripe fruit which the reapers have not gathered
The true harvest of the year,
Which it bears forever,
With fondness annually watering & maturing it.
And man never severs the stalk
Which bears this palatable fruit.

Men no where, east or west, live as yet a natural life, round
which the vine clings, and which the elm willingly shadows. A
life of equal simplicity and sincerity with nature, and in
harmony with her grandeur & beauty. The natural world has
no inhabitant. Man would desecrate the temple by his touch—
and so the beauty of the world remains veiled to him.

Who shall say what would be impossible to a natural man?

I love to hear some men speak though I hear not what they
say—men who are felt rather than understood—because they
are being most rapidly developed—they stand many deep.
They are great natures, and it takes a good deal to support
their life. Theirs is no thin diet. The very air they breathe

seems rich and perfumed, and the sound of their voices falls on the ear, as naturally as the rustling of leaves or the crackling of fire.

The distinctions of right and wrong—of sense and nonsense—seem petty—when such great and healthy indifference comes along. They have the heavens for their abettors, as if they had never stood from under them. They look at the stars with an answering ray. Their words are rich and voluminous for they proceed out of a deep though unconscious sympathy with the nature of things. They are earth-born—γηγενη—as was said of the giants & Titans of old time.

Their eyes are like glow-worms—   Their motions graceful and flowing as if a place were already found for them—like rivers flowing through vallies.

Those indicate slightly what might be the life of men on earth.

An immortal life should not be destitute of an immortal abode.

When we withdraw a little from the village and perceive how it is imbosomed in nature its roofs perchance gleaming in the setting sun, we wonder if the life of its inhabitants also might not be thus natural reflecting the sun of nature.

> All things are current found
>   On earthly ground,
> Spirits and elements
>   Have their descents.
>
> Night and day—year on year,
>   High & low—far and near,
> These are our own aspects,
>   These are our own regrets.
>
> Ye gods of the shore
> Who abide evermore,

I see your far headland
Stretching on either hand.

I hear the sweet evening sounds
From your undecaying grounds
Cheat me no more with time,
Take me to your clime.

Thus we go home to find some autumnal work to do—&
help in the revolution of the seasons. Perhaps nature may
condescend to make use of us, even without our knowledge, as
when we help to scatter her seeds in our walks, or carry burrs
and cockles on our clothes from field to field.

As it waxed late in the afternoon and we rowed leisurely up
the gentle stream shut in between fragrant and blooming
banks where we had passed our first night, and drew nearer to
the fields where our lives had passed, we seemed to detect the
hues of our native sky in the south west horizon. The sun was
just setting with warm purple colors behind the fringed edge
of a wooded hill.— So rich a sunset as would never have
ended but for some mysterious reason unknown to men, and
surely to be marked with brighter colors than ordinary in the
scroll of time   the evenings have no principle of decay in
them. Though the shadows of the hills were beginning to steal
over the stream, the whole river valley undulated with mild
light, purer—deeper and more memorable than the noon
— So does day bid farewell to solitary vales where no men reside.

Two blue herons with their long and slender limbs relieved
against the sky were seen travelling high over our heads
— The lofty and silent flight of these birds wending their way
at evening surely not to alight in any marsh on the earth's
surface, but perchance on the other side of our atmosphere,
was a symbol for the ages to study—whether impressed upon
the sky—or sculptured amid the hyeroglyphics of Egypt.
Bound to some northern meadow—they held on their stately
stationary flight like the storks in the picture, and disappeared

at length behind the clouds. It was like a vision of Styria or Cayster. And dense flocks of black birds were winging their way along the river course, as it were on a short evening pilgrimage to some shrine of theirs—or to celebrate so fair a sunset.—   And after the night had set in our boat awakened the clamors of some geese which had settled in this part of the river.

The sun setting presumes all men at leisure and in a contemplative mood.

But the farmers boy only whistles as he drives his cows home from pasture in the twilight—and the teamster refrains from cracking his whip so frequently—and guides his team with a lower voice—

The last vestige of day light at length disappeared—

"et invito processit Vesper Olympo"

As we rowed silently along with our backs toward home— through the darkness, only a few fine stars being visible—we had little to say but suffered any thoughts to be soothed by the monotonous sound of our oars.

"Pulsae referunt ad sidera valles"

And as we looked up in silence to those distant lights in the firmament—it seemed a fine imagination which first taught that the stars were worlds—and so conferred a great favor on mankind.

The celestial phenomena are a necessary link between the actual—and real—and answer to the ideal in man. The stars are distant and unobtrusive, but bright and enduring—like our fairest and most memorable experience.

As the truest society approaches always nearer to solitude— so the most excellent speech finally falls into Silence. We go about to find Solitude and Silence, as though they dwelt only

in distant glens and the depths of the wood, venturing out
from these fortresses at midnight—and do not dream that she
is then imported into them when we wend thither— As the
butcher busied himself with looking after his knife when he
had it in his mouth. For where man is there is silence. And it
takes a man to make any place silent.

It is the communing of a conscious soul with itself
— When we attend for a moment to our own infinity—
audible to all men—at all times—in all places— It is when
we hear inwardly—sound when he hear outwardly.

Creation has not displaced her but is her visible frame work
and foil— She is always at hand with her wisdom, by road
sides and street corners—lurking in belfries, the cannon's
mouth, and the wake of the earthquake, gathering up and
fondling their puny din in her ample bosom. Silence is ever
less strange and startling than noise, and is any where intense
and profound just in proportion as we find ourselves these.

All sounds are her servants and purveyers, proclaiming not
only that their mistress is, but is a rare mistress, and earnestly
to be sought after. The thunder is only the signal of her
coming.

All sound is nearly akin to silence—it is a bubble on her
surface which straightway bursts, an evidence of the strength
and prolificness of the under current. It is a faint utterance of
silence—and then only agreeable to our auditory senses when
it contrasts itself with and relieves the former. In proportion as
it does this, and is a heightener and intensifier of the Silence—
it is harmony and purest melody.

Accordingly every melodious sound is an ally of silence—a
help and not a hindrance to abstraction.

Silence is the universal refuge. The sequel to all dull
discourses, and all foolish acts—as balm to our every chagrin—
as welcome after satiety as disappointment. That background
which the painter may not daub, be he master or bungler, and

which, however awkward a figure he may have made in the foreground, remains ever our inviolable asylum.

Where no indignity can assail no personality—disturb us.

The orator puts off his individuality and is then most eloquent, when most silent. He listens while he speaks and is a hearer along with his audience.

Who has not hearkened to her infinite din? She is Truth's speaking trumpet— She is the sole oracle, the true Delphi and Dodena, which kings and courtiers would do well to consult, nor will they be balked by an ambiguous answer. Through her all revelations have been made— Just in proportion as men have consulted her oracle they have obtained a clear insight, and their age been marked as an enlightened one. But as often as they have gone gadding abroad to a strange Delphi and her mad priestess, their age has been Dark or Leaden. These have been garrulous and noisy eras which no longer yield any sound, but the Grecian or silent & melodius era, is ever sounding and resounding in the ears of men.

A good book is the plectrum with which our silent lyres are struck. We not unfrequently refer the interest which belongs to our own unwritten sequel to the written and comparatively lifeless body of the work. Of all books this sequel is the most indispensable part. It should be the authors aim to say once and emphatically "he said" 'εφη' ε This is the most the book maker can attain to   If he make his volume a foil whereon the waves of silence may break it is well.

It were vain for me to interpret the silence—she cannot be done into English. For six thousand years have men translated her with what fidelity belonged to each, and still is she little better than a sealed book. A man may run on confidently for a time—thinking he has her under his thumb, and shall one day exhaust her—but he too must at last be silent, and men remark only how brave a beginning he made. For when he at length dives into her—so vast is the disproportion of the told to the untold, that the former will seem but the bubble on the surface where he disappeared.

Never the less will we go on, like those Chinese Cliff swallows, feathering our nests with the froth, which may one day be bread of life to such as dwell by the sea shore.

And now our boat was already grating against the bullrushes of its native port—and its keel again recognized the Concord mud where the flattened weeds still preserved some semblance of its own outline having scarce yet recovered themselves since its departure. And we leaped gladly on shore—drawing it up and fastening it to the little apple tree whose stem still bore the mark which its chain had worn—in the chafing of the spring freshets.

Textual Notes

Appendix

Index

Textual Notes

The following notes record all emendations (marked by an asterisk), all marginal notes and significant ink marks not reproduced in the text, all ink revisions, relevant pencil revisions, and significant physical peculiarities of the manuscript, including missing leaves, torn or fragmentary leaves, and leaves Thoreau incorporated or later inserted in the draft.

The format of the notes is intended to allow the reader to reconstruct Thoreau's manuscript revisions. Where he altered a single word by adding a letter or letters, for example changing "occasional" to "occasionally" (23.18), by canceling a letter or letters, for example changing "differently" to "different" (23.33), or by writing over a letter or letters, for example changing "saw" to "see" (15.34), I use the rubric "altered from," giving both the original and the revised manuscript reading. Otherwise I describe his process of revision in exact detail, reporting all cancellations, interlineations, and other additions, and the location of carets and other signs indicating the insertion and/or the transposition of material. Where I report that Thoreau indicated transposition by drawing vertical lines in the left margin and numbering portions of the text, I mean that he drew a single vertical line in the left margin beside each of two passages in the manuscript and then numbered each passage to the left of the vertical line. I do not specify whether the two passages are written on the same page, on the recto and verso of the same leaf, or on different leaves unless one of the two passages was a later addition. When Thoreau revised a passage after interlining or otherwise adding it to the draft, his revisions are recorded in notes following the note to the passage as a whole. When Thoreau revised a passage before canceling it, his revisions are indicated in the notes by angle brackets enclosing any words he had previously canceled and by up-and-down arrows enclosing any words he had previously interlined. For example:

25.35   ingenious] followed by canceled '— <and>
               ↑ but ↓ disingennuous'

indicates that Thoreau first wrote "—and disingennuous," then canceled "and" interlining "but," and finally canceled the whole phrase.

For clarity and convenience, I have used certain reference marks and abbreviations in the notes. As in the example above, single quotation marks set off manuscript readings from editorial comments. Square brackets enclosing a portion of a word indicate a conjectural editorial expansion of an abbreviation or of a word Thoreau canceled before completing. A virgule (/) indicates the end of a line and a reference mark (¶) indicates the end of a paragraph in the manuscript (MS). I refer to chapters in the draft by their titles in the published version, i.e., "Saturday" rather than "Sat Aug 31st 1839." All other abbreviations are identified in the list of Abbreviations.

As indicated, all notes are keyed to page and line numbers in the text. In counting lines, I have included blank spaces, represented by an additional line space in the text (see above, Note on the Text).

1.1–2	Were . . . plough.] added at the top of the page in smaller script
1.1	Heaven] altered from 'heaven'
1.7	river] followed by canceled 'on which it is situated'
1.9	'ground' "] followed by canceled 'and hence justly applied to the country through which it flows, and afterward to the stream itself'
1.10	though] preceded by canceled 'did'
1.12	meadows] interlined with a caret before canceled 'and open uplands'
1.18	Westborough,"] quotation mark added in pencil

1.28	"At] quotation mark added in pencil
2.1–19	The current . . . varieties] This is written on the recto of a leaf HDT inserted into the manuscript, noting 'v[ide] s[heet *or* scrap]' below paragraph 1.37–38
2.2	by it] interlined with a caret
2.2	of the town] preceded by canceled 'of C[oncord?]'
2.3	by the wind] interlined with a caret
2.4	meadows,] followed by canceled 'bet[ween?]'
*2.4	part, . . . oaks] MS: 'interspersed with oaks' interlined with a caret after 'part'
2.4–5	the cranberry] preceded by canceled 'the'. Above, HDT interlined 'Pc[?]', but his intention is unclear.
*2.6	bed,] MS: 'bed'. See following note
2.6–8	a fruit . . . acres] interlined with a caret after 'bed'
*2.7	being] MS: 'is being'
2.9	present] followed by canceled 'to <his> a friend'
2.9–10	is said . . . friend] interlined with a caret between canceled 'was' and canceled 'thankfully received'
2.11	A row] preceded by canceled 'Farther on nearer to the'
2.13	trees] interlined above canceled 'plants'
2.14	bearing . . . season] interlined with a caret
2.18	huckle-berry] preceded by canceled 'former'
2.18	alone] interlined with a caret
*2.18–19	blue—white] MS: 'blue / white'
2.21	volume] interlined above canceled 'phenomenon'
2.23	levels] As an alternate reading HDT interlined 'places', later canceling 'levels' in pencil.
2.25	they not] interlined with a caret
2.31	annual] interlined with a caret

2.34   Rivers] preceded by canceled 'By a natural
            impulse the dwellers'
3.2   the ground] interlined with a caret
3.5   the most populous] preceded by canceled
            'through'
3.9–23   Many . . . escort.] Drawing vertical lines in
            the left margin, HDT numbered this section
            '1' and the poem at 3.25–28 "2", indicating
            transposition.
3.22   put] As an alternate reading HDT interlined
            'trust', later canceling 'put' in pencil.
3.25–28   I . . . dream.] See note to 3.9–23.
3.25   River] altered from 'river'
3.26   My] altered from 'Thy'
5.18   farewell] 'fare- / well'
6.1–3   The tortoises . . . trees.] Drawing vertical lines
            in the left margin, HDT numbered this
            paragraph '1' and paragraph 6.4–9 '2',
            indicating transposition.
6.4–9   The . . . well.] See note above.
6.7   this circumstance] preceded by canceled
            'even'
6.16   in the midst] preceded by canceled 'especially'
6.16   dense fields] followed by canceled 'and
            masses'
6.20   arrow-head] 'arrow- / head' followed by a
            canceled comma
6.21   shallow parts] followed by canceled 'of the
            river'
6.24–27   The snake-Head . . . array.] Drawing vertical
            lines in the left margin, HDT numbered this
            paragraph '1' and paragraph 6.29–34 '2',
            indicating transposition.
6.26   red flower] preceded by canceled 'rank'
6.29–34   The bright . . . Traces.] See note to 6.24–27.
6.29   (purple?)] interlined with a caret
6.32   and . . . bank] interlined with a caret

6.34	Traces] interlined above canceled 'Tresses'
6.37	and . . . lodged] interlined with a caret
6.38	from . . . prime.] HDT first wrote 'where the tansy was in its prime.', later interlining 'from' above canceled 'where', 'ranks of' with a caret before 'tansy', and 'now' above canceled 'was'.
7.1–3	Indeed . . . water—] See note to 7.4–16.
*7.1	Indeed nature] MS: 'Indeed' added in the left margin before 'Nature'
7.4–16	But . . . Lord.] HDT added this paragraph, which he partially circled and numbered '2', beginning it at the bottom of the page and completing it at the top of the following page above paragraph 7.1–3, which he numbered '1', indicating transposition.
7.7–8	so long—] preceded by canceled 'till its season is passed'
7.17–18	floating . . . meadows] interlined above canceled 'gliding out of sight of the village spire'
*7.20	And we] MS: 'And' added in the left margin before 'We'
7.22	flower] preceded by canceled 'plan[t?]'
7.23	but] written over 'and'
7.28	blossom] interlined above canceled 'flower'
7.31	not indeed] preceded by canceled 'where we found'
7.32	voyage] interlined above canceled 'adventure'
7.32	gather] interlined above canceled 'pick'
8.3	new scenes and adventures] preceded by canceled 'the' and followed by canceled 'which awaited us'
8.7	we had] followed by canceled 'already formed'
8.13	bordered] followed by canceled 'on each side'
8.13	beyond which are] interlined with a caret before canceled 'and'
8.14	pads] followed by canceled 'and'

8.17	its . . . on] interlined with a caret
8.37	finds] preceded by canceled 'can'
9.1	employment] interlined above canceled 'occupation' preceded by canceled 'employ[ment?] pursuit'
9.5	these august days] interlined with a caret
9.9	highest noon] interlined above canceled 'the first phospher dawn'
9.11	under . . . sun] interlined above canceled 'at high noon'
9.12	scenting] As an alternate reading HDT interlined 'amid'.
9.14	land] altered from 'lands'
9.19	Honor] altered from 'honor'
9.27	of all] followed by canceled 'our fishes'
*9.31	green—red] MS: 'green / red'
9.33	such] preceded by canceled 'the'
*10.10	element,] MS: 'element.' followed by canceled 'It'
10.14	In] preceded by canceled 'It is'
10.18	probably prey] preceded by canceled 'prey'
10.20–21	without nibbling] interlined with a caret
10.21	sculling] preceded by canceled 'sailing'
10.36–37	with . . . book] interlined with a caret
10.37	bites] altered from 'bitten' preceded by canceled 'had'
11.11	suspicious guiltiness] preceded by canceled 'a'
11.14	water] followed by a caret without a corresponding interlineation
11.23	lurking] preceded by canceled 'loving'
11.28	exceedingly ravenous] preceded by canceled 'an'
11.34–35	The . . . large.] added in the space between paragraphs
12.8	an hour] preceded by canceled 'hours'
12.14	bait] followed by canceled 'by chance'

12.15–16	Though . . . spring.] interlined below canceled 'and so are they hooked'
12.31–32	—as large as] preceded by canceled 'composed of stones as large as a hen's egg'
12.33–34	of . . . larger] interlined with a caret
13.28	'good loaf sugar' or 'good brown'] quotation marks added in pencil
13.30	June] preceded by canceled 'Apri[l]'
13.30	promptly] interlined with a caret
*13.31	full . . . date.] MS: 'at the last date' added in the right margin and between lines following 'full.'
15.6	instinct] interlined above canceled 'faith'
15.32	breeze rising] 'rising' interlined above 'breezing' altered to 'breeze'
15.32–33	but . . . grows] interlined with a caret
15.33	For] added on line before canceled 'And'
15.33	having] interlined below canceled 'we had'. See following note.
*15.34	we] MS: 'We' preceded by canceled 'and were gliding <through> ↑ into ↓ the meadows of Billerica.'
15.34	see] altered from 'saw'
15.35	cut] interlined above canceled 'mowed'
16.8	At length] preceded by canceled 'It seemed insensibly to grow lighter as the night shut in, and the farthest hamlet began to be revealed, which before lurked in the shadows of the noon.' See 16.15–18.
16.18	noon.] At the end of this paragraph, HDT later noted 'v[ide] s[heet or scrap]' in a sideways caret, but the manuscript contains no corresponding leaf, nor is there any indication that a leaf is missing, so it was probably not included in the original stitched gathering.
16.25	hill-side] 'hill- / side'

17.6	throttled] interlined with a caret
17.18	with so much interest] As an alternate reading HDT interlined 'so favorably', later canceling 'with so much interest' in pencil.
17.21	roof] preceded by canceled 'lowest'
17.21	mastiff] preceded by canceled 'terrier'
17.22	wow—wow—ow—w—w–w] interlined with a caret
17.24–25	more impressive] preceded by canceled 'sweet and'
17.26	line] followed on line by canceled 'I ha[d?]'
18.5	and the] preceded by canceled 'the'
18.9–12	remembered . . . sprite.] To avoid using an additional leaf, HDT wrote this in the left margin.
18.11	sleeps] interlined above canceled 'wakes'
19.11	birth] followed by canceled 'hast trod'
19.25	the various] interlined with a caret after canceled 'two'
19.26	we] preceded by canceled 'which'
19.26	gave] interlined above canceled 'named'
19.26	them names as the] 'names as the' interlined with a caret after 'the' altered to 'them'
19.27	or] written above canceled '<and afterwards> & more which we named'
19.27	the sisters—] followed by canceled 'there being still no farm house in sight to disturb the wildness of the scenery'
19.27	one fine] interlined above canceled 'ere long another'
19.28	surrounded] preceded by canceled 'a perfect jun[gle?]'
19.29	overrun] 'over- / run'
19.29–30	which . . . it] interlined with a caret before canceled 'which'
19.31	Grape] altered from 'grape'
19.31–32	It . . . America] added on line at the end of the paragraph

19.33	We . . . Fox island] added in the space between paragraphs
19.35	still] interlined with a caret
19.36	more] interlined with a caret
19.38	there] written over 'were'
19.38	is] written over 'are'
19.38–39	house . . . field] interlined above and below canceled 'traces of a village'
20.1–15	It was . . . but] This is written on the recto of a leaf HDT inserted into the manuscript, noting 'v[ide] scrap' in a sideways caret in the right margin beside canceled 'It <proved a fine and as it were a natural sunday> ↑ was in nature too a sunday ↓ —' at 20.15 (see notes).
20.2	with the grape] preceded by canceled 'gr[ape?]' and followed by canceled 'vine'
20.4	king-fisher] 'king- / fisher'
*20.6	above,] MS: 'above.' See following note.
20.6–8	and . . . bosom.] interlined with a caret after 'above.'
20.8–10	The heavens . . . herself.] HDT added this sentence at the bottom of the page, but he then circled it and drew a line to a caret after 'bosom.' at 20.8.
20.10	The dead limbs] In the left margin HDT wrote but later canceled, 'The robins were continually crossing and recrossing the river higher in the air in company with the blackbirds', adding but then canceling a caret after 'robin' at 20.5, and then adding a sideways caret in the left margin beside 'The' to indicate its position. See paragraph 22.17–22 and note to 20.15.
*20.13	supporter,] MS: 'supporter.,'
20.14	balls] preceded by canceled 'now brownish'
20.15	There . . . but] This is written above and below canceled 'As it wax[ed?]', a phrase used in paragraph 22.17–22, where HDT may have

	initially planned to use the material on the inserted leaf. See notes to 20.1–15 and 20.10.
*20.15	the air]. MS: 'The air'. See note to 20.1–15.
*20.17	world, &] MS: 'world.' followed by '&' interlined above canceled 'It'
20.19–24	In . . . villas.] Drawing vertical lines in the left margin, HDT numbered this paragraph '1' and paragraphs 20.26–21.11 '2', indicating transposition.
20.26–21.11	It was . . . itself.] See note above.
20.33	that they seem] interlined above canceled 'and'
20.35	the Parthenon] 'the' added on line in pencil
21.2	whether . . . painted] interlined with a caret
21.2	painted] preceded by canceled 'merely'
21.3	and] interlined above canceled 'that'
21.3	duly] preceded by canceled 'have been'
*21.3	observed,] MS: 'observed.'
*21.4	reality,] MS: 'reality.'
21.18–22.20	river . . . later] HDT later removed this leaf from the stitched gathering, shifting it to "Wednesday," where he evidently decided to use the passage on character. See note to 71.20–22.
21.18	once] preceded by canceled 'thus'
21.23	thoughts.] followed by canceled 'But she sails here no more.'
21.28–29	It . . . with.] interlined with a caret
21.28	&] interlined in pencil to clarify the reading
21.31–33	Methinks . . . cloud] added in the left margin with a sideways caret
21.38	orbit] interlined above canceled 'path'
22.7	unfolding] followed by canceled 'itself'
22.11	star-lit clime] interlined above canceled 'trackless night'
22.17	For amusement] preceded by canceled 'As it waxed later in the day the cattle stood'
22.19	especially over] preceded by canceled 'in the'

22.31	to avoid difficulty] interlined with a caret
22.38–23.5	The clear . . . prey.] added at the bottom of the page below paragraph 22.34–37
23.7	without a ripple] interlined with a caret
23.11	interrogating] preceded by canceled 'even interrupting'
*23.12	But as] MS: 'But' added on line before 'As'
23.17	When] preceded by canceled 'As we drew nearer to the'
23.18	occasionally a] HDT first wrote 'an occasional', later canceling 'an' and adding 'a' on the line after 'occasional' altered to 'occasionally'.
23.19	whether] preceded by canceled 'the vil[lage?]'
23.25	In such a scenery] preceded by canceled '↑ The inhabitants are clearly cultivators of the earth and live under an organized political government. ↓ But in civilization as in a southern latitude the race of man degenerates at length, and yields to the incursions of Northern barbarians— / "Some nation yet shut in / With hills of ice.' " See 24.32–36.
23.33	different] altered from 'differently'
23.37	it is] preceded by canceled 'that'
24.13	breaks] followed by canceled 'and tames'
24.15	as his gods] preceded by canceled 'with'
*25.2	poetry we have read.] MS: 'poetry. (we have read)'. HDT later canceled '(we have read)' in pencil.
25.8	strong temptations] preceded by canceled 'a'
*25.14	healthy,] MS: 'healthy.,'
25.35–27.30	These modern . . . brothers.] This section is written on two leaves, pages 131–34, HDT excised from the Long Book (J 2:74–75) and incorporated in the manuscript, noting 'These modern &c v[ide] s[heets?]' in the space following 25.32–33. The section begins on the verso of the first leaf, which remains in the

manuscript, and continues on the recto and verso of the second leaf, which HDT later transferred to the *Walden* manuscript (HM 924, Before A).

25.35	ingenious] followed by canceled '—<and> ↑ but ↓ disingennuous'
25.35	sciences and arts] HDT first wrote 'arts and sciences', but he later underlined 'arts' and 'sciences', numbering them '2' and '1', indicating transposition.
25.36	do those] preceded by canceled 'th[ose?]'
25.37	husbandry] HDT interlined but later canceled 'of war & peace & the like' with a caret after 'husbandry'.
26.4	According to Gower] interlined above the quotation
26.7	toke.] period preceded by canceled comma
26.29–32	The gifts . . . discovery] interlined with a caret before canceled 'The potatoe seems to have been one of these gifts which fell into a crevice when first bestowed.'
26.31	ancient] preceded by canceled 'men have long known'
26.32–37	"The boat . . . Providence."] HDT added the quotation at the bottom of the verso of the leaf, noting 'v[ide] n[ext] p[age]' following 'discovery' at 26.32 on the recto and 'v[ide] n[ext] p[age] veeshnoo Sarma' above the quotation on the verso.
27.2–3	a great deal] preceded by canceled 'It was'
27.4	conveniences.] preceded by canceled 'advantages.'
27.13	invented] preceded by canceled 'first'
27.14	portable cave] followed by canceled 'and lo! the plains and valleys too were populated'
*27.17	languages.] MS: 'languages,.'
27.18	And] followed by canceled 'lo! the'
27.21	thereby] interlined with a caret

27.37	we arrived] 'we' preceded by canceled 'here' and followed by 'arrived' interlined above canceled 'are'
27.37	falls] interlined with a caret
28.13	fed] preceded by canceled 'supplied'
28.24	pass] altered in pencil from 'pas'
28.28–29.6	The people . . . state.] This is written on the recto of a leaf HDT inserted into the manuscript without indicating the intended position of the paragraphs, which, however, is clear from the context. See also *W* 63.
28.29–32	They . . . N.H.] HDT added 'They . . . parts,' in the space following 'under.' at 28.29, drawing a line to the bottom of the page, where he added 'according to the historian of N.H.' See note to 28.33–35.
28.30	as formerly] interlined with a caret
28.33–35	"In . . . that] HDT added this at the bottom of the page, noting '&c v[ide] above' to indicate that it should replace canceled 'It is still true what the old historian of <the state> ↑ N.H. ↓ said' and uncanceled 'that' at the beginning of the paragraph. See note to 28.29–32.
*28.35	that] MS: 'that that'. See note above.
29.2	but were naturally] interlined above canceled 'and consequently were'
29.3	among the rest] interlined above canceled 'to any great extent'
29.4	it is said] interlined with a caret
29.4	a weak] preceded by canceled 'but they are'
29.6	the state.] HDT placed a parenthesis before this and interlined 'place of the former' as an alternate reading.
29.12–14	so . . . understood—] HDT interlined 'v[ide] n[ext] p[age]' with a caret after 'locks—' at 29.12, indicating that this passage, added between paragraphs on the verso of the leaf,

	where it is enclosed by large parentheses and followed by the note 'v[ide] e[arlier]. p[age]', was to be inserted here.
29.12	so] written over 'a'
29.12	&] added on line
29.13	in . . . nature] This originally followed 'understood—' at the end of the added passage (see note to 29.12–14), but HDT later circled it and drew a line to canceled 'man' following 'liberal' at 29.13 to indicate its position.
29.14	noise] interlined above canceled 'din'
29.15	&] added on line
29.16	conjectures] interlined above canceled 'opinions'
29.17	of ———] as in MS
29.18	prescribed] added on line in smaller script
29.25	humanity] preceded by canceled 'little trait of'
29.25	we had experienced] interlined with a caret
29.37	&] preceded by canceled 'a[nd?]'
30.5	Squire] altered from 'squire'
*30.6	to bear] MS: 'bear'
30.9	quarter] preceded by canceled 'part'
30.22	on shore] 'on' preceded by canceled 'by' and followed by canceled 'the'
30.29	should] preceded by canceled 'could'
*31.3	its] MS: 'it'
31.4–5	should . . . boundary] preceded by canceled '<should have a> ↑ is ↓ properly bounded'
31.7	by the] preceded by canceled 'of the'
31.8	Notch] altered from 'notch'
31.11	east 35] preceded by canceled '35'
31.11	Rising] preceded by canceled 'In its swift descent to the sea it has numerous falls and rapids'
31.13	form] interlined above canceled 'spread itself out into'
31.14	broad] followed by canceled 'mea[dows?]'

31.14	hurried] preceded by canceled 'rather rushing through ↑ the ↓ numerous'
31.17	high] interlined above 'interval'
31.17–18	formerly . . . hills] interlined with a caret
31.19–21	The Nashua . . . river—] interlined above 'valuable to the farmers.' at 31.19
31.19–20	taken advantage] preceded by canceled 'found'
31.22–23	The Pemigewasset . . . freshet] added in the space between paragraphs
31.22	has been known to] interlined above canceled 'sometimes'
31.22	rise] altered from 'rises'
31.24–25	A small . . . completed.] added in the left margin with a sideways caret before 'It is navigable' at 31.25–26
31.24	steam boat] preceded by canceled 'river s[teamer?]'
31.24–25	between Lowell & Nashua] interlined with a caret
31.28	For . . . Plymouth.] interlined above 'mouth.' at 31.28
31.29	almost] interlined with a caret
31.31	abundant] preceded by canceled 'at present'
31.31–32	though at one time] preceded by canceled 'are <at present> ↑ still ↓ rare.'
31.35	one] preceded by canceled 'which is'
32.5–7	A rather . . . stream.] HDT added this in the space between paragraphs. See note to 32.7–12.
32.6	Bellow's falls] Below this HDT interlined 'Walpole', a town in New Hampshire close to Bellows Falls, but his intention is unclear.
32.7–12	"On . . . seen.] HDT added these sentences in the left margin without indicating their intended position. See W 88–89.
32.11	made . . . stones] interlined below 'remains'
32.16	some] interlined with a caret

*32.20   which . . . hemispheres,] HDT added this, with a period rather than a comma, at the end of the sentence, later circling it in pencil and adding a penciled caret before 'growing' at 32.21.

32.25   Navigator.] altered from 'navigator.' followed by a canceled caret

32.26–29   Beaver river . . . NE.] HDT added this in the space above the paragraph, but he circled it and drew a line to a caret after 'poetry.' at 32.26. 'Beaver river' is preceded by canceled 'As', an indication that he had originally begun the paragraph there but had then decided to leave a blank space.

32.28–29   according . . . authority] interlined with a caret

32.33–34   and sometimes beneath?] interlined with a caret

32.35   stones,] MS: 'stones.' See following note.

32.35–36   which . . . conclude] interlined with a caret after 'stones.'

33.1–3   —"jam . . . poma"] written in the left margin

33.3   poma"] preceded by canceled 'jacent pomae'

33.5   languages] altered from 'language' in pencil and preceded by canceled 'na[tions?]'

*33.5   recognition of] MS: 'recognition'

33.5   still] HDT placed this in parentheses and later canceled it in pencil.

33.6   Such] preceded by canceled 'These are'

33.15   as . . . country] interlined with a caret

33.17   such] followed by canceled 'su[ch?]'

33.20   more.] preceded by canceled 'new.'

33.28   civilized life] preceded by canceled 'life'

33.35   now] interlined with a caret

33.36   before] preceded by canceled 'now'

*33.38   it is,] MS: 'it is.' followed by canceled 'They'

34.12   stout] interlined above canceled 'servicable'

34.30	finest] As an alternate reading HDT interlined 'faintest'.
34.36	near] preceded by canceled 'we'
34.38	or] interlined with a caret
34.38	stream] preceded by canceled 'rill'
34.38–35.1	the site] preceded by canceled 'perchance'
35.9–10	the unsympathizing . . . direction] interlined with a caret
35.21	by the boisterous] Above this HDT interlined but then canceled 'by camped'.
35.24	done,] followed by canceled 'till late in the night,'
35.27	with . . . hist–st] interlined with a caret
35.30	buffaloes] preceded by canceled 'Blank[ets?]'
35.30	which . . . Indians] interlined with a caret
35.32	skin] followed by canceled 'of'
*35.34	Having] MS: 'having' preceded by canceled 'Usually'
35.34	a] interlined above canceled 'some'
35.37	a buffaloe] 'a' interlined above canceled 'our' followed by 'buffaloes' altered to 'buffaloe'
35.37	had] interlined above canceled 'drew'
35.38	for his] HDT first wrote 'over him for', later interlining 'for' above canceled 'over', altering 'him' to 'his', and canceling 'for'.
36.1	from the boat] interlined with a caret
*36.2	just over the] interlined above canceled 'a few feet from the ground—and' followed by uncanceled 'a'
36.3–7	so . . . voyage,] To avoid using an additional leaf, HDT wrote this in the left margin. See note to 36.7–8.
36.3	near] interlined with a caret
*36.7	voyage,] MS: 'voyage.' See following note.
36.7–8	or . . . us.] added in the right margin. See note to 36.3–7.
*37.15	1725.] MS: '1725,'

37.25	materials] preceded by canceled 'in[cidents?]'
*37.25	shaggy] MS: 'shagy' altered from 'shady'
*37.27	returned] MS: 'return returned' preceded by canceled 'of the'
37.27	the fruits] 'the' altered from 'their'
*38.3	path,] MS: 'path.'
38.3–4	in disgraceful] preceded by canceled 'in perhaps'
38.6	valor] followed by canceled 'or worth'
38.12–17	2 . . . wounds] added in the space between the quotation and the following paragraph
*38.15	in a pond] MS: 'in pond'
38.19	were advancing] interlined above canceled 'rowed steadily on'
38.19–20	into the country and into the day] HDT first wrote 'into the day and into the country', later drawing lines indicating transposition.
38.20	which last] interlined above canceled 'and occ-[asionally?] / the day'
38.21	bustle] interlined above canceled 'stir'
38.21	monday] preceded by canceled 'natural'
38.22	of nature] interlined with a caret
38.22–26	Now . . . of.] added in the left margin with a sideways caret and a line to another caret before 'Occasionally' at 38.27
38.27	a change] interlined above canceled 'variety'
38.29	the other followed] 'the other' interlined with a caret before 'following' altered to 'followed'
38.29–30	from time to time] interlined with a caret
38.30	scaring up . . . summer duck—] Above this HDT interlined 'navigator?', but his intention is unclear.
38.30	king-fisher] 'king- / fisher'
38.31	hear] altered from 'hearing'
39.1	inhabitants of the] interlined with a caret
39.3	experience] HDT later altered this to 'experienced' in pencil. But see W 123.

39.7   beast] Below this HDT interlined 'horse' as an
                alternate reading.
39.7   large] interlined below canceled 'white'
39.8–10   And . . . more] HDT first wrote, 'And we
                found ourselves in the current of commerce
                once more, and then another and another
                glided into sight', but he later underlined the
                two clauses, numbering them '2' and '1',
                indicating transposition.
39.12   At length we] interlined above canceled
                'When we'
39.12   junks] preceded by canceled 'prows'
39.13–14   In . . . we] interlined above canceled 'We
                would occasionally'
39.14   rested] altered from 'rest'
39.15   drew] altered from 'draw'
*39.18   us,] MS: 'us.' See following note.
39.18–20   while . . . still.] interlined with a caret after
                'us.'
39.20   All . . . thought.] added at the end of the
                paragraph
39.21–24   It . . . measure.] HDT drew a vertical line in
                the left margin from this paragraph to
                paragraph 39.33–34, numbering them '2';
                however, since he also drew vertical lines in
                the left margin beside paragraphs 39.25–32
                and 39.35–40.5, both of which he numbered
                '1', his intention is unclear, so his original
                order has been retained.
39.23   in] added on line after canceled 'by'
39.23   longer] interlined above canceled 'infinite'
39.24   we] interlined above canceled 'man'
39.25–32   The hardest . . . year.] See note to 39.21–24.
39.33–34   But . . . stream.] See note to 39.21–24.
*39.34   ocean,] MS: 'ocean.'
39.35–40.5   There . . . thought.] See note to 39.21–24.

39.35	practical desires] As an alternate reading HDT interlined 'stated toil', later canceling 'practical desires' in pencil.
39.36	be becalmed] As an alternate reading HDT interlined 'cease'.
*39.37	Laborers] MS: 'laborers' preceded by canceled 'All crafts[men?]'
39.37	sailor] followed by canceled 'especially'
*40.1	So] MS: 'so' preceded by canceled 'And'
40.1	have] written over 'ceased'
40.2	and float] 'and' preceded by canceled 'and leave off' and followed by canceled 'flo[at] submit to'
40.3	and . . . shore] HDT placed this in parentheses and later canceled it in pencil.
40.4	varying] preceded by canceled 'ever'
40.4	wind and current] HDT placed 'wind' and 'current' in parentheses and interlined 'air' and 'water' as alternate readings, later canceling 'wind' and 'current' in pencil.
40.11	But] As an alternate reading HDT interlined 'And'.
40.12	Thebes . . . today.] Below this, in the space between paragraphs, HDT noted 'V[ide] S[heet *or* scrap]', which he later altered to 'v[ide] Veeshnoo' in pencil. The manuscript contains no corresponding leaf, but see *W* 124.
40.16	the past—] followed by canceled 'not an unquestionable witness—'
40.20	more] altered from 'most'
40.20	importance . . . rest] interlined above canceled 'to the parties'
40.20–21	is it] added in the left margin
40.21	the gods] interlined above canceled 'heaven'
*40.21	faintest] MS: 'fantest'
40.22	articles] As an alternate reading HDT

interlined 'clauses', later canceling 'articles' in
pencil.

40.22   ever] interlined with a caret

40.25   to] interlined above canceled 'before you can'

40.26   the Delphic priestess did] preceded by
           canceled 'did'

40.30   under these willows] interlined above
           canceled 'here'

40.36   betel] preceded by canceled 'the'

*41.1   tree,] MS: 'tree.'

41.1   tops] followed by canceled 'and'

41.27   saxon-wise] interlined with a caret

41.37   sea-bord] 'sea- / bord'

42.1–2   or . . . forever] interlined with a caret

42.4   and . . . mankind] HDT interlined 'ready to
           mix with mankind' with a caret, later adding
           'and were' in pencil to clarify the reading.

42.8   under] preceded by canceled 'in a'

42.13–43.5 We will not . . . as] This is written on the
           recto and verso of the first of two leaves HDT
           extracted from an unpublished 1842 essay on
           Hindu scripture and incorporated in the
           manuscript. He tore the second leaf in half:
           the top half, which contains the conclusion of
           paragraph 42.29–43.13 (recto) and the
           conclusion of paragraph 46.3–17 (verso),
           follows the first leaf from the essay; the
           bottom half, which contains the opening of
           paragraph 46.3–17 (recto) and the whole of
           paragraph 46.18–29 (verso), was placed at the
           end of the chapter, where HDT marked those
           paragraphs for insertion (see note to 46.3–29).
           Notes to the text of these two leaves
           distinguish between original pen revisions
           (ca. 1842) and pen revisions for A Week.

42.13   We will not inquire] preceded by the canceled
           paragraph 'Again, for there is an orientalism

in the most restless pioneer, and the farthest
west is the farthest east. Through Pawnee
and Blackfoot you come to Japannese and
Hindoo again.' (original revision)

*42.24   contains.] MS: 'contains,' followed by
canceled 'or Sir William Jones has unlocked.'
(original revision)

43.13   remoter . . . also.] When HDT tore this leaf in
half, he interlined 'moter star we call that
new also.' above the line ending 're-' to
conclude the penultimate sentence of the
paragraph on the top half of the recto. He
later canceled the final sentence of the
paragraph, 'These old truths are new as
Uranus or the Asteroids.', on the bottom half
of the recto, in pencil. See note to 42.13–43.5.

43.15–18   Suddenly . . . hear.] HDT interlined this
sentence twice, first between lines 46.3–5
(see note), and later at the top of the page
above paragraph 43.19–27.

43.18   muskrats] preceded by canceled 'ret[ired?]'

43.22   last—] followed by canceled 'which overhangs
the water,'

43.29   In] preceded in the space between paragraphs
by canceled 'In'

43.30–31   and rushes] 'and' interlined with a caret

43.38   in] interlined above canceled 'in her'

44.1   her territories] interlined above canceled
'nature'

44.2   It] preceded by canceled 'which'

44.3   garment] preceded by canceled 'clothing'

44.4   and] altered from 'an' in pencil

44.7   the universe] preceded by canceled
'u[niverse?]'

44.9   as it were] 'as' altered from 'a' in pencil

44.9   in the bare] preceded by canceled 'the bare'

44.10–11   which . . . pulp] interlined with a caret

44.12   soil] preceded by canceled 'vegetable'

44.14	of Tasso's] preceded by canceled 'of the'
44.19–20	and . . . fields—] In the left margin HDT added two question marks, later canceling the passage in pencil.
*44.21	to be] MS: 'to to be'
44.26	ages] interlined above canceled 'thousand'
44.35	far enough] preceded by canceled 'under its Dock'
44.36	a haymaker] preceded by canceled 'the'
44.37	eel] altered from 'eels'
44.38	forms] preceded by canceled 'which'
45.1	and we] 'and' interlined above canceled 'which'
45.2	this before] interlined above canceled 'before'
45.3	his fishy lore] HDT placed this in parentheses and interlined 'he knew' as an alternate reading, later canceling 'his fishy lore' in pencil.
45.4	our eyes . . . contentedly and] interlined with a caret
45.10–22	Salmon Brook . . . endure?] In the manuscript the two stanzas are written side by side. See also note to 93.12.
45.10	Brook] altered from 'brook'
45.20	fly] followed by canceled comma
45.24	village of] interlined with a caret
45.24	Nashua] followed by canceled 'one of the larger tributaries, and the village of the same name'
45.24–25	the river . . . name] interlined above canceled 'its banks'
45.26–30	While one . . . argo.] Drawing vertical lines in the left margin, HDT numbered this sentence '1' and the sentence at 45.30–34 '2', indicating transposition.
45.26	his companion] preceded by canceled 'the'
45.27	above] interlined with a caret
*45.28	sheep, the] MS: 'sheep the'

45.30–34   The nashua . . . it.] See note to 45.26–30.
45.30–31   one . . . tributaries] interlined with a caret
45.34   it.] HDT interlined '&' to connect this
        sentence with 45.26–30, which follows in the
        manuscript, but he later numbered the
        sentences, indicating transposition (see note
        to 45.26–30). At the end of the paragraph, he
        later noted in a different ink 'v[ide] s[heet *or*
        scrap]', possibly a reference to the earliest
        surviving version of the passage beginning,
        "As late as 1724 there was no house on the
        north side of the Nashua" (*W* 166 ff.), drafted
        on a leaf of the same paper used for most of
        the first draft. The leaf, now in HM 13195
        ("Monday," 3), has no pinholes in the margin,
        so it was not part of the pinned gathering of
        the chapter, but it appears to have been
        folded along the margin, so HDT possibly
        inserted it later.
45.36   for our] preceded by canceled 'to pr[epare?]'
46.1   the muskrats] preceded by canceled 'only'
46.3–29   Here . . . by.] These two paragraphs begin on
        the recto and conclude on the verso of the
        bottom half of the leaf HDT inserted in the
        manuscript, noting 'V[ide] Menu V[ide]'
        following 'stream.' at 46.1. He probably
        decided to shift these paragraphs to the end
        of the chapter because each contains a
        reference to "evening" (see 46.8 and 46.19),
        while the initial part of the digression takes
        place at "noon" (see 42.7). See note to 42.29–
        43.13.
46.3–5   Here . . . south west.] Above this sentence
        HDT interlined, 'Suddenly a boatman's horn
        was heard echoing from shore to shore to give
        notice of his approach to the farmer's wife
        with whom he was to take his dinner—
        though in that retired place only the muskrat

and kingfisher seemed to hear.' Probably after he tore the leaf in half, he later interlined the sentence with two minor variants at 43.15–18. See note above and note to 42.29–43.13.

46.14   So] preceded by canceled 'So'

46.17   blows.] followed by canceled 'Silenter and silenter grows the memory as the wanderer looks back.'

46.18   mind gazing] HDT interlined 'mind' in ink and later wrote 'gazing' in the left margin in pencil, probably to replace words obscured or lost when he tore the leaf in half. See note to 42.29–43.13.

46.31–32   on the west bank] preceded by canceled 'under'

46.34   protecting arms] 'arms' interlined above 'protectingly' altered to 'protecting'

47.8   yellow] HDT placed this in parentheses and later canceled it in pencil.

47.10   & everlasting] HDT placed this in parentheses and later canceled it in pencil.

*47.11   nature, & our] MS: '&' added in the left margin between 'nature. / Our'

47.15   &] interlined with a caret

47.19   Compton] HDT's spelling here and in the Long Book, but emended to "Campton," a town in northern New Hampshire, in the *Journal* (see *J*:2 TN 13.13).

47.20   line] followed by computations unrelated to the text

47.27   there.] followed by computations unrelated to the text

47.33–35   When . . . hour.] Drawing vertical lines in the left margin, HDT later numbered this paragraph '2', revising it in order to combine it with paragraph 47.37–48.2, which he twice numbered '1', possibly to indicate transposition within the paragraph. But his intentions are unclear, so the original order and wording of the paragraphs have been retained.

47.33   When . . . if] With the exception of the word 'as', HDT canceled the whole of this passage in pen as part of the revision described in the note above.

47.38–48.2   Occasionally . . . know.] See note to 47.33–35.

47.37   sound] As an alternate reading, HDT interlined 'music', later revising it to read 'sound from a distant sphere' in pencil.

*47.38   sense, far] MS: 'sense. / far'

*48.1   the] MS: '(the'. See note to 47.33–35.

48.2   larger] preceded by canceled 'wider'

48.8   fluent & flexible] interlined with a caret

48.15–23   There . . . usual.] HDT originally wrote this passage on the recto of the final leaf in "Monday," beginning "Tuesday" on the verso. But he later recopied the passage on another leaf, probably to separate the manuscripts of the two chapters. Three minor variants are recorded in the following notes.

48.17   corn-fields] HDT originally wrote 'corn fields'. See note above.

48.20   security,] HDT originally wrote 'security—'. See note to 45.15–23.

48.21   rippled,] HDT originally wrote 'rippled'. See note to 45.15–23.

49.5   heat] preceded by canceled 'mid[day?]'

49.14–18   Dr Belknap . . . night."] HDT added this between lines and in the left margin with a caret after 'mountains' at 49.22. He then canceled the caret, drawing a line from 'Dr' to an inverted caret after 'it.' at 49.14.

49.18   night."] MS: 'night.'

49.28   was spread] preceded by canceled 'spread'

49.28–29   for a hundred miles] preceded by canceled 'as f[ar?]'

49.30	country] preceded by canceled 'vap[or?]'
49.33	gleaming] preceded by canceled 'and sha[dy?]'
50.1–2	had . . . also] interlined with a caret before canceled 'had risen to my level'
50.3–4	it was inserted in] interlined above canceled 'according to'
50.27–51.5	The same . . . the] This is written on the recto of a leaf HDT inserted into the manuscript, noting 's[heet *or* scrap]' within a sideways caret in the space following the poem at 50.26.
51.4–5	Our tent . . . the] HDT cut off the bottom third of the leaf. Probably to fill the gap, he later interlined 'Such was the heaviness of the dew that we were obliged to leave our tent spread over the boat till the sun had dried it to avoid mildew' in pencil. See W 192.
51.5	spread] As an alternate reading, HDT interlined 'left'.
51.10	distinguish] preceded by canceled 'see'
51.14–15	The trees . . . banks.] In the space above this sentence, HDT added 'The sun's rays struggled through the mist and showed the pines dripping with dew.', probably as an alternate reading. But he did not cancel the original reading or a related observation at 51.24–25 until he revised the passage in pencil. See also 64.3–5 and note to 64.3–26.
51.15	banks.] altered from 'bank.'
51.24–25	Streaks . . . river—] See note to 55.14–15.
51.24	fog] interlined above canceled 'mist'
51.26–27	The river . . . pleasing] added above the paragraph
52.14	soon] interlined with a caret
52.15	change] followed by canceled 'to'
52.20	were] preceded by canceled 'could'
*52.21	floated] MS: 'foated'

52.22–24	Any . . . stream.] interlined with a caret
52.29	reached] interlined above canceled 'passed'
52.30	passing] interlined above canceled 'coming'
52.36	wrinkles] interlined above canceled 'countenance'
53.2	manner] interlined above canceled 'manner'
53.4–57.21	There . . . owner."] This section is written on five leaves, pages 165–74, HDT excised from the Long Book (*J* 2:95–101) and incorporated in the manuscript. The recto of the first leaf (page 165) contains an earlier version of paragraphs 52.29–53.2 as well as an unrelated entry. The verso of the last leaf (page 174) also contains an unrelated entry.
53.6	any . . . all.] HDT first wrote 'any core—or sap wood.', later interlining 'or' above canceled 'any', 'any' above canceled 'or', and 'at all' above the dash between the phrases, which he underlined and numbered '2' and '1', indicating transposition.
*53.8	strangers, whose] MS: 'strangers.' followed by 'whose' interlined above canceled 'Their'
53.10	who] interlined above canceled 'they'
53.11	accustomed] As an alternate reading HDT interlined 'wont'.
53.12	sun light] preceded by canceled 'of'
53.14	down] interlined above canceled 'out'
53.18	in] interlined above canceled 'through'
53.20	when I reached] interlined above canceled 'through'
53.21	with] interlined above canceled 'where dwelt'
53.22	who . . . that] interlined with a caret before canceled 'while'
53.23–25	dwelt . . . themselves] interlined with a caret
53.23	less] preceded by canceled 'different &'
53.24	polished] interlined above canceled 'cultivated'
53.24	of settlers] interlined with a caret

53.24–25	who . . . themselves] As an alternate reading HDT interlined 'with whom they had little &c'.
53.25	directly] interlined with a caret
53.26	they could] HDT first interlined 'the traveller could' above canceled 'I', later altering 'the' to 'they' and canceling 'traveller'.
53.26	hear] altered from 'heard'
53.29	my kind hosts] preceded by canceled 'I took leave of' and followed by canceled '—who'
53.29	the nearest] preceded by canceled 'one Rice the' interlined above canceled 'the'
53.30	these] altered from 'this'
53.30	settlers . . . Rice] interlined above canceled 'race—whom we will call Satyrus'
53.32–33	"What . . . kindly?"] added in the space between paragraphs
53.35	valley] altered from 'vale'
53.36	his] interlined above canceled 'the'
*53.36	dwelling.] MS: 'dwelling' followed by uncanceled 'of' and canceled '<Satyrus my host.> this man'
53.37	to his abode] HDT placed this in parentheses, an indication that he considered omitting it.
53.37	rude] interlined above canceled 'savage'
53.38	anticipated] interlined above canceled 'feared'
53.38	many cattle] interlined above canceled 'herds'
53.39	had] interlined with a caret
54.1	more than all] interlined with a caret
*54.10–11	There . . . before] MS: 'Before' preceded by 'There was no sign post' interlined with a caret
54.11	it] interlined above canceled 'the front was'
54.11	nor any] 'any' interlined with a caret after 'no' altered to 'nor'
54.13	owner's] As alternate readings HDT interlined 'Masters' and 'Landlord's'.

54.17	about it] interlined with a caret
54.18	map] interlined above canceled 'chart'
*54.20	length] MS: 'lenght'
54.21–22	the master of the house] HDT placed this in parentheses and interlined 'Rice', which he then canceled, and 'landlord' as an alternate reading. He later canceled 'the master of the house' in pencil.
54.30	find no] interlined with a caret before canceled 'neither'
54.37	and] interlined above canceled 'then'
54.37	leaving] interlined above canceled 'and left'
55.4	at the spring] interlined with a caret
55.11	breathing] preceded by canceled 'and'
55.16	that] written over 'it'
55.21	smoothness] interlined above canceled 'level'
55.22	hills, there's] HDT first wrote 'hills," said he, "there's', later canceling both 'said he' and the quotation marks.
55.28	it—] followed by canceled 'that it was a place between certain other places—and the books and maps were all wrong—for he had lived there longer than anybody.'
55.32	content] altered from 'contentment'
56.2	somewhat] interlined with a penciled caret
56.6	the few hours] preceded by canceled 'of'
56.6	day-] interlined with a caret
56.13	understand] preceded by canceled 'be expected to'
56.14	stayed] interlined above canceled 'lingered a'
56.25	lighted the lamp] followed by canceled 'and handed'
56.28	passed] preceded by canceled 'passed' interlined above canceled 'worked'
56.30	asleep] preceded by canceled 'sound'
56.33–34	half way over] preceded by canceled 'over'
56.37	country] preceded by canceled 'fields and pastures of my hoste'

57.1	old] interlined above canceled 'aged'
57.3	near] preceded by canceled 'with'
57.4	answered] interlined above canceled 'inquired'
57.4	low] followed by canceled 'lo[w?]'
57.5	take any notice of me] As an alternate reading HDT interlined 'regard my presence', later canceling 'take any notice of me' in pencil.
*57.7	proceeded] MS: 'proceed'
57.8	near] added in the left margin before 'to'
57.11	unjust,] followed by canceled 'would not'
57.24	made] interlined with a caret
57.34	contemplation] followed by canceled 'of nature'
58.3	not like] preceded by canceled 'like an'
58.10	&] interlined above canceled 'amid'
58.14	stately] As an alternate reading HDT interlined 'majestic'.
58.18–23	It . . . them] added at the bottom of the page in the space below paragraph 58.13–17
*58.28	to conquer] MS: 'conquer'
58.30	traverse.] At the end of the paragraph HDT wrote 'Shag bark trees', probably a reference to a passage in the Long Book later revised for *A Week*. See *J*:2 32 and *W* 215.
58.34	bank] interlined above canceled 'shore'
58.36–37	us—] followed by canceled 'which made boat building'
59.3–6	The whole . . . argo.] Drawing vertical lines in the left margin, HDT numbered this paragraph '1', indicating that it should precede 59.6–8, originally the final line of the preceding paragraph, which he numbered '2'.
59.6–8	We . . . bridge.] See note above.
59.13	hornets] preceded by canceled 'hornest'
59.22–32	Sometimes . . . roof.] This is written on the recto of a leaf HDT inserted into the manuscript, noting 'routine scrap' within a

sideways caret in the space following the
poem at 59.21.

59.22   manifest] HDT placed this in parentheses and
later canceled it in pencil.

59.29   the genial darkness of] HDT placed this in
parentheses and later canceled it in pencil.

60.3   This intention] In *A Week* the quotation
concludes: "being communicated to
Cromwell, he buried his wealth and made his
escape. Within a few hours after his flight, a
party of the Penacook tribe arrived, and not
finding the object of their resentment, burnt
his habitation" (W 196–97).

60.21   without effort] HDT placed this in
parentheses, an indication that he considered
omitting it.

60.26   We] preceded by canceled 'The'

60.27–28   as . . . time to time] HDT placed this in
parentheses and later canceled it in pencil.

60.36–61.16   We . . . falls—]HDT first wrote, 'In the
afternoon we went on our way, passing
another ferry and more falls—', later revising
and expanding the paragraph as described in
the following notes.

60.36–61.4   We . . . long.] added in the space between
paragraphs

*61.1   is sometimes] interlined with a caret after
uncanceled 'is'

61.1–2   to be accompanied] preceded by canceled 'to
produce'

61.4–13   With . . . commerce] added in the left margin
with a sideways caret

61.11   the roar of] interlined with a caret

61.13   & we soon . . . again] interlined below
canceled 'In the afternoon'

61.14   & we went] '&' added in pencil. See note
above.

61.14–15   driving . . . us] interlined with a caret

*61.15   us,] MS: 'us'. See note above.
61.17–22   This . . . water.] Drawing vertical lines in the
                left margin, HDT numbered this paragraph '1'
                and paragraph 61.23–26 '2', indicating
                transposition.
61.19   damsel] altered from 'damsels'
61.20   stood awhile to] interlined with a caret
61.23–26   Occasionally . . . behind.] See note to 61.17–
                22.
61.31   in] followed by canceled 'to'
61.34–62.2   The Pythagoreans . . . framing"] interlined
                with a caret
61.37   perceive"] followed by canceled 'that'
62.1   composed] followed by canceled 'by it'
62.12   nations] preceded by canceled 'f[lowers?]'
*62.28   if we were] MS: 'if were'
62.32–33   As he . . . eye] interlined with a caret
64.1   Wednesday Sept. 4th] The title, based on a
                reference to "Sept 4th Wednesday" in the
                Long Book (J 2:16) and on the format of the
                other chapter titles in the first draft, is
                supplied by the editor, since the first leaf in
                the reconstructed manuscript of this chapter
                is untitled (see following note). A leaf of the
                same paper used in the draft bears the title
                "Wednesday," followed by a quotation from
                Cotton ("Man is man's foe, and destiny.") and
                the poem "Upon the bank at early dawn"
                (HM 13195, "Wednesday," 1; cf. CP 203–5).
                The leaf has no pinholes in its margin, so it
                was not part of the pinned gathering of the
                chapter, but it appears to have been folded
                along the left margin, so HDT possibly
                inserted it later. He also later made cuts in
                the margin, indicating that the title page was
                incorporated in the second draft but probably
                removed when HDT decided to omit his poem
                from A Week.

64.3–26   We . . . man.] This is written on a leaf, pages
               129–30, HDT excised from the Long Book (*J*
               2:71–72) and incorporated in the manuscript,
               drawing vertical use marks through two
               unrelated entries on the verso. Probably
               sometime later he also drew a vertical use
               mark through the first paragraph on the recto
               (64.3–5), part of which he interlined in
               "Tuesday" (see note to 51.14–15). However,
               since he did not perfect the reading in
               "Tuesday" until he revised the chapter in
               pencil, the first paragraph has been retained.
64.4   mist] preceded by canceled 'fo[g?]'
64.14   seek] HDT placed this in parentheses and
               interlined 'another flight to' as an alternate
               reading.
64.28–66.3   We passed . . . surface] The surviving
               manuscript continues '[sur-]face is strewn
               with their relics.' at 66.3. However, F. B.
               Sanborn apparently had access to the missing
               leaves, which he edited as part of *The First
               and Last Journeys of Thoreau*, I:35–38. Since
               HDT first drafted most of the missing portion
               in the Long Book, he obviously intended to
               include it in the first draft, so Sanborn's text
               is reprinted here as 64.28–66.3. A study of
               Sanborn's text of surviving portions of the
               manuscript indicates that while he
               normalized HDT's capitalization, punctuation
               and spelling, his readings are fairly reliable.
66.4   chisels] interlined with a caret
66.16   relics] preceded by canceled 'imple[ments?]'
66.16–17   circles of] interlined with a caret
66.22   fracture.] preceded by canceled 'structure.'
66.35   preserve] preceded by canceled 'have'
67.4   his] interlined above canceled 'our'
67.5   chisel,] comma added in pencil
67.10   An] altered from 'And'
67.13   arrow-head] 'arrow- / head'

67.33–68.27   Some . . . art.] This is written on the recto
and verso of a leaf HDT inserted into the
manuscript, noting 'v[ide] s[heet *or* scrap]'
below canceled 'The descent of these falls is
54 feet in half a mile. We locked ourselves
through with much ado, consuming much
river water for our behoof' at 67.33.

67.36   race] interlined above canceled 'life'

67.37   and] preceded by 'and' canceled in pencil

68.3   swept] As an alternate reading HDT interlined
'drifted', later canceling 'swept' in pencil.

68.6–7   Spherical . . . conjectured.] HDT added this at
the bottom of the page, noting 'Adz.' following
'stones' at 68.5. Later he clarified his
intention by numbering each passage '1' in
pencil.

68.8   of stone] followed by canceled 'with a short
neck'

68.9   whose] preceded by canceled 'but its'

68.11   Sometimes the] interlined above canceled
'Sometimes a cornfie[ld?]'

68.18   shafts] As an alternate reading HDT
interlined 'bondage'.

68.20   in stone] interlined with a caret

68.24   without their shafts] As an alternate reading
HDT interlined 'whose shafts have crumbled
into dust', later canceling 'without their
shafts' in pencil.

68.26   implements] preceded by canceled
'utens[ils?]'

68.29   holes] interlined above canceled 'hloes'

68.31   royal] preceded by canceled 'Royal'

68.35   white] interlined with a caret

69.6–7   fresh stones] preceded by canceled 's[tones?]'

69.9   bottom] preceded by canceled 'si[de?]'

69.9   prison] followed by canceled 'of'

69.9–10   some . . . nature] As an alternate reading
HDT interlined 'some more violent freshet'.

69.10   There] preceded by canceled 'They'

69.11	sizes] followed by canceled 'some'
69.12	instance] followed by canceled 'I s[aw?]'
69.12	they] preceded by canceled 'I saw where'
69.13	rock] As an alternate reading HDT interlined and then canceled 'hole'.
69.13	—so that] preceded by canceled 'in one part'
69.13–14	river . . . fall.] preceded by canceled 'water flowed that way anticipating the fall.'
69.16–17	by the roadside] interlined with a caret
69.18	basin] preceded by canceled 'deep'
69.20	or more] interlined with a caret before canceled 'at least'
69.20	it is] interlined above canceled 'the basin is'
69.21	deep] interlined with a caret
69.21	scarcely . . . width] interlined above 'cut directly opposite'
69.29–70.33	The manchester . . . again.] Except for one paragraph (see note to 69.31–70.5), this section is written on a leaf, pages 91–92, HDT excised from the Long Book (*J* 2:48–49) and incorporated in the manuscript of "Wednesday," although it is now bound in with the manuscript of "Tuesday" (HM 956). Drawing vertical use marks through the first three paragraphs on the recto, he apparently recopied the first two at 64.35–65.4 (see note to 64.28–66.3). He recopied the third and then canceled it (see note to 67.33–68.27).
69.30	about 1 mile long—] 'about 1 mile long' interlined above the dash
69.31–70.5	Above . . . passed—] This paragraph is written on the recto and verso of a fragmentary leaf that followed the leaf from the Long Book in the original gathering of "Wednesday" (see note to 69.29–70.33). The paragraph replaces two canceled passages (see notes to 70.6 and *70.17). Drawing a vertical line in the left margin beside each paragraph, HDT

numbered the paragraph on the fragmentary
leaf '2', indicating that it should follow
paragraph 69.29–30, which he numbered '1'.

70.2   came to anchor at] preceded by canceled 'at'

70.3   where] preceded by canceled 'to'

70.6   Presently came] HDT first wrote 'We could
see', which he later canceled, interlining
'Presently came'. He then canceled 'Presently
came' and interlined 'By and by came'.
Finally, he canceled 'By and by' and wrote
'Presently' below the line. The sentence is
preceded by canceled 'Above the falls the
river spreads out into a lake—stretching up
toward Hooksett—'. See note to 69.31–70.5.

*70.6–7   a quarter of a mile] added in the right margin
following uncanceled 'a < ↑ half ↓ > mile <or
more>'

70.7–8   and . . . above] interlined with a caret

*70.8   Their] MS: 'their' preceded by canceled 'With'

70.11–14   It reminded . . . shuffling.] added in the left
margin with a line to a caret after 'steady.' at
70.11

70.13   expressing . . . progress] interlined above
canceled 'progressing'

70.15–16   Their sails . . . set.] added at the bottom of the
recto below canceled 'For the most part . . .
getting'. See following note.

*70.17   At] MS: 'at' preceded on recto and verso by
canceled 'For the most part they were
returning empty, or at most with a few
passengers aboard. As we rowed near to one
which was just getting under way, the steers
man offered to take us in tow—but when we
came along side we found that he intended to
take us on board, as otherwise we should
retard his own voyage too much—but as we
were too heavy to be lifted aboard—we left
him and proceeded up the stream a half a

	mile to the shade of some maples to spend our noon ¶ In the course of half an hour several boats passed up the river'. See 69.31–70.5 and note.
*70.17	length] interlined above 'intervals of half a mile—and among them', all of which HDT canceled except 'of'. See note above.
70.18	with a fair wind] interlined with a caret
70.19	ironically] interlined with a caret before canceled 'in'
70.20–26	But . . . little] interlined to replace canceled ' ↑ yet ↓ until our preparations were made—by which time they were a <quarter> ↑ half a mile ↓ of a mile ahead. Then with our own'
70.26	sails] followed by 'set' canceled in pencil. See note above.
70.26–28	shot . . . aid] interlined above and below canceled 'were soon along side of them'
*70.29–30	the side . . . air,] MS: 'their side,' followed by 'of our acquaintances whose sail was heard panting for a breath of air' interlined with a penciled caret
70.29	whose sail was] HDT first wrote 'their sails were', later writing 'whose' over 'their' and altering 'sails' to 'sail' and 'were' to 'was'.
70.30	panting] preceded by canceled 'flapping and the[n?]'
70.31	throw us a rope] preceded by canceled 'take us in tow'
70.32–33	gradually . . . again.] This was originally written at the top of page 93 of the Long Book. HDT later recopied it at the bottom of page 92, probably when he excised the leaf from the notebook. See note to 69.29–70.33.
70.35–36	& . . . the] interlined with a caret before canceled 'those'
70.36–37	that tributary] preceded by canceled 'the banks of'

70.37	stream] preceded by canceled 'same' interlined above canceled 'very'
*70.37	us.] MS: 'us—' followed by 'even with some advantage—without harsh & unfriendly interruptions.' all of which HDT canceled except 'without harsh &'.
71.1	Though] preceded at the beginning of the paragraph by canceled 'Like the stars our thoughts will go down in our friends' horizon still.'
71.1	floted] interlined above canceled 'wandered'
71.1	that river] 'that' altered from 'these' followed by 'river' interlined with a caret after canceled 'familiar ↑ streams ↓'
71.2	still] interlined with a caret
71.3	our breasts] interlined below canceled '<us both> ↑ each ↓'
71.6	rise up] interlined above canceled 'go down'
*71.8	We are] MS: 'am' preceded by 'We' interlined above canceled 'I'
71.9	which reflects] preceded by canceled 'which surely memory cannot retain.'
*71.10	heat, &] MS: 'heat.' followed by '&' interlined in pencil above canceled 'I'
71.10	our] interlined above canceled 'my'
71.11	us] interlined above canceled 'me'
71.12	us] written below canceled 'me'
*71.12	unnoticed.] MS: 'unnoticed.,' followed by canceled 'so pure that they presented no object to my eyes—so generous and universal that I did not detect them.'
71.13	us not] interlined with a caret after canceled 'me'
71.13	we were] interlined above canceled 'I was not'
71.13	we aspired] 'we' interlined above canceled 'I'
71.14	us perchance] interlined above canceled 'me'
71.15	we] written over 'I'
71.16	us] interlined above canceled 'me'

71.17	hour] followed by canceled 'I have awakened'
71.17	we] written over 'I'
71.17	at midnight,] followed by canceled 'at rare intervals,'
71.18	moments] preceded by canceled 'some'
71.20–22	My friends . . . free] HDT added these verses in the space between paragraphs, later noting in pencil 'v[ide] character', apparently a reference to a passage in "Sunday" and a related passage in "Wednesday." See notes to 21.18–22.20 and 73.4–14.
71.29	we] preceded by canceled 'with the pleasure and not the displeasure of the gods'
*71.33	fibre,] MS: 'fibre.'
71.34	Friends] preceded by canceled 'Are not'
*72.1	bring] MS: 'brink'
72.5–18	There . . . Eve.] HDT placed this section in large parentheses, an indication that he considered omitting it. He later added another parenthesis in pencil after 'lovers?' at 72.25.
72.14–15	Only . . . aright] interlined with a caret
72.18	is the garden of] interlined above canceled 'belongs to'
*72.22	them, & the] MS: '&' interlined above 'them. The'
72.25	dwell there] interlined above partially canceled 'thereunder' interlined above canceled 'is sheltered there'
72.27–31	Yet . . . summers.] HDT added this paragraph at the bottom of the page below paragraph 72.25. See note 73.2.
72.29	It is] interlined above canceled 'How'
72.29	evanescent] followed by canceled 'it has been'
72.30	—&] '&' interlined above the dash
73.2	man.] HDT interlined 'Yet without any outrage to the tenderest ties which exist, compared with his dream, one is ever ready to say that friendship is <still> unrealized' with

a caret after 'man.' Drawing a vertical line in the left margin, he numbered the sentence '1' but later canceled and recopied it at 72.27–31 (see note).

73.4–14   There . . . friendship.] This paragraph is preceded by the canceled paragraph 'The friend is some fair floating isle of palms, cheering the mariner in the Pacific sea, near whose coast<s> he in vain stands off and on, sounding for some safe entrance within its coral reef.' (see 75.30–33 and note). Between the paragraphs HDT later noted 'character' in pencil and tore the leaf in two, though it is now taped back together. See note to 71.20–22.

73.6   highest] HDT altered 'higher' to 'highest' and interlined 'divinest' as an alternate reading, later canceling 'highest' in pencil.

*73.6   But ignorance] MS: 'But' interlined with a caret before 'Ignorance'

73.7   love] HDT placed this in parentheses and as an alternate reading interlined with a caret 'this innocent fire', which he later canceled in pencil.

73.12–14   Comparatively . . . friendship.] HDT added this at the end of the paragraph in a different ink, so it probably postdates his other ink revisions.

73.17–20   There . . . religion.] Drawing vertical lines in the left margin, HDT numbered this paragraph '1' and paragraph 73.22–23 '2', indicating transposition.

73.20   religion.] followed by canceled 'The wisest books of the ancient world do not contain its code—nor do the scriptures inculcate it.'

73.22–23   He . . . stopping.] See note to 73.17–20.

73.25–26   he has not seen] HDT first wrote 'we have seen only', later writing 'he' over 'we', interlining 'not' with a caret after 'have' altered to 'has', and canceling 'only'.

73.29–74.20   I walk . . . stature.] HDT placed this poem in large parentheses, possibly indicating that he considered omitting it. See note to 74.22–75.25.

74.13   sure foundation] preceded by canceled 'f[oundation?]'

74.22–75.25   The Friend . . . mystery.] This poem is written on the recto and verso of a leaf, pages 163–64, HDT excised from the Long Book (*J* 2:93–94) and incorporated in the manuscript, noting 'V[ide] Great Friend' below 'stature.' at 74.21. "Great Friend" is the title of the poem printed at 73.29–74.20 (see *CP* 144), but he evidently had in mind the first line of "The Friend," which begins 'The great friend/ Dwells at lands end'. On the leaf excised from the Long Book, the poem is preceded on the recto by the poem "Morning," which HDT used as an epigraph to "Sunday" (19.6–16), and is followed on the verso by an unrelated passage that he recopied in "Monday."

74.25   he] followed by canceled 'next to'

75.2   speak;] followed by canceled 'In every beholder's eye/A sailing vessel doth descry'. See 75.7–8 and note.

75.3   some] written over 'this'

*75.5   the] MS: 'the the'

75.7–8   In . . . descry] added at the bottom of the page. See note to 75.2.

75.7   companions] interlined above canceled 'beholder's'

75.27   None] altered from 'No' followed by canceled 'man'

*75.28   For it] MS: 'For' interlined with a caret before 'It'

75.29   But] interlined above canceled 'It is'

75.30–33   The friend . . . reef.] HDT added this
                paragraph at the bottom of the page, but
                drawing vertical lines in the left margin he
                numbered it '1', indicating that it should
                precede paragraph 75.35–76.4, which he
                numbered '2'. See note to 73.4–14.

75.35–76.4   The friend . . . reprobates.] See note above.

75.37   Our suspicions] preceded by canceled 'There
                can be no fairer recompense than this.'

*75.38   them, & by] MS: '&' added on line between
                'them. By'

76.6–11   But . . . enough.] This is written on the recto
                of a leaf HDT inserted into the manuscript,
                noting 'v[ide] scrap' with a caret after
                'intercourse.' at 76.6.

*76.6   But my] MS: 'But' added in the left margin
                before 'My'

76.9–10   He . . . good will.] HDT added this below the
                paragraph, but in pencil he later circled it and
                drew a line to a caret after 'worthy—' at 76.9
                to indicate that it was intended to replace
                canceled 'for so I should put a bar between
                us. ↑ nor ↓ '

76.12   remembers] interlined above canceled 'seems
                to be aware'

76.24   My friend] HDT placed this in parentheses
                and interlined 'He' as an alternate reading,
                later canceling 'My friend' in pencil.

76.24   degree] interlined above canceled 'measure'

76.26   what] preceded by canceled 'that'

76.28–30   "Although . . . connected."] added at the
                bottom of the page below paragraph 74.24–
                27

76.30   broken] preceded by canceled 'alter[ed?]'

76.38   survive . . . &] interlined with a caret

*77.1   law, & the] MS: '&' added in the left margin
                between 'law. / The' to connect two
                paragraphs

77.2	the same] interlined with a caret
77.7	The balance of extremes] added below the line with an inverted caret
77.9	simply] interlined with a caret
77.13–15	All . . . intercourse.] added in the space between paragraphs
77.15	this intercourse] 'intercourse' preceded by 'the' altered to 'this' and followed by canceled 'of friends'
77.21–23	"Metals . . . sight."] added at the end of the paragraph
77.36	scalps.] followed by the canceled paragraph 'And if Wawatam would drink the fire water— or <feast on human> ↑ sip his bowl of soup ↓ made of his English prisoners—with his tribe he first <put his friend in> ↑ finds ↓ a place of safety for his friend.'
77.38	while] preceded by canceled 'bu[t?]'
77.38–39	if not indifferent] interlined with a caret
78.2–3	or interpret . . . silent] interlined above 'of wise friends and relations.'
78.2	interpret] preceded by canceled 'understand'
*78.5	I . . . it] MS: 'I would have such remember that' interlined above canceled 'It'
78.6	superior . . . opens] HDT placed this in parentheses and interlined 'as well as' as an alternate reading, later canceling 'superior to that which opens' in pencil.
78.12	is the wanderer's] interlined with a caret
78.15	with] preceded by canceled 'as it were'
78.15	as it were] interlined with a caret
78.19	the atmosphere like electricity.] In A Week the complete sentence reads: 'Friendship is not so kind as imagined; it has not much human blood in it, but consists with a certain disregard for men and their erections, the Christian duties and humanities, while it

purifies the air like electricity' (*W* 275–76; cf. *J* 2:88).

*78.24	it, & no] MS: '&' added in the left margin between 'it. / No'
78.26–27	That . . . treaty.] interlined with a caret
78.30	Without . . . it] interlined above canceled 'It is in some sense'
78.30–31	an essentially Heathenish] 'essentially' interlined with a caret between 'a' altered to 'an' and 'heathenish' altered to 'Heathenish'
78.35	has] interlined above canceled 'there is'
79.3	a sympathy] 'a' interlined in pencil with a caret
79.6	Other religions teach] 'Other religions' interlined above canceled 'Christianity' followed by 'teaches' altered to 'teach'
79.6	tolerance] preceded by canceled 'kin[dness?]'
*79.8	grown,] MS: 'grown.' See following note.
79.8–9	& exists . . . future] interlined with a caret after 'grown.'
79.8	&] added before canceled 'It'
79.8	at all only] interlined with a caret
79.9	anticipation] preceded by canceled 'by'
79.9	remotest future] Below this HDT interlined 'bare possibilities' as an alternate reading.
*79.10	nobleness,] MS: 'nobleness.' See following note.
79.10–11	its bravery trust] interlined above 'nobleness.'
79.11–13	While . . . trust.] interlined with a caret
79.13	boundless trust] preceded by canceled 'a'
*79.15	even,] MS: 'even.'
*79.16	representative] MS: 'representive'
79.18	a] interlined above canceled 'and'
79.20	sometimes] interlined with a caret
79.26–28	It remains . . . pair"] added at the top of the page above paragraph 79.30–35
79.26	It remains] preceded by canceled 'I doubt if'

79.33	in some sense] interlined with a caret
79.33–34	among men] interlined with a caret
80.2	friend] altered from 'friends'
80.3	This . . . friends.] added in the space between paragraphs
80.6	or commerce] interlined with a caret
80.8	powerful] As an alternate reading HDT interlined 'respectable'.
80.9	beyond the sea] interlined with a caret
80.9	Greeting.] HDT apparently planned to end this section here, for at the top of the verso of the leaf he wrote, 'Thus we saild between the territories of Manchester & Goffstown.' However, he then added the paragraphs on 80.11–81.9, beginning in the space below 'Greeting.', continuing below the sentence on the verso, and concluding on the recto of an additional leaf. The sentence on the verso has therefore been printed at the end of the chapter at 81.11–12.
80.11–81.9	If ye . . . met] See note above.
80.15	useful] followed by canceled 'and well disposed'
80.15	admirable] preceded by canceled 'beautiful and'
80.15–16	at head] 'at' preceded by canceled 'in' and followed by canceled 'the'
80.16	or . . . part] interlined above 'head—'
80.16	hit] followed by canceled 'it'
80.17	your own tack] 'own' interlined with a caret before 'tack', which is followed by canceled 'and keep your bearings'
81.4–9	Commonly . . . met] This paragraph is written in a different ink, so it probably postdates the other additions. It is preceded by the canceled paragraph 'Know ye that we can afford to spend our best wealth most freely', written in the same ink. See note to 80.9 Greeting.

81.4–5	which . . . qualities,] interlined above canceled 'or its greater qualities', which HDT interlined with a caret and a comma after 'life'
81.11–12	Thus . . . Goffstown.] See note to 80.9 Greeting.
82.4	rain drops] preceded by canceled 'd[rops?]'
82.17–19	It . . . hours] This is added in the space between paragraphs, where HDT first wrote but then canceled 'tree sparrow'.
82.21	in the rain] interlined with a caret
82.21	last] preceded by canceled 'farthest'
82.22–23	long and numerous] interlined with a caret
82.25–26	and climbing] preceded by canceled 'still with'
82.27	brightest] interlined with a caret
82.28	genial] interlined with a caret
82.29–30	& . . . feet] HDT originally placed '& cheered by the tones of invisible waterfalls' in parentheses, then canceled the parenthesis after 'waterfalls' and added a parenthesis after 'feet', probably an indication that he considered omitting the whole passage.
82.29	&] interlined above 'cheered'
82.29	invisible waterfalls] 'invisible' interlined with a caret before 'waterfalls', which is followed by canceled 'which we'
*82.35	followed] MS: 'folled'
83.4–5	until . . . agiocochook] interlined with a caret
83.8–9	many . . . side.] HDT originally wrote this at the top of a separate leaf, but he recopied it in the left margin in order to conserve paper. See note to 88.8.
84.4	favor] preceded by partially wiped out 'favor'
84.10	loss] HDT later interlined 'of time' in pencil to clarify the reading.
84.11	high] interlined with a caret
84.11	above] preceded by canceled 'high'
84.14	as a strange craft] interlined with a caret

84.17–21	In . . . departed.] Drawing vertical lines in the left margin, HDT numbered this paragraph '1' and paragraph 84.22–26 '2', indicating transposition.
*84.19	nature.] MS: 'nature,'
84.22–26	The . . . awakened.] See note 84.17-21.
84.23	vision] interlined above canceled 'sight'
84.33	The savage . . . sea] added in the space between paragraphs
*84.34	On . . . there] MS: 'On the other hand' interlined with a caret before 'There'
84.35	sylvan] interlined above canceled 'primitive'
85.8	recognized] preceded by canceled 'passed rapidl[y]'
85.9	had] added in the left margin before 'rested'
85.12–35	Our boat . . . stars."] This is written on the recto of the first of two leaves HDT inserted into the manuscript, noting 'H' in the margin and 'v[ide] scrap H' in a sideways caret after 'portages—' at 86.3. He then drew a line to indicate that the passage should precede rather than follow paragraph 85.37–86.3. See also note to 86.17–87.34.
85.29	or] preceded by canceled 'a[nd?]'
85.32–35	"It . . . stars."] added below 'So we sailed this afternoon.' at 85.31
86.1	as] followed by canceled 'the rip[ples?]'
86.2	keeping] preceded by canceled 'and carr[y?]'
86.2	boat] preceded by canceled 'cr[aft?]'
86.2	in the] preceded by canceled 'fr[om?]'
86.5	ringlets] preceded by canceled 'the rin[glets?]'
*86.5	child,] MS: 'child.'
86.11–15	How . . . ship.] HDT added this in the space between paragraphs, probably to form a transition to additional material he marked for inclusion here. See note to 86.17–87.34.
*86.14	his element] MS: 'the his element'
86.17–87.34	Nature . . . flower.] This follows 85.12–35 (see note) on the first leaf and continues on a

second leaf HDT inserted into the
manuscript. Drawing vertical lines in the left
margin, he marked this section "I" to
distinguish it from the preceding section,
noting 'Vide I' below paragraph 86.11–15 (see
note). There he also noted 'Τὸ Καλον', but his
intention is unclear. See 95.31 ff.

86.38	they] As an alternate reading HDT interlined 'the laws of nature'.
87.1	actions] As an alternate reading HDT interlined 'characterized deeds'.
87.2–8	And . . . faithfully.] HDT added this at the bottom of the page, drawing a line to indicate that it should follow 'life—' at 87.2. See also note to 87.8–14.
87.3	efforts] interlined below and with a caret after canceled 'inquiries'
87.8–14	Science . . . end."] HDT added this in the left margin, drawing a line to an inverted caret after 'life—' at 87.2. See also note to 87.2–8.
87.14	in this study] interlined with a caret
*87.15	faculties] MS: 'facuties'
*87.20	personally— The] MS: 'personally— / —The'
87.23	intellectual] preceded by canceled 'physical'
87.30–32	Some dig . . . nature.] preceded by canceled 'Some say it is always concealed in the flower and who plants the flower gets the seed with it. Some <prefer> ↑ pluck ↓ the root— some—the stalk—some the flower—some the kernel'
*87.31	kernel,] MS: 'kernel.'
*88.6	cool] MS: 'col'
88.8	fragrance.] followed, at the bottom of the page, by 'many a rude blast would have to be encountered on the mountain side!' written inverted. See note to 83.8–9.
89.30	hue."] preceded by canceled 'hue. hue'
89.32–35	"And . . . year."] HDT added the poem in the left margin with a sideways caret in the space

between paragraphs, where he noted 'attempered suns arise', a reference to a passage from Thomson's *The Seasons,* portions of which are quoted at 96.33–97.5.

*89.37   The woods & fields] MS: 'fields &' interlined with a canceled caret after 'The' and a caret after 'woods'

90.7–21   Dense . . . traveller.] Drawing vertical lines in the left margin, HDT numbered these paragraphs '1' and paragraph 90.23–31 '2', indicating transposition.

90.11–14   The lark . . . them.] Above this HDT interlined 'sept 29th'. In the Long Book, page 95, the entry is dated 'Sept 29—42' (*J* 2:50).

90.15   early in october] interlined with a penciled caret

90.23–31   By . . . meadows.] See note to 90.7–21.
*90.23   especially if the] MS: 'especially' interlined with a caret before canceled 'if the'

90.29   veins] interlined above canceled 'veins'
90.34–35   of . . . button-woods] interlined with a caret
90.39   campaign.] Probably to form a smoother transition to the section on the cattle show (see following note), below this HDT later added in pencil, 'This fair (festival) when men are gathered in crowds in the streets as naturally as the leaves rustle and cluster by the way-side is naturally associated in my mind with the fall of the year.' See also note to 92.33.

91.1–92.33   The low . . . festival.''] This is written on three leaves, pages 143–46 and the bottom half of pages 147–48, HDT excised from the Long Book (*J* 2:80 ff.) and incorporated in the manuscript, drawing vertical use marks through unrelated entries on the recto of the first leaf (page 143) and the verso of the third leaf (page 148). The verso of the second leaf (page 146) contains three epitaphs, portions of which he later added to *A Week* (*W* 170).

91.1–2 The low . . . leaves.] added above paragraph 91.3–13. See note to 92.22.

91.6 as yet] HDT placed this in parentheses, an indication that he considered omitting it.

91.9 amid] As an alternate reading HDT interlined 'among'.

91.11 not yet] HDT placed this in parentheses and interlined 'never' as an alternate reading.

*91.15 to the plain."] MS: 'to the" plain.'

91.18 rushing] followed by canceled 'in herds'

91.19 that] As an alternate reading HDT interlined 'lest'.

91.23–24 "wise . . . hurl'd."] added in the space between paragraphs

91.23 Nature's] altered from 'nature's'

91.26 fattest] altered from 'fairest'

91.26 and their] 'their' interlined with a caret

91.28–29 in crowds] In the right margin HDT added '(in the fall of the year)', possibly as an alternate reading.

91.33 adays] interlined with a caret

91.39 procession] preceded by canceled 'goat'

92.4 & skolars] interlined with a caret

92.8 naturally] preceded by canceled 'bees'

92.11 vegetables] As an alternate reading HDT interlined 'plants'.

92.15 like] preceded by canceled 'for'

92.22 dug up?] Below this, at the bottom of the page, HDT added but then canceled, 'The low of the cattle in the street sounds like a low symphony or running base to the hurry scurry of the leaves. v[ide] n[ext] p[age] but 1'. He apparently intended to use the line to introduce paragraph 92.24–31, written on the verso of the following leaf, but he then decided to shift the line to the opening of the section. See 91.1–2 and note.

92.25	at the heels] preceded by canceled 'hastening'
92.26	the melodies] preceded by canceled 'all'
92.33	Went] As an alternate reading HDT interlined 'came', later canceling 'Went' in pencil.
92.33	festival."] Below this, probably to form a transition to the following poem, HDT added in pencil, 'But to return to the Autumn'. Canceling this, he added but then canceled, 'Our annual cattleshow is associated with the fall of the year when men are gathered in crowds in the streets as naturally as leaves cluster and rustle by the wayside.' See note to 90.39.
92.35–93.4	I mark . . . year.] Below this poem HDT drew two large sideways carets and noted 'v[ide] fall of leaf' in the right margin, probably a reference to his poem "The Fall of the Leaf" (*CP* 236–38). Although the first draft contains no draft of the poem, other surviving manuscripts indicate that HDT later incorporated extended portions of it before he finally decided to omit all but one stanza from *A Week* (*W* 349). Above the reference to the poem he later noted 'Birds' in pencil, probably a reference the digression he began to draft in 1846. See Appendix, no. 12.
93.12	regret—] Following this, HDT noted 'verses', probably a reference to the poem at 45.10–22, which he later shifted to "Friday." See *W* 351–52.
93.15	a slight] followed by 'but slight' later canceled in pencil
93.15	and familiar] interlined with a penciled caret
93.16–17	Many . . . voyage.] added between paragraphs
93.19	for] interlined above canceled 'to'
93.19	soon] preceded by canceled 'was'
93.35–94.21	There . . . nature.] This is written on the verso of a leaf, pages 101–2, HDT excised from the Long Book (*J* 2:54–55) and

incorporated in the manuscript, noting 'v
[ide]. s[heet *or* scrap]' following 'winter' at
93.33. He drew vertical use marks through
three unrelated entries on the recto of the
leaf.

*93.35–94.4   There . . . grow.] This entry is dated 'Oct 30th
—42'. See note above.

*93.36–37   blossoms . . . November.] MS: 'blossoms . . .
November' interlined above canceled 'is now
in bloom' followed by a comma rather than a
period. See note above.

94.2–3   Surely . . . man's] interlined with a caret

94.7   to heal our] HDT first wrote 'which heal the',
immediately interlining 'to' above canceled
'which' and canceling 'the' before continuing
the sentence with 'our'.

94.9   our lives are] preceded by canceled 'are'

94.16   overlooked their existence] HDT placed this
in parentheses, later canceling 'existence' in
pencil.

94.19–21   and health . . . nature.] HDT originally
completed the paragraph at the top of page
103 of the Long Book, where he wrote: 'and
health in (present) nature; which is not to be
found in any religion—and cannot be
contemplated in antiquity— I suppose that
what in other men is religion is in me love of
nature.' But he revised and recopied the
passage in smaller script at the bottom of
page 102 when he excised the leaves from
the Long Book. See notes to 93.35–94.21 and
99.34–100.20.

94.24   Hudson] interlined with a caret

*95.7   sail,] MS: 'sail.'

95.11   when] interlined in pencil with a caret

95.20   Eschylus] preceded by canceled 'Anacreon.'

95.23   at that season] Above this HDT interlined 'oct
21st'. In the Long Book, page 100, the entry
is dated 'Oct 21st 42' (*J* 2:53).

95.23   that the lights] preceded by canceled 'that a
                 candle set in the'

95.26–28   The ancients . . . flower.] interlined with a
                 caret

95.30   now] preceded by canceled 'to'

*95.33   his] MS: 'the his'

96.5   a midsummer . . . taper] interlined with a
                 caret

*96.5   taper—] MS: 'taper'. See note above.

*96.9   sun] MS: 'sun / sun'

96.15   Hunters] altered from 'hunters'

96.17–25   I never tire . . . science.] HDT originally wrote
                 this on page 101 of the Long Book (see note
                 to 93.35–94.21) but recopied it on the verso of
                 another leaf (pages 43–44; see *J* 2:24), which
                 he excised from the notebook and
                 incorporated in the manuscript, later noting
                 'v[ide] n[ext] p[age,] b[ut] 1 we never tire' in
                 pencil following 'forgotten.' at 96.15. See also
                 note to 97.7–27.

96.25   science.] The earlier version of this paragraph
                 on page 101 of the Long Book reads 'study to
                 the intellect.' See note above.

*96.27–28   in whom . . . is] interlined with a caret before
                 canceled 'and' followed by uncanceled 'is'

96.29   so] added on line

96.37   —gives us his blaze again,] HDT later
                 clarified this by adding '<Scarcely> ↑ Not ↓
                 secondary to the sun, she' in pencil.

97.7–27   What an impartial . . . surrounds.] This is
                 written on a leaf, pages 43–44, HDT excised
                 from the Long Book and incorporated in the
                 manuscript, noting 'v[ide] s[heet *or* scrap]'
                 below the quotation at 97.6. He drew vertical
                 use marks through an unrelated passage on
                 the verso, which also contains paragraphs
                 96.17–25 (see note).

97.11   pale,] altered from 'paler,' followed by
                 canceled 'more'

97.11   light,] followed by canceled 'than the sun'

97.12–13   In this light . . . old.] HDT wrote this at the
               end of the passage on the verso of the leaf
               but noted 'v[ide] n[ext] p[age]' within a caret
               following 'ruins.' at 97.12 on the recto. See
               note to 97.7–27.

97.14   It is therefore] interlined above canceled 'The
               moonlight is'

97.23   around] altered from 'aroung'

97.29   When we reached] preceded by canceled 'By
               noon we reached the locks at Middlesex—
               and'

97.38   current] interlined above canceled 'tide'

98.1   rawness] interlined above partially wiped out
               'rawness'

98.7   autumn] preceded by canceled 'winter'

98.10–17   On fields . . . haze.] Drawing vertical lines in
               the left margin, HDT numbered this poem '1'
               and the paragraph and poem on 98.19–99.4
               '2', indicating transposition.

98.19–99.4   There is . . . relief.] See note above.

98.38   winter] preceded by canceled 'lurk[ing?]'

99.18   have not gathered] 'gathered' written above
               'have not'

99.29   touch] interlined above canceled 'step'

99.30   remains] interlined above canceled 'is'

99.34–100.20   I love to hear . . . abode.] This is written on a
               leaf, pages 103–4, HDT excised from the
               Long Book (J 2:55–56) and incorporated in
               the manuscript, noting 'I love to hear some
               &c v[ide] s[heet *or* scrap]' at 99.34. He drew
               vertical use marks through unrelated
               passages on the recto and verso. See also note
               to 94.19–21.

99.35–36   men . . . deep.] interlined below 'though I
               hear not what they say—'

100.19–20   An immortal . . . abode.] added below
               paragraph 100.17–18

*100.19	An] MS: 'an' preceded by canceled 'A true life shall not fail'
100.19	destitute] preceded by canceled 'depriv[ed?]'
100.24	also] interlined with a caret
100.25	sun] As an alternate reading HDT interlined 'aspects', later canceling 'sun' in pencil.
101.15–102.9	As it waxed . . . mood.] This is written on a leaf, pages 87–88, HDT excised from the Long Book (*J* 2:45–46) and incorporated in the manuscript, noting 'v[ide] s[heet *or* scrap]' preceding 'But the farmers boy only whistles' at 102.11. He drew vertical use marks through a portion of an unrelated passage between paragraph 101.15–28 (recto) and paragraphs 101.30–102.9 (verso).
101.17	where . . . night] interlined with a caret
*101.22	men,] MS: 'men.' See following note.
101.22–23	and surely . . . them] interlined with a caret after 'men.'
*101.27	light,] MS: 'light'. See following note.
101.27	purer . . . noon] interlined with a caret after 'light'
101.32–102.2	The . . . Cayster.] HDT wrote this below the paragraph, drawing a line to a caret following 'heads—' at 101.31–32 to indicate its position. See also notes to 101.15–102.9 and 102.8–9.
102.4	—or] 'or' interlined above the dash
102.8–9	The . . . mood.] HDT added this at the bottom of the page, probably to form a transition between the paragraphs on the leaf from the Long Book and the paragraph that follows in the manuscript. See note to 101.15–102.9.
102.15	at length] interlined with a caret
102.28	the stars] HDT placed this in parentheses and interlined 'they' as an alternate reading.
102.35–105.7	As the truest . . . shore.] HDT drafted this on three leaves (pages 191–96) in the Long Book (*J* 2:112–15), two of which he excised from the notebook and incorporated in the manuscript, drawing vertical use marks

through unrelated material on the recto of the first leaf. Probably because the third leaf also contains a passage on Marlowe not used in the first draft, HDT left the leaf in the notebook. See also note to 105.9–16.

103.1   wood] As an alternate reading HDT interlined 'forest', later canceling 'wood' in pencil.

*103.5   silence.] MS: 'silence,'

103.7   It] interlined above canceled 'Silence'

103.8   infinity—] followed by canceled 'then and there is silence—'

103.11–17   Creation . . . these.] 'Silence is ever less strange and startling than noise.' was originally the first sentence in the paragraph, but HDT numbered it '2', drawing a vertical line in the left margin beside the remainder of the paragraph, which he numbered '1', indicating transposition. He then added 'and is any where intense and profound just in proportion as we find ourselves these.' at the end of the paragraph, apparently as a continuation of the first sentence.

*103.16   noise,] MS: 'noise.' See note above.

103.20–21   of her coming.] Above this HDT interlined 'to attend to her communications', but his intention is unclear.

103.34   dull] interlined above canceled 'dry'

104.13–14   in proportion] preceded by canceled 'as f[ar?]'

104.28   the book] preceded by canceled 'book'

105.9–16   And now . . . freshets.] HDT drafted the concluding paragraph on page 197 of the Long Book (J 2:116). It is the last entry in the notebook he numbered for inclusion in the first draft, but, probably because the leaf also contains poems and other entries not used in the first draft, he left the leaf in the notebook. See also note to 102.35–105.7.

105.10   keel] preceded by canceled 'hull'

105.14   tree] interlined with a caret

Appendix:

Passages Omitted from *A Week*

The surviving manuscripts contain a substantial amount of material Thoreau omitted from *A Week* as he worked on the second draft during 1846–49. A number of passages are quoted in Part 1. What follows are the texts of fourteen other passages, all of which I refer to or discuss in Part 1. Since this appendix is intended simply as a supplement to my study of the writing of *A Week,* I have not gathered all of the extended passages Thoreau omitted from the book. I have instead included passages that illuminate what I view as his major thematic concerns in *A Week*.

In a headnote to each passage, I describe the manuscript, give its location, and identify other surviving versions of the passage. Wherever possible, I have numbered paper types according to Howarth's descriptions of the various types of paper Thoreau used (*LMHDT* 376–79), though my dating of leaves occasionally varies from Howarth's conjectured dates for a given paper type. I also discuss the context of each passage in the second draft in relation to the published version of *A Week*. Except where otherwise noted, I have followed all revisions in pen and pencil Thoreau made before removing the leaf or leaves from the manuscript, adjusting his punctuation and capitalization in only a few places where he added a word or phrase at the beginning of a sentence or interlined "&" to connect two sentences.

1 "Sunday" [Two Yankee Priests]

> This passage followed the poem "I make ye an offer"
> plus an interlined quotation from Saadi (*W* 69) and
> preceded a paragraph on the New Testament (*W* 71–
> 72). Thoreau deleted the passage by drawing vertical
> pencil lines through it, interlining "V[ide] S[heet?]
> Most people &c," a reference to the paragraph
> beginning "Most people with whom I talk" (*W* 69–71),
> which replaced the deleted passage. The omitted leaf
> of blue wove paper (type 9) probably dates from 1847.
> It is in the Houghton Library (MH 15, R).

It might seem that I had some spite against the priest,
but not so, I am on as good terms with him as with another
man.

I once knew a good specimen of a Yankee priest—a man
who beside being as shrewd at a bargain and as shifty under
all circumstances as any of his parishoners, was also gifted in
prayer. He very properly had his society completely under his
thumb, and regulated not only their spiritual but temporal
affairs. He was truly independent with all, and could afford to
doff his ministerial surplice during the week or even on
Sunday. He fatted a pig on the contributions of his neighbors
which he collected himself in his own swill-pail. I have heard
some of his parishoners congratulate themselves upon having
got a man at last who could swap horses without being
cheated. One who lived near the meeting house said that one
Sunday when the priest was belated and the congregation
were all within, he saw him arrive and fasten his horse, open
the mouths of his parishoners horses & look at their teeth, and
then walk into the church at his leisure to unite with them in
prayer.

He was a better man in all respects than any in his parish.

This reminds me of another praying Yankee who performed
in the very next parish, to the last who was unequalled at a

practical joke—whose best and most practical jokes were his prayers.

As he was descending the pulpit stairs with the benidiction lingering upon his lips he whispered to his sprightly young cousin who met him half way—the next time she met her cousin Alice to run a pin into her clear up to the head.

2 "Monday" [Lovewell's Hunting Expedition]

> This passage, based on the accounts in Belknap's
> *History of New-Hampshire* (II:51–52) and Penhallow's
> *Indian Wars* (*CNHHS*, I [1824]: 112–113), followed a
> quotation from Fox's *History of Dunstable* at the
> conclusion of Thoreau's account of Lovewell's Fight in
> "Monday" (*W* 122). The omitted leaf of gray wove
> paper (type 6) probably dates from 1848. It is in the
> Huntington Library (HM 13195, "Monday," 1).

One of the most remarkable and successful hunting expeditions which ever took place in these parts, was got up and led by Lovewell a few months before this in February 1725. Forty men, according to Belknap, some say fifty-eight, who had been induced to undertake this enterprise by the generous bounty on Indian scalps, discovered ten Indians asleep at midnight round a fire by the side of a frozen pond, since called Lovewell's pond, near Winnepiseogee lake. They ordered their fire so as to make sure of the whole party. One who was only wounded "attempted to escape by crossing the pond, but was seized by a dog and held fast till they killed him." Thus says the historian "some attempt against the frontiers of New Hampshire was prevented; for the Indians were marching from Canada, well furnished with new guns, and plenty of ammunition; they had also a number of spare blankets, mockaseens & snow-shoes for the accomodation of the prisoners whom they expected to take, and were within two days march of the frontiers"—"The action is spoken of by elderly people, at this distance of time, with an air of exultation;"—"it was a capital exploit." To us at *this* distance of time, it seems to have been fair enough, as the world goes, considering the intentions of the Indians, but not particularly heroic; four to one, and that one asleep! "The brave company" continues the historian, "with the ten scalps stretched on hoops, and elevated on poles, entered Dover in triumph, and proceeded thence to Boston; where they received the bounty of one hundred pounds for each, out of the public treasury."

Penhallow says that "the guns were so good & new that most of them were sold for seven pounds apiece. The plunder was but a few skins [he was not thinking of the scalps,] but during the march our men were well entertained with moose, bear and deer, together with salmon trout, some of which were three feet long, and weighed twelve pounds apiece."

3 "Monday" [Graveyards]

This passage is a far longer version of the paragraph beginning, "A man might well pray that he may not taboo or curse any part of nature by being buried in it," at the end of the digression on graveyards in "Monday" (W 170–71). Thoreau wrote at least three distinct versions of the digression during 1846–48. The first, drafted on three leaves of blue wove paper (type 1), is in the Houghton Library (MH 15, J). A second, expanded version, drafted on four leaves of a different blue wove paper (type 3), is evenly divided between the Houghton Library (MH 15, J) and the Huntington Library (HM 13195, "Monday," 4). Two leaves from a third, compressed version drafted on white wove paper (type 5) are in the Houghton Library (MH 15, J). The following passage, the concluding portion of the second version, is written on the two leaves in the Huntington Library. A missing portion of the preceding leaf, now in the Houghton Library, probably contained the opening of the passage, portions of which Thoreau deleted with vertical pencil strokes. Neither his initial deletions nor his related pencil revisions are followed in the text below.

They are too highly manured. If I held, as I do not, to the
practice which is prevalent of manuring highly, I should
remove all the stones,—for though there is commonly a good
crop of grass, you cannot mow there conveniently between the
stones—and then plough deep and plant corn for a first crop,
and so on ploughing deeper and deeper every year. As it is, I
should recommend to a village to collect together and grind or
burn up all its bones, and distribute the dust to its several
families to be spread broadcast on the land as a top-dressing.
The first settlers of Dunstable owed their bodies to the soil
which fed them; why then were they not returned to it? Why
should this single hill be so fattened, and all our other hills so
impoverished? The farmer who has skimmed his farm should
at least leave his body to nature, to be ploughed in and in
some measure restore its fertility. Men should not retard but
forward the economies of Nature. She incessantly demands
manures. Every carcass should be husbanded, nothing be lost.
Keep the ball a moving. Instead of a stinking graveyard, let us
have blooming and fertile fields. Any body can smell a
slaughter-house. When Caspar Hauser went abroad he smelt
the graveyards. If an angel were to come on earth he would
smell the graveyards everywhere, and inquire—Why dont you
dispose of your dead? Aye, he would smell the living also, and
ask—Why dont you bury these too?

I have no taste for such collections as they have at the
Catacombs, Pere la Chaise, Mount Auburn, and this Dunstable
graveyard. For my part I had rather walk where there is no
carrion. Nothing but great antiquity can make graveyards
interesting to me. I have no friends there.

I think that the ancient practice of burning the dead is far
the most tasteful and beautiful, for so the body is most speedily
and cleanly returned to dust again, and its elements dispersed
throughout nature. Those Saints who have been burnt at the
stake, and their ashes cast into some stream have made the
cleanest departure. God says plainly, for even I hear him, lay
not up this matter, but disperse it. Go into a museum and look
at the mummy and consider whether the man that did that
work of embalming has not got something to answer for. Aye,
the nation, with its fingers ever in its entrails, like the dog

returning to his vomit. The most fearful thought of all is that there may, nay must, be a soul, a real living entity somewhere ghastly and funest as that corpse.

When the master of a household dies let his children assemble and burn his body, and carrying the dust to the house top, let the wind take it, or else spread it in the fields around the house—or disperse it from the cannon's mouth, so only it be broadcast, and so celebrate your Independence.

These condemned, these damned bodies. Think of the living men that walk on this globe, and then think of the dead bodies that lie in graves beneath them, carefully pact away in chests as if ready for a start! Whose idea was that to put them there? Is there any race of beetle-bugs that disposes of its dead thus? In a sort of chrysalis state deep in the earth, as if any butterfly were about to issue thence! I believe in a speedy resurrection of the body in some other form, in corn for fodder, in wood for fuel, in grain or flowers for use or beauty. Every wind blows the last trump, which should call the lost atoms together. The last thing I should wish to preserve is an old man's body which now for thirty years has been wracked with gout and rheumatism and nameless ills. Waste no time at funerals. Let the dead bury their dead   *propera viator, memento vivere.* Make haste traveller, remember that you have got to live.

4 "Tuesday" [Morning Courage]

> This passage, most of it drawn from the early Journal (*J* 1:69, 122), is an expanded version of a paragraph in the first draft (FD 49). Thoreau deleted the passage, which followed the description of the brothers' preparations at the opening of "Tuesday" (*W* 179), by drawing vertical pencil lines through it. The leaf of blue wove paper (type 3) probably dates from 1848. It is in the Huntington Library (HM 13195, "Tuesday," 1).

Buonaparte exaggerates the three o'clock in the morning courage; fear does not awake so early. Few men are so degenerate as to baulk Nature by not beginning the day well.

In the morning we do not believe in expediency, but will start afresh without botching. The afternoon man has an interest in the past, and sees indifferently well either way. The morning dew breeds no cold. Disease is a sluggard that overtakes, never encounters us. We have the start each day, and may fairly distance him before the dew is off; but if we recline in the bowers of noon he will come up with us after all.— I have always found an early morning walk to be a blessing for the whole day. To our neighbors who have risen in mist and rain, we tell of a clear sunrise and the singing of birds, as some traditionary mythus. We look back to those fresh but now remote hours as to the dawn of time, when a solid and blooming health reigned, and every deed was simple and heroic.

5 "Tuesday" [Etiquette]

> This passage followed the quotation at the end of Thoreau's account of his encounter with an old man at the conclusion of the Rice story (*W* 209). The leaf of blue wove paper (type 1), paged 265–66, dates from 1846–47. It is in the Houghton Library (MH 15, 0). Thoreau deleted roughly half of the paragraph on etiquette in pen before removing the leaf from the manuscript. His initial deletions are not followed in the text below.

It is the saddest thought of all, that what we are to another, that we are much more to ourselves; uncivil, avaricious, mean, irascible, affected, we are the sufferers. If our rudeness offends our companion, it much more offends ourselves, though our lives are never so private and solitary.

Our etiquette is for little men. Men commonly do not meet on the ground of their real acquaintance and actual understanding of one another, but degrade themselves into the puppets of convention. They do as if in given circumstances they had agreed to know each other only so well. If Zoroaster, or Homer, or Socrates should come on earth again, would they

need letters of introduction to the prominent characters? The
foundations of all sincerity are very deep. Even stone walls
have their foundations below the frost. The best intercourse or
communion men have is in silence above and behind their
speech. We should be very simple to rely on words. I cannot
easily remember what any man has said, but how can I forget
what he has been to me? We know each other after all better
than we are aware or can tell. We are admitted to startling
privacies with every man we meet, and in some emergency we
shall find how well we are acquainted. To our solitary &
distant thought our neighbor is shorn of his mists & halo and
is seen as privately and barely as a star through a glass.

6 "Tuesday" [Fashion]

> Drawing upon entries in the Journal (*J* 1:250–52;
> 2:317–18), Thoreau wrote two versions of this passage
> for *A Week* in 1846–47, later reworking the material
> again for *Walden*. The earliest version, which followed
> a description of the boatman's life (*W* 211), was
> drafted on two leaves of blue wove paper (type 1): the
> first is in the Houghton Library (MH 16); the second
> is in the Huntington Library (HM 13182, III, 2). The
> later, expanded version printed below, drafted on two
> leaves of the same blue wove paper paged 252–53 and
> 254–55 (Thoreau later renumbered the latter 273–74),
> followed the description of canalboats on Concord
> River (*W* 211–12). These leaves are in the Houghton
> Library (MH 16). In each version the remarks on
> fashion follow a paragraph beginning, "It was pleasant
> to hail" (cf. *W* 214), in which Thoreau originally
> praised the "manifest wisdom" of the boatman's
> "simple attire," concluding, "We shall have far to seek
> to find a gentleman who is so wisely dressed."

When we see a fine lady or a gentleman dressed at the top
of the fashion, we naturally wonder what they would do if an
earthquake should happen, or a fire suddenly break out, for

they seem to have counted only on fair weather, and that all things will go on smoothly without jostling. Those curls and jewels so nicely adjusted expect an unusual deference from the elements. There is something skittish as well as foolish in all finery. Our dress should be such at any rate as will hang conveniently about us, and fit equally well in good and in bad fortune. It is true, all costume off a man is grotesque. It is the serious eye, and the sincere life passed within it, which restrain laughter and consecrate the costume of any people. Let Harlequin be taken with a fit of the colic in the midst of his buffoonery, and his trappings and finery will have to serve that mood too. When the soldier is hit by a cannon ball rags are as becoming as purple, and purple is perhaps as becoming as rags. As soon, in fact, as a man engages to eat, drink, walk, work, and sit, and meet all the contingencies of life therein, his costume is hallowed, and may be the theme of poetry.

The taste for dress was probably first exercised upon the bare body. In warm latitudes, among primitive races, where clothing is not required, comparatively speaking tattooing is not necessarily the hideous custom it is described to be. It is the same taste that prints the calico which the wearer puts off and on, and the skin itself which is always worn, and the consistent objection is rather to the fashion of the print than to the practice itself. It is not therefore barbarous because the printing is skin deep. For our own part, it is true, we love plain patterns, but it seems natural that the savage warrior or hunter should imprint some indelible device, some emblem of his profession on his ever naked body, since he has scarcely other ground whereon these symbols can be displayed.

7 "Wednesday" [Guns]

This was the second paragraph in "Wednesday," following Thoreau's description of the masons who stumble upon the brothers' camp (W 235). The draft of the opening of the chapter, written on two leaves of gray wove paper (type 6), probably dates from 1848. It is in the Huntington Library (HM 13195,

"Wednesday," 2). Thoreau deleted portions of the
paragraph before canceling all of it with additional
vertical pencil strokes. His initial deletions are not
followed in the text below.

These men tarried awhile to examine our equiptments,
which lay scattered about on the grass,—and to see where we
had slept. They handled our guns with especial pleasure, and
thought that they should like to join us for the sake of the
game. Indeed, there are few tools to be compared with a gun
for efficiency and compactness. We do not know of another so
complete an *arm*. It is almost a companion like the dog. The
hunter has an affection for the gun which no laborer has for
the tool which he uses, his axe or spade. We have seen the
time when we could carry a gun in our hand all day on a
journey, and not feel it to be heavy, though we did not use it
once. In the country a boy's love is commonly divided between
a gun and a watch; but the more active and manly choose a
gun. Men love to be *armed*, without reference to self defence,
as to carry a cane though it may be always under their arms.
Like the first settlers who rarely went to the field, or even to
church, without their guns, we their descendents have not yet
quite outgrown this habit of pioneers, and even today the
villager whose way leads him far through a piece of wood, or
over a plain where game is sometimes met with, will deliberate
whether he shall not take his gun, because, as he says, he
"may see something." If the Indian and the bear are
exterminated, the partridge and rabbit are left. Even in the
streets and suburbs of cities you may hear occasionally the
sound of guns by which men keep up their reminiscence of
the hunter life—

8 "Wednesday" [General Stark's Captivity]

The two surviving drafts of Thoreau's tribute to Stark
date from 1846–47. The first, a rough draft on a leaf of
blue wove paper (type 1), is in the Houghton Library
(MH 15, P). The second, on a leaf of the same paper

paged 320–21, is in the Huntington Library (HM
13195, "Wednesday," 9). In that version, the following
passage, deleted with a vertical pencil stroke, falls
between a reference to Stark's death "in 1822 at the
age of 94" and a description of his monument on the
banks of the Merrimack, which Thoreau revised after
visiting the spot in 1848 (cf. W 253).

It is said that when a prisoner among the Indians, being
compelled to run the gauntlet, he snatched a club from the
nearest one, and laying it lustily about him, by his courage and
activity escaped almost without a blow, greatly to the delight of
the old men of the tribe who were looking on. When set to hoe
corn by them, understanding well the Indian character, he
took care not to exhibit any skill in this labor, to which he had
been accustomed on his father's farm, but cut up the corn and
left the weeds, and when this did not avail him, he threw his
hoe into the river declaring that "it was the business, not of
warriors, but of Squaws, to hoe corn." This conduct at length
gained him the respect of the Indians, and the title of young
chief, with the honor of adoption into the tribe. He in some
measure retained his free ranger habits to the last, and at the
time of the battle of Bennington was acting as an independent
and partizan commander over forces which had been
assembled mainly by his exertions and the influence of his
name, holding himseif responsible only to his native state, and
refusing to recognise the authority of General Schuyler, who
had ordered him to cross the Hudson & join him.

9 "Wednesday" [Mercy Killing]

Two versions of this passage survive, both in a folder
in the Houghton Library containing six leaves of draft
material for the digression of sickness and health (MH
15, I). The later version, printed below, concluded the
digression, which in *A Week* ends with the only line
salvaged from the passage, "Now he falls between two
stools" (W 257). Like the other leaves in the folder, the
leaf of blue wove paper (type 1) dates from 1846–47.

Poor suffering sick children, that cannot live, such as I have heard of, should be killed, as also some very old and infirm folks, whose life is a burden, and who have none to love them but come upon the cold charity of the town, and all idiotic and greatly deformed persons, and those who complain perpetually. This is not nearly as barbarous as most think. It is astonishing to me that killing makes no part of the avowed practice of the physician—but he never gives it up, though he should strive right against nature. He seems always to think that a man ought not to die, that's a mistake at any rate, anything but that, and so—he kills him

The physician thinks only of preserving the body—the priest of preserving the soul—but none thinks ever of preserving the soul by the sacrifice of the body, and so it falls between two stools—   Is not Death a soverign remedy? For certain diseases I should write—"Kill the patient." I would put him out of misery as I would an insect. To insult and defile and poke at a sick man with your medicines—sick unto death,—how much kinder and cleaner it would often be to cut his thread.

—   Turn out the physician and the priest and let a man die in peace—without dirty drugs to defile or prophane words to disturb him. If his sun sets serenely, stand aside and wait in patience. If it is likely to be too prolonged an agony, shocking to humanity to witness, gently cut his thread and let him go— if you respect *life,* if that is sacred in your eyes.

You may not ask this yourself, through impatience, at the hands of your friends, but kindness will not fail to prompt *your* hands when their condition shall require it.

What is kindness else but partiality and weakness? May not a man be kind heroically, and as the fates are kind?

I have heard of some who were 15 years a dying—a shiftless business for which neither gods nor mortals have any sympathy to spare.

At any rate, I rather like to hear of a man's dying as he has lived, though it were never so loudly   There was one of my neighbors who bothered his watchers—when he was hourly expected to die, by trying to sell them his hay—   After an earnest & natural conversation about hay grain & oats & their prices, he would break out with, "And now O Lord teach me to

pray—Prepare me for this great change"— And having given
this subject the attention it deserved return to the more
interesting one, what oats were agoing to fetch this fall.

10 "Thursday" [Conversation]

> Most of this passage is a revised and expanded version
> of "Conversation," an unpublished essay probably
> written in 1843. A four-page draft of the essay,
> portions of which he copied into the Long Book (*J*
> 2:67–69) and all of which he later revised in pencil, is
> in the Starr Library, Middlebury College. The following
> version, written on four leaves of white wove paper
> (type 14), probably in late 1847 or 1848, is in
> Houghton Library (MH 15, F). In the manuscript, the
> passage is followed by the paragraph beginning, "We
> were hospitably entertained in Concord" (*W* 303), and
> the observation "It was here that the Herald of
> Freedom was published at this time. We had" (4v),
> Thoreau's introduction to the revised version of
> "Herald of Freedom," also omitted from *A Week*.

As we were entering this village it chanced that we overtook
a man travelling slowly who wanted to enter into conversation
with us. He talked as if from his stomach. Words came from
him as if he belched them, and his very atmosphere was
mephitic. He had broken three of his ribs and he wanted us to
walk and talk both at his pace. But we did not wish to talk for
that phenomenon was no novelty to us, and he wanted only a
soothing, simmering, salving kind of talk, too lazy to go after
an idea, which would suffice to knit his ribs together again.
A man who wishes to talk in his sleep may as well talk to
himself

One thing, unfortunately, he remembered, which we had
forgotten, the year when Buonaparte died, and this fact he
repeated many times, telling us precisely how he remembered
it, and this seemed to him a good excuse for continuing the
conversation, as if it might not be unprofitable to us. He
prayed silently that we might be detained, but we resolved that

until we also had broken three of our ribs, we would never talk with him.

What is called talking is a remarkable though universal phenomenon of human society. Some nations, it is true, are said to articulate less distinctly than others, yet the rule holds with those who have the fewest letters in their alphabet. Men of any race cannot stay long together without *talking:*—by a common consent they fall to using the invention of speech, nor without a very obvious reason, must long intervals of silence occur.— I have seen a hundred men and women at once—all friends and acquaintances, that is such as eat drink, sleep and transact the business of living within the circuit of a mile— wholly given over to talk—chattering like a flock of blackbirds in the spring, endeavoring to cement society and hasten on the millennium. From the lively gestures and voices of the company it appeared to me that many fine and memorable things were said, which would be repeated to me another day, after the din had subsided. I have read that among the Finlanders it is the custom, at an assemblage—"when one has succeeded in rendering himself agreeable, for all the women present to give him a sudden slap on the back, when it is least expected; and the compliment is in proportion to the weight of the blow." From the actions of some who were here assembled I thought that some such custom prevailed among them also. But what I had supposed to be nectar and ambrosia proved on a nearer inspection to be mere bohea and short ginger-bread. When next I went to the woods, it seemed to me that the trees, having heard of this, all set their leaves a rustling, and I said to myself I shall not be able to hear when the wind blows—whereupon they suddenly stopped. But the aspen has rustled ever since. Thomas Fuller relates that "In Merionethshire, in Wales, there are high mountains, whose hanging tops come so close together that shepherds on the tops of several hills may audibly talk together, yet will it be a day's journey for their bodies to meet, so vast is the hollowness of the vallies between them." So, though we may audibly converse together, we may be many days journey from a veritable communication.

There is a terra firma in society however as well as in geography—some whose ports you may make by dead reckoning in all weather, but most are but floating and fabulous isles which sometimes skirt the western horizon and impose on sea-sick mariners. I sometimes see them and sail for them, but alas! alas! I man my tow-boats, and fire my stern chasers in vain.

Not that there are not some artless and sincere communications from our country acquaintances—   My friend, my friend, I'd speak so frank to thee that thou wouldst pray me to keep back some part for fear I robbed myself.

I have sometimes heard a conversation beginning again when it should have ceased for want of fuel. They who cannot live near me with pleasure unless I am talking I do not wish to live near. What would Ye my friends! I have not much, at least, not much to speak of. Zeno said,"On this account have we two ears and but one mouth, that we may hear more and speak less." And herein we may see how it is more natural as well as noble to hear than to speak   But the wisest man might apologize that he only said thus or so, to *hear* himself talk. That would be modest certainly. It is true if all men were to listen in this proportion to their speech it would for the most part be silence audible, and they would have an opportunity to hear that summer simmering with which the air is filled, and also the incessant tinkering called hum of industry, which however is wont to be little better than the hum of voices—for if we are truly *industrious,* or *building within,* the passers by will not be likely to hear the hum. But we will not pursue our advantage too far and cruelly this way, for I have heard that

"Misery heaves
The dust of sin above the *industrious* sky,
And lets it not to dust and ashes fly."

When I remember some persons who have talked at me, I think that if we had been all the world, talking is an invention that would have slumbered with me. They have forgotten what the design of the original inventor was.

By a well directed silence however you may rout threatening and troublesome people, such as to avoid your society would fain take refuge in conversation with you— So much humanity over against one without any disguise,—not even the disguise of speech! They cannot stand it nor sit against it.

But it is saddest when you have to go silent, as it were by a decree of fate, in the presence of a fellow being, not having got the handle to him, until some mutual enemy introduces you. "This is Mr Merops Anthropos, that possesses an articulating voice"—and you are expected to unburden your breasts. They stand upon ceremony who have no other ground to stand on. Not only must men talk, but, if they are scholars, for the most part about talk, even about books or dead and buried talk. I have thus seen very near & intimate—very old friends, in fact, introduced by very old strangers, with liberty given to talk.

But a man might be an object of interest to me though his tongue were pulled out by the roots. I have heretofore listened so attentively to the whole expression of a man, that I did not hear one word he was saying, and saying too with more vivacity, observing my attention. And so it has happened that when I met with an eloquent man, I have heard through him Him that spoke to him, and overlooked the orator.

Answer honestly all the questions that are put to you and you will speedily silence the inquirers, though you may earn a bad reputation thus.

Some people will put stupid or impertinent questions to you, and when having no particular answer, you give them a universal one, take you to be a quiz.— Or it will frequently happen that, as they are not contented, either that you should have a peculiar opinion, or that you should have none—you kindly give them several to choose between.

The most successful mode of dealing with shopkeepers is to tell them the whole truth at once, for this they are least prepared for. They will be nonplussed, and may have to tell you the truth in return.— "What do you want Sir?" "I wish to see the best sack coat you have of a certain description for 10 dollars." They will not be inclined to show you it, but this will be the quickest way to come to terms with them.— It is easy to circumvent falsehood with falsehood, but not truth with falsehood.

Once at a tea-table, forgetting where I was, I whistled—whereupon the company could not be convinced that it was not meant for a hint that their conversation was frivolous—   I thought that their suspicion was the best proof that it was so.

By this time, as the reader may suppose, our transient fellow traveller was well out of sight.

11 "Thursday" [Lives of Quiet Desperation]

> This passage occasioned the digression on traveling, which in the manuscript begins with a quotation from Saadi (W 304) and concludes, "There are may ways in which a man can live on the road without carrying a barrel organ." Thoreau deleted that sentence, recopied the remarks on traveling for A Week, and revised the remainder of the passage for Walden (see S 52–53). Since his revisions were for Walden, they have not been followed in the text below. The two leaves of white wove paper (type 14), probably drafted in 1848, are in the Huntington Library (HM 924, D).

We were astonished to meet away up here in New · Hampshire an Italian with his hand organ, so far from Rome, for no youth had yet been born here who could bring his mind to follow this kind of life.

Here was also a poor wretch asking for a lodging, whom it was almost no pleasure to befriend he was so helpless. He said that he came from New York and was seeking work. He did not know where he lodged the night before, nor where he was then—"What place is this sir?"—but only that he had travelled 30 miles that day. He could do work about a stable, but he declared in a disconsolate voice that there was no work for him, as if the fates had a spite against him. He thought that he had seriously injured himself by lying out.

I asked him why he travelled so far in a day, and farther

each successive day—if he was any better off at night than in the morning? Why 3 miles would not do as well as 30 and better. He allowed that I had the right of it.

I concluded that he was a desperate man, who had committed some crime, or whose life was a crime, who was endeavoring to escape from himself. He travelled far superficially because he would not budge an inch in the direction of reform and a good conscience. He thought that nobody wished to employ or would respect him, because he felt himself unfit to be employed and did not respect himself. If he could have had one half hour of sanity he would have found a job at the next door, and all the world would have appeared kind to him.

He had travelled 250 miles from New York in a straight line with desperate steps 25 or 30 miles a day, offering himself with a down look anticipating failure, to do stable work at such stable yards as that radius happened to intersect, doing his part, as he would fain have believed toward getting work—but there was none for him. He only wished to convince the fates that he was willing to do his part when he knew that he was not. And so he would go on if his constitution held out to the Gulf of St. Lawrence, where he would probably jump in. It had never occurred to him how few stable yards such a radius might [*illegible word, possibly* strike], or that a shorter radius describing a circle might have advantages.

It is the sum of all wisdom not to do desperate things. The great mass of mankind lead lives of quiet desperation. What is called resignation is confirmed desperation— From the desperate city you go into the desperate country and have to console yourself with the bravery of minks and muskrats.

12 "Friday" [Birds]

A leaf of rough notes and three complete versions of this passage have survived. The leaf of notes, jotted down on the same paper used in the first draft, probably in late 1845 or 1846, is laid into a notebook identified as "Nature and Bird Notes" in the Berg

Collection of the New York Public Library. The first
version, drafted on two leaves of blue wove paper (type
1) paged 369–72, is in the Huntington Library (HM
13182, III, 5–6). The second version, drafted on two
leaves of the same blue wove paper paged 415–18, is
in the Houghton Library (MH 15, E, Q). The third and
final version, drafted on two unpaginated leaves of a
different blue wove paper and canceled with vertical
pencil strokes, is also in the Houghton Library (MH
15, E, P). The first version followed the long poem
"The Fall of the Leaf," one stanza of which Thoreau
retained in *A Week* (W 349). The second version,
beginning, "Birds are the truest heralds of the
seasons," and the third version, printed below, followed
the passage beginning, "Yet the universe is a sphere"
(W 349–50). The third version probably dates from
1848.

Occasionally a pair of summer ducks sailed out from a
recess in the shore, and swam and dove before us, to escape
our attention. Just before immersion they appeared to give
each other a significant nod, as if to insure a common
understanding as to when and where they should come up.
When they reappeared it was obvious to observe with what a
self satisfied darn-it-how-we-nicks-'em air they paddled off to
repeat the experiment; but our rapid approach soon compelled
them to use their wings. The few birds which flitted across the
river seemed to have already commenced their migration.
  Birds are the truest heralds of the seasons, since they
appreciate a thousand delicate changes in the atmosphere
which is their own element, of which man and the other
animals cannot be aware. The occasional and transient notes
of such birds as migrate early, heard in mid-summer, or later,
are among the earliest indications of the advancing year. The
clear whistle of the oriole is occasionally heard among the elms
at this time as if it were striving to reawaken the love season,
or as if, in the long interval since the spring it had but paused
a moment to secure its prey, and now resumed its song. It

harmonizes with the aftermath springing under our feet. The
faint flitting note of the gold finch marks the turning point of
the year, and is heard in the gardens by the middle of August,
as if this little harbinger of the Fall were prompting Nature to
make haste. Its lisping peeping note, so incessant and
universal that it is hardly distinguished, more than the creak of
the crickets, is one of nature's ground tones and is associated
with the rustling of the leaves and the swift lapse of time. The
lark, too, sometimes sings again down in the meadow, as in
the spring, and the robin occasionally peeps—and the
bluebirds, old and young, revisit their boxes and hollow trees,
as if they would fain repeat the summer without the
intervention of winter. Dense flocks of bobolinks, russet &
rustling, like leaves floating on the wind, or like some ripe
meadow grain threshed out by the gale, rise before us in our
walk. Each tuft gives up its bird. The purple finch, or
American linnet is seen early in October moving south in
straggling flocks, and alighting on the apple trees, reminding
us of the pine and spruce, juniper & cedar, on whose berries it
feeds. In its plumage are the crimson hues of October
evenings, as if it had caught and preserved some of their
beams. Many a serene evening lies snugly packed under its
wing. Thus one after another these little passengers wing their
way seasonably to the haunts of summer, with each a passing
warning to man.

13 "Friday" [Museums]

This paragraph, a revision of two Journal entries
copied into the Long Book (J 1:465–66, 472; 2:77, 78–
79), is written on a leaf of blue wove paper (type 1)
paged 425–26. The paragraph is preceded the passage
beginning, "Asters and goldenrods were the livery
which nature wears at present," drafted on the recto of
a leaf of the same blue wove paper paged 427- [verso
blank] (cf. W 354). Both leaves are in the Houghton
Library (MH 15, G). The paragraph originally began,
"We saw now along the shore, and on the hills and

meadows mostly dried specimens of a summer, but
still sweet and clean & invigorating to our senses—all
whose death and decay was pregnant with new life."
After at least two separate revisions, first in pen and
later in pencil, the sentence read, "The summer
though decayed was still sweet and clean &
invigorating to our senses—a sort of natural museum,
all whose death was pregnant with new life." Thoreau
then canceled the sentence, evidently before removing
the leaf from the manuscript of *A Week*. The leaf
probably dates from 1847.

I hate Museums, such as feed on the wonder of men in
large towns without ever awakening any love for nature; there
is nothing so weighs upon the spirits. They are the catacombs
of nature. One green bud of spring, one willow catkin, one
faint warble from some migrating sparrow, would set the world
on its legs again. The life that is in a single green weed is of
more worth than all this death. They are very much like the
written history of the world, & I have read Rollin & Ferguson
with the same feelings. Men have a strange taste for death
who prefer to behold the cast-off garments of life, rather than
the life itself. Where is the proper herbarium, the cabinet of
shells, the museum of skeletons, but in the meadow where the
flower bloomed, by the sea-side where the tide cast up the fish,
and on the hills where the beast laid down its life. We love to
see things in their places—but for the most part natural
curiosities have rather lost than gained in value by being
brought near to their collector. Where the skeleton of the
traveller reposes in the grass, there it may be profitably
studied. If a mummy be found in a salt peter cave leave it in a
salt peter cave and do not bring it into the parlor. Let those
who are curious about the dust & ashes of our race, go to
Egypt and Italy where bones are the natural product of the
soil, which is a tomb & catacomb. Would you live in a dried
specimen of a world—a pickled world? Embalming is a sin
against heaven & earth; against heaven which has recalled the
soul, and set free the servile elements; against earth which is

thus robbed of her dust. I know not whether I muse most at the bodies stuffed with cotton & saw-dust, or those stuffed with bowels & fleshy fibre outside the cases. I have had my sight-perceiving sense so disturbed in these haunts, as for a long time to mistake a veritable living man in the attitude of repose, musing like myself, as the place requires, for a stuffed specimen.

14 "Friday" [English Poets]

This passage, a revision of two early Journal entries copied into the Long Book (J 1:437, 467; 2:52, 78–79), is written on a leaf of white wove paper in the Houghton Library (MH 4, C). Although its exact place in the manuscript of A Week cannot be determined, the concluding remark, "But we are getting too near home for such a theme," indicates that it was intended for insertion at the end of "Friday," in which Thoreau inserted related digressions on Ossian and Chaucer. The leaf probably dates from 1846 or 1847.

Gower writes like a man of common sense & good parts, who has undertaken with steady rather than high purpose to do narrative with rhyme. With little or no invention following in the track of the old fablers, he employs his leisure and his pencraft to entertain his readers, and speak a good word for the right. He has no fire or rather blaze, though occasionally some brand's end peeps out from the ashes, especially if you approach the heap in a dark day. And if you extend your hand over it you experience a slight warmth there more than elsewhere. In fair weather you may see a slight smoke go up here and there. He narrates what Chaucer sometimes sings. He tells his story with a fair understanding of the original, and sometimes it gains a little in blunt plainness & point in his hands. Unlike the early Saxon and later English, his poetry is but a plainer & directer speech than other men's prose. He might have been a teamster, and written his rhymes on his wagon seat, as he went to mill with a load of plaster.

After all we draw on very gradually in English literature to Shakspeare, through Peele & Marlowe, to say nothing of Raleigh Spenser & Sidney. They have the same cheerful and elastic wit, and we hear the same grand tones sounding which he freighted with such a genial human wisdom. The works of Marlowe are so much poetical pabulum or food for poets, water from the Castalian spring—some of the atmosphere of Parnassus, raw & blustering it is true, but pure and bracing. Few have so rich a phraseology. He had enthusiasm the rarest quality of genius. He had drunk deep of the Pierion spring, though not deep enough, and had that fine madness, as Drayton says

"which justly should possess a poet's brain."

The more one reads the literature of those times, the more does acquaintance divest the genius of Shakspeare of the false mystery which has thickened around it, and leave it shrouded in the grander mystery of daylight. It does not detract from but rather describes his genius to say that much of what is regarded as peculiarly Shakspearean in his writings was without doubt adopted from the popular wit & phraseology. The critic of Shakspeare has for the most part made Shakspeare's and his own contemporaries less, that he might make Shakspeare more.— We have no doubt that there were mystics in England in that day, whose light was darkness to Shakspeare himself.— But we are getting too near home for such a theme.

Index

NOTE: In this index all titles of books, essays, poems, or lectures are by Thoreau unless otherwise specified.

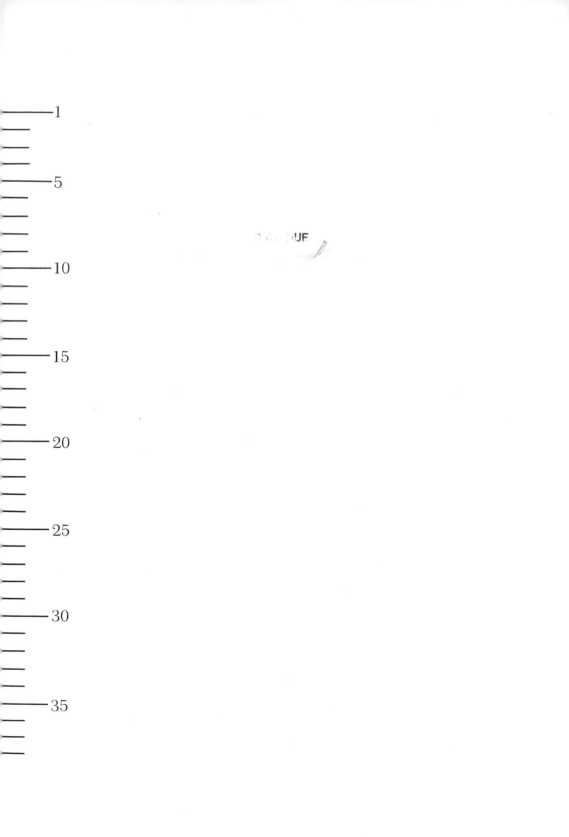